FROMMER'S

COMPREHENSIVE TRAVEL GUIDE

NASHVILLE & MEMPHIS

1ST EDITION

W9-AON-718

by Karl Samson
with Jane Aukshunas

PRENTICE HALL TRAVEL

NEW YORK • LONDON • TORONTO • SYDNEY • TOKYO • SINGAPORE

FROMMER BOOKS

Published by Prentice Hall General Reference
15 Columbus Circle
New York, NY 10023

ISBN 0-671-86980-9
ISSN 1074-8415

Design by Robert Bull Design
Maps by Ortelius Design

Frommer's Editorial Staff
Editorial Director: Marilyn Wood
Editorial Manager/Senior Editor: Alice Fellows
Senior Editors: Sara Hinsey Raveret, Lisa Renaud
Editors: Charlotte Allstrom, Thomas F. Hirsch, Peter Katucki, Theodore
    Stavrou
Assistant Editors: Margaret Bowen, Chris Hollander, Alice
    Thompson, Ian Wilker
Editorial Assistants: Gretchen Henderson, Douglas Stallings
Managing Editor: Leanne Coupe

Special Sales
Bulk purchases (10+ copies) of Frommer's Travel Guides are available to
corporations at special discounts. The Special Sales Department can produce
custom editions to be used as premiums and/or for sales promotion to suit
individual needs. Existing editions can be produced with custom cover
imprints such as a corporate logo. For more information write to Special Sales,
Prentice Hall Travel, Paramount Communications Building, 15 Columbus
Circle, New York, NY 10023.

Manufactured in the United States of America

CONTENTS

LIST OF MAPS

INVITATION TO THE READERS

In researching this book, I have come across many wonderful establishments, the best of which I have included here. I'm sure that many of you will also come across appealing hotels, inns, restaurants, guesthouses, shops, and attractions. Please don't keep them to yourself. Share your experiences, especially if you want to comment on places that have been included in this edition that have changed for the worse. You can address your letters to:

Karl Samson
Frommer's Nashville & Memphis
c/o Prentice Hall Travel
15 Columbus Circle
New York, NY 10023

A DISCLAIMER

Readers are advised that prices fluctuate in the course of time and travel information changes under the impact of the varied and volatile factors that affect the travel industry. Neither the author nor the publisher can be held responsible for the experiences of readers while traveling. Readers are invited to write to the publisher with ideas, comments, and suggestions for future editions.

SAFETY ADVISORY

Whenever you're traveling in an unfamiliar city or country, stay alert. Be aware of your immediate surroundings. Wear a moneybelt and keep a close eye on your possessions. Be particularly careful with cameras, purses, and wallets, all favorite targets of thieves and pickpockets.

INTRODUCING NASHVILLE

If you had a data base of all the songs recorded in the United States over the past 30 years and searched for the word "Nashville," I suspect that it would show up more frequently than any other city name in the world. More often than New York, more often than L.A., more often than Paris. If you could stop a German on the street in Frankfurt, a Scotsman in a pub in Edinburgh, an Italian in a caffè in Rome, and ask them "What's the country music capital of the world?" they could all tell you. And when you put together all the different types of music that come under the heading of country music—contemporary, honky tonk, cowboy, cowboy swing, Cajun, bluegrass, rockabilly—there wouldn't be too many people left in the United States who wouldn't have to say "Well, I guess I'm a fan of country music."

Nashville, Tennessee (despite stiff competition in recent years from upstart Branson, Missouri), is now, and has been for nearly 70 years, the capital of country music, a city that can, without hesitation, wear the moniker "Music City USA." Music, country and otherwise, is ubiquitous in Nashville. However, despite the fact that some people think Nashville's history began the day the "Grand Ole Opry" first went on the air, this city has a recorded past that dates back to the early 1700s. The city also seems to have a bright future. Nashville today is solidly a city of the New South. It is a sun-belt city sprawling across the hills of middle Tennessee fueled by the country-music industry and a newfound diversity of businesses, including nearby Saturn and Nissan car-manufacturing plants, an American Airlines hub, and 16 colleges and universities.

Nashville may be the country-music capital of the world, but it's also the capital of the state of Tennessee. Government offices kept a breath of life in the city's downtown during the 1950s, '60s, and '70s as the population and businesses fled to the suburbs. Though many of downtown's old buildings were abandoned during this period, in recent years many of these buildings have been renovated and new life breathed into them. This area of restored buildings, known as the District, has become the city's main entertainment center and is packed with nightclubs, restaurants, and interesting shops.

However, far more visitors spend time several miles east of downtown in an area called Music Valley, which is home to Opryland USA, Nashville's country-music theme park. Imagine Disneyland gone Nashville and you'll have a good idea of what Opryland USA is all about. The "Grand Ole Opry," the radio show

WHAT'S SPECIAL ABOUT NASHVILLE

After Dark

- ☐ The "Grand Ole Opry," the show that started it all and the longest-running radio program in the U.S.
- ☐ The Bluebird Café, Nashville's most famous venue for new songwriters.
- ☐ The District, a restored section of downtown Nashville that's the heart of the city's nightlife.
- ☐ Clubs all over the city featuring up-and-coming country musicians.

Architectural Highlights

- ☐ Nashville's Parthenon is the only full-scale replica of this famous Greek building.
- ☐ The Opryland Hotel, with two huge atriums that are covered by several acres of glass.

Museums

- ☐ The Country Music Hall of Fame and Museum, the nation's definitive exhibition on the music that made Nashville famous.

Plantation Homes

- ☐ The Hermitage, home of President Andrew Jackson.
- ☐ Belle Meade, a stately antebellum mansion.

Events/Festivals

- ☐ Fan Fair, a festival for fans of country music.

- ☐ Harlan Howard Birthday Bash, an end-of-summer country-music fund-raiser on Music Row.

For the Kids

- ☐ Opryland USA, Nashville's country-music theme park—fun for kids of all ages.

Regional Food and Drink

- ☐ Jack Daniels and George Dickel Tennessee whiskey, known throughout the world.
- ☐ Barbecued pork, hickory-smoked ham, and fried catfish—the staff of life hereabouts.

Shopping

- ☐ Hatch Show Print, the oldest poster print shop in the country.
- ☐ Manuel, big-bucks clothing for country-music stars.

Offbeat Oddities

- ☐ More than a dozen small museums focusing on specific country-music stars or country music in general.

Activities

- ☐ Cruising the Cumberland River aboard the *General Jackson* paddlewheel showboat.

that started the whole country-music ball rolling, moved to a new theater in Music Valley in 1974, two years after Opryland opened. Together these two establishments form the core of the Nashville's country-music attractions. However, in this same area there are several other related attractions, including the impressive Opryland

Hotel, a showboat, a country-music television network, and more than half a dozen museums with country-music themes.

Both by day and by night, Nashville has much to offer. Country-music fans will be in hog heaven, and even if you aren't a fan of country music, you just might find yourself tapping your toes to that old Nashville sound.

1. GEOGRAPHY, HISTORY & CULTURE

GEOGRAPHY & PEOPLE

Nashville is located in roughly the geographic center of Tennessee in the region known as middle Tennessee. That region, midway between the Appalachian Mountains and the Mississippi River, is characterized by rolling limestone hills covered with hardwood forests and farmlands. The city itself developed on a bluff above a bend in the Cumberland River, and for the city's first century or so the river was the most important transportation link to the rest of the country. It was the river that initially made Nashville an important trading center, a prominence that continued into the era of railroads. Today, with three different Interstate highways passing through the city, Nashville has become a transportation hub and is rapidly becoming one of the business centers of the South.

Tennessee is a part of the Mid-South and is bordered by the Deep South states of Mississippi, Alabama, and Georgia. This placement has historically given the state its southern attitudes, though commerce with the North has tempered these attitudes. Race relations during the height of the civil rights movement were not as strained as they were in the states south of Tennessee, perhaps in part because Nashville was the first Southern state capital to fall to the Union army during the Civil War and thus recovered sooner from the war and adapted better to the changes wrought by the Emancipation Proclamation.

For the most part Nashvillians, as the city's inhabitants are known, today share the traditional values, outlook, and attitudes of other southerners. Wealthy Nashvillians seem to cling tightly to the traditional image of the plantation home surrounded by green lawns. Clothing styles are casual but traditional, with women generally wearing more "feminine" apparel than is the norm in cities of the North and West. Country music has played a large role in shaping Nashville fashions—as the stars dress, so dresses a large portion of the city's population, both male and female. Folks here still stick by their meat-and-three, the traditional American meal of simply prepared meat accompanied by three vegetables. Pork barbecue and hickory-smoked hams are other favorites. When it comes time to relax, Nashvillians prefer horseback riding to hiking, boating to bungee-jumping. Golf and tennis are favorite sports in Nashville.

However, this is not to say that the city does not have its more forward-thinking populations. It does. As a magnet for young musicians from around the country and a center for higher education, Nashville is constantly infused with youthful vigor that adds a healthy balance to the city's more traditional side.

DATELINE

- **9000 B.C.** Paleo-Indians inhabit area that is now Nashville.
- **A.D. 1000–1400** Mississippian Period Indians develop advanced society characterized by mound-building and farming.
- **1710** French fur trader Charles Charleville establishes a trading post in the area.
- **1765** A group of long hunters camp at Mansker's Lick, north of present-day Nashville.
- **1772** The Wautauga Association becomes the first form of government west of the Appalachians.
- **1775** The Transylvania Purchase stimulates settlement in middle Tennessee.
- **1778** James Robertson scouts the area and decides to found a settlement.
- **1779** Robertson's first party of settlers arrives on Christmas Eve.
- **1780** Second of Robertson's parties of settlers, led by Col. John Donelson, arrives by boat in
  (continues)

HISTORY

FRONTIER DAYS Long before the first Europeans set foot in middle Tennessee, Native Americans had populated this region of rolling hills, dense forests, and plentiful grasslands. Large herds of deer and buffalo had made the region an excellent hunting ground. However, by the late 18th century when the first settlers arrived, continuing warfare over access to the area's rich hunting grounds had forced the various battling tribes to move away from the area. Though there were no native villages in the immediate area, this did not eliminate conflicts between Native Americans and settlers. For their first few years, the pioneers were constantly forced to defend themselves against Indian attacks.

The first white men to arrive in middle Tennessee were French fur trapper and trader Charles Charleville, who established a trading post at a salt lick, and another Frenchman named Timothy Demonbreun, who made his home in a cave on a bluff above the Cumberland River. By the middle part of the century, the area that is now Nashville came to be known as French Lick because of the salt lick.

Throughout the middle part of the century, the only other whites to explore the area were so-called long hunters. These hunters got their name from the extended hunting trips, often months long, that they would make over the Appalachian Mountains. These hunters would bring back stacks of buckskins, which at the time sold for $1. Thus a dollar came to be called a "buck." Among the most famous of the long hunters was Daniel Boone, who may have passed through French Lick in the 1760s. It was about this same time, in 1765, that long hunters Henry, Charles, and Richard Skaggs and Joseph Drake camped at another nearby salt lick known as Mansker's Lick. Today there is a living-history center called

Manskers Station near this site in present-day Goodletsville.

The Indian Treaty of Lochaber in 1770 and the Transylvania Purchase in 1775 opened up much of the land west of the Appalachians to settlers. Several settlements had already sprung up on Cherokee land in the Appalachians, and these settlements had formed the Watauga Association, a sort of self-government. However, it was not until the late 1770s that the first settlers began to arrive in middle Tennessee. In 1778 James Robertson, a member of the Watauga Association, brought a scouting party to the area in his search for a place to found a new settlement. The bluffs above the Cumberland River appealed to Robertson, and the following year he returned with a party of settlers. This group had traveled through Kentucky and arrived at French Lick on Christmas Eve, 1779. This first group of settlers was comprised of men only. The women and children, under the leadership of John Donelson, followed by flatboat, traveling 1,000 miles by river to reach the new settlement and arriving in April 1780. This new settlement of nearly 300 people was named Fort Nashboro after North Carolinian Gen. Francis Nash. As soon as both parties were assembled at Fort Nashboro, the settlers drew up a charter of government called the Cumberland Compact. This was the first form of government in middle Tennessee.

Fort Nashboro was founded while the Revolutionary War was raging, and these first settlers very soon found themselves battling Cherokee, Choctaw, and Chickasaw Indians whose attacks were incited by the British. The worst confrontation was the Battle of the Bluffs, which took place in April 1781 when settlers were attacked by a band of Cherokees.

By 1784 the situation was quieter, and in that year the settlement changed its name from Nashboro to Nashville. Twelve years later, in 1796, Tennessee became the 16th state in the Union. Nashville at that time was still a tiny settlement in a vast wilderness, but in less than 20 years, the nation would know of Nashville through the heroic exploits of one of its citizens. In 1814, at the close of the War of 1812,

DATELINE

April; in May the settlement of Nashboro founded.

- **1781** Battle of the Bluffs fought with Cherokee Indians.
- **1784** The small settlement's name changed from Nashboro to Nashville.
- **1796** Tennessee becomes the 16th state.
- **1814** Andrew Jackson, a Nashville resident, leads the Tennessee militia in the Battle of New Orleans and gains national stature.
- **1840** Belle Meade plantation home built.
- **1843** The state capital moved from Murfreesboro to Nashville.
- **1850** Nashville is site of convention held by nine Southern states that jointly assert the right to secede.
- **1862** Nashville becomes the first state capital in the South to fall to Union troops.
- **1864** Battle of Nashville, the last major battle initiated by the Confederate army.
- **1866** Fisk University, one of the nation's first African-American universities, founded.
- **1873** Vanderbilt University founded.
(continues)

Andrew Jackson, a Nashville lawyer, led a contingent of Tennessee militiamen in the Battle of New Orleans. The British were soundly defeated and Jackson became a hero. A political career soon followed, and in 1829 Jackson was elected seventh president of the United States.

In the early part of the 19th century, the state government bounced back and forth between eastern and middle Tennessee, and was twice seated in Knoxville, once in Murfreesboro, and had once before been located in Nashville before finally staying put here on the Cumberland. By 1845 work had begun on a capitol building, which would not be completed until 1859.

THE CIVIL WAR & RECONSTRUCTION

By 1860, when the first rumblings of secession began to be heard across the South, Nashville was a very prosperous city, made wealthy by its importance as a river port. Tennessee had reluctantly sided with the Confederacy and had become the last state to secede from the Union. This decision sealed Nashville's fate. The city's significance as a shipping port was not lost on either the Union or Confederate army, both of which coveted the city as a means of controlling important river and railroad transportation routes. In February 1862 the Union army occupied Nashville, razing many homes in the process. Thus Nashville became the first state capital to fall to the Union troops.

Throughout the Civil War, the Confederates repeatedly attempted to reclaim Nashville, but to no avail. In December 1864 the Confederate army made its last stab at retaking Nashville, but during the Battle of Nashville they were roundly rebuffed.

Though the Civil War left Nashville severely damaged and in dire economic straits, the city quickly rebounded. Within a few years the city had reclaimed its important shipping and trading position and also developed a solid manufacturing base. However, it was in the area of education that the city made its greatest gains. Fisk University, one of the nation's first African-American universities, was founded in 1866. Vanderbilt

University was founded in 1873, and in 1876, Meharry Medical College, the country's foremost African-American medical school, was founded. With this proliferation of schools of higher learning, Nashville came to be known as the "Athens of the South." Thus, at the turn of the 20th century, Nashville was firmly established as one of the South's most important cities.

COUNTRY MUSIC   As early as 1871, a Nashville musical group, the Fisk University Jubilee Singers, had traveled to Europe to sing African-American spirituals. By 1902 the city had its first music publisher; the Benson Company, which is still active today, helped make Nashville an important center for gospel music. Nashville is still important in the world of gospel music, but this musical tradition has been overshadowed by country music.

The history of Nashville in the 20th century is, for the most part and for most people, the history of country music. Though traditional fiddle music, often played at dances, had been a part of the Tennessee scene from the arrival of the very first settlers, it was not until the early 20th century that people outside the hills and mountains began to pay attention to this "hillbilly" music.

In 1925, WSM-AM went on the air and began broadcasting a show called "The WSM Barn Dance." This program featured live performances of country music; two years later it became the "Grand Ole Opry," which has been on the air ever since and is the longest-running radio show in the country. The same year that the "Grand Ole Opry" began, Victor Records sent a recording engineer to Tennessee to record the traditional country music of the South. These recordings helped expose this music to a much wider audience than it had ever enjoyed before, and interest in country music began to grow throughout the South and across the nation.

In 1942 Nashville's first country-music publishing house opened, followed by the first recording studio in 1945. By the 1960s there were more than 100 music publishers in Nashville and dozens of recording studios. The 1950s and early 1960s saw a rapid rise in the popularity of country music, and all the major record companies eventually opened offices here. Leading the industry at this time were brothers Owen and Harold Bradley, who opened the city's first recording studio not affiliated with the "Grand Ole Opry." CBS and RCA soon followed suit. Many of the industry's biggest and most familiar names first recorded in Nashville at this time. Among the famous performers to record here during this seminal period were Patsy Cline, Hank Williams, Brenda Lee, Dottie West, Floyd Cramer, Porter Wagoner, Dolly Parton, Loretta Lynn, George Jones, Tammy Wynette, Elvis Presley, the Everly brothers, Perry Como, and Connie Frances.

During this period, country music also changed quite a bit from its hillbilly music origins. With growing competition from rock 'n' roll, record producers developed a cleaner, more urban sound for country music. Production values went up and the music took on a new sound, the "Nashville sound."

In 1972 the Opryland USA theme park, with its emphasis on

country music, opened on the east side of Nashville. In 1974, the "Grand Ole Opry" moved from the Ryman Auditorium, its home of 31 years, to the new Grand Ole Opry House just outside the gates of Opryland. In recent years country music has once again been changing in order to maintain its listenership. Rock 'n' roll influences have crept into the music and caused a rift between traditionalists (who still like the old Nashville sound) and fans of the new country music, which for the most part is faster and louder than the music of old. However, in Nashville, every type of country music, from Cajun to contemporary, bluegrass to cowboy, honky tonk to cowboy swing, is heard with regularity. And if you turn on your car radio anywhere in America and run quickly through the AM and FM dials, you'll likely pick up a handful of country-music stations playing music that got its start in Nashville.

ART, ARCHITECTURE & CULTURAL LIFE

The art of Nashville is country music, and it's on display everywhere. You can hardly walk down a street without hearing the strains of a country melody. In bars, restaurants, hotel lobbies, on trolleys, in the airport, and on the street corners, country musicians sing out in hopes that they, too, might be discovered and become the next big name in country music. Nashville's reputation as Music City attracts thousands of hopeful musicians and songwriters every year, and though few of them make it to the big time, they provide the music fan with myriad opportunities to hear the occasional great, undiscovered performer. Keep your ears tuned to the music that's the pulse of Nashville and you just might be able one day to say "I heard her playing at this little bar in Nashville years ago."

Though Nashville is not known as a city of the visual arts, it has its share of art galleries and museums. There are also a fair share of artists living here and throughout the state who show and sell their work in Nashville. Traditional crafts of the Appalachian Mountains, such as pottery and basketry, make their way to a few shops and galleries around town. If you're interested in such crafts, see Chapter 7, "Nashville Shopping."

The post–Civil War years of the late 19th century brought a newfound prosperity to Nashville. These healthy economic times left the city with a legacy of grand classically styled buildings, which can be seen around the downtown area. However, the city's single most endearing building was constructed as a temporary structure for the Tennessee Centennial Exposition in 1897. The centerpiece of the exposition was a full-size reconstruction of the Parthenon. Though Nashville's Parthenon was meant to last only the duration of the exposition, it proved so popular that the city left it in place. Over the years the Parthenon deteriorated until it was no longer safe to visit. At that point the city was considering demolishing this last vestige of the Centennial Exposition, but public outcry brought about the reconstruction, from more permanent materials, of the Parthenon. Today, this building houses a museum and the largest indoor sculpture in the country and is Nashville's most striking landmark.

IMPRESSIONS

Good to the last drop.
—TEDDY ROOSEVELT, SPEAKING OF THE COFFEE AT NASHVILLE'S
MAXWELL HOUSE HOTEL

About the same time the Parthenon was built, the city also received its Union Station, a Roman-Gothic train station that is now a luxury hotel. The station's grand waiting hall is roofed by a stained-glass ceiling, and, with its gilded plasterwork and bas-reliefs, Union Station is a symbol of the waning glory days of railroading in America. Another lodging, the Opryland Hotel, has become the city's most breathtaking modern structure. With two huge atriums full of tropical plants, the 1,800-room hotel is an attraction unto itself. Within the atriums, which are covered with several acres of glass, there are waterfalls, streams, ponds, fountains, restaurants, and lounges.

People the world over know that Nashville is the capital of country music, and the city has adopted the epithet "Music City USA" in recognition of this important role. Not only is this city the home of the "Grand Ole Opry," but that long-running country-music radio show has even generated a country-music theme park—Opryland USA. There are also dozens of clubs around the city that feature live country music of various genres. However, country has moved beyond music and become a lifestyle. Stores all over the city sell more western wear and cowboy boots than it would take to clothe all the cowboys and cowgirls in Montana, Wyoming, Colorado, and Texas put together. In recent years, with the growing national reputation of southwestern and cowboy styling, the look of Nashville has taken on a slightly more consciously fashionable appearance as country stars and country fans don the bright colors of Santa Fe.

---

2. FAMOUS NASHVILLIANS

As you would expect, or as you already know, there are many famous country-music stars living in or near Nashville. The homes and former homes of many of the people listed below can be seen on various Nashville city tours. See Chapter 6, "What to See and Do in Nashville," for details.

Eddy Arnold (b. 1918) Raised on a farm in Tennessee, Arnold became the most successful country singer between 1946 and 1970. Hits included "Tennessee Stud," "My Everything," and "Kentucky Waltz."

Chet Atkins (b. 1924) Became a member of the "Grand Ole Opry" in 1950. His guitar-picking style has made his instrumental albums immensely popular. He was a producer for Elvis Presley, Perry Como, and Waylon Jennings.

Johnny Cash (b. 1932) Part Cherokee and born into a poor family, Cash started out as a rockabilly singer but soon switched to country and folk music. His distinctive gravelly, rumbling bass made hits of "Folsom Prison Blues," "I Walk the Line," "Ring of Fire," and "Orange Blossom Special."

Andrew Jackson (1767–1845) Seventh president of the United States. Jackson became a hero at the Battle of New Orleans in 1814 and later entered politics as a champion of the common man. His plantation home in Nashville, the Hermitage, is open to the public.

Andrew Johnson (1808–75) Vice-president under Abraham Lincoln, Johnson became the nation's 17th president upon Lincoln's death. Was nearly removed from office after being impeached.

George Jones (b. 1931) Both of Jones's parents were musicians, so he became a musician at a young age. During his long career he sang pure country, honky tonk, and heartache ballads. In the early 1970s he was married to Tammy Wynette.

Brenda Lee (b. 1942) An exuberant performer, her hoarse, raspy voice had a cracking emotionalism that made her popular as both a country and a pop singer.

Loretta Lynn (b. 1943) A coal-miner's daughter and child bride from Butcher Holler, Kentucky, Lynn became the most popular female country singer in the country. Her songs tell the story of a woman who has risen above her difficult past.

Reba McEntire (b. 1954) Popular country-music singer who was discovered when she sang the "Star Spangled Banner" at a rodeo. Was named the 1984 Female Artist of the Year by the Country Music Association.

Ronnie Milsap (b. 1944) A blind child prodigy, Milsap was trained in classical music, but later found success in country music. In 1977 he was the Country Music Association Entertainer of the Year.

Dolly Parton (b. 1946) Born poor, Parton moved to Nashville after high school to become a country-music songwriter. Her songs, filled with heartfelt tragedy, frequently became hits and launched her on her own singing career. Music eventually led her to a successful film acting career.

Minnie Pearl (b. 1912) Comedienne with the "Grand Ole Opry." Most famous for her flowered straw hat with the price tag still on it and her high-pitched greeting, "Howdee! I'm just so proud to be here."

James K. Polk (1795–1849) The 11th president of the United States, Polk was an expansionist. He brought Texas and Oregon into the Union and waged war on Mexico for California, New Mexico, and Arizona.

Hank Snow (b. 1914) Born in Canada, Snow ran away from home at 12 and soon entered the country-music business. He moved to the United States to further his career, and became a member of the "Grand Ole Opry."

Conway Twitty (1933–93) Second only to Merle Haggard in number one country-music hits, he sang duets with Loretta Lynn. His home, Twitty City, just outside Nashville, is open to the public and is a major tourist attraction.

Porter Wagoner (b. 1930) Best known for his duets and television appearances with Dolly Parton, Wagoner had hits with such songs as "Green Green Grass of Home" and "Satisfied Mind." His sequined outfits and bleached pompadour made him a visually memorable performer.

William Walker (1824–60) Doctor, lawyer, and journalist from Nashville. With U.S. government support, Walker invaded several Central American nations, proclaiming himself president and attempting to set up a slave state. He was executed in Honduras.

Hank Williams (1923–52) Influenced by blues and gospel music, Williams had a distinctively mournful vocal delivery and incorporated yodeling into his tunes. His early death was pointed out as the wages of the rock music and honky-tonk lifestyle.

Tammy Wynette (b. 1942) Used her hoarse, emotional voice to sing songs of heartache. Her hits have included "Stand by Your Man," "D-I-V-O-R-C-E," and other songs based on her own personal experiences.

3. FOOD & DRINK

Down-home American cooking still reigns supreme in the South, and nowhere is it more available than in Nashville, where hordes of country-music tourists work up powerful hungers traipsing around Opryland. "Meat and three" is a term you may hear bandied about around these parts, and what it means is a meat main dish with your choice of three vegetables on the side. Your three vegetables might include fried okra, collard greens, purple-hull peas, black-eyed peas, or candied yams, among others. This is down-home comfort food like your mama used to cook—right down to the cans the vegetables come out of.

Pork has always been a favored meat in the South. You can take some home with you as hickory-smoked ham, or eat your fill while you're in town. More readily available than ham, however, is pork barbecue. Though Memphis is better known for its barbecue, you can still find some decent barbecue here in Music City. See Chapter 10, "Introducing Memphis," for a full description of barbecue and its many permutations.

The waters of the South yield a bounty of catfish that has kept southerners well fed for generations, and you'll find it on the menu of any good southern-cooking restaurant. Breaded and fried is the traditional way to have it, though you might even run across Cajun-style blackened catfish. A basket of hush puppies (cornbread fritters) are the perfect accompaniment.

If fried foods are anathema to you, don't despair. There is an alternative. New Southern cuisine is the South's answer to the current taste for imaginative regional cuisine. Basically, New Southern dishes take such traditional ingredients as pork, pecans, greens, corn meal, even catfish, and rethink them. Pork chops may be served *au poivre* instead of with country gravy, or an otherwise familiar French sauce will be flavored with Jack Daniel's. The salsa might be made with black-eyed peas, or it will be trout instead of pork that gets hickory smoked. You just never know.

Some uninformed people have the silly notion that the whiskey they make in Tennessee is called bourbon. Wrong! A Tennessean will be quick to point out that the Jack Daniel's and George Dickel distilleries produce Tennessee sour mash sippin' whiskey. "What's the difference?" you ask. Well, it's all in the charcoal. You see, here in Tennessee, folks just weren't content with that firewater they made up in Bourbon County, Kentucky, so they decided to improve it. By letting the whiskey drip through hard-maple charcoal, they take out the harshness of the whiskey and make a smooth sippin' whiskey. If you're already a fan of these libations, you may want to tour their distilleries (see Chapter 9, "Easy Excursions from Nashville").

4. RECOMMENDED BOOKS, FILMS & RECORDINGS

BOOKS

GENERAL If you'd like to learn more about Nashville history, you'll find some in *Paths of the Past* (University of Tennessee Press, 1988) by Paul H. Bergeron. This brief history of Tennessee between the years 1770 and 1970 includes quite a bit on Nashville itself. For a more thorough look at Tennessee and Nashville history, read *Tennessee, A Short History* (University of Tennessee Press, 1990) by Stanley J. Folmsbee, Robert E. Corlew, and Enoch L. Mitchell, or *Tennessee: A History* (W. W. Norton & Co., 1984) by Wilma Dykeman.

COUNTRY MUSIC Books on country music abound and you'll find good selections at most of the bookstores in Nashville. For a very thorough history of country music, read the scholarly *Country Music* (University of Texas Press, 1985) by Bill Malone. *Finding Her Voice: The Saga of Women in Country Music* (Crown Publishers, 1993), by Mary A. Bufwack and Robert K. Oermann, is the essential history of women country singers and covers the topic right up to 1991. The book is organized both by genres and time periods. *Grand Ole Opry* (Henry Holt, 1989), by Chet Hagan, is the official Opryland USA history of this country-music tradition. The book includes lots of great old photos.

There are numerous country-music encyclopedias on the market. The *Encyclopedia of Country & Western Music* (Exeter Books, 1985), by Rick Marschall, has lots of good photos and very succinct write-ups. *The New Country Music Encyclopedia* (Simon & Schuster, 1993), by Tad Richards and Melvin B. Shestack, is up-to-date and has lengthy profiles of more than 200 country-music stars. In *Country Musicians* (Grove Press, 1987), editor Judie Eremo assembled informative country-music profiles by various writers. *Nash-*

ville: Music City USA (Harry N. Abrams, 1985), by John Lomax III, is a similar book that focuses specifically on Nashville and its music. The book has lots of great photos.

If you want to know what it's really like in the country-music business, read *Music City Babylon* (Carol Publishing Co./Birch Lane Press, 1992), a revealing look by industry insider Scott Fagagher. If this latter book only whets your appetite for some really juicy gossip, you'll want to read *Nashville Babylon* (Congdon & Weed, Inc., 1988), by Randall Riese, which has the low-down, inside scoop on all the greats and what they've gotten themselves into over the years.

Biographies of country-music stars abound. The following are biographies of some of the stars who lived or still live in Nashville: *Man in Black* (Warner Books, 1976) by Johnny Cash; *Coal Miner's Daughter* (Warner Books, 1976) by Loretta Lynn with George Vecsey; *Stand By Your Man* (Pocket Books, 1979) by Tammy Wynette with Joan Dew; *Dolly* (Reed Books, 1978) by Alanna Nash; *A Satisfied Mind: The Country Music Life of Porter Wagoner* (Rutledge Hill Press, 1992) by Steve Eng; *Minnie Pearl* (Simon & Schuster, 1980) by Minnie Pearl with Joan Dew; *Your Cheatin' Heart: A Biography of Hank Williams* (Simon & Schuster, 1981) by Chet Flippo; and *Hank Williams, Country Music's Tragic King* (Scarborough Books, 1981) by Jay Caress.

FICTION Peter Taylor, a winner of the Pulitzer Prize, is one of the few Nashville writers to garner a national reputation. His works of Southern fiction have been well received both in the South and elsewhere. In *A Summons to Memphis* (Ballantine Books, 1986) he tells a story of a southerner haunted by an unhappy childhood in Nashville and Memphis who returns to the South from New York City. *In the Miro District* (Ballantine Books, 1990) and the more recent *The Oracle at Stoneleigh Court* (Alfred Knopf, 1993) are both collections of Taylor's short stories.

FILMS

Coal Miners Daughter (1980), starring Sissy Spacek, is the story of country star Loretta Lynn and is considered one of the best films to use the country-music industry as its background. *Sweet Dreams* (1985), starring Jessica Lange, is a similar film which focuses on the life of Patsy Cline. Back in 1975, director Robert Altman turned his balefully ironic eye on Nashville in the film *Nashville,* which covered a day in the life of the city and several typically Nashvillian characters. More recently, *The Thing Called Love* (1993), starring River Phoenix and Samantha Mathis, presented a picture of love and songwriting in Music City.

RECORDINGS

Walk into nearly any record store in America and say "Where's the country-music section?" and you'll likely be directed to a vast selection of recordings. Country music is as large and varied as rock 'n' roll. Genres that fall under the umbrella of country music include contemporary (or new country), honky-tonk (drinkin' and truckin' and losin'-your-baby music), bluegrass, western swing, cowboy, Cajun, and even rockabilly and country rock. There are several record stores in Nashville that specialize in country music (see Chapter 7, "Nashville Shopping," for details).

CHAPTER 2

PLANNING A TRIP TO NASHVILLE

As the country-music capital of the world, Nashville is a major tourist destination. Consequently it has a solid infrastructure for the visitor. This chapter gives you all the essentials that will be necessary to plan a trip to Nashville. Some of the important questions that you'll find answered here are, what will a trip cost? what airlines fly to Nashville? where can I get more information about Nashville?

1. INFORMATION & COSTS

SOURCES OF INFORMATION

Before heading to Music City, you can get more information on the city by contacting the **Nashville Convention & Visitors Bureau,** 161 Fourth Ave. N., Nashville, TN 37219 (tel. 615/259-4700). For information on the State of Tennessee, contact the **Tennessee Department of Tourism Development,** P.O. Box 23170, Nashville, TN 37202-3170 (tel. 615/741-2158).

COSTS

What will a trip to Nashville cost? Probably less than you thought it would. Because this is the country-music capital of the world and a major tourist destination, Nashville has an abundance of hotel rooms. Tourism is big business here and, for the most part, people visiting Nashville don't come here intending to spend a lot of money. The majority of the hotel and motel rooms in the city are in the $50 to $80 range, and $20 to $25 will buy you a great meal in many of the city's best restaurants.

If you do want to splurge, you certainly can. The music industry has produced its fair share of wealthy individuals and consequently there are hotels such as the Opryland Hotel where you can spend $200 a night for a room. At a few of the city's restaurants you can spend as much as $100 for dinner. Such prices are, however, exceptions.

If you're used to exorbitantly overpriced downtown hotels, you'll be pleasantly surprised to learn that hotels in downtown Nashville are for the most part very reasonably priced. On the other hand, you'll find that hotels and motels in the Opryland area do tend to be overpriced. You're paying for convenience. If you're looking for the cheapest acceptable room for the night, head east out of the city on I-40 and you'll find a string of budget motels a few miles past the airport.

A credit or charge card is the most convenient way to pay for hotel rooms and restaurant meals, and if you plan to rent a car, you'll need a credit or charge card for the deposit. However, most hotels, restaurants, and many shops also accept traveler's checks, and, of course, personal checks.

WHAT THINGS COST IN NASHVILLE	U.S. $
Taxi from the airport to the city center	14.00–17.00
Bus ride between any two downtown points	1.15
Local telephone call	.25
Double room at the Sheraton Music City (deluxe)	130.00
Double room at the Wyndham Garden Hotel (moderate)	64.00
Double room at the Red Roof Inn (budget)	34.00
Lunch for one at the Mad Platter (moderate)	16.00
Lunch for one at El Palenque (budget)	8.00
Dinner for one, without wine, at the Wild Boar (deluxe)	38.00
Dinner for one, without wine, at the Cakewalk Restaurant (moderate)	20.00
Dinner for one, without wine, at Uncle Bud's Catfish (budget)	10.00
Bottle of beer	2.50
Coca-Cola	1.00
Cup of coffee or ice tea	.95
Roll of ASA 100 Kodacolor film, 36 exposures	4.90
Movie ticket	5.75
Theater ticket for the Tennessee Repertory Theatre	12.00–26.00

2. WHEN TO GO — CLIMATE & EVENTS

CLIMATE

Summer is the peak tourist season in Nashville and is also when the city experiences its worst weather. During July and August, and often in September as well, temperatures can be up around 100° Fahrenheit, with humidity of close to 100%. Can you say "muggy"? Spring and fall, however, are both quite pleasant and last for several months. Days are often warm and nights cool, though during these two seasons the weather is changeable so bring a variety of clothes. Heavy rains can hit any time of year, and if you spend more than three or four days in town, you can almost bet on seeing some rain. Winters can be cold, with daytime temperatures staying below freezing, and snow is not unknown.

Nashville's Average Monthly Temperatures and Rainfall

	Jan	Feb	Mar	Apr	May	June	July	Aug	Sept	Oct	Nov	Dec
Temp. (°F)	37	41	49	59	68	76	80	79	72	60	48	40
Temp. (°C)	3	5	9	15	20	25	27	26	22	15	9	4
Days of Rain	11	11	12	11	11	9	10	9	8	7	10	11

NASHVILLE CALENDAR OF EVENTS

FEBRUARY

☐ **Annual Americana Spring Sampler Craft, Folk Art & Antique Fair,** Tennessee State Fairground. About 200 craft and antiques professionals from over 30 states display their wares. Call 227-2080. Mid-February.

APRIL

☐ **Annual Opryland American Music Festival,** Grand Ole Opry House and Acuff Theater. Opryland-sponsored national competition for choruses and high school bands. Call 889-6600. Late April.

MAY

☐ **Sara Lee Classic LPGA Golf Tournament,** Hermitage Golf Course. Old Hickory. Professional golf competition featuring about 140 internationally known women players. Call 847-5017. First week in May.

☐ **Tennessee Renaissance Festival,** in Triune (20 miles south of downtown Nashville). Maidens, knights, gypsies, jugglers, and jousting are some of the people and activities you'll find at this medieval fair held on the grounds of the Castle Gwynn. Call 320-9333. Weekends in May, including Memorial Day.

☐ **Annual Tennessee Crafts Fair,** Centennial Park. With the largest display of Tennessee crafts, this fair opens the summer season. Food, demonstrations, and children's craft activities. Call 665-0502. Early May.

☐ **Annual Running of the Iroquois Steeplechase,** Percy Warner Park. This horse race has been a Nashville ritual for more than 50 years. The race is accompanied by tailgate picnics. Call 322-7284 or 322-7450. Second Saturday in May.

☐ **Opryland Gospel Jubilee,** Opryland. A dozen or so top gospel groups open the summer season at Opryland. Call 889-6700. Memorial Day weekend.

JUNE

☐ **Summer Lights Festival,** downtown Nashville. Four days of art, dance, and music encompassing many styles, including country, jazz, classical, and gospel. Call 862-6720. Early June.

۞ INTERNATIONAL COUNTRY MUSIC FAN FAIR *A chance for country artists and their fans to meet and greet each other in a week-long music celebration. Glitzy stage shows and picture/autograph sessions with country-music stars are all part of the action. A Texas barbecue and tickets for sightseeing are included in the price of a ticket, along with a bluegrass concert and the Grand Masters Fiddling Championship. This event is very big and popular, so book your tickets way in advance.*

*Where: Tennessee State Fairgrounds and Opryland.
When: Early June. How: Contact the Fan Fair Office (tel. 615/889-7503) for ticket information.*

☐ **Annual American Artisan Festival,** Centennial Park. Artisans from 35 states present a wide range of crafts from blown glass to leather and quilts. Children's art booth and music, too. Call 298-4691. Mid-June.

☐ **Bellevue Center Balloon Classic,** Edwin Warner Park. Brilliantly colored hot-air balloons parade, chase, and race. Call 329-7807. Mid-June.

JULY

☐ **Independence Celebration at Opryland,** Opryland. Four-day celebration at the Opryland theme park featuring patriotic music, flags, and fireworks. Call 889-6700. Around July 4.

- ☐ **Independence Day Celebration,** Riverfront Park. Family-oriented alcohol-free event attracts 100,000 people for entertainment, food, and fireworks. Call 862-8400. July 4.
- ☐ **Uncle Dave Macon Days,** Cannonsburg Village. Murfreesboro (30 miles southeast of downtown Nashville). Entertaining old-time music and dance featuring banjo, fiddle, and buck dancing. Motorless parade and food. Write to P.O. Box 5016, Murfreesboro, TN 37133-5016, for details. Second weekend in July.

AUGUST

- ☐ **Annual Americana Summer Sampler Craft, Folk Art & Antique Fair,** Tennessee State Fairgrounds. Retail and wholesale art fair with over 170 craftspeople, lectures, demonstrations, and exhibits. Call 227-2080. First weekend in August.
- ☐ **Annual Franklin Jazz Festival,** in Franklin (15 miles south of downtown Nashville). Jazz, Dixieland, and big-band music are performed on the elegant town square in downtown Franklin. Call 790-7094. Early August.
- ☐ **Annual Tennessee Walking Horse National Celebration,** Celebration Grounds, Shelbyville (40 miles southeast of downtown Nashville). The World Grand Championship of the much-loved Tennessee walking horse, plus trade fairs and dog shows. Call 684-5915. Late August.

SEPTEMBER

- ☐ **Italian Street Fair,** Maryland Farms Office Complex, Brentwood. A benefit for the Nashville Symphony Orchestra, featuring Italian food, arts and crafts, children's crafts, and musical performances. Call 329-3033. Labor Day weekend.
- ☐ **Belle Meade Fall Fest,** Belle Meade Plantation. Antiques, crafts, children's festival, garage treasures, and food from local restaurants. Call 356-0501. Mid-September.
- ☐ **Tennessee State Fair,** Tennessee State Fairgrounds. Sprawling livestock and agriculture fair, with 4-H Club members and Future Farmers well represented. And a midway, of course. Call 862-8980. Mid- to late September.
- ☐ **National Quartet Convention,** Nashville Municipal Auditorium. Dozens of popular gospel artists are featured in this week-long event, which is comparable to the Country Music Fan Fair celebration. Call 320-7000. Late September.

OCTOBER

- ☐ **Riverfest,** Riverfront Park. A fireworks display tops off a day of food and entertainment. Call 259-4750. First weekend in October.
- ☐ **Annual Oktoberfest,** Historic Germantown, at the corner of Seventh Avenue North and Monroe Street. Tours of German-

town, polka dancing, accordion players, and lots of authentic German food. Call 256-2729. Early October.

☐ **Southern Festival of Books,** Legislative Plaza. Readings, panel discussions, and book signings by authors from the U.S. and especially from the Southeast. Call 320-7001. Second weekend in October.

☐ **Annual NAIA Pow Wow** (call for location). Native Americans from the U.S. and Canada gather for this pow-wow sponsored by the Native American Indian Association. Call 726-0806. Mid-October.

☐ **Birthday of the "Grand Ole Opry,"** Opryland. Three-day party with performances, a country buffet, and autograph and picture sessions with Opry stars. Call 889-3060. Mid-October.

NOVEMBER

☐ **Annual Americana Christmas Sampler Craft, Folk Art & Antique Fair,** Tennessee State Fairgrounds. Shop for Christmas treasures and handcraft arts. Call 227-2080. Early November.

☐ **Longhorn World Championship Rodeo,** Nashville Municipal Auditorium. Professional cowboys and cowgirls participate in this full-scale rodeo to win championship points. Colorful costumes and music add to the excitement. Call toll free 800/477-6336 or 876-1016. Third weekend in November.

DECEMBER

☐ **Rudolph's Red Nose Run and Nashville Gas Christmas Parade,** downtown Nashville. After a five-kilometer race which begins at 1pm, the Christmas parade of 100 floats, bands, and clowns starts at 2pm at Ninth and Broadway. Call 734-1754. First Sunday in December.

☐ **Annual Dickens of a Christmas,** in Franklin (15 miles south of downtown Nashville). Historic Franklin is the perfect setting for a Victorian Christmas. Caroling and hot wassail, of course! Call 790-7094. Second weekend in December.

3. INSURANCE

Before going out and spending money on various sorts of travel insurance, check your existing policies to see if they'll cover you while you're traveling. Make sure your health insurance will cover you when you are away from home. Most credit cards offer automatic flight insurance when you purchase an airline ticket with that credit card. These policies insure against death or dismemberment in the case of an airplane crash. Also, check your credit cards to see if any of them pick up the collision damage waiver (CDW) when you rent a car.

The CDW can run as much as $10 a day and can add 50% or more to the cost of renting a car. Check your automobile insurance policy, too; it might cover the CDW as well. If you own a home or have renter's insurance, see if that policy covers off-premises theft and loss wherever it occurs. If you are traveling on a tour or have prepaid a large chunk of your travel expenses, you might want to ask your travel agent about trip-cancellation insurance.

If, after checking all your existing insurance policies, you decide that you need additional insurance, a good travel agent can give you information on a variety of different options. **Teletrip** (Mutual of Omaha), 3314 Harney Street, Omaha, NE 68175 (tel. 402/351-8000), offers many different types of travel insurance policies for 1 day to a year. These policies include medical, baggage, trip cancellation or interruption insurance, and flight insurance against death or dismemberment.

4. WHAT TO PACK

CLOTHING It's a good idea to take along an umbrella for unexpected summer thunderstorms and heavy rains any time of year. Lightweight and breathable clothing are your best choice in summer's high temperatures and equally high humidity. Layered clothing works well for days in the fall, and a jacket or coat is necessary for winter days. You might want to bring a dress-up ensemble for dining out or other events.

OTHER ITEMS Most hotels and motels will give you a wake-up call or have an alarm clock in the room, but you may want to carry a little travel alarm clock just in case. A small flashlight can prove invaluable in the event of an emergency after dark, especially if your car breaks down. A Swiss army knife is another item that everyone should carry. They are handy for countless unexpected little tasks.

5. TIPS FOR THE DISABLED, SENIORS, SINGLES, FAMILIES & STUDENTS

FOR THE DISABLED Many hotels and motels in Nashville offer handicapped-accessible accommodations, but when making reservations be sure to ask. Additionally, the public transit systems found in Nashville have either handicapped-accessible regular vehicles or offer special transportation services for the disabled. To find out more about special services, call **Access Ride** (tel. 327-0240).

The **Disability Information Office,** 700 Second Ave. S. (tel. 615/862-6492), is a referral and information office for disabled visitors. Call their office to get the free book *Access to Nashville,* which lists restaurants, hotels, and other places that are barrier-free. This booklet also contains transportation information.

FOR SENIORS   Many airlines offer discounts to senior citizens, so whenever making reservations, always be sure to ask. You should also carry some sort of photo ID card (driver's license, AARP membership card, passport, etc.) to avail yourself of senior-citizen discounts at attractions, hotels, motels, and on public transportation.

If you're not already a member, the **American Association of Retired Persons (AARP),** 601 E St. NW, Washington, DC 20049 (tel. toll free 800/424-3410), is a good source of information for senior citizens. Membership is only $8 for a married couple.

American Express (tel. toll free 800/282-1700) offers a $20 discount on their regular charge cards if you are 62 years or older. When you sign up, you get a packet of discount coupons and a quarterly newsletter containing discounts coupons as well.

Older travelers who want to learn something from their trip to Nashville, or who simply prefer the company of like-minded older travelers, should look into programs by **Elderhostel,** 75 Federal St., Boston, MA 02110 (tel. 617/426-7788). To participate in an Elderhostel program, either you or your spouse must be at least 60 years old. In addition to one-week educational programs, Elderhostel offers short getaways with interesting themes.

FOR SINGLE TRAVELERS   There's no doubt about it, single travelers are discriminated against by hotels and motels. A lone traveler often has to pay the same room rate as two people, and if you want to spend time at an expensive hotel, this can make a vacation a very costly experience. Unless you're dead set on staying at a particular hotel, you might be able to save some money by finding a comparable hostelry that offers separate rates for single and double rooms.

If you're looking for someone to travel with, **Travel Companions Exchange,** P.O. Box 833, Amityville, NY 11701-0833 (tel. 516/454-0880), provides listings of possible travel companions categorized under such headings as special interests, age, education, and location. It costs a minimum of $36 for a six-month membership and subscription to the service. It's also possible to subscribe to the organization's bimonthly newsletter without becoming a member. The newsletter costs $24 for a six-month subscription or $36 for a full year.

FOR FAMILIES   At many hotels and motels, children stay free in their parents' room if no additional bed is required. Always be sure to ask about a lodging's children's policy when making a reservation or booking a room. Children's menus are also available at many restaurants. Nashville is a great place for a family vacation. There are several miniature-golf courses, a water amusement park, and biggest and best of all, the Opryland USA theme park. Always be sure to ask about special family rates at various attractions.

FOR STUDENTS   Student discounts are available at many museums, theaters, and concert halls. Be sure to carry an ID and ask about discounts. Unfortunately, there are no American Youth Hostels in the state of Tennessee.

6. GETTING THERE

BY PLANE

THE AIRPORT   The **Nashville International Airport** (tel. 615/275-1662) is located east of downtown Nashville and south of I-40. It takes about 15 minutes to reach downtown Nashville from the airport.

THE MAJOR AIRLINES   Nashville is served by the following airlines: American Airlines (tel. toll free 800/433-7300), Delta (tel. 615/244-9860, or toll free 800/221-1212), Northwest (tel. toll free 800/225-2525), Southwest (tel. toll free 800/435-9792), TWA (tel. 615/244-9010, or toll free 800/221-2000), United Airlines (tel. toll

---

 FROMMER'S SMART TRAVELER:
AIRFARES

1. Watch the papers for special seasonal discounts. In the ongoing airfare wars, airlines frequently offer substantial discounts, but they are often only available for a short period of time.
2. Shop all the airlines that fly to Nashville. Though rates are usually fairly uniform, you may happen upon the odd special.
3. To save money on your airfare, try to fly during the week.
4. If you're flying any time near a major holiday, ask when the holiday rates are in effect. If you can fly before or after these higher rates are in effect, you can save a considerable amount of money.
5. Be sure to book your ticket as far in advance as possible. Most airlines offer their lowest rates for two-week advance-purchase tickets.
6. If you live in a major city, check the Sunday travel section of your daily paper for advertisements of ticket wholesalers, who are able to sell airline tickets for less because of various deals they are able to make.
7. Calling a travel agent may help you find out about some special fare that you may not yet be aware of.

free 800/241-6522), and USAir (tel. 615/361-4030, or toll free 800/428-4322).

REGULAR AIRFARES   At the time of this writing, round-trip 14-day advance-purchase excursion (APEX) fares from New York to Nashville were about $347. Full coach fares were running about $932 and first-class fares were about $1,466. Round-trip 14-day advance-purchase excursion fares from Los Angeles to Nashville were about $420. Full coach fares were about $1,428 and first-class fares about $1,742.

OTHER GOOD-VALUE CHOICES   You may be able to fly for less than the standard APEX fare by contacting a ticket broker (also known as a "bucket shop"). These companies advertise in the Sunday travel sections of major city newspapers with small box ads listing numerous destinations and ticket prices. You won't always be able to get the low price they advertise, but you are likely to save a bit of money off the regular fare. Call a few and compare prices, making sure you find out about all the taxes and surcharges that may not be included in the initial fare quote.

BY TRAIN

There is no Amtrak service to Nashville.

BY BUS

Greyhound Lines (tel. toll free 800/231-2222) offers service to Nashville from around the country. These buses operate along Interstate corridors or local routes. The fare between New York and Nashville is $106 one-way and $198 round-trip; the fare between Chicago and Nashville is $66 one-way and $119 round-trip. The Greyhound bus station in Nashville is at 200 Eighth Ave. S. (tel. 256-6141 or 255-1691).

BY CAR

Nashville is a hub city intersected by three Interstate highways. **I-65** runs north to Louisville, Kentucky, and south to Birmingham, Alabama. **I-40** runs west to Memphis and east to Knoxville, Tennessee. **I-24** runs northwest toward St. Louis and southeast toward Atlanta.

Here are some driving distances from selected cities (in miles)· Atlanta, 250; Birmingham, 190; Chicago, 442; Cincinnati, 291; Memphis, 206; New Orleans, 549; and St. Louis, 310.

PACKAGE TOURS

Companies that offer tours with stops in Nashville include **Globus** and **Cosmos Tourama,** both of which are owned by the same parent company and work only with travel agents.

The **Delta Queen Steamboat Company,** 30 Robin St. Wharf, New Orleans, LA 70130-1890 (tel. 504/586-0631), offers paddlewheel steamboat tours that include Nashville in the itinerary.

Tours that focus on Nashville are offered by **Domenico Tours,**

751 Broadway, Bayonne, NJ 07002 (tel. toll free 800/554-8687); **USA Super Cities,** 139 Main St., Cambridge, MA 02142 (tel. toll free 800/333-1234); **American Airlines Fly Away Vacations** (tel. toll free 800/321-2121); **Our Town Tours,** P.O. Box 148287, Nashville, TN 37214 (tel. 615/889-0525, or toll free 800/624-5170); **Country and Western/Gray Line Tours,** 2416 Music Valley Dr., Nashville, TN 37214 (tel. 615/227-2270, or toll free 800/251-1864); and **Music Valley Tour & Travel,** 2401 Music Valley Dr., Nashville, TN 37214 (tel. 615/883-1560, or toll free 800/843-6995).

CHAPTER 3

GETTING TO KNOW NASHVILLE

Getting one's bearings in a new city is always the hardest part of taking a trip, but in the following pages you'll find everything you need to know in order to get settled in after you arrive in town. This is the sort of nuts-and-bolts information that will help you, the visitor, get familiar with Nashville.

1. ORIENTATION

ARRIVING

BY PLANE   The **Nashville International Airport** (tel. 615/275-1662) is located about eight miles east of downtown Nashville and is just south of I-40. If you're driving a rented car, plan on about 15 minutes to reach downtown. See "Getting There," in Chapter 2, for information on airlines serving Nashville.

Getting Downtown   The **Downtown Airport Express** (tel. 615/275-1180) operates two shuttle routes between the airport and downtown and West End hotels. These shuttles operate from the airport every 15 minutes daily between 6am and 11pm; they stop at the hotels every 30 minutes. The downtown shuttle stops at the following hotels: Union Station, Clubhouse Inn, Stouffer Nashville, Holiday Inn Crowne Plaza, Days Inn–Downtown Convention Center, the Hermitage Hotel, and the Doubletree Hotel Nashville. The West End shuttle stops at the following hotels: Shoneys, Quality Inn, Vanderbilt Plaza, Holiday Inn Vanderbilt, Hampton Inn, Days Inn–Vanderbilt, and the Regal Maxwell House. Rates are $8 one-way and $14 round-trip.

Metropolitan Transit Authority **buses** connect the airport and downtown Nashville. The no. 18 Elm Hill Pike bus runs between 8:13am and 10:35pm Monday through Friday; departure times vary on weekends. The fare is $1.15 each way, with exact change required, and the ride takes approximately 40 minutes. Buses from the airport leave at the ground-level curbside. Buses for the airport leave from Shelter C on Deaderick Street. For the most current schedule information, call 242-4433 Monday through Friday between 6:30am and 6pm.

A **taxi** from the airport into downtown Nashville will cost you between $14 and $17. Taxis are available on the ground level of the airport terminal; ask the cab starter to find a taxi for you, or take the first available taxi in line.

BY BUS The Greyhound Lines bus station is located in downtown Nashville at 200 Eighth Ave. S. (tel. 256-6141 or 255-1691). For schedules and information, call toll free 800/231-2222.

BY CAR Nashville is a hub city intersected by three Interstate highways. **I-65** runs north to Louisville, Kentucky, and south to Birmingham, Alabama. **I-40** runs west to Memphis and east to Knoxville. **I-24** runs northwest toward St. Louis, Missouri, and southeast toward Atlanta, Georgia. Downtown Nashville is the center of the hub, encircled by Interstates 40, 65, and 265. Briley Parkway on the east, north, and west, and I-440 on the south form a larger "wheel" around this hub.

If you're heading into downtown Nashville, follow the signs for I-65/24 and take either Exit 84 or Exit 85. If you're headed to the Opryland USA area (Music Valley), take I-40 east to the Briley Parkway exit and head north. If your destination is the West End/Music Row area, take I-40 around the south side of downtown and get off at the Broadway exit.

TOURIST INFORMATION

Tourist information on Nashville and the surrounding area can be picked up at the **Nashville Convention & Visitors Bureau,** 161 Fourth Ave. N., Nashville, TN 37219 (tel. 615/259-4700). This location is convenient if you're in the downtown area. It's open Monday through Friday from 8am to 5pm.

If you're driving, the **Tourist Information Center** (tel. 615/259-4747) at the James Robertson Parkway exit (Exit 85) off I-65 may be more accessible. This office is open daily during daylight hours. Look for the Tourist Information Center sign.

If you want to pick up information when you arrive at the airport, or you have some questions, the **Nashville International Airport Welcome Center** (tel. 615/275-1674) is on the baggage-claim level. This center is open from 6:30am to 11pm daily.

IMPRESSIONS

Take of London fog 30 parts; malaria 10 parts; gas leaks 20 parts; dewdrops gathered in a brickyard at sunrise 25 parts; odor of honeysuckle 15 parts. Mix. The mixture will give you an approximate conception of a Nashville drizzle.
—O. Henry, "A Municipal Report," in *Strictly Business*, 1910

For information on the State of Tennessee, contact the **Tennessee Department of Tourism Development**, P.O. Box 23170, Nashville, TN 37202-3170 (tel. 615/741-2158).

CITY LAYOUT

Nashville was built on a bend in the Cumberland River, and it is this and other bends in the river that have defined the city's expansion over the years. The area referred to as **downtown** is located on the west side of the Cumberland and is built in a grid pattern. Numbered avenues run parallel to the river on a northwest-southeast axis. Streets perpendicular to the river are named. Though the grid pattern is interrupted by I-40 it remains fairly regular until you get to Vanderbilt University in the West End area.

For the most part, Nashville is a sprawling modern city. Though there are some areas downtown that are frequented by pedestrians, the city is primarily oriented toward automobiles. The city's main tourist attraction, Opryland USA, is about 10 miles (by highway) northeast of downtown. However, despite the sprawl, you can easily and efficiently get from an Interstate to an inner city pike, and then to a neighborhood, without having to fight a lot of traffic congestion. The only thing to watch out for is the numerous divisions of the Interstate highway as it encircles Nashville. If you don't pay very close attention to what lane you're supposed to be in, you can wind up heading in the wrong direction.

MAIN ARTERIES & STREETS   The main arteries in Nashville radiate out from downtown like spokes on a wheel. **Broadway** is the main artery through downtown Nashville and leads southwest from the river. Just after crossing I-40, Broadway forks, with **West End Avenue** being the right-hand fork. West End Avenue eventually becomes Harding Road out in the Belle Meade area. If you stay on Broadway (the left fork), the road curves around to the south becoming 21st Avenue and then Hillsboro Pike.

Eighth Avenue is downtown's other main artery and runs roughly north-south. To the north Eighth Avenue becomes **MetroCenter Boulevard** and to the south it forks, with the Eighth Avenue fork becoming the **Franklin Pike** and the other fork becoming Lafayette Road and then the Nolensville Pike.

There are also several roads that you should become familiar with out in the suburbs. **Briley Parkway** describes a large loop that begins just south of the airport, runs up the east side of the city past Opryland USA, and then curves around to the west passing well north of downtown. On the south side of the city, **Harding Place** connects I-24 on the east with Belle Meade on the west. Don't confuse Harding Place with Harding Road.

FINDING AN ADDRESS   Nashville's address-numbering system begins in downtown at Broadway and the Cumberland River and increases as you move away from this point. In the downtown area, and out as far as there are numbered avenues, avenues include either a north or south designation. The dividing line between north and south is the Broadway and West End Avenue corridor.

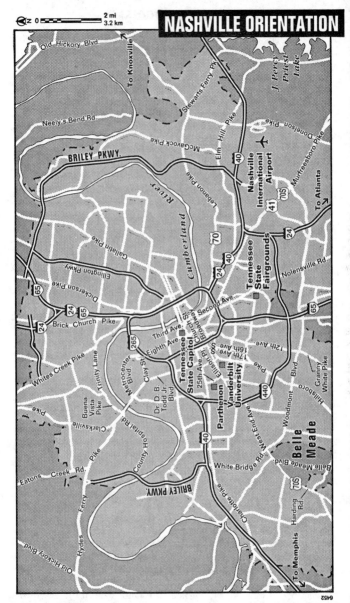

NASHVILLE ORIENTATION

STREET MAPS   You can get a map of the city from the **Tourist Information Center** (tel. 615/259-4747) at the James Robertson Parkway exit off I-65 (Exit 85) or at the **Airport Welcome Center** (tel. 615/275-1674) on the baggage-claim level at the Nashville International Airport.

If you happen to be a member of **AAA,** you can get free maps of Nashville and Tennessee from your local AAA office or from the Nashville office at 2501 Hillsboro Rd., Suite 1 (tel. 615/297-7700).

They're open Monday through Friday from 8:30am to 5:30pm (on Thursday until 7pm).

NEIGHBORHOODS IN BRIEF

Nashville has few neighborhoods in the traditional sense of the word. What it does have is named areas and communities.

The District   This downtown historic district is the most urban area of Nashville, with restored buildings housing interesting shops, restaurants, and nightclubs. The District is Nashville's main entertainment area.

The West End   Located adjacent to Vanderbilt University, this upscale neighborhood is home to many small shops, good restaurants, and several hotels. The youthful college inhabitants make this a lively part of the city.

Music Row   Recording studios and record companies make this neighborhood located around the corner of 16th Avenue South and Demonbreun Street, the center of the county-music recording industry. The Country Music Hall of Fame and Museum and numerous country stars' souvenir shops make this a major tourist neighborhood as well.

Belle Meade   This community, located seven miles out West End Avenue from downtown, is one of the wealthiest in the Nashville area and is home to several of the city's best restaurants and upscale shops. Mansions abound in Belle Meade and many are owned by country stars.

Music Valley   This area on the east side of Nashville is where you'll find the Opryland USA theme park, the Grand Ole Opry House, and numerous other country-theme tourist attractions.

2. GETTING AROUND

BY PUBLIC TRANSPORTATION

BY BUS   Nashville is served by the extensive and efficient **Metropolitan Transit Authority (MTA)** bus system. The MTA information center (tel. 242-4433) and ticket booth, located on Deaderick Street at Fifth Avenue, is open Monday through Friday from 7am to 5pm and on Saturday from 7am to 3:30pm. MTA bus stops are marked with a blue-and-white sign; in the downtown area, signs include names and numbers of all the routes using that stop. All express buses are marked with an X following the route number.

Adult **bus fares** are $1.15 ($1.45 for express buses); children under 4 ride free. You can ride for 25¢ on any MTA bus within the downtown area bordered by James Robertson Boulevard, Demonbreun Street, the Cumberland River, and I-40; just ask the bus driver for a **RUSH card** and return it when you leave.

Discount Passes You can purchase a weekly pass good for unlimited local rides from Sunday through Saturday for $14; a picture ID is required. Disabled or elderly riders qualify for a 55¢ fare with an MTA Golden Age or Medicare card.

BY TROLLEY The **Nashville Trolley Company** (tel. 242-4433) operates three trolley routes between March and October and one route during the other months of the year. These aren't really trolleys—just buses built to look like old-fashioned trolley cars. However, they're a bit more fun than the regular buses, and they go to places that you're likely to want to visit. The fare is 75¢.

The **downtown route** passes by many points of interest in downtown Nashville, and is a good way to get acquainted with the city. In summer this route operates Monday through Thursday from 11am to 8pm, on Friday and Saturday from 11am to 10pm, and on Sunday from 11am to 6pm; no service off-season. This route originates at Riverfront Park.

The **Music Row route** operates Sunday through Saturday from 11am until 8pm in the summer and has musicians performing on the trolley every Saturday between noon and 4pm. In the off-season it operates Saturday from 11am to 4pm. It also originates at Riverfront Park.

The **Music Valley route** operates only during the summer season; call the Trolley Company for the schedule for this route. To get to the Music Valley Drive trolley route, take the MTA no. 6 "Donelson/Opryland" bus, at Deaderick (Petway) Transit Mall, Shelter A.

BY TAXI

For quick cab service, call **Music City Taxi** (tel. 262-0451), **Yellow Cab** (tel. 256-0101), or **Nashville Cab** (tel. 242-7070). The flag-drop rate is $1.50; after that it's $1.50 per mile.

BY CAR

Because the city and its many attractions are quite spread out, the best way to get around Nashville is by car. It's surprisingly easy both to find your way around the city and to find parking, even downtown. The only time driving is a problem is during morning and evening rush hours. At these times, streets leading south and west out of downtown can get quite congested.

RENTAL CARS For the very best deal on a rental car, make your reservation at least one week in advance. It also pays to shop around and call the same companies a few times over the course of a couple of weeks. Quoted rates frequently change based on availability. If you decide on the spur of the moment that you want to rent a car, check to see whether there are any weekend or special rates available. If you're a member of a frequent-flyer program, be sure to mention it: You might get mileage credit for renting a car. Currently daily rates for a subcompact are around $35 and weekly rates are around $135. These rates include unlimited mileage.

All the major auto-rental companies and several independent companies have offices in Nashville. Fortunately, many of the companies have desks conveniently located on the lower level at the Nashville International Airport. Major car-rental companies in Nashville include: **Alamo Rent-A-Car,** at the airport (tel. 615/ 275-1050, or toll free 800/327-9633); **Avis Rent-A-Car,** at the airport (tel. 615/361-1212, or toll free 800/831-2847); **Budget Rent-A-Car,** at 1406 Broadway, 300 N. 1st St., the Opryland Hotel, and at the airport (tel. 615/366-0800, or toll free 800/527-0700); **Dollar Rent-A-Car,** at the airport (tel. 615/275-1081, or toll free 800/800-4000); **Hertz,** at the airport (tel. 615/361-3131, or toll free 800/654-1831); **National Car Rental,** at the airport (tel. 615/361-7467, or toll free 800/227-7368); **Payless Rent-A-Car,** 733 Briley Pkwy. and at the airport (tel. 615/361-8896, or toll free 800/ PAYLESS); and **Thrifty Car Rental,** 1315 Vultee Blvd. and at the airport (tel. 615/361-6050, or toll free 800/367-2277).

PARKING In downtown Nashville there is an inexpensive public parking lot on 1st Street South at the end of Broadway. Parking is 25¢ an hour, with no maximum limit; drop your money into the self-service machine at the end of the parking lot. Downtown parking is also available in other municipal and private lots and parking garages.

When parking on the street, be sure to check the time limit on parking meters. Also be sure to check whether or not you can park in a parking space during rush hour (between 4 and 5:30pm) or your car may be ticketed and towed.

DRIVING RULES A right turn at a red light is permitted after coming to a full stop, unless posted otherwise, but drivers must first yield to vehicles that have a green light or pedestrians in the walkway. Children under 4 years of age must be in a children's car seat or other approved restraint when in the car.

Tennessee has a very strict DUI (Driving Under the Influence of alcohol) law, and recently passed a law which states that a person driving under the influence with a child under 12 years of age may be charged with a felony.

ON FOOT

Downtown Nashville is the only area where you're likely to do much walking around. In this area you can visit numerous attractions, do some shopping, have a good meal, and go to a club, all without having to get in your car. The suburban strips can't make that claim.

 NASHVILLE

Airport The Nashville International Airport is located 15 minutes east of downtown Nashville (tel. 615/275-1662); see "Orientation," earlier in this chapter.

American Express The American Express Travel Service

office is at 4400 Harding Rd. (tel. 385-3535, or toll free 800/528-4800), and is open Monday through Friday from 9am to 5pm.

Area Code   The telephone area code in Nashville is 615.

Babysitters   Call Merry Poppins Nannies (tel. 824-0257) for a bonded professional nanny to care for your children in your hotel room.

Business Hours   Banks are generally open Monday through Thursday from 9am to 4pm, on Friday from 9am to 5 or 6pm, and on Saturday morning. Office hours in Nashville are usually Monday through Friday from 8:30am to 5pm. In general, **stores** in downtown Nashville are open Monday through Saturday from 10am to 6pm. Shops in suburban Nashville malls are generally open Monday through Saturday from 10am to 9pm and on Sunday from 1 to 6pm. **Bars** in Nashville are frequently open all day long and are allowed to stay open until 3am, but may close between 1 and 3am.

Car Rentals   See "Getting Around," earlier in this chapter.

Climate   See "When to Go," in Chapter 2.

Currency   See "money" in "Preparing for your Trip" in the Appendix.

Currency Exchange   See "Money" in "Preparing for Your Trip," in the Appendix.

Dentist   If you should find yourself in need of a dentist while you're in Nashville, contact Dental Referral Service (tel. 333-2372).

Doctor   If you need a doctor, call Medline (tel. 342-1919), open Monday through Friday from 8am to 5pm; or contact the Vanderbilt University Medical Center Physician Referral Service (tel. 322-3000), open Monday through Friday from 7:30am to 4:30pm.

Documents Required   See "Preparing for Your Trip," in the Appendix.

Driving Rules   See "By Car" in "Getting Around," earlier in this chapter.

Drugstores   Walgreen Pharmacies has several locations in the Nashville area, at 517 Donelson Pike (tel. 883-5108), 5412 Charlotte Ave. (298-5594), and 2622 Gallatin Rd. (tel. 226-7591); or call toll free 800/925-4733 for the Walgreen's nearest you. Certain Walgreen locations are open Monday through Saturday from 8am to 10pm and on Sunday from 9am to 7pm; some are open 24 hours a day. Super X Pharmacy, 303 E. Thompson Lane (tel. 361-3636), is also open 24 hours.

Embassies/Consulates   See "Fast Facts: For the Foreign Traveler," in the Appendix.

Emergencies   Phone **911** for fire, police, emergency, or ambulance. If you get into really desperate straits, call Travelers' Aid of the Nashville Union Mission, 129 Seventh Ave. S. (tel. 780-9471). It's primarily a mission that helps destitute people, but if you need help in making phone calls or getting home, they might be able to help.

Eyeglasses   If you have problems with your glasses, call Horner Rausch, which has one-hour service. They have several locations. One is downtown at 968 Main St. (tel. 226-0251) and is open Monday through Friday from 8am to 7pm and on Saturday from 8am to 5pm. Another store is at 4117 Hillsboro Rd. (tel. 298-2669).

Hairdressers/Barbers   The Heads Up Hair Cutting Center cuts hair for the entire family, and they have salons at 7071 U.S. 70, Bellevue Valley Plaza (tel. 662-0141), 2122 Green Hills Village Dr. (tel. 292-8049), 73 Whitebridge Rd. (tel. 352-4570), and several other locations.

Holidays   See "Fast Facts: For the Foreign Traveler," in the Appendix.

Hospitals   The following hospitals offer emergency medical treatment: Baptist Hospital, 2000 Church St., in the Vanderbilt area (tel. 329-5114); HCA Donelson Hospital, 3055 Lebanon Rd. (tel. 871-3600); and Vanderbilt University Medical Center, 1211 22nd Ave. S., in the downtown/Vanderbilt area (tel. 322-3391).

Hotlines   The 24-hour Info Line for Nashville (tel. 244-9393) is the number to call for entertainment, events calendar, national sports scores, and the weather. The Suicide Prevention/Crisis Intervention Center hotline is 244-7444.

Information   See "Orientation," earlier in this chapter.

Laundry/Dry Cleaning   Coin Laundry Express self-service laundries are open 24 hours, and they have locations at 2130 21st Ave. S. (tel. 297-6871), 1506 Dickerson Pike (tel. 226-9307), and 1206 Gallatin Rd. (tel. 226-9308). For dry cleaning downtown, try Nicholson Cleaners, 127 Fourth Ave. S. (tel. 255-7450) or 206 Fourth Ave. N. (tel. 255-7019), open Monday through Friday from 7am to 6pm and on Saturday from 8am to 1pm.

Libraries   The public library of Nashville and Davidson County is at 225 Polk Ave. (tel. 862-5800). It's open Monday through Friday from 9am to 8pm and on Saturday from 9am to 5pm.

Liquor Laws   The legal drinking age in Tennessee is 21. Bars are allowed to stay open until 3am every day. Beer can be purchased at a drug, grocery, or package store, but wine and liquor are sold through package stores only.

Lost Property   If you left something at the airport, call the airport authority at 275-1675; if you left something on an MTA bus, call 862-5969.

Luggage Storage/Lockers   There is a luggage-storage facility at the Greyhound Lines bus station at 200 Eighth Ave. S.; lockers cost $1 for 24 hours.

Mail   You can receive mail c/o General Delivery ("Poste Restante") at the post office (see "Post Office," below).

Maps   Maps of Nashville are available at the Chamber of Commerce, 161 Fourth Ave. N., and the Tourist Information Center, Exit 85 off I-65.

Money   See "Preparing for Your Trip," in the Appendix.

Newspapers/Magazines   *The Tennessean* is Nashville's morning daily and Sunday newspaper. The *Nashville Banner,* published Monday through Friday, is the afternoon newspaper. The arts and entertainment weekly is the *Music City Entertainment Guide,* distributed through hotels and attractions, and the alternative weekly is the *Nashville Scene.*

Photographic Needs   Dury's, with locations at 3001 West End Ave. (tel. 327-3001), 73 White Bridge Rd. (tel. 356-3275), and 720 Sixth Ave. S. (tel. 255-3456) offers one-hour film processing, complete photographic supplies, services, and equipment.

Police   For police emergencies, phone 911.

Post Office   The post office located at 901 Broadway (tel. 255-9447) is convenient to downtown and the West End, and will accept mail addressed to General Delivery. It's open Monday through Friday from 7:30am to 7pm and on Saturday from 8am to 2pm. There's also a post office in the downtown arcade at 16 Arcade (tel. 255-3579), open Monday through Friday from 7:30am to 5pm and on Saturday from 9am to 2pm.

Radio   Nashville has over 30 AM and FM radio stations. Some specialize in a particular style of music, including gospel, soul, big band, and jazz. Of course there are several country-music stations, including WSM (650 AM), the station that first broadcast the "Grand Ole Opry." WPLN (90.3 FM) is Nashville's National Public Radio station.

Religious Services   For an extensive listing of churches, look under "Churches" in the Greater Nashville yellow pages; they're arranged by locality. Or ask at your hotel for locations and hours of services.

Restrooms   There are public restrooms at the parking lot on First Avenue South and also at hotels, restaurants, and shopping malls.

Safety   Even though Nashville is not a huge city, it has its share of crime. Take extra precaution with your wallet or purse when you're in a crush of people—pickpockets take advantage of crowds. Whenever possible, try to park your car in a garage, not on the street, at night. When walking around town at night, stick to the busier streets. The lower Broadway area, though popular with visitors, also attracts a rather unruly crowd to its many bars. See also the "Safety" section in the Appendix.

Shoe Repairs   If your shoes break down, take them to the Golden Boot, 2817 West End Ave. (tel. 320-5223), open Monday through Friday from 8am to 5:30pm and on Saturday from 8am to 2pm. Downtown, visit Tony's Shoes Service in the Nashville Arcade (tel. 256-8590).

Taxes   In Tennessee the state sales tax is 8.25%. This tax applies to goods as well as all recreation, entertainment, and amusements. However, in the case of services, the tax is often already included in the price of admission. The Nashville hotel and motel room tax is 4%, which when added to the 8.25% makes for a total hotel-room tax of 12.25%.

Taxis   See "Getting Around," earlier in this chapter.

Television   The seven local television channels are 2 (ABC), 4 (NBC), 5 (CBS), 8 (PBS), 17 (Fox), and 30 and 39 (both Independent).

Time   Tennessee is in the central time zone—central standard time (CST) or central daylight time, depending on the time of year, making it two hours ahead of the West Coast and one hour behind the East Coast.

Tipping   In restaurants, 15% to 20% is the rule if service has been good. Taxi drivers expect about 10%. Airport porters and bellhops should be tipped about 50¢ per bag, and $1 per night is appropriate for chamber staff.

Transit Information   Call 242-4433 for information on the MTA bus system, and 242-4433 for information on the trolleys.

Useful Telephone Numbers Info Line for Nashville (tel. 244-9393) is the 24-hour number to call for entertainment, events calendar, national sports scores, and the weather. The Suicide Prevention/Crisis Intervention Center hotline is 244-7444.

Weather For a local forecast, call the National Weather Service (tel. 754-4633) Monday through Friday from 8am to 4pm, or the 24-hour Info Line for Nashville (tel. 244-9393).

3. NETWORKS & RESOURCES

FOR STUDENTS If you don't already have one, get an official student ID from your school. Such an ID will entitle you to discounts at museums, theaters, and attractions around town.

There are many universities and colleges in the Nashville area, but the main ones are **Vanderbilt University,** on West End Avenue (tel. 322-7311), a private four-year research-oriented university; **Tennessee State University,** 3500 John A. Merritt Blvd. (tel. 320-3131), a public four-year university; **Belmont University,** 1900 Belmont Blvd. (tel. 383-7001), a Baptist liberal arts university; and **Fisk University,** 1000 17th Ave. N. (tel. 329-8500), a private four-year African-American university.

West End Avenue around Vanderbilt University is a college neighborhood full of restaurants, cafés, and shops. The area around Belmont University also has some college-type hangouts.

FOR GAY MEN & LESBIANS The **Center for Lesbian and Gay Community Services,** 703 Berry Rd. (tel. 297-0008), is open Monday through Saturday from 5 to 10pm. They have a good library and many on-going activities.

Local gay and lesbian publications available in Nashville include *Query* (tel. 327-3273), a weekly newspaper, and the *Triangle Journal News* (tel. 901/454-1411), a monthly Memphis-based newspaper. Both are usually available at Davis-Kidd booksellers and other establishments around the Nashville area.

FOR WOMEN The **Nashville Women's Alliance,** The Center, 703 Berry Rd. (tel. 297-0008), has weekly women's discussion groups and a good library. **Tower Books,** 2400 West End Ave. (tel. 327-8085), has an extensive woman's-book section.

The local **Rape Crisis Center** is at 327-1110.

CHAPTER 4

NASHVILLE ACCOMMODATIONS

1. DOWNTOWN
- **FROMMER'S SMART TRAVELER: HOTELS**
2. THE OPRYLAND AREA
3. THE AIRPORT AREA
- **FROMMER'S COOL FOR KIDS: HOTELS**
4. MUSIC ROW & THE WEST END
5. THE NORTH SIDE

Whatever your reason for being in Nashville, you'll likely find a hotel that's convenient for you. Because the city caters to a lot of country-music fans, there is an abundance of inexpensive and moderately priced hotels, especially near Opryland USA. And part of the Opryland complex is the largest hotel in Nashville— the 1,800-room Opryland Hotel. There are also several good luxury hotels, including two in historic buildings, in downtown Nashville. If you want to be close to the city's best restaurants and wealthiest neighborhoods, book a room in a West End hotel.

The rates quoted below are the published rates, sometimes called "rack rates" in hotel-industry jargon. At expensive business and resort hotels, rack rates are what you are most likely to be quoted if you walk in off the street and ask what a room will cost for that night. However, it's often not necessary to pay this high rate if you plan ahead or ask for a discount. It's often possible to get low corporate rates even if you aren't visiting on business. Frequently there are also special discount rates available. Many hotel and motel chains now have frequent-guest and other special programs that you can join. These programs often provide savings off the regular rates.

The rates quoted here don't include the Tennessee sales tax (8.25%) or the Nashville room tax (4%), which together will add 12.25% onto your room bill. Keep this in mind if you're on a tight budget. I have used the following rate definitions for price categories in this chapter (rates are for double rooms): "Very Expensive," $125 and up; "Expensive," $90 to $125; "Moderate," $60 to $90; "Inexpensive," under $60. However, in placing hotels into categories, I calculated what they would cost with the tax included. Therefore a hotel that charges $85 a night for a double room is listed in the "Expensive" category rather than the "Moderate" category because with the tax added in, you'll be paying more than $95.

1. DOWNTOWN

VERY EXPENSIVE

HOLIDAY INN CROWNE PLAZA, 623 Union St., Nashville, TN 37219. Tel. 615/259-2000, or toll free 800/HOLIDAY. Fax 615/742-6057. 479 rms, 16 suites. A/C TV TEL

$ Rates: $119–$129 single or double; $279–$600 suite. Weekend rates available. AE, CB, DC, DISC, ER, JCB, MC, V. **Parking:** $5 self-park, $7 valet.

Located across the street from the Tennessee State Capitol building and two blocks from the Nashville Convention Center, this new high-rise is popular with both state politicians and convention-goers. The atrium lobby has a modern elegance that draws on traditional and contemporary hotel architecture. There's plenty of polished marble all around and hand-carved, dark-wood furniture. A glass elevator provides city views as it whisks you up to your floor.

Though the rooms are for the most part clean and comfortable without being remarkable, the northside rooms overlooking the Capitol have the best views. These rooms are also popular with state politicians.

Dining/Entertainment: Way up on the hotel's 25th floor you'll find the Pinnacle restaurant, a revolving restaurant that features steaks and great views. There are also Cajun dishes, and even buffalo steaks and burgers. On the mezzanine level there's the more casual Speakers Restaurant, which is open for three meals a day and has a great salad bar. In the lobby there's a sunken lounge area.

Services: Room service, valet/laundry service.

Facilities: Indoor pool, fitness center, gift shop.

EXPENSIVE

DOUBLETREE HOTEL NASHVILLE, 315 Fourth Ave. N., Nashville, TN 37219. Tel. 615/244-8200, or toll free 800/528-0444. Fax 615/244-4894. 337 rms, 38 suites. A/C TV TEL

$ Rates: $69–$134 single; $79–$144 double; $125–$475 suite. AE, CB, DC, DISC, ER, MC, V. **Parking:** $6 per day.

This strikingly angular high-rise is only a couple of blocks from downtown Nashville's main entertainment areas, yet is also conveniently located for anyone in town on state-government business. I find the corner rooms, with their sharply angled walls of glass, the most appealing rooms in the hotel. You should also ask for a room facing the street; these rooms get more light. Rooms on the ninth floor offer additional amenities.

Dining/Entertainment: The Hunt Room, an elegant dining room serving continental and traditional American dishes at lunch and dinner, is tucked in a corner off the lobby and offers the warmest atmosphere in the hotel. In the high-ceilinged lobby, you'll find the casual Union St. Grill, which is open for all three meals. The Reflections Lounge is a large, glitzy place with lots of chrome and mirrors. There's a dance floor and recorded Top 40 and country dance music nightly. The Gallery Lounge is in the atrium section of the lobby and features evening piano music.

Services: Room service, valet/laundry service, airport shuttle, tour services.

Facilities: Indoor pool, sauna, exercise room, gift shop.

THE HERMITAGE HOTEL, 231 Sixth Ave. N., Nashville, TN 37219. Tel. 615/244-3121, or toll free 800/251-1908, 800/

FROMMER'S SMART TRAVELER: HOTELS

1. Always ask what the rate will be with the tax figured in. At a total of 12.25%, taxes in Nashville can add a shocking amount to the bill at a luxury hotel.
2. On weekends, luxury hotels tend to offer discounts while budget restaurants tend to raise their rates. With rates converging in this way, you may find that for only a little bit more than you'd spend at a budget hotel, you can stay in a much nicer hotel.
3. At the more expensive hotels, rates fluctuate based on occupancy. If the hotel isn't full and doesn't expect to fill up, you stand a good chance of getting the room at a lower rate. Thus, if you book farther in advance, you're more likely to get the room at a lower rate—and if you're making a last-minute booking, you may be able to bargain. Just tell them that the rate quoted you is too much and tell them what *you* want to spend.
4. If you plan to stay downtown, be sure to ask about parking charges. These can add as much as $10 or so to your daily bill.
5. For some strange reason, the less money you spend on a room, the more likely you are to get free local phone calls and a continental breakfast (coffee, doughnuts, fruit, and juice).
6. Families should consider staying in an all-suite hotel. These hotels are proliferating in Nashville and offer two-room suites for about the same price as a regular hotel room at many luxury hotels. This can be a real bonus if you've got kids with you and plan to be in town for a few days.
7. Many chain hotels and motels are now instituting advance-reservation discounts similar to those offered by airlines. You may be able to save quite a bit of money by making your reservation two weeks or a month in advance.
8. Members of the American Automobile Association (AAA) and senior citizens often can get discounts at inexpensive motels. At more expensive hotels, be sure to ask about special packages or discount rates.

342-1816 in Tennessee. Fax 615/254-6909. 112 suites. A/C TV TEL
$ Rates: $90 suite for one person, $100 suite for two people; $69 suite for one or two people on weekends. AE, CB, DC, DISC, MC, V. **Parking:** $6.50 per day.

 This historic downtown hotel was built in 1910 in the classic beaux arts style, and the lobby is nearly as elegant as that of the Union Station hotel. Marble columns are topped by gilded

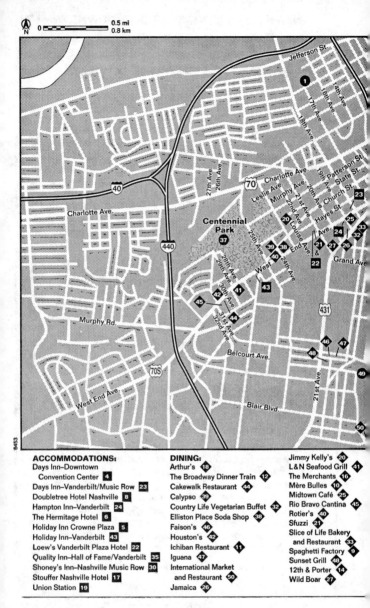

ACCOMMODATIONS:

Days Inn–Downtown
  Convention Center **4**
Days Inn–Vanderbilt/Music Row **23**
Doubletree Hotel Nashville **8**
Hampton Inn–Vanderbilt **24**
The Hermitage Hotel **6**
Holiday Inn Crowne Plaza **5**
Holiday Inn–Vanderbilt **43**
Loew's Vanderbilt Plaza Hotel **22**
Quality Inn–Hall of Fame/Vanderbilt **35**
Shoney's Inn–Nashville Music Row **30**
Stouffer Nashville Hotel **17**
Union Station **19**

DINING:

Arthur's **18**
The Broadway Dinner Train **12**
Cakewalk Restaurant **44**
Calypso **39**
Country Life Vegetarian Buffet **32**
Elliston Place Soda Shop **38**
Faison's **46**
Houston's **42**
Ichiban Restaurant **11**
Iguana **47**
International Market
  and Restaurant **50**
Jamaica **26**

Jimmy Kelly's **20**
L&N Seafood Grill **41**
The Merchants **16**
Mère Bulles **10**
Midtown Café **25**
Rio Bravo Cantina **45**
Rotier's **40**
Sfuzzi **21**
Slice of Life Bakery
  and Restaurant **33**
Spaghetti Factory **9**
Sunset Grill **48**
12th & Porter **14**
Wild Boar **27**

plasterwork that frames a stained-glass ceiling. A marble floor, Persian-style carpets, and heavy draperies complete this picture of classic sophistication.

Unfortunately, the rooms don't continue the lobby's rich decor. All the rooms are suites, with separate sitting areas, but the furnishings are a bit dated and the carpeting is desperately in need of replacing. However, there are clock radios and hairdryers in all the rooms, and because each room is different, you can't be sure whether

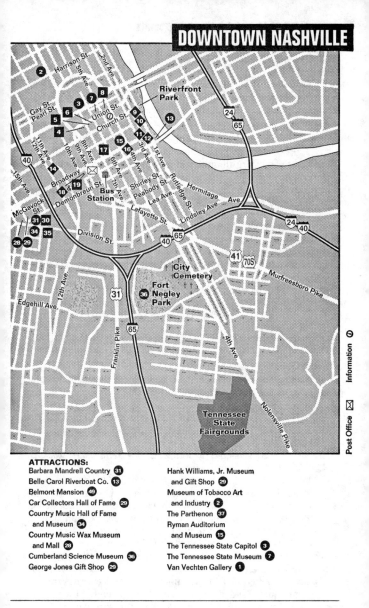

DOWNTOWN NASHVILLE

Riverfront Park

Harrison St.
2nd Ave.
5th Ave.
Gay St.
Pearl St.
Union St.
Church St.
11th Ave.
12th Ave.
10th Ave.
8th Ave.
9th Ave.
7th Ave.
6th Ave.
4th Ave.
3rd Ave.
1st Ave.
Broadway
Demonbreun St.
Bus Station
Shirley St.
Peabody
Hermitage Ave.
Lea Ave.
Lafayette St.
Rutledge St.
Lindsley Ave.
McGavock St.
Division St.
Edgehill Ave.
12th Ave.
Franklin Pike
City Cemetery
Fort Negley Park
Murfreesboro Pike
4th Ave.
Nolensville Pike

Tennessee State Fairgrounds

Post Office ⊠   Information ⊘

ATTRACTIONS:

Barbara Mandrell Country ③①
Belle Carol Riverboat Co. ⑬
Belmont Mansion ㊾
Car Collectors Hall of Fame ㉙
Country Music Hall of Fame
  and Museum ㉞
Country Music Wax Museum
  and Mall ㉘
Cumberland Science Museum ㊱
George Jones Gift Shop ㉙

Hank Williams, Jr. Museum
  and Gift Shop ㉙
Museum of Tobacco Art
  and Industry ②
The Parthenon ㊲
Ryman Auditorium
  and Museum ⑮
The Tennessee State Capitol ③
The Tennessee State Museum ⑦
Van Vechten Gallery ①

---

you'll get one with attractive furnishings or not. North-side rooms have good views of the Capitol.

Dining/Entertainment: Down in the basement, you'll find the Grille Room, which has a vaulted ceiling that gives it the feel of a wine cellar. Also in the basement is a dark and woody lounge with an outrageously ornate plasterwork ceiling.

STOUFFER NASHVILLE HOTEL, 611 Commerce St., Nash-

ville, TN 37203-3707. Tel. 615/255-8400, or toll free 800/HOTELS-1. Fax 615/255-8202. 673 rms, 34 suites. A/C TV TEL

$ Rates: $99–$139 single or double; $269–$788 suite. AE, CB, DC, DISC, MC, V. **Parking:** $10 per day.

Because it's directly connected to the Nashville Convention Center, this large, modern hotel is often filled with conventioneers. However, the hotel does offer all the luxuries one would expect, which makes it the city's top downtown hotel choice.

The guest rooms are all quite roomy and feature wingback chairs and dark-wood furnishings. Walls of glass let in plenty of light. For business travelers, there are computer hookups in all the rooms, and in the king rooms there are well-lighted work desks. The upper floors offer additional amenities, including a concierge, private lounge, bathrobes, express check-out, complimentary continental breakfast and evening hors d'oeuvres, and evening turn-down service.

Dining/Entertainment: The Commerce St. Bar and Grille, located off the lobby, can only be described as having a Southern plantation deco styling. The menu features classic Southern dishes as well as more contemporary and health-conscious offerings. There are breakfast and lunch buffets. The Bridge Lounge and Deli is in the greenhouselike sky bridge that connects the hotel to the Church Street Centre shopping mall.

Services: 24-hour room service, concierge, valet/laundry service, complimentary shoeshine, complimentary morning coffee and newspaper.

Facilities: Indoor pool, exercise room with weight machines, hot tub, sauna, sun deck, gift and sundries shop.

UNION STATION, 1001 Broadway, Nashville, TN 37203. Tel. 615/726-1001, or toll free 800/331-2123. Fax 615/248-3554. 126 rms, 12 suites. A/C TV TEL

$ Rates: $85–$135 single or double; $160–$250 suite. AE, CB, DC, DISC, MC, V. **Parking:** $7.

This hotel is the most elegant in Nashville and is housed in the former Union Station railway terminal. Though trains no longer stop here, the hotel, which was completely renovated in 1986, still has the feel of a turn-of-the-century train station. When Union Station was built in 1900 railroads were at the peak of their popularity and the building's lavish decor reflects this. The building was designed in the Romanesque Gothic style and features a clock tower that's a Nashville landmark. Inside, the lobby has a soaring, vaulted ceiling of stained glass, and everywhere you look there's exquisite gilded plasterwork. At either end of the hall are large bas-relief panels, and at one end, the obligatory clock.

No two guest rooms here are alike, but in all of them you'll find such attractive touches as gilded mirror and picture frames and original woodwork. One of the only drawbacks is that in most rooms the bathrooms are a bit small. My personal favorite rooms are the gallery deluxe rooms, which have 22-foot-high ceilings and huge arched walls of glass that overlook the lobby. These rooms best capture the hotel's railroad heritage.

Dining/Entertainment: Arthur's, which was once the

women's smoking room, is the hotel's premiere restaurant and is considered the best restaurant in the city (see "Downtown," in Chapter 5, for details). For breakfast, there's the vaultlike McKinley Room, with its arched windows, stone walls, and Spanish floor tiles. The Broadway Bistro is a combination lounge and casual dining room serving a mix of American, Cajun, and southwestern dishes.

Services: Room service, complimentary morning newspaper, complimentary downtown shuttle.

Facilities: Gift and sundries shop.

INEXPENSIVE

DAYS INN–DOWNTOWN CONVENTION CENTER, 711 Union St., Nashville, TN 37219. Tel. 615/242-4311, or toll free 800/627-3297. Fax 615/242-1654. 100 rms. A/C TV TEL

$ Rates: $39–$69 single; $43–$79 double. AE, CB, DC, DISC, MC, V. **Parking:** Free.

$ Though this downtown motel has seen better days, it's still a good choice if you're on a budget but want the convenience of being downtown. The convention center, Printers Alley, and Tennessee Performing Arts Center are all within a few blocks. There are good views from the upper-floor hallways and rooms on the north side of the motel. The guest rooms have all been recently refurbished. The bathrooms, unfortunately, are quite small.

2. THE OPRYLAND AREA

VERY EXPENSIVE

OPRYLAND HOTEL, 2800 Opryland Dr., Nashville, TN 37214. Tel. 615/889-1000. Fax 615/871-7741. 1,891 rms. 120 suites. A/C TV TEL

$ Rates: $169–$209 single or double; $279–$740 suite. Special packages available. AE, CB, DC, DISC, MC, V. **Parking:** Free self-park, $8 valet.

✪ Each day thousands of visitors stop by this hotel just to wander through its tropical atriums. What most people come to see—and why this is *the* place to stay in Nashville if you can afford it—is the Cascades atrium, which is topped by a 2½-acre glass roof. This tropical greenhouse takes its name from the 40-foot-tall waterfall that cascades down an artificial rock outcropping. There are also an ever-changing fountain that's lit with colored lights at night, bridges and meandering paths, palm trees and other tropical plants, a revolving gazebo bar, and a deluxe patio restaurant. The Conservatory atrium is even larger and is filled with many more exotic plants.

To balance out this tropical fantasy, there are several very traditional lobbies. The largest and grandest of these is the Magnolia lobby, which has as its focal point a classically proportioned double staircase worthy of the most elegant antebellum mansion.

Guest rooms, while modern and comfortable, do not, however,

live up to the promise of the public areas. Though colonial American decor and tasteful floral wallpaper gives them a touch of classic elegance, they are still of average size and not overly plush. Wingback chairs, however, provide an extra measure of comfort. The more expensive rooms are those overlooking the Conservatory or the Cascades atriums.

Dining/Entertainment: Whatever your craving, you'll find just the right restaurant under the roof of the Opryland Hotel. The Cascades Restaurant offers the most spectacular setting, while the Old Hickory Restaurant features the most sophisticated atmosphere. Both these restaurants serve continental cuisine. For traditional Southern dining, there is Rhett's, which is adjacent to the Conservatory atrium and has an "outdoor" patio. Rachel's Kitchen offers lighter, less expensive meals. During the warm months, you can dine on the Veranda beside the pool, and any time of year you can enjoy Sunday brunch in the Magnolia lobby. Ice cream, pastries, and coffee are the fare at the Conservatory Café.

There are also five lounges around this huge hotel. Most popular is the Cascades Lounge with its revolving gazebo patio. In the Cascades lobby you'll find the less crowded and quieter Lobby Bar. The Stagedoor Lounge offers live entertainment (mostly country music) and dancing in the evening. The Pickin' Parlor also offers live music, in this case primarily acoustic country guitar music. In the Jack Daniel's Saloon, Tennessee sippin' whiskey is the drink of choice.

Services: Room service, safe-deposit boxes, travel agency, car-rental desk, Opryland ticket sales.

Facilities: 18-hole golf course, two large outdoor swimming pools, fitness center, saunas, hot tubs, tennis courts, pro shop, 20 specialty shops, beauty salon.

EXPENSIVE

RAMADA INN ACROSS FROM OPRYLAND, 2401 Music Valley Dr., Nashville, TN 37214. Tel. 615/889-0800, or toll free 800/2-RAMADA. Fax 615/883-1230. 300 rms, 5 suites. A/C TV TEL

$ Rates: $81–$91 single or double; $130 suite. AE, CB, DC, DISC, MC, V. **Parking:** Free.

This Ramada Inn is located right across the road from the entrance to the Opryland Hotel, and is the next most luxurious hotel in the area. The colonial American–style lobby immediately gives the impression that this is a country inn. That feeling is quickly dispelled, however, when you walk into the hotel's large, though strangely empty, atrium, which houses the pool and a lounge.

Guest rooms that open onto the atrium are rather dark, so I'd ask for one that has windows to the outside. Many of the rooms have been recently redecorated and these are also worth asking for.

Dining/Entertainment: Briley's restaurant is a moderately priced place with a classic southern decor and buffets for breakfast, lunch, and dinner. Pennington's Lounge is in the atrium and features a large-screen TV for sports broadcasts.

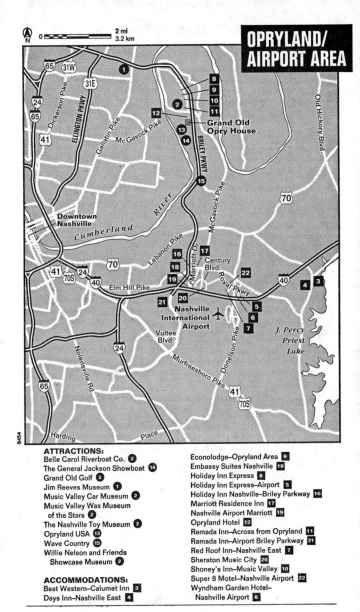

OPRYLAND/ AIRPORT AREA

ATTRACTIONS:
Belle Carol Riverboat Co. **2**
The General Jackson Showboat **14**
Grand Old Golf **2**
Jim Reeves Museum **1**
Music Valley Car Museum **2**
Music Valley Wax Museum
  of the Stars **2**
The Nashville Toy Museum **2**
Opryland USA **13**
Wave Country **15**
Willie Nelson and Friends
  Showcase Museum **2**

ACCOMMODATIONS:
Best Western–Calumet Inn **3**
Days Inn–Nashville East **4**

Econolodge–Opryland Area **9**
Embassy Suites Nashville **18**
Holiday Inn Express **8**
Holiday Inn Express–Airport **5**
Holiday Inn Nashville–Briley Parkway **16**
Marriott Residence Inn **17**
Nashville Airport Marriott **19**
Opryland Hotel **12**
Ramada Inn–Across from Opryland **11**
Ramada Inn–Airport Briley Parkway **21**
Red Roof Inn–Nashville East **7**
Sheraton Music City **20**
Shoney's Inn–Music Valley **10**
Super 8 Motel–Nashville Airport **22**
Wyndham Garden Hotel–
  Nashville Airport **6**

Services: Room service, complimentary airport and Opryland Hotel shuttle, valet/laundry service.
Facilities: Indoor pool, hot tub, giftshop/newsstand.

MODERATE

**SHONEY'S INN–MUSIC VALLEY, 2420 Music Valley Dr.,
Nashville, TN 37214. Tel. 615/885-4030,** or toll free
800/222-2222. Fax 615/391-0632. 185 rms. A/C TV TEL

$ Rates: $69–$89 single or double. AE, CB, DC, DISC, MC, V.
Parking: Free.

This modern hotel is one of the first lodgings along Music
Valley Drive, which puts it just a little bit closer to Opryland
and the Opryland Hotel than some of the other choices here.
Guest rooms are done in the same pastels as the lobby. The
pickled-pine furniture and chairs upholstered with colorful floral fabrics give the rooms considerably more character than most
hotel rooms in this price category have. Local phone calls are
free.

Dining/Entertainment: There's a Shoney's restaurant adjacent
to the hotel, and a cocktail lounge just off the hotel lobby.

Facilities: Indoor pool, outdoor hot tub, gift shop.

INEXPENSIVE

**ECONOLODGE–OPRYLAND AREA, 2460 Music Valley
Dr., Nashville, TN 37214. Tel. 615/889-0090,** or toll free
800/424-4777. 86 rms. A/C TV TEL
$ Rates: $36–$60 single; $46–$60 double. Higher rates are for
weekends. AE, CB, DC, DISC, MC, V. **Parking:** Free.

Located less than a mile from Opryland, this Music Valley
Drive motel offers basic accommodations at low rates. The
guest rooms are surprisingly large, though the bathrooms are
quite small. With a miniature-golf course right next door, this is a
good choice for families. There's also a small pool in front of the
hotel. Unfortunately, the highway traffic noise isn't conducive to
relaxing by the pool.

**HOLIDAY INN EXPRESS, 2516 Music Valley Dr., Nash-
ville, TN 37214. Tel. 615/889-0086,** or toll free 800/
HOLIDAY. Fax 615/889-0086. 121 rms. A/C TV TEL
$ Rates (including continental breakfast): $44–$64 single; $50–
$70 double. AE, CB, DC, DISC, MC, V. **Parking:** Free.
This is currently the last hotel in the strip of Music Valley Drive
motels catering to Opryland visitors. This also happens to be the least
expensive motel in the area. The rooms are quite basic, with standard
budget-motel furnishings. There's a small pool out front, though it
gets a lot of traffic noise from the highway. You'll also get free local
phone calls if you stay here.

3. THE AIRPORT AREA

VERY EXPENSIVE

**EMBASSY SUITES NASHVILLE, 10 Century Blvd., Nash-
ville, TN 37214. Tel. 615/871-0033,** or toll free 800/
EMBASSY. Fax 615/883-9245. 284 suites. A/C TV TEL
$ Rates (including full breakfast): $119–$139 suite for one or two

people; $89–$99 suite midweek and off-season. AE, CB, DC, DISC, JCB, MC, V. **Parking:** Free.

This all-suite hotel makes a great choice and a good value for families, as well as business travelers. Not only are the two-room suites well designed for comfort and convenience, but there are also plenty of activities for the kids. Of particular interest is the supervised youth activities program. The center-piece of the hotel is its large atrium, which is full of tropical plants, including palm trees. A rocky stream runs through the atrium and there are caged tropical songbirds adding their cheery notes to the pleasant atmosphere.

All guest rooms are two-room suites with two TVs and two phones, a wet bar, small refrigerator, coffee maker, and microwave ovens on request. A couch, easy chairs, and a table for four make these suites far more comfortable than standard hotel rooms.

Dining/Entertainment: The Ambassador Grille restaurant is located amid the tropical plants in the atrium and serves moderately priced meals. Also in the atrium are the lounge where the evening manager's reception is held and a dining area where the complimentary breakfast is served. There is also a sports bar off the atrium.

Services: Room service, complimentary airport shuttle, complimentary morning newspaper, complimentary evening manager's reception.

Facilities: Indoor pool, exercise room, hot tub, sauna, games room, gift shop.

SHERATON MUSIC CITY, 777 McGavock Pike, Nashville, TN 37214-3175. Tel. 615/885-2200, or toll free 800/325-3535. Fax 615/871-0926. 412 rms, 3 suites. A/C TV TEL

$ Rates: $125 single; $130–$140 double; $550 suite. Weekends and advance-reservation rates available. AE, CB, DC, DISC, ER, JCB, MC, V. **Parking:** Free.

Set on 23 attractively landscaped acres in a modern business park near the airport, this Sheraton sits atop a hill with a commanding vista of the surrounding area. Classic Georgian styling sets the tone for the hotel, and when you walk through the front door, you'll step into an elegant lobby with marble floors. The warm glow of burnished cherrywood paneling surrounds you, and in the center of the room stands a lion's-head fountain.

Because the four-story hotel is built around a large courtyard, hallways are quite long. If you don't want to do a lot of walking, request a room close to the lobby. The rooms themselves are well designed and have the business traveler in mind. There are three phones in every room, large work desks, and plenty of closet space, as well as a couple of comfortable chairs. The colonial American–style furnishings are made with bird's-eye maple. In the big bathrooms, you'll find a nice assortment of toiletries, a coffee maker, and a phone.

Dining/Entertainment: The Belair Room is steeped in southern elegance with white linen and paneled walls. The menu features deluxe southern fare with an emphasis on steaks and seafood. The service is excellent and prices for entrees are between $14 and $20. The Veranda Lounge is down a couple of steps from the lobby and sports a gardenlike atmosphere. This is the place if you're searching for a quiet place to enjoy a drink and a bit of conversation. For dancing to live or recorded popular and country music, there's McGavock's Place II, a big, lively lounge with lots of flashing lights.

Services: 24-hour room service, concierge, valet/laundry service, complimentary airport shuttle, massages.

Facilities: A courtyard off the lobby contains a large outdoor pool that's quiet and protected from the noise of the nearby Interstate. There's an indoor pool as well. You'll also have access to two tennis courts and a health club with hot tub, sauna, weight machines, free weights, and other exercise equipment. Other facilities include a gift shop and a games room.

EXPENSIVE

HOLIDAY INN NASHVILLE—BRILEY PARKWAY, 2200 Elm Hill Pike, Nashville, TN 37210. Tel. 615/883-9770, or toll free 800/HOLIDAY. Fax 615/391-4521. 385 rms, 4 suites. A/C TV TEL

$ Rates: $89 single; $99 double; $148–$240 suite. Lower advance-reservation rates available. AE, CB, DC, DISC, MC, V. **Parking:** Free.

If you're looking for someplace that's convenient to the airport and not too far from Opryland, this Holiday Inn just off the Briley Parkway is a good bet. The lobby features two atriums, which together provide a cheery, sunny atmosphere. One atrium houses the reception desk, car-rental desk, and a couple of seating areas, while the other contains the swimming pool, a lobby lounge area, and a terraced restaurant.

Guest rooms for the most part are fairly standard, with Holiday Inn reliability one of their strong points. There are, however, big TVs and plenty of counter space in the bathrooms. The king rooms have a bit more space and are designed with business travelers in mind. On the 14th-floor executive level, you'll also receive complimentary coffee and morning newspaper and a continental breakfast.

Dining/Entertainment: Jackson's Veranda is a colorful and casual restaurant set to one side of the back atrium. The Sweetwater lounge hosts live country and rock music Tuesday through Saturday nights. On Sunday night there's a show featuring new musicians and songwriters.

Services: Room service, airport shuttle, valet/laundry service, car-rental desk, Opryland ticket sales.

Facilities: Indoor pool, hot tub, exercise room, sauna, games room with video games and table tennis.

MARRIOTT RESIDENCE INN, 2300 Elm Hill Pike, Nashville, TN 37214. Tel. 615/889-8600, or toll free 800/331-3131. Fax 615/871-4970. 168 suites. A/C TV TEL

$ Rates (including continental breakfast): $84–$124 suite for one or two people. AE, CB, DC, DISC, MC, V. **Parking:** Free.

⑤ This hotel is built to resemble a modern apartment complex: All the rooms are suites with kitchen facilities. For this reason the Marriott Residence Inn appeals to both families and business travelers who expect to be in town for a while.

In addition to plenty of space and comfortable seating areas, there are fireplaces in most of the rooms. The penthouse suites have two bedrooms, the second being a loft area. These suites also have two bathrooms. Most rooms also have a small balcony or deck so that you can sit outside and enjoy good weather and the attractively landscaped grounds of the hotel.

Dining/Entertainment: There's no restaurant on the premises.

Services: Airport shuttle, manager's hospitality hour.

Facilities: The small sports court is set up both for basketball and some racquet sports.

NASHVILLE AIRPORT MARRIOTT, 600 Marriott Dr., Nashville, TN 37214-5010. Tel. 615/889-9300, or toll free 800/228-9290. Fax 615/889-9315. 399 rms, 6 suites. A/C TV TEL

$ Rates: $82–$144 single or double; $274–$555 suite. Weekend rates available. AE, CB, DC, DISC, ER, JCB, MC, V. **Parking:** Free.

This is one of Nashville's most resortlike hotels and features lots of recreational facilities. So if you like to stay in shape while you're out of town on business or on a vacation, this is an excellent choice. The hotel grounds cover 17 mostly wooded acres, though the proximity to the Interstate keeps the grounds rather noisy.

All the guest rooms were recently remodeled and now feature very elegant, classically styled furnishings. For business travelers, there are large work desks, modem hookups, voice mail, and express check-in and check-out. Families will do well to ask for a lower-level poolside room; for extra space, try one of the corner rooms, which are 30% larger than standard rooms.

Dining/Entertainment: Lots of polished brass and exposed brick give the Village Green restaurant a classy, classic feel, while a wall of glass overlooking a grove of trees provides a relaxing, natural setting. The menu features American and continental dishes and prices are fairly moderate. Albert's is a quiet lounge that has live guitar music a few nights each week. The Terrace Lounge overlooks the swimming pool area.

Services: Room service, concierge, valet/laundry service, tour desk, complimentary morning newspaper and coffee on weekdays, complimentary airport shuttle, babysitting service, safe-deposit boxes.

Facilities: Indoor/outdoor pool, hot tub, health club, saunas, tennis courts, picnic area, basketball court, volleyball court, gift shop.

MODERATE

HOLIDAY INN EXPRESS–AIRPORT, 1111 Airport Center Dr., Nashville, TN 37214. Tel. 615/883-1366, or toll free 800/HOLIDAY. Fax 615/889-6867. 206 rms. A/C TV TEL

$ Rates (including continental breakfast): $45–$55 single; $53–$63 double. AE, CB, DC, DISC, MC, V. **Parking:** Free.

Though you might expect from the name that this is a basic motel, it's far from that. From the minute you pull up to the grand entry portico, you'll recognize that this is a great value. Step through the door and you'll find yourself in the lobby of a remote mountain lodge. There are moose-antler chandeliers hanging from exposed roof beams, a flagstone floor, and a river-rock fireplace. The guest rooms are all fairly spacious, with country-pine furniture and extra-large bathrooms. Many rooms have little balconies overlooking the courtyard gardens.

Dining/Entertainment: There's no restaurant or lounge on the premises, but several are within walking distance.

Services: Access to nearby full-service health club.

Facilities: Outdoor pool.

RAMADA INN–AIRPORT BRILEY PARKWAY, 733 Briley Pkwy., Nashville, TN 37217. Tel. 615/361-5900, or toll free 800/2-RAMADA. Fax 615/367-0339. 200 rms, 8 suites. A/C TV TEL

$ Rates: $45–$64 single; $50–$70 double; $85–$145 suite. AE, CB, DC, DISC, MC, V. **Parking:** Free.

This 11-story hotel is one of the closest accommodations to the airport, and makes a good choice if you plan to arrive late at night or if you have an early flight out. Guest rooms are fairly large, though the bathrooms are not. Big windows are a plus, especially if you're up on a higher floor. The king rooms have comfortable little sofas.

Dining/Entertainment: McRedmond's Restaurant, located off the lobby, serves moderately priced American standards. Also off the lobby is Conroy's Pub, a sports bar that features live country music and dancing on the weekends.

Services: Room service, complimentary airport shuttle, Opryland shuttle, car-rental desk.

Facilities: Outdoor pool.

WYNDHAM GARDEN HOTEL–NASHVILLE AIRPORT, 1112 Airport Center Dr., Nashville, TN 37214. Tel. 615/889-9090, or toll free 800/822-4200. Fax 615/885-1564. 180 rms, 24 suites. A/C TV TEL

$ Rates: $64–$79 single or double; $89 suite. AE, CB, DC, DISC, MC, V. **Parking:** Free.

There's something comfortingly old-fashioned about the lobby of this modern hotel. Just inside the front door, you'll find a seating area in front of a wood-paneled wall. A fireplace and bookshelves beckon you to sit down and relax a while. Behind this librarylike seating area is a second and similar area that has more chairs and couches and a lounge off to one side.

The guest rooms all feature cherrywood furniture that gives the rooms a classic feel. You'll also find two phones, clock radios, remote-control TVs, and coffee makers. The bathrooms have plenty of space, big counters, and hairdryers. The king rooms are nicely laid out with the beds facing out the window and separated from the seating/work area by a bureau arranged perpendicular to the wall. The overall feeling in these rooms is of a minisuite.

Dining/Entertainment: The Garden Café, which serves three meals a day, is a casual place with moderate prices. The menu has an international flavor. A lobby lounge is set behind the library seating area just inside the front door.

Services: Room service, complimentary airport shuttle, laundry/valet service, safe-deposit boxes.

Facilities: Indoor pool, hot tub, exercise room.

INEXPENSIVE

BEST WESTERN–CALUMET INN, 701 Stewart's Ferry Pike, Nashville, TN 37214. Tel. 615/889-9199, or toll free 800/528-1234. 80 rms, 4 suites. A/C TV TEL

$ Rates (including continental breakfast): $38–$69 single; $44–$85 double; $85–$156 suite. AE, CB, DC, DISC, MC, V.

This new motel is located just south of I-40 at Exit 219 and is across the street from Uncle Bud's catfish restaurant. The plushest rooms are the king suites, which come with whirlpool tubs. Facilities include an outdoor swimming pool.

DAYS INN–NASHVILLE EAST, 3445 Percy Priest Dr., Nashville, TN 37214. Tel. 615/889-8881, or toll free 800/325-2525. 70 rms, 5 suites. A/C TV TEL

$ Rates: $30–$56 single; $32–$58 double; $69–$94 suite. AE, CB, DC, DISC, MC, V. **Parking:** Free.

Located right next door to the popular Uncle Bud's catfish restaurant, this older motel has open hallways along the outside of the building and rooms with fairly small windows. However, if you don't plan to spend much time in your room, this shouldn't be a problem—and think of all that great catfish just steps

---

Ⓕ FROMMER'S COOL FOR KIDS: HOTELS

Opryland Hotel (see p. 43) The kids can run all over this huge hotel's two tropical atriums, exploring waterfalls, hidden gardens, fountains, whatever, and then head for one of the pools. There are also enough restaurants under this one roof to keep everyone in the family happy.

Nashville Airport Marriott (see p. 49) Set on spacious grounds, this hotel gives the kids plenty of room to run around. There's an indoor/outdoor pool and even a basketball court.

Embassy Suites Nashville (see p. 46) With a supervised youth-activity program, an indoor pool, and a garden atrium, there is plenty to keep the kids distracted here.

away. Facilities include a small outdoor pool and a hot tub, and there are also suites with whirlpool tubs available.

RED ROOF INN–NASHVILLE EAST, 510 Claridge Dr., Nashville, TN 37214. Tel. 615/872-0735, or toll free 800/THE-ROOF. Fax 615/871-4647. 120 rms. A/C TV TEL

$ Rates: $28–$34 single; $34–$42 double. AE, CB, DC, DISC, MC, V. **Parking:** Free.

This chain of basic motels offers accommodations comparable to those at more familiar budget chains such as Motel 6. You'll find this particular Red Roof Inn motel just off I-40 at the Donelson Parkway exit. To reach the motel, head north on Donelson Parkway and turn left on Shacklett Drive.

SUPER 8 MOTEL–NASHVILLE AIRPORT, 720 Royal Pkwy., Nashville, TN 37214. Tel. 615/889-8887, or toll free 800/800-8000. Fax 615/889-8887. 110 rms. A/C TV TEL

$ Rates (including continental breakfast): $40 single; $46–$56 double. AE, CB, DC, DISC, MC, V. **Parking:** Free.

Located just off Donelson Parkway, this is a newer Super 8 Motel and is a modern brick building rather than the familiar half-timbered structures so familiar to Interstate travelers. The rooms are all very clean and feature modern furnishings and good, firm mattresses.

---

4. MUSIC ROW & THE WEST END

EXPENSIVE

LOEW'S VANDERBILT PLAZA HOTEL, 2100 West End Ave., Nashville, TN 37203. Tel. 615/320-1700, or toll free 800/23-LOEWS. Fax 615/320-5019. 338 rms, 3 suites. A/C MINIBAR TV TEL

$ Rates: $89–$165 single or double; $112–$600 suite. AE, CB, DC, DISC, MC, V. **Parking:** $5 self-park, $7 valet.

This high-rise hotel across the street from Vanderbilt University stays busy with conferences and conventions, but even at its busiest it manages to maintain an air of quiet sophistication. Before ever setting foot in this hotel, you begin to sense the luxuriousness. The parking lot is attractively landscaped, and a huge flower arrangement is the first thing you see when you step into the travertine-floored lobby, which is decorated with European tapestries and original works of art.

Guest rooms are decorated with a contemporary European styling. I like the lower rooms with the angled walls that slope inward. These have a charmingly unique feel to them that sets them apart from other hotel rooms. In these rooms, you'll find a wall of curtains that gives a very cozy and romantic feel. Furnishings in all the rooms are antique reproductions, and TVs and minibars are hidden in cherrywood armoires. The more spacious and luxuriously appointed concierge-level guest rooms also have coffee makers and hairdryers, and telephones in the bathrooms. Concierge-level guests can enjoy complimentary breakfast and evening hors d'oeuvres in an elegant club lounge with a fireplace and great views of the city. Business travelers will appreciate the large work desks, computer hookups, voice mail, and dual phone lines.

Dining/Entertainment: Sfuzzi, one level below the lobby, is decorated to look a bit like a Roman ruin with faux marble walls and columns. The menu features Italian bistro fare (see "Music Row and the West End," in Chapter 5, for details). Just off the lobby is the more casual Plaza Grill, which also serves Mediterranean fare at moderate prices. The Garden Lounge is a lively place with live music nightly.

Services: Room service, concierge, valet/laundry service, shoeshine service.

Facilities: Exercise room, gift shop, hair salon; unfortunately, there's no swimming pool, but there are plans to add one soon.

MODERATE

HAMPTON INN–VANDERBILT, 1919 West End Ave., Nashville, TN 37203. Tel. 615/329-1144, or toll free 800/HAMPTON. Fax 615/320-7112. 171 rms. A/C TV TEL

$ Rates (including continental breakfast): $58–$61 single; $65–$68 double. AE, CB, DC, DISC, MC, V. **Parking:** Free.

This reliable chain motel is located one block from Vanderbilt University and six blocks from both Music Row and the Parthenon. Guest rooms are all furnished with modern appointments, and you'll find the king rooms particularly spacious. With the university so close by, it's not surprising that there are quite a few good restaurants within walking distance.

Facilities: Outdoor pool, exercise room.

HOLIDAY INN–VANDERBILT, 2613 West End Ave., Nashville, TN 37203. Tel. 615/327-4707, or toll free 800/HOLIDAY. Fax 615/327-8034. 300 rms, 3 suites. A/C TV TEL

$ Rates: $60–$75 single; $60–$98 double; $156–$252 suite. AE, CB, DC, DISC, MC, V. **Parking:** Free.

With the Vanderbilt University football stadium right outside this hotel's back door, it isn't surprising that this is a favorite with Vanderbilt alumni and football fans. However, if you stay here, you're also right across the street from Centennial Park.

Couples and business travelers will do well to ask for a king room. These are considerably more comfortable than rooms with two beds in them, and have work desks with phones, bedside phones, coffee makers and clock radios. If you ask for a room on the park side of the hotel, you may be able to see the Parthenon from your room. All the rooms here have private balconies.

Dining/Entertainment: The Commodore Restaurant serves American favorites at moderate prices amid traditional decor heavy on the brass and beveled glass. In the Commodore Lounge there's live music (mostly country, but some rock and pop) most nights of the week.

Services: Room service, business services (secretaries, faxes, copies).

Facilities: Outdoor pool, fitness center.

QUALITY INN–HALL OF FAME/VANDERBILT, 1407 Division St., Nashville, TN 37203. Tel. 615/242-1631, or toll free 800/221-2222. Fax 615/244-9519. 103 rms, 5 suites. A/C TV TEL

$ Rates: $49–$65 single; $59–$75 double; $64–$100 suite. AE, CB, DC, DISC, MC, V. **Parking:** Free.

Along with the Shoney's Inn mentioned below, this is the closest lodging to Music Row and the Country Music Hall of Fame. Keep in mind that many of the people staying here are in town for some partying, so expect a bit of noise. The standard rooms are what you'd expect from a moderately priced Quality Inn. However, if you're here with your family or plan to be in town for a while, the large suites, which have twice the space of a regular room, are a particularly good deal.

Dining/Entertainment: There's an inexpensive restaurant and a large lounge with live country music most nights of the week.

Facilities: Outdoor pool.

SHONEY'S INN–NASHVILLE MUSIC ROW, 1521 Demonbreun St., Nashville, TN 37203. Tel. 615/255-9977, or toll free 800/222-2222, 800/233-4667 in Canada. Fax 615/242-6127. 147 rms, 7 suites. A/C TV TEL

$ Rates: $49 single; $59 double; $79–$89 suite. AE, CB, DC, DISC, MC, V. **Parking:** Free.

If you want to stay right in the heart of Music Row and possibly spot a few country-music stars while you're in town, try this Shoney's. This is sort of a modern antebellum-style motel. In the lobby you'll find walls covered with dozens of autographed photos of country-music stars who have stayed here. The rooms are fairly standard, though they are all quite clean and comfortable. You'll get free local phone calls if you stay here.

Dining/Entertainment: There's a Shoney's restaurant right next door to the hotel.

Services: Complimentary morning coffee and newspaper, airport shuttle.

Facilities: Outdoor pool.

INEXPENSIVE

DAYS INN–VANDERBILT/MUSIC ROW, 1800 West End Ave., Nashville, TN 37203. Tel. 615/327-0922, or toll free 800/325-2525. Fax 615/327-0102. 151 rms. A/C TV TEL

$ Rates: $39–$60 single; $39–$70 double. AE, CB, DC, DISC, MC, V. **Parking:** Free.

Though this motel dates back 30 years or so, the rooms have been refurbished in recent years making it a good choice if you're on a budget. For a bit more money you can opt for a room with a whirlpool tub and a steam bath. Music Row and Vanderbilt University are both within walking distance. Facilities include a casual restaurant with inexpensive meals, a lounge that features live country music, and an outdoor swimming pool.

5. THE NORTH SIDE

EXPENSIVE

REGAL MAXWELL HOUSE, 2025 MetroCenter Blvd., Nashville, TN 37228. Tel. 615/259-4343, or toll free 800/222-8888, 800/233-9188 in Canada. Fax 615/242-4967. 289 rms. 12 suites. A/C TV TEL
$ Rates: $94–$114 single; $104–$124 double; $165–$300 suite. Weekend rates available. AE, CB, DC, DISC, ER, JCB, MC, V. **Parking:** Free.

Located just off I-265 and convenient to both downtown and Opryland, this high-rise hotel has a commanding view of the Nashville skyline from its upper floors. The original Maxwell House Hotel was in downtown Nashville, and it was there that President Theodore Roosevelt once commented that the hotel's coffee was "good to the last drop."

Glass elevators on the outside of the building take full advantage of the unobstructed views from this northern Nashville location. Guest rooms have large windows to take in some of those same views. Furnishings feature traditional styling, including wooden headboards and wingback chairs. Each room has a large armoire that hides the TV and also serves as a desk.

Dining/Entertainment: The Crown Court Restaurant, up on the 10th floor has the best view of any restaurant in town. Open for dinner only, the restaurant serves a mix of American classics and southern specialties. The dishes are all well prepared and the service is excellent. For breakfast and lunch, there is Pralines, just off the lobby. Maxwell's is a lively lounge with recorded Top 40 and country dance music in the evenings.

Services: Room service, concierge, valet/laundry service.
Facilities: Outdoor pool, two lighted tennis courts, indoor hot tub, steam room, exercise room.

INEXPENSIVE

LA QUINTA INN–METROCENTER, 2001 MetroCenter Blvd., Nashville, TN 37228-0001. Tel. 615/259-2130, or toll free 800/531-5900. Fax 615/242-2650. 121 rms. A/C TV TEL
$ Rates (including continental breakfast): $43–$56 single; $50–$63 double. AE, CB, DC, DISC, MC, V. **Parking:** Free.

With its southwestern styling, this modern motel on the north side of downtown may seem out of place, but I'm sure you'll find the La Quinta both attractive and comfortable. For couples and business travelers, the king rooms are the best bet here. These rooms include recliners, full-length mirrors, and remote-control TVs. There's an outdoor swimming pool, and local calls are free.

NASHVILLE DINING

The rest of the country may make fun of southern cooking, with its fatback and chitlins, collard greens, and fried everything, but there is more to southern food than these stereotypes. You'll find that southern fare, in all its diversity, is a way of life here in Nashville. This is not to say that you can't get good Italian, French, German, Japanese, Chinese, or even Vietnamese—you can. However, as long as you're here below the Mason-Dixon Line, you owe it to yourself to try a bit of country cookin'. Barbecue and fried catfish are two inexpensive staples well worth trying, and if you enjoy good old-fashioned American food, try a "meat-and-three" restaurant, where you get your choice of three vegetables with your meal. However, to find out what southern cooking is truly capable of, try someplace serving New Southern or New American cuisine. This is the equivalent of California cuisine, but made with traditional, and not-so-traditional, southern ingredients.

I have divided the following restaurant listings into four different general locations: **"downtown,"** which is roughly the area within 12 blocks of the Cumberland River between Broadway and Jefferson Street; **"Music Row and the West End,"** which refers to the area along West End Avenue and Broadway beginning about 20 blocks from the river; **"south of downtown"** which refers to the large area of the city's southern suburbs, with many of the restaurants clustered around the Mall at Green Hills; and **"Belle Meade,"** which is roughly along Harding Road, which itself is a western extension of West End Avenue.

For these listings, I have classified a restaurant as "Expensive" if a meal without wine or beer would cost $25 or more. At a restaurant in the "Moderate" category, you can expect to pay between $15 and $25 for a complete dinner (once again, without beer or wine), and at a "Budget" restaurant, a complete meal can be had for less than $15.

1. DOWNTOWN

EXPENSIVE

ARTHUR'S, in the Union Station hotel, 1001 Broadway. Tel. 255-1494.
  Cuisine: CONTINENTAL. **Reservations:** Highly recommended; jacket and tie required for men.

$ Prices: Six-course fixed-price dinner $45. AE, CB, DC, DISC, MC, V.

Open: Dinner only, Mon–Thurs 5:30–10pm, Fri–Sat 5:30–11pm, Sun 5:30–9pm.

 The Union Station hotel is quite simply the most elegant hotel in Nashville, which makes Arthur's a contender for most elegant restaurant in the city. Tucked into its own room off the hotel's immense lobby, this restaurant breathes southern gentility. There are huge plantation-style shutters on the windows, gilded plasterwork and stained glass, lots of lace and walnut paneling, a stone fireplace, and comfortable banquettes. The very first thing you'll see when you arrive at Arthur's is the cart of cordials and liqueurs. This alone should give you an idea of what dinner here entails. Set aside at least two or three hours for a meal—you'll want to savor every course. The menu changes daily and is always given verbally. However, you can count on such dishes as rack of lamb, chateaubriand, and tournedos of beef to make regular appearances. Quail, pheasant, and duck are also served frequently, and on a recent evening, stuffed pheasant breast in grape leaves was among the main courses. Sauces, such as beurre blanc and sauce dijonnaise, are always rich and full of flavor. Flambéed desserts and coffees are a specialty of Arthur's and shouldn't be missed.

THE MERCHANTS, 401 Broadway. Tel. 254-1892.
  Cuisine: NEW AMERICAN/NEW SOUTHERN. **Reservations:** Recommended.
$ Prices: Appetizers $3–$7.25; main courses $15–$20. AE, DC, MC, V.

🅕 FROMMER'S SMART TRAVELER: RESTAURANTS

1. If you're looking to save money, head for a "meat-and-three" restaurant or try some barbecue. Either of these meals is a good bet for inexpensive and filling regional specialties. If you've got friends or the family with you, consider ordering take-out barbecue by the pound.
2. If you have a CEO's tastes but a working stiff's wallet, try doing lunch at the gourmet restaurants. Prices (and portions) are smaller during the midday meal. You'll get to sample some outstanding culinary delights and still have money for dinner.
3. Whenever you eat, keep an eye on the bar tab, which can add quite a bit to your bill—even if you only have one or two drinks.
4. Some restaurants offer less expensive meals if you dine between 5 and 6pm. It's worth checking on if you're planning a meal in advance.

Open: Upstairs, lunch Mon–Fri 11am–2pm; dinner Sun–Thurs 5–10pm, Fri–Sat 5–11pm. Sidewalk café and grill, Mon–Fri 11am–11pm, Sat noon–11pm (bar open until midnight Fri–Sat).

The old South meets ancient Rome at the Merchants, one of the finest restaurants in Nashville. This restaurant tastefully manages to blend contemporary Mediterranean styling (alabaster wall sconces and a grape motif) with traditional southern design elements such as ceiling fans and louvered shutters. A favorite power-lunch spot and after-work hangout for the young executive set, Merchants has a loyal clientele. However, once you step through the doors at the Merchants, you'll completely forget the world outside. The restaurant's first floor consists of a bar, a café, and an outdoor patio seating area. The bar and café sport contemporary Italianate influences that place Merchants firmly in the realm of the Mediterranean styling that's currently en vogue. Upstairs is an even more elegant dining room.

A dinner here might begin with quail Andrew, which is served with foie gras croûtons and a madeira demi-glace or shrimp Wellington, which is made with spinach, feta cheese, garlic, and lemon butter. From here you could move on to fresh grouper in corn husk with poblano chili butter, grilled corn, and pico de gallo salsa, or perhaps hickory-grilled pork chops au poivre made with a shallot-cognac demi-glace.

MODERATE

ICHIBAN RESTAURANT, 109 Second Ave. N. Tel. 254-7185.

Cuisine: JAPANESE. **Reservations:** Not required.

$ Prices: Appetizers $1.95–$3.75; main courses $7.95–$14.50. AE, MC, V.

Open: Lunch Mon–Fri 11:30am–2pm; dinner Mon–Thurs 5–10:30pm, Fri–Sat 5–11pm, Sun 5–10pm.

As you walk by this restaurant, you'll see traditional Japanese food displayed in the window—it looks tempting even though it's plastic. Located in the historic Lower Broadway district, this simply decorated restaurant has a spare yet comfortable feeling, further enhanced by the conviviality of the staff.

Some nicely prepared vegetable appetizers I can recommend are the grilled or broiled eggplant with a miso sauce, or try some clam or flounder sushi with ponzu sauce. The bento box is an artfully arranged meal, with your choice of teriyaki, tempura, kushikatsu, or negimaki, and is served with a variety of extras such as pot stickers or shrimp rolls.

THE MAD PLATTER, 1239 Sixth Ave. N. Tel. 242-2563.

Cuisine: NEW AMERICAN/NEW SOUTHERN. **Reservations:** Recommended.

$ Prices: Appetizers $4.95–$6.95; main courses $14.25–$23.50. AE, DISC, MC, V.

Open: Lunch Mon–Fri 11am–2pm; dinner Tues–Sat 5:30–11pm.

★ Located in an old brick corner store in a historic neighborhood full of Victorian buildings and renovated houses, the Mad Platter has the feel of a corner hangout restaurant and is casual yet upscale. A wall of bookshelves filled with knickknacks and old *National Geographics* and a front table covered with old children's books are evidence that the owners are collectors, as well as the operators of a restaurant that serves fun and delicious food.

The menu changes daily, but you can always find something on it to delight your taste buds. If it's on the menu, try the thick, flavorful, and rich peasant stew. We ordered pasta and gnocchi, and when the plate came it was heaped high with sun-dried tomatoes and chicken and marvelously accented with pesto. Crab cakes were full of crabmeat with a delicious Maryland-style seasoning. For dessert you can choose between a light espresso ice or Death by Chocolate—either way, you can't lose. Lunch here is a good deal.

MERE BULLES, 152 Second Ave. N. Tel. 256-1946.
   Cuisine: NEW AMERICAN/NEW SOUTHERN. **Reservations:** Recommended.
 $ **Prices:** Appetizers $5.95–$8.95; main courses $9.95–$20.95; Sun brunch $12.95 adults, $6.95 for children under 10. AE, DC, DISC, MC, V.
   Open: Lunch Mon–Sat 11am–3pm; dinner Mon–Thurs 6–10pm, Fri–Sat 6–11pm, Sun 6–9pm; brunch Sun 11:30am–3pm. Lounge, Sun–Thurs 11am–midnight, Fri–Sat 11am–2am.

This old Maxwell House Coffee warehouse has been renovated as the home of "Mother Bubbles," the woman etched on the glass wall at the back of this extremely spacious restaurant. The most prominent feature here is a lounge area with a long bar, cushy chairs, and soft lighting that illuminates colorful paintings on the exposed brick walls. Take a booth in this cavernous and comfortable space and listen to some live jazz while you're waiting for your food to arrive.

Try the house special salad, an appetizing concoction of crabmeat, artichokes, hearts of palm, mushrooms, and peppers with a basil vinaigrette, to start a meal. After this flavorful beginning, you can choose from among enticing main courses such as filet mignon with a red-pepper coulis, salmon grilled with a crust of herbs, or chicken sautéed with Jack Daniel's sauce and wild mushrooms. There usually is a good selection of veal and pasta dishes on the menu as well. On Thursday from 5 to 7pm, Mère Bulles offers, for $10 per person, wine tastings with complimentary appetizers. Call for reservations.

BUDGET

12TH & PORTER, 114 12th Ave. N. Tel. 254-7236.
   Cuisine: NEW AMERICAN/NEW SOUTHERN. **Reservations:** Accepted only for parties of six or more (unless attending a show).
 $ **Prices:** Appetizers $4.25–$6.95; main courses $9.95–$13.95; shows $3–$10. AE, MC, V.

Open: Lunch Mon–Fri 11:30am–2pm; dinner Mon–Sat 5:30pm–1:30am.

It's hip, it's retro, it's 12th & Porter. If you dig the turquoise-and-black checkerboard styling of the 1950s and like imaginative cooking, you should be sure to check this place out. 12th & Porter is primarily a nightclub, and suffers some hard use at the hands (and feet) of Friday-night dance crowds, but it's worth putting up with the bar atmosphere to enjoy such dishes as spicy potato pie with salsa, sour cream, and green onions, or roasted eggplant crostini with feta cheese, garlic, and red pepper. And that's just for starters. Main courses include such tempting dishes as rasta pasta, which is made with shrimp, scallops, and blackened chicken on fettuccine. Each night there are special pizzas (such as roast duck) and calzones. You'll find 12th & Porter in the warehouse district behind the offices of *The Tennesseean* newspaper. There is valet parking, so you don't need to look for a parking space.

THE GERST HAUS, 228 Woodland St. Tel. 256-9760.

Cuisine: GERMAN. **Reservations:** Not accepted.

$ Prices: Appetizers $1.95–$5.25; main courses $5.95–$10.95. No credit cards.

Open: Mon–Sat 11am–10pm, Sun 3–9pm.

Every day is Oktoberfest at this big, rather scruffy old beer hall of a restaurant. You can sit at a long table and order pig's knuckles or sauerbraten, clink glasses with your neighbor, and join in the boisterous fun. On Saturday and Sunday from 5pm on there's a live polka band (and a cover charge), which makes it even livelier. Meals are simple and come with a choice of extras such as potato salad or boiled cabbage. There are some German-style barbecue items too, if you feel as if you just can't get enough of the local barbecue.

THE OLD SPAGHETTI FACTORY, 160 Second Ave. N. Tel. 254-9010.

Cuisine: ITALIAN. **Reservations:** Not accepted.

$ Prices: Main courses $4.25–$8.95. DISC, MC, V.

Open: Lunch Mon–Fri 11:30am–2pm; dinner Mon–Thurs 5–10pm, Fri–Sat 5–11pm, Sun 4–10pm.

With its ornate Victorian elegance, you'd never guess that this restaurant was once a warehouse. Where boxes and bags were once stacked, diners now sit surrounded by burnished wood. There's stained and beveled glass all around, antiques everywhere, and plush seating in the waiting area. The front of the restaurant is a large and very elegant bar. Now if they'd just do something about that trolley car that someone parked in the middle of the dining room.

A complete meal—including a salad, French bread, spumoni ice cream, and beverage—won't set you back very much. The choices are spaghetti, spaghetti, and spaghetti, which comes with a variety of sauces. Oh yes, they also serve lasagne, ravioli, and tortellini.

2. MUSIC ROW & THE WEST END

EXPENSIVE

WILD BOAR, 2014 Broadway. Tel. 329-1313.
 Cuisine: NEW AMERICAN/NEW SOUTHERN. **Reservations:** Required.
 $ Prices: Appetizers $5.95–$10.95; main courses $25.95–$32.95. AE, CB, DC, DISC, MC, V.
 Open: Lunch Mon–Fri 11am–2pm; dinner Mon–Thurs 6–10pm, Fri–Sat 6–10:30pm.

Exotic floral arrangements, high-backed booths upholstered in tapestry, burgundy awnings and flags over the tables, and trophy heads underlit with spotlights provide a lavish medieval setting for the Wild Boar's high-dining experience. Men in suits and sophisticated ladies meet here to take their seats in private dining rooms decorated with Flemish-style paintings. Though the food is wonderful, it's the wine list that truly sets the restaurant apart. In fact, the Wild Boar was recently written up by *Wine Spectator* magazine as having one of the three best restaurant wine cellars in the United States. If you happen to be an oenophile, you'll most certainly want to sample a bit of wine from the inventory of over 18,000 bottles.

The menu changes frequently, but chef Boris usually offers a tasting menu with six or so courses, each accompanied by a complimentary wine. Creations such as bluefin tuna sushi and salmon tartare with flying fish caviar are offered with a Roederer Brut Premier; the soufflé is accompanied by a 1991 Sergio Cerutti Luva. You get the idea. The cost for the tasting menu is $98 per person with the wines and $75 without wine. Both the dinner and lunch menus offer similar kinds of imaginative cuisine, but lunch is much less expensive. There's live piano music Wednesday through Saturday from 8pm on.

MODERATE

CAKEWALK RESTAURANT, 3001 West End Ave. Tel. 320-7778.
 Cuisine: NEW AMERICAN/NEW SOUTHERN. **Reservations:** Highly recommended.
 $ Prices: Appetizers $4–$6.25; main courses $9–$19.50. AE, CB, DC, DISC, MC, V.
 Open: Lunch Mon–Fri 11am–3pm; dinner Sun–Thurs 5:30–10pm, Fri–Sat 5:30–11pm; brunch Sun 11am–3pm.

Geometric cutouts on a curving faux-finished wall create an art deco effect at this bistrolike restaurant tucked into the back of a tiny shopping plaza. Changing art exhibits complement the colors of the blue walls, which seem to infuse the interior with a blue light. Soft candlelight on the tables adds an additional romantic touch, and the cozy lounge is a relaxing place to have a drink.

The menu pulls its gastronomic references from all over the

world, adding creative seasonings to traditional dishes. Chicken shows up in several ways. One worthy of note is chicken Kathmandu, with tamarind-raisin sauce and curried vegetables. Paella comes on a spicy saffron rice, and catfish Clovis has a tortilla crust and is served with a black-eyed-pea salsa. The dance contests for which this restaurant is named offered cakes as prizes, but probably not like the award-winning cake that's offered for dessert here now—a flourless chocolate cake with dense rich chocolate crème and a raspberry glaze. I'd visit here just for the cake—I'd even walk. Sunday-brunch offerings include traditional egg dishes and gourmet specials.

FAISON'S, 2000 Belcourt Ave. Tel. 298-2112.

> **Cuisine:** INTERNATIONAL/SOUTHERN. **Reservations:** Recommended.
>
> **$ Prices:** Appetizers $3.75–$7; main courses $9–$16. AE, DC, MC, V.
>
> **Open:** Lunch Mon–Fri 11am–2pm; dinner Sun–Thurs 5–10pm, Fri–Sat 5–11pm; brunch Sun 11:30am–2:30pm.

Operated by the same folks who brought Nashville the Sunset Grill, which many people consider the best restaurant in town (see below), Faison's is a more traditional sort of place. The restaurant is in an old renovated house with hardwood floors and a New Orleans–style brick patio under the trees out front. On a warm summer evening, you can have a seat on the patio. A restaurant has to have a lot of guts to offer such cross-cultural assimilations as potato skins stuffed with caviar or artichoke fritters with bacon bits and mustard-cream sauce. The wacky names on the menu (broken-heart fettuccine, bow Thai, and que pasta) should clue you in that dinner here isn't meant to be a serious event. For late-night dining, there's some of Nashville's unusual hot food. "Hot" in this case means spicy, and you can get hot lamb, hot chicken, even hot smoked duck. These dishes can be fixed medium, hot, or masochistic (no mild, no way).

HOUSTON'S, 3000 West End Ave. Tel. 269-3481.

> **Cuisine:** STEAKS. **Reservations:** Not accepted.
>
> **$ Prices:** Main courses $7.25–$15.75. AE, MC, V.
>
> **Open:** Sun–Thurs 11am–10pm, Fri–Sat 11am–midnight.

S West End Avenue is home to quite a few good restaurants, most of which are moderately priced and appeal to college students from nearby Vanderbilt University. Houston's is one such place, and you can be sure that it'll be packed on a weekend night. Despite the fact that this is a new building, interior brick arches and exposed beams give the restaurant the feel of a renovated warehouse. The salads and burgers here are consistently voted the best in town, but they also do a good job on prime rib and barbecue. A few surprising dishes, such as chicken with couscous and catfish beignets, also find their way onto the menu. There's also a dark oak bar with lots of brass and pine.

JAMAICA, 1901 Broadway. Tel. 321-5191.

> **Cuisine:** JAMAICAN. **Reservations:** Recommended for parties of eight or more.
>
> **$ Prices:** Appetizers $3.75–$8.50; main courses $7.95–$15.75. AE, CB, DC, MC, V.

Open: Mon–Sat 11am–11pm, Sun 5–10pm (bar open until 1am daily).

Visiting Jamaica is like visiting Jamaica (well, almost). Murals of a marketplace, people fishing, village and jungle scenes in the softly lit dining room are convincingly real. Choose from several different ambiences here—on one side you can share your table with an aquarium of tigerfish and eels; on the other, a colorful bar studded with boat prows and psychedelic corals. When the owners visit Jamaica, they like to bring back recipes, which means that the menu has a good deal of authenticity about it.

How does conch fritters or mango salad sound? I decided to order the jerk chicken with Daddy Dee's beans and peas, and it didn't let me down. The Negril grilled fish, which was marinated in lime juice and served with a sweet-potato salad, was also delicious.

JIMMY KELLY'S, 217 Louise Ave. Tel. 329-4349.

Cuisine: STEAK/SEAFOOD. **Reservations:** Recommended.
$ Prices: Appetizers $5.75–$6.75; main courses $12.75–$26.75. AE, DC, MC, V.
Open: Dinner only, Mon–Sat 5pm–midnight.

Tradition is the name of the game at Jimmy Kelly's, so if you long for the good old days of gracious southern hospitality, be sure to schedule a dinner here. The restaurant is in a grand old home with neatly trimmed lawns and a valet-parking attendant waiting out front. There's a big magnolia tree by the front door, so you know this is the real South. Inside you'll almost always find the dining rooms and bar bustling with activity as elderly African-American waiters in white jackets navigate from the kitchen to the tables and back. Though folks tend to dress up for dinner here, the several small dining rooms are surprisingly casual.

Jimmy Kelly's kitchen turns out well-prepared traditional dishes such as chateaubriand in a burgundy-and-mushroom sauce and blackened catfish (not too spicy, to accommodate the tastes of middle Tennessee). Whatever you have for dinner, don't miss the cornbread—it's the best in the city.

L&N SEAFOOD GRILL, 2817 West End Ave., Park Place Mall. Tel. 327-9610.

Cuisine: SEAFOOD/STEAK. **Reservations:** Recommended.
$ Prices: Appetizers $2.50–$6.50; main courses $7.95–$14.95. AE, CB, DC, DISC, MC, V.
Open: Mon–Thurs 11am–10pm, Fri–Sat 11am–11pm, Sun 11am–9pm.

It might be a chain restaurant in a shopping mall, but Nashville thinks it's the best seafood around. This well-lit "glass and brass" place is classy and cozy with a nice cherrywood bar, dark forest-green ceiling and wallpaper, and lots of window tables. Just inside the front door is a tank full of Maine lobsters, should you be in the mood for a splurge. As you might expect, there are plenty of pictures of fish and ships (not fish and chips) on the walls. The fish served here is so fresh that just about any seafood dish is good, but I particularly like the blackened catfish with smoky jalapeño sauce.

MIDTOWN CAFE, 102 19th Ave. S. Tel. 320-7176.

Cuisine: NEW AMERICAN/NEW SOUTHERN. **Reservations:** Recommended.

$ Prices: Appetizers $2.95–$5.95; main courses $8.95–$16.95. DC, DISC, MC, V.

Open: Mon–Thurs 11am–10pm, Fri–Sat 11am–11pm, Sun 5–10pm.

Neutral colors and a spareness of furnishings are a good backdrop for changing art exhibits at this West End restaurant. A striped awning over a small bar even manages to give the restaurant an atmosphere of New York in the 'burbs. The appetizer list here is so appealing that you may want to forgo ordering an entree in favor of a bit of grazing. Ordering this way will also allow you to leave room for the chocolate-raspberry truffle. You could start with lemon-artichoke soup, which is as good as its reputation around town. Another good choice is the smoked salmon spiral, with artichokes, black olives, capers, and cream cheese, and served with salsa. Still hungry? Try the crab cakes with cayenne hollandaise (which is also available as a main course).

SFUZZI, in the Loew's Vanderbilt Plaza Hotel, 2100 West End Ave. Tel. 329-9500.

Cuisine: ITALIAN. **Reservations:** Recommended.

$ Prices: Appetizers $4.25–$6.25; main courses $8.50–$15.95. AE, DC, MC, V.

Open: Lunch Mon–Sat 10:30am–5pm; dinner Sun–Thurs 5:30–10pm, Fri–Sat 5:30pm–midnight; brunch Sun 10:30am–3:30pm.

As you walk into this Italian bistro, located in the lower level at Loew's Vanderbilt Plaza, your taste buds can't help but get excited as the aroma of pizzas and pastas greets you. Weathered-looking concrete archways and antiqued friezes on the walls give you the impression that you have wandered into a ruined Italian villa, and at the bar the latest in halogen spotlights counterbalance neoclassic antiquity. The main dining room is open and airy, but if you prefer to be more cloistered, there are dining rooms in back that are reminiscent of an old wine cellar.

The open kitchen serves up such specialties as grilled beef tenderloin with black pepper–chianti sauce and mashed potatoes with garlic and marinated shrimp with lemon, garlic, and saffron orzo. Desserts displayed on marble-topped tables are not only classic looking, they're mouth-watering. An outdoor patio on a busy streetcorner serves the same good food, with a different atmosphere, and a limited menu is available in the main dining room between 3:30 and 5pm. Sunday brunch includes an antipasti bar for $9.50, and for an additional $4, choices of pizza, pasta, egg specialties, a drink, and dessert.

SUNSET GRILL, 2001 Belcourt Ave. Tel. 386-FOOD.

Cuisine: NEW AMERICAN/NEW SOUTHERN. **Reservations:** Recommended.

$ Prices: Appetizers $3–$9; main courses $7–$23. AE, CB, DC, DISC, MC, V.

Open: Lunch Mon–Fri 11am–2:30pm; dinner Mon–Thurs 5–

10pm, Fri–Sat 5pm–midnight; late-night menu Mon–Thurs 10pm–1:30am, Fri–Sat midnight–1:30am.

Located in the West End neighborhood called Hillsboro Village, the Sunset Grill offers an extensive wine list and a menu that highlights healthy dining choices low in fats and with calories and sodium contents noted. But don't let that make you think the food is boring. Among the items starred with the health symbol are a piquant hickory-smoked bucksnort trout, served with capers, red onion, lemon yogurt, and garlic toast and a teriyaki stir-fry including bok choy, daikon, purple cabbage, and red peppers (all served over brown rice).

When I last visited, the green-plate special was a scrumptious combination of sautéed chanterelles, crimini, and lobster mushrooms, red onions, yellow tomatoes, and angel-hair pasta. As you might be able to tell, the food is also very visually appealing. Neo-industrial style predominates, in black, gray, and white, with industrial rubber flooring, white twinkle lights draped through exposed girders in the ceiling, and paintings to soften and warm the atmosphere. Outside, the dining patio faces a park; in pleasant weather the patio's always lively with well-to-do patrons.

BUDGET

BOBBI'S DAIRY DIP, 5301 Charlotte Ave. Tel. 385-4661.
   Cuisine: FAST FOOD. **Reservations:** Not accepted.
$ Prices: Main courses $1–$2.70. No credit cards.
   Open: Mon–Sat 7am–10pm, Sun 11am–10pm.
This '50s drive-in is not just kitsch for effect, it's the real thing. Hanging planters are filled with plastic flowers, and in the front window there is cotton candy that people actually buy, to eat even. "Rock Around the Clock" plays on the stereo, and you might even see a '57 Chevy or other vintage car pull up. But the fare isn't the usual drive-in type—we had cantaloupe milkshakes and tomatoes stuffed with tuna salad, good and basic and very cheap. Other amazing daily special values include a bowl of white beans and cornbread or a pimento cheese sandwich for 50¢. I hear the Arctic Swirls are top-notch.

CALYPSO, 2424 Elliston Place. Tel. 321-3878.
   Cuisine: CARIBBEAN. **Reservations:** Not accepted.
$ Prices: Appetizers $3.50–$4.60; main courses $3.80–$6.40. AE, DISC, MC, V.
   Open: Mon–Thurs 11am–9pm, Fri 11am–10pm, Sat 11am–9pm, Sun noon–8pm.
If you're looking for a good, healthy, inexpensive meal in the West End, I can think of no better place to send you than Calypso. This casual place is located in a small shopping plaza and has the brightness of a fast-food restaurant. The rôtisserie chicken, in a sauce made from more than 30 ingredients, is the most popular item on the menu, but they also have good vegetarian meals. The Caribbean salads—such as tropical chicken salad with pineapple and raisins and black-bean salad topped with beef or chicken,

Cheddar cheese, green onions, and barbecue sauce—are among my favorites.

There's another Calypso at 4910 Thoroughbred (tel. 370-8033).

COUNTRY LIFE VEGETARIAN BUFFET, 1917 Division St. Tel. 327-3695.

Cuisine: VEGETARIAN. **Reservations:** Not accepted.

$ Prices: Buffet $2.99 a pound. No credit cards.

Open: Lunch only, Mon–Thurs 11:30am–2:30pm, Fri 11:30am–2:15pm.

Elbow your way in with the rest of the patrons to partake of this bountiful vegetarian buffet. You can pile up your plate with such healthy and delicious offerings as fettuccine Alfredo, steamed broccoli, black-eyed-pea soup, corn on the cob, and salads, both fruit and vegetable. Just down from Music Row, the place is modest and small, but you can't beat the quality of the food. People sit outside on picnic benches to eat their vegetable feasts. This place is only open for lunch.

ELLISTON PLACE SODA SHOP, 2111 Elliston Place. Tel. 327-1090.

Cuisine: AMERICAN. **Reservations:** Not accepted.

$ Prices: Sandwiches $1.75–$3.15; main courses $3.65–$7.25. No credit cards.

Open: Mon–Fri 6am–7:45pm, Sat 7am–7:45pm.

One of the oldest eating establishments in Nashville, the Elliston Place Soda Shop has been around since 1939, and it looks it. The lunch counter, black-topped stools, and signs advertising malted milks and banana splits all seem to have been here since it originally opened. It's a treat to visit this place, almost like visiting a museum of the '50s, with its red-and-white tiled walls, old beat-up Formica tables, and individual booth jukeboxes. The soda shop serves "meat-and-three" meals. Of course you can also get club sandwiches, steaks, fish, hamburgers, and salmon croquettes. They also make the best chocolate shakes in town.

IGUANA, 2000 Belcourt Ave. Tel. 383-8920.

Cuisine: MEXICAN/SOUTHWESTERN. **Reservations:** Recommended for groups.

$ Prices: Appetizers $3–$4.50; main courses $7–$9. AE, DC, MC, V.

Open: Mon–Thurs 11am–10pm, Fri 11am–11pm, Sat–Sun 5–11pm.

Belcourt Avenue is the site of three of my favorite Nashville restaurants, and they're all run by the same people, which means that somebody is doing something right around here. So if the Sunset Grill is too crowded and Faison's just isn't wild enough for you, try the Iguana. New southwestern fare and Tex-Mex like no Texas cowpoke ever saw are the specialties here. The atmosphere is laid-back, the music is loud, and the bar is busy. You get the picture. Now, when it comes time to order, don't miss the hickory-smoked honeysuckle brisket tacos, and the sushi burritos aren't bad either (they're made with crab, avocado, and cheese). If you're in the mood for lighter fare, try the "South by Southwest" salad, made with grilled shrimp, grapefruit, avocado, corn relish, pecans, and raisins, all on a bed of greens and topped with chili-honey dressing. If you prefer your Mexican food to beans and cheese rather than crab and corn relish, you can order one of their more traditional dishes.

INTERNATIONAL MARKET AND RESTAURANT, 2010 Belmont Blvd. Tel. 297-4453.

Cuisine: THAI/CHINESE. **Reservations:** Not accepted.

$ Prices: Appetizers 90¢–$1.50; main courses $3.50–$5.50. AE, CB, DC, MC, V.

Open: Mon–Sat 10:30am–9pm, Sun 11am–9pm.

For some Thai home-cooking (and Chinese, too), visit this small and simple restaurant in a residential neighborhood full of schools. Asian packaged snack food and grocery items are available alongside a counter full of hot food to go or to be dished up immediately, cafeteria style. The owners have been here since the mid-'70s, making this the first Thai restaurant in Nashville. Daily specials, such as kang kai (chicken, curry, potato, and coconut milk) and ocean perch with fresh ginger are on the menu for as little as $1.50.

RIO BRAVO CANTINA, 3015 West End Ave. Tel. 329-1745.

Cuisine: MEXICAN. **Reservations:** Not accepted.

$ Prices: Appetizers $2.95–$7.95; main courses $5.95–$12.95. AE, CB, DC, DISC, MC, V.

Open: Mon–Thurs 11am–11pm, Fri–Sat 11am–midnight, Sun 11am–10pm.

The food is inexpensive and the margaritas are great. What more is necessary to keep a Mexican restaurant near a university packed? Located near the Vanderbilt University campus, Rio Bravo is one of Nashville's better Mexican restaurants and stays busy all day long. You'll find all your favorites on the menu, as well as a few lesser-known dishes such as spinach-and-cheese soup, layered deep-fried beans, cheese, and chicken with pico de gallo, black olives, peppers, and onions. If it's still on the menu when you're here, try the Tijuana shrimp, which is sautéed in jalapeño butter and served with a roasted tomato salsa. There are daily specials, too. In the warmer months, the patio here is a great place to hang out or linger over a meal.

ROTIER'S, 2413 Elliston Place. Tel. 327-9892.

Cuisine: BURGERS/SANDWICHES. **Reservations:** Not accepted.

$ Prices: Appetizers $1.95–$4.50; sandwiches/main courses $2–$8.95. No credit cards.

Open: Mon–Sat 9am–10:30pm.

If you're a fan of old-fashioned diners, don't miss Rotier's. This little stone cottage is surrounded by newer buildings, but has remained a world unto itself. Sure, it looks like a dive from the outside, and the interior doesn't seem to have been upgraded in 40 years, but the food is good and the prices are great. The cheeseburger here is reputed to be the best in the city, and the milkshakes are pretty good, too. For bigger appetites, there is that staple of southern cooking—the meat and three. With this dish you get a portion of meat (minute steak, pork chops, fried chicken, whatever) and three vegetables of your choice. They also do daily blue-plate specials and cheap breakfasts.

SLICE OF LIFE BAKERY AND RESTAURANT, 1811 Division St. Tel. 329-2525.
   Cuisine: HEALTH-CONSCIOUS. **Reservations:** Not accepted.
$ Prices: Appetizers $2.25–$6.95; main courses $5.95–$10.95. AE, CB, DC, DISC, MC, V.
   Open: Mon–Fri 7am–9:30pm, Sat–Sun 8am–9:30pm.

If you're looking for a laid-back spot to eat a salad and relax, this is it. Around the corner from Music Row, this place has a light and natural feeling in the exposed brick, wood paneling, skylight, and wall of glass blocks. It's a cool escape in the summer, and in winter a small fireplace keeps it cozy. At night there is frequently live music. Choose from a large selection of soups and salads at lunch, plus vegetable stir-fries, steamed vegetables, and chili. You can get similar items at dinner, with additions such as black beans and tofu. But it's not just vegetarian here—well prepared seafood and chicken dishes are also served. The bakery provides a focaccia of the day at dinner. And sweets tooths are definitely indulged, as evidenced by the huge chocolate-chip cookies and muffins in the case up front.

---

3. SOUTH OF DOWNTOWN (GREEN HILLS)

EXPENSIVE

F. SCOTT'S, 2210 Crestmoor Ave. Tel. 269-5861.
   Cuisine: NEW AMERICAN/NEW SOUTHERN. **Reservations:** Recommended.
$ Prices: Appetizers $4.50–$11; main courses $14–$24.95. AE, DC, DISC, MC, V.
   Open: Lunch Mon–Fri 11:30am–2:30pm; dinner Sun–Thurs 5:30–10pm, Fri–Sat 5:30–11pm; brunch Sun 11:30am–2:30pm.

The Green Hills area south of downtown is a land of shopping centers and malls, where you wouldn't expect to find an outpost of urban chic. However, here it is. The classic movie-palace marquee out front announces in no uncertain terms that this place is different, and inside everything is tastefully sophisticated. Art deco is the chosen style for the interior, with black-and-white tile floors, glass-blocks, Erte-inspired art on the walls, and tapes of old jazz radio broadcasts playing over the stereo. In the evenings there's even live piano music.

Basically there are three categories on the menu—thin-crust phyllo pizzas, small plates, and large plates—so whatever the size of your appetite, you'll find a meal to fit. Small plates include such delicious dishes as Andalusian gazpacho, escargots with vermouth and goat cheese, warm salad of duck confit, shallots, and wine. I like to go with a small plate so I can save room for dessert. Large plates, on the other hand, are a bit more substantial. You might order grilled swordfish with roasted nuts and raisins or fried oysters with a large Caesar salad. There are also daily specials.

MODERATE

LA PAZ, 3808 Cleghorn Ave. Tel. 383-5200.

Cuisine: MEXICAN/SOUTHWESTERN. **Reservations:** Not accepted.

$ Prices: Appetizers $3.25–$9.95; main courses $8.95–$12.95. AE, DC, DISC, MC, V.

Open: Lunch Mon–Fri 11am–2pm; dinner Sun–Thurs 5–10pm, Fri–Sat 5–11pm.

This Green Hills Mexican restaurant is a big place that from the outside looks a bit like the Alamo. There's even a cactus garden by the front door. Inside, however, you'll find big dining rooms and a bar that opens onto a deck, a concession to the southern tradition of the veranda. Rough-board floors and a partially rock wall give the interior an aged look that belies the restaurant's shopping-mall surroundings. The menu features much more than the standard Mexican fare, and owes a lot to the modern cuisine of New Mexico. I like the Santa Fe enchiladas, which are made from layered blue-corn tortillas, broiled chicken, and cheese that are baked with a green salsa, sour cream, and avocado. Also worth trying are the green-corn tamales, which are prepared several different ways.

SHINTOMI, 2184 Bandywood Dr. Tel. 386-3022.

Cuisine: JAPANESE. **Reservations:** Recommended.

$ Prices: Appetizers $3.50–$4.75; main courses $8.75–$26. AE, CB, DC, MC, V.

Open: Lunch Mon–Fri 11:30am–2pm; dinner Mon–Thurs 5:30–10pm, Fri–Sat 5:30–10:30pm, Sun 5–10pm.

Shintomi is located in a small shopping plaza just downhill from the Mall at Green Hills, and is a great place for lunch or dinner. The decor is contemporary, minimalist Japanese, and the lighting is bright. If you'd like, you can sit at the sushi bar rather than at a table. The Zen dinners, which include several courses, are about the best deal at Shintomi; you'll get a taste of quite a few dishes, and can choose between tempura and a grilled dish. The lunch special, at $4.75, is a particularly good deal; you get tempura with sushi, sashimi, or gyoza, miso soup, a small salad, and fruit.

BUDGET

CHINATOWN RESTAURANT, 3900 Hillsboro Rd. Tel. 269-3275.

Cuisine: CHINESE. **Reservations:** Recommended Fri–Sat for parties of six or more.

$ **Prices:** Appetizers 95¢–$4.25; main courses $5.95–$11.75. AE, DISC, MC, V.

Open: Sun–Thurs 11am–10pm, Fri–Sat 11am–11pm.

This large restaurant is in a shopping mall, but don't let that put you off. The inside is surprisingly sophisticated with pale-green and pink walls, recessed lighting, and etched-glass booth dividers that provide a relaxing setting. The serving staff speaks Chinese, which bodes well for the authenticity of the cooking. As on just about any Chinese menu, the offerings are extensive. Try the chef's inspiration meal, if it's available. About 40 inexpensive lunch specials are offered daily from 11am to 3pm.

EL PALENQUE, 4407 Nolensville Pike. Tel. 832-9978.

Cuisine: MEXICAN. **Reservations:** Not accepted.

$ **Prices:** Appetizers $2.15–$4.50; main courses $6.25–$8.75. AE, DISC, MC, V.

Open: Lunch Mon–Thurs 11am–2pm, Sun 11am–3pm; dinner Mon–Thurs 4:30–10pm, Fri 11am–10pm, Sat noon–10pm, Sun 4:30–9pm.

This family-run restaurant is the most authentic Mexican restaurant in Nashville. The decor is minimal and atmosphere is lacking, but by giving up happy hour, margarita parties, and walls covered with Mexican glitz, you get delicious, traditional food at rock-bottom prices. The menu is simple and straightforward. This is Mexican home-cooking at its best.

There's a second El Palenque—just as authentic Mexican–at 4121 Hillsboro Rd. (tel. 386-3822).

SYLVAN PARK RESTAURANT, GREEN HILLS, 2201 Bandywood Ave. Tel. 292-6449.

Cuisine: AMERICAN. **Reservations:** Not accepted.

$ **Prices:** Main courses $4.25–$4.50. No credit cards.

Open: Mon–Sat 11am–8pm.

The Sylvan Park has been serving Nashville residents with good old-fashioned southern cooking for more than 50 years, and the restaurant's continuing popularity is proven by the proliferation of Sylvan Park restaurants around the city. The "meat-and-three" concept is at the heart of the Sylvan Park experience—choose a meat serving from the list of daily specials such as baked ham or barbecued chicken and add to it your choice of three vegetables. Vegetable choices include turnip greens, lima beans, candied yams, and cranberry sauce. It's American food, like mom used to make.

This restaurant is kind of homey, like a dining room in a suburban home, with oilcloth tablecloths and a blue-and-white tiled floor. Don't forget a slice of homemade pie.

There are many Sylvan Park locations, including 4502 Murphy Rd. (tel. 292-9275), 221 Sixth Ave. N. (tel. 255-1562), and 5207 Nolensville Rd. (tel. 781-3077).

4. BELLE MEADE

EXPENSIVE

106 CLUB, 106 Harding Place. Tel. 356-1300.
   Cuisine: NEW AMERICAN/NEW SOUTHERN. **Reservations:** Recommended.
$ Prices: Appetizers $4–$18.50; main courses $14.50–$21. AE, CB, DC, DISC, MC, V.
   Open: Dinner only, Sun–Thurs 5:30–10pm, Fri–Sat 5:30–11pm.

If you're in the mood for a romantic dinner amid classically contemporary sophistication, the 106 Club is the place. Deep-blue carpets, walls, and ceiling give the dining room and bar a tastefully urban chic, while art deco decor, complete with a curving wall of glass blocks, sets the tone. Walls are decorated with large black-and-white photos that provide still more visual interest. A pianist plays quiet jazz melodies while waiters in tuxedo shirts and bow ties unobtrusively attend to diners' needs. Halogen light fixtures illuminate every table as if it were a stage.

Every dish is skillfully prepared and artfully arranged, so a meal here is as much a visual treat as a gustatory adventure. To start out, you might try goose foie gras, here prepared with port-brandy sauce and caramelized apples. A salad of vine-ripened tomatoes with asiago cheese and basil makes for a lighter yet equally flavorful start. Main dishes are rich in flavor and contrast as witnessed by such dishes as prawns and artichoke hearts over cilantro salsa with avocado-and-lime vinaigrette.

BELLE MEADE BRASSERIE, 101 Page Rd. Tel. 356-5450.
   Cuisine: NEW AMERICAN/NEW SOUTHERN. **Reservations:** Recommended Fri–Sat.
$ Prices: Appetizers $3.95–$8.50; main courses $9.50–$22. AE, MC, V.
   Open: Dinner only, Mon–Thurs 5:30–10pm, Fri–Sat 5:30–11pm.

Belle Meade is the Nashville area's wealthiest community, and this is one of its favorite places to dine. Despite the decidedly residential and suburban feel of the surrounding neighborhoods, the Belle Meade Brasserie has managed to create a stylish urban sophistication. Pink tablecloths and black chairs set the tone, and changing art exhibits and big black silhouette cutouts provide a decidedly artistic atmosphere. You can dine in one of the intimate dining rooms, or when the weather's good you can have a seat on the deck.

The menu makes frequent use of Cajun and Créole seasonings, so be prepared for some lively flavors. Corn fritters with pepper jelly are a reworking of a couple of southern classics and make for an appetizer to wake up your mouth. Main dishes roam the globe and bring it all back home to the South. You could try roast duck on a bed of peaches laced with ginger and scallions or grilled swordfish with gazpacho beurre blanc. There are always several pasta dishes,

FROMMER'S COOL FOR KIDS: RESTAURANTS

Uncle Bud's Catfish   *(see p. 75)* The fun country decor and the all-you-can-eat catfish and fried chicken make this place a hit with families. The kids will love all the hats on the ceiling.

The Old Spaghetti Factory   *(see p. 61)* Kids love the spaghetti, that's all there is to it. Adults will enjoy the Victorian decor and the old trolley car in the middle of the dining room.

Elliston Place Soda Shop   *(see p. 67)* Bring the kids by for a burger and a shake and tell them stories of how you and their dad used to hang out in a place just like this one when you were lovestruck teenagers.

The Gerst Haus   *(see p. 61)* The basic German fare is simple enough for kids to like it and the oom-pah-pah bands on the weekend will have the little ones dancing in the aisles.

such as garden angel hair with smoked salmon, and meat dishes such as marinated pork chops with maple apples. You'll find the brasserie just off Harding Road at the start of Harding Place, behind the Exxon station.

MODERATE

BENKAY JAPANESE RESTAURANT, Lion's Head Village, 40 White Bridge Rd. Tel. 356-6600.
   Cuisine: JAPANESE. **Reservations:** Recommended.
$ Prices: Appetizers $1–$7.50; main courses $7.25–$18.45. AE, DC, DISC, JCB, MC, V.
   Open: Lunch Mon–Sat 11:30am–2pm; dinner Mon–Thurs 5:30–10pm, Fri–Sat 5:30–10:30pm, Sun 5–10pm.
Located in the Lion's Head Village shopping center, which is north off Harding Road near Belle Meade, Benkay is a casual and popular place. Though small, it manages to have several tatami rooms. Plenty of natural wood throughout the restaurant provide a Japanese flavor and paper lanterns hang from the ceiling. There's a sushi bar at the back where solo diners will feel comfortable. Both the menu and the setting have an authentic feel about them. Appetizers include plenty of types of sushi and sashimi, as well as a variety of Japanese pickles and such unusual dishes as cold boiled spinach with dried fish. The bento lunch box is a good deal, as are the udon and soba noodle dishes.

FINEZZA TRATTORIA, 5404 Harding Rd. Tel. 356-9398.
   Cuisine: ITALIAN. **Reservations:** Not accepted.

$ Prices: Appetizers $3.50–$8.50; main courses $5.95–$13.50.
CB, DC, MC, V.
Open: Dinner only, Mon–Thurs 5–10pm, Fri–Sat 5–11pm, Sun
5–9pm.

Look closely to find the sign for Finezza because it gets lost in
the confusion of a highway junction. Once inside, you'll find a
comfortable low-ceilinged room filled with the sound of
dining conversations. Green marble-topped tables and a copper-
topped bar add an air of class, and crusty loaves of bread piled on a
shelf outside the open kitchen are a rustic touch.

Italian country dishes, very reasonably priced, are offered here.
For starters, order some fried calamari or a polenta dish with sausage
and mushrooms. There are dinners on the menu that you won't
usually find at most Italian restaurants, such as fettuccine con carciofi
(wide pasta with artichokes, tomatoes, green onions, and olive oil)
and spezzatino con peperoni (pork with roasted red peppers and
crushed red peppers). Tiramisu, made with mascarpone cheese and
lady fingers, is a specialty. There's a kid's menu, and children eat free
on Sunday if accompanied by an adult.

BUDGET

**DALT'S, Lion's Head Village, 38 White Bridge Rd. Tel.
352-8121.**
　Cuisine: BURGERS/SANDWICHES. **Reservations:** Not accepted.
$ Prices: Appetizers $2.95–$4.95; sandwiches/main courses
$4.95–$11.95. AE, CB, DC, DISC, MC, V.
　Open: Sun–Thurs 10:30am–11pm, Fri–Sat 10:30am–midnight.
If you've ever been in an old-fashioned oyster bar someplace like
Chicago or New York, you know what to expect at Dalt's. The
surprise is that this place is fairly new and is located in the Lion's
Head Village shopping center adjacent to the Benkay Japanese
Restaurant. To one side there's a sports bar, but most of the
restaurant is taken up by a single large dining room. There's lots of
dark wood, pillars with old gas-light-style lamps, and a floor that
imitates the classic little white tiles that were always found in old bars.
For the most part, this is a family place and a burger, fries, and a
milkshake is the meal of choice. However, they also have more
imaginative daily specials such as shrimp fajitas and blackened
halibut. During warm weather, the patio is a great place to eat.

LOVELESS CAFE, 8400 Tenn. 100. Tel. 646-9700.
　Cuisine: AMERICAN. **Reservations:** Recommended.
$ Prices: Main courses $6.95–$12.95. No credit cards.
　Open: Breakfast/lunch Tues–Sun 8am–2pm; dinner Tues–Sat
5–9pm, Sun 2–9pm.
For country cooking in a country atmosphere, take a trip to the
Loveless Motel and Café. You'll find this casual but popular
Nashville institution out Tenn. 100 about 7½ miles south of Belle
Meade and the turnoff from U.S. 70S. People rave about the cooking
here because the country ham with red-eye gravy, southern fried

chicken, and homemade biscuits with fruit jams are made just the way granny used to make them back when the Loveless opened 35 years ago. This restaurant may be a little out of the way, but it's worth it if you like down-home cookin'.

5. SPECIALTY DINING

LOCAL FAVORITES

CORKY'S BAR-B-Q, 100 Franklin Rd, Brentwood. Tel. 373-1020.
Cuisine: BARBECUE. **Reservations:** Not accepted.
$ Prices: Main courses $6–$7. AE, DC, DISC, MC, V.
Open: Mon–Thurs 11am–9:30pm, Fri–Sat 11am–10:30pm, Sun 11:30am–9:30pm.

Sure Nashville ought to have its own style of barbecue, but the barbecue they make in Memphis seems so much better. That's why Corky's, a Memphis institution, is starting a Nashville tradition by serving Memphis-style slow-smoked, pulled pork, ribs, brisket, and chicken. This is a casual barbecue joint, but the waiters still wear bow ties and serve both professionals with portable phones and day laborers in denim. Corky's has the largest barbecue pit in Tennessee, and a toll-free 800 number (tel. 800/9-CORKYS) to call for getting their delicious ribs shipped "anywhere." Barbecued pork or beef sandwiches or dinners, which come with beans, cole slaw, and bread, are the primary attraction here.

UNCLE BUD'S CATFISH, 714 Stewart's Ferry Pike. Tel. 872-7700.
Cuisine: SOUTHERN. **Reservations:** Not accepted.
$ Prices: Main courses $5.95–$14.50. DISC, MC, V.
Open: Mon–Thurs 4–9pm, Fri 4–10pm, Sat 11:30am–10pm, Sun 11:30am–9pm.

Located near the airport, Uncle Bud's has a country-kitchen atmosphere, with old farm tools and a covered wooden porch out front. Inside, red-and-white checked curtains and table-cloths, rough-hewn wood paneling, fish nets, and old signs on the walls make you feel right at home. Thousands of ball caps hang from the ceiling, and if you bring one in, you can trade it for one of Uncle Bud's caps. But that's not the best reason to visit here—the raison d'être of this place is Uncle Bud's succulent fried catfish, served in a basket with crunchy hush puppies. They'll just keep bringing out all the catfish or fried chicken you can eat, along with as much as you want of the additional fixin's. Uncle Bud caters to kids, which makes this a great place for a family dinner.

WHITT'S BARBECUE, 5310 Harding Rd. Tel. 356-3435.
Cuisine: BARBECUE. **Reservations:** Not accepted.
$ Prices: Main courses $3.30–$4.95; barbecue $5.20–$7 per pound. No credit cards.

Open: Mon–Sat 10:30am–8pm.

Walk in, drive up, or get it delivered—Whitt's was voted "Best Barbecue" by *Nashville Scene* readers, and here's your chance to taste for yourself. There's no in-restaurant seating here, so plan to take it back to the motel or have a picnic somewhere. You can buy succulent barbecued pork, beef, and even turkey by the pound, or order sandwiches and plates with the extra fixin's.

Other locations are at 2535 Lebanon Rd. (tel. 883-6907) and 114 Old Hickory Blvd. E. (tel. 868-1369).

A DINNER TRAIN

THE BROADWAY DINNER TRAIN, First and Broadway (P.O. Box 25085, Nashville, TN 37202-5085). Tel. 254-8000, or toll free 800/274-8010.
  Cuisine: CONTINENTAL. **Reservations:** Required.
$ Prices: $39.50 per person. AE, DISC, MC, V.
  Open: Boarding at 6:30pm with departure at 7pm; Sat only Jan–Mar, Thurs–Sat Apr–Dec.

There may no longer be Amtrak service to Nashville, but you can still catch a train here. The Broadway Dinner Train, which has its depot at Riverfront Park on the banks of the Cumberland River, pulls out of downtown Nashville regularly and spends 2½ hours rolling slowly through Nashville and out into the rolling pastures of middle Tennessee. In the community of Old Hickory, the train turns around and heads back to the city. Along the way a four-course meal is served. If you're a railroading fan, the dinner train is well worth the cost.

LIGHT, CASUAL, & FAST FOOD

Try **Calypso,** 2424 Elliston Place (tel. 321-3878), for some fast and healthy Caribbean food. If you like old-fashioned drive-ins, **Bobbi's Dairy Dip,** 5301 Charlotte Ave. (tel. 385-4661), is sure to please. Get good and cheap Chinese fast food at **Ling-Ling's,** 3941 Nolensville Rd. (tel. 331-2822). See above for full descriptions of these restaurants.

BREAKFAST/BRUNCH

For a country-style breakfast, head out to the **Loveless Café,** 8400 Tenn. 100, (tel. 646-9700). It's a ways out of town, but worth the experience.

Some of Nashville's best Sunday brunches are to be had at the following restaurants: **Sfuzzi,** 2100 West End Ave. (tel. 329-9500), serves from 10:30am to 3:30pm, and has an antipasti bar and Italian specialties. **Cakewalk Restaurant,** 3001 West End Ave. (tel. 320-7778), serves a gourmet brunch from 11am to 3pm. The elegant atmosphere of **Mère Bulles,** 152 Second Ave. N. (tel. 256-1946), is the site of yet another excellent brunch from 11:30am to 3pm. Last, there is **F. Scott's,** 2210 Crestmoor Ave. (tel. 269-5861), which serves brunch from 11:30am to 2:30pm. See the listings above for complete descriptions of the restaurants.

LATE-NIGHT/24-HOUR
RESTAURANTS

The following restaurants serve food up until about 1:30am: **12th & Porter,** 114 12th Ave. N. (tel. 254-7236); **Sportsman's Grill,** 1601 21st Ave. S. (tel. 320-1633); and **Sunset Grill,** 2001 Belcourt Ave. (tel. 386-FOOD). See above for full descriptions of these restaurants.

CHAPTER 6

WHAT TO SEE & DO IN NASHVILLE

Nashville, Music City USA, the Country Music Capital of the World. There's no doubt as to why people visit Nashville, but what might come as a surprise is that there's more to see and do here than just chase country stars. Sure, you can go to a country-music theme park, attend the "Grand Ole Opry," linger over displays at the Country Music Hall of Fame, take a tour past the homes of the country stars, visit Conway Twitty's house and Johnny Cash's museum, and hear the stars of the future at any number of clubs. Nashville, however, is also the state capital of Tennessee and has plenty of museums and other attractions that have nothing to do with country music. There's the Tennessee State Museum, the Tennessee State Capitol, a combination botanical garden and art museum, even a full-size reproduction of the Parthenon. So, whether you own a Loretta Lynn album or have never even heard of Vince Gill, you'll find something to keep you busy while you're in town. However, if you do own every album ever released by Tammy Wynette or Tanya Tucker, you'll be in hog heaven on a visit to Nashville.

SUGGESTED ITINERARIES

IF YOU HAVE ONE DAY Start your day at Waterfront Park on the edge of the District in downtown Nashville. Visit Fort Nashboro to learn about the city's history, then check out the shops along North Second Avenue. A few blocks over is the Tennessee State Museum, for more history. After touring this museum, head over to the Ryman Auditorium for some country-music history. You can stop in at Tootsie's, around the corner, to hear a bit of live country music. Catch the trolley to Music Row and tour the Country Music Hall of Fame and Museum and then wander over to Studio B for a bit more country-music history. If you still have time left and are so inclined, you can visit some of the other country-music museums and gift shops here in the Music Row area. In the evening, if it's a Friday or Saturday, you can catch a performance of the "Grand Ole Opry"; other days of the week, you might catch some up-and-coming singer-songwriters performing at the Bluebird Café in the Green Hills area.

IF YOU HAVE TWO DAYS   Follow the outline above for your first day. If you've got the kids with you, you'll want to spend the entire second day at Opryland USA, Nashville's music-oriented theme park. On the other hand, if you have an interest in art, old mansions, or botanic gardens, you'll find more than enough to fill your day. Start out on the east side of town at the Hermitage, which was the home of President Andrew Jackson. Next, head across to the west side of town, stopping at the Parthenon en route, and tour Belle Meade Plantation, a classic antebellum plantation home. After finishing here, visit Cheekwood, the Tennessee Botanical Gardens and Museum of Art. Catch a performance at the Bluebird Café or Opryland, or do a sunset cruise on the *General Jackson* showboat.

IF YOU HAVE THREE DAYS   Follow the suggestions above for your first two days. If you spent your second day at Opryland USA, on Day 3 you may want to visit the historic buildings and museums mentioned above. If you skipped Opryland USA and haven't yet had your fill of historic sites, head north of the city to Mansker's Station, a living-history center depicting life in pioneer Tennessee. From there, head back into the city to the Belmont Mansion. You can finish your historic tour at Traveler's Rest.

IF YOU HAVE FIVE DAYS OR MORE   Follow the itineraries outlined above on your first three days. If you have more time, and if you're a country-music fan, spend a day visiting some of the numerous museums and gift shops devoted to individual country stars. If you're a history buff head south to the historic town of Franklin, which is a charmingly restored little town full of antique malls and historic homes. If you have the kids along, visit one of Nashville's two zoos or the Cumberland Science Museum. You might also find one or more of the city's small specialty museums of interest.

1. THE TOP ATTRACTIONS

OPRYLAND USA, 2802 Opryland Dr. Tel. 889-6611.
Whether or not you're a fan of country music, whether you're a grownup or a kid, you'll have a great time at Opryland USA, Nashville's country-music theme park. When Disneyland meets the "Grand Old Opry," what you get is roller coasters and log-flume rides interspersed with performances by country stars, bluegrass concerts, gospel singing, even Broadway-style musical shows. You can spend the day on the white-knuckle rides or go from show to show. There are special shows and rides for the littlest kids, and of course lots of restaurants and snack bars. In the Chevrolet/GEO Celebrity Theater there are daily concerts by such country stars

as Crystal Gayle, Louise Mandrell, Ricky Skaggs, Tanya Tucker, and Tammy Wynette. These concerts are usually held at 7:30pm and admission is *not* included in the price of your park admission ticket.

Outside the front gates of the park, you'll find still more attractions, including the new Grand Ole Opry House, which is the site of the live radio broadcasts of the famous country music show (see "The Performing Arts," in Chapter 8, for details). There are also three country-music museums—the Grand Ole Opry Museum, the Roy Acuff Museum, and the Minnie Pearl Museum—here at the Opryland entrance. This is also where you'll find the Star Walk, which commemorates famous country-music performers. On Sunday morning the Acuff Theater, here by the front gate, is the site of an informal worship service that includes plenty of gospel music.

Admission (includes all rides and all shows except the country star concerts, which are $5 extra): One-day pass, $23.95 adults, $12.95 children 4–11; two-day pass, $35.95 adults, $19.45 children 4–11. Three-day Opryland USA Passport, $75.95 (includes park admission, *General Jackson* showboat cruise, "Grand Ole Opry" matinee, Nashville city tour, ticket to attend taping of the Nashville Network's "Nashville Now" television show, and country star concert at Opryland USA). There are also frequent special discount programs in effect; be sure to call and find out if any are in effect when you plan to visit.

Open: Late Mar to early May and late Sept to late Oct, Sat–Sun 10am–9pm; early to late May and early to late Sept, Fri–Sun 10am–9pm; late May to early Sept, daily 10am–9pm. **Closed:** Late Oct–early Mar.

COUNTRY MUSIC HALL OF FAME AND MUSEUM, 4 Music Sq. E. Tel. 255-5333.

If you're a fan of country music, this is *the* museum in Nashville. If you aren't a country-music fan, visit this museum and you may find out that you really do like country music. The museum is pretty loose with its definition of country music, so you'll find displays on bluegrass, cowboy music (à la Roy Rogers), country swing, rockabilly, Cajun, honky tonk, and contemporary country music. Among the exhibits here are a large display on the history of the "Grand Ole Opry," and as you peruse the pieces of memorabilia from this most famous of country-music shows, you can listen to "Grand Ole Opry" recordings. There are also videos of old television broadcasts that were inspired by the "Grand Ole Opry."

Among the more fascinating displays are Elvis Presley's solid-gold Cadillac (which isn't really solid gold) and his gold-leaf-covered

---

IMPRESSIONS

For the last hour we have been listening to music taken from the Grand Opera, but from now on we will present "Grand Ole Opry."
—GEORGE D. HAY, 1927

baby-grand piano. Several cases are filled with costumes and clothing once worn by famous stars. One room is devoted exclusively to Johnny Cash. Another section of the museum is devoted to country music in the movies and includes the black Trans Am from *Smokey and the Bandit,* the mechanical bull from *Urban Cowboy,* and a dress made by Loretta Lynn when she was 14 and worn by Sissy Spacek in *Coal Miner's Daughter.* Last of all, you can walk through the Hall of Fame Gallery and read about each of the stars who have been inducted. Your ticket also gives you admission to the Studio B recording studio, two blocks away.

Admission: $7.50 adults, $2 children 6–11.

Open: Sun–Thurs 9am–5pm, Fri–Sat 8am–6pm.

BELLE MEADE PLANTATION, 5025 Harding Rd. Tel. 356-0501.

Called the "Queen of Tennessee Plantations," Belle Meade was built in 1853 after this plantation had become famous as a stud farm that produced some of the best race horses in the South. Today the Greek Revival mansion is the centerpiece of the affluent Belle Meade region of Nashville and is surrounded by 30 acres of manicured lawns and shade trees. A long driveway leads uphill to the mansion, which is fronted by six columns and a wide veranda. Inside, the restored building has been furnished with 19th-century antiques that hint at the elegance and wealth that the southern gentility enjoyed in the late 1800s. Also on the grounds are a large carriage house and stable that were built in 1890 and now house a large collection of antique carriages. A log cabin, smokehouse, and creamery are other buildings that you can have a look inside during your visit. Belle Meade's parklike grounds make it a popular site for festivals throughout the year.

Admission: $5.50 adults, $5 senior citizens, $3.50 children 13–18, $2 children 6–12, free for children under 6.

Open: Mon–Sat 9am–5pm, Sun 1–5pm.

THE HERMITAGE, Old Hickory Blvd., Hermitage. Tel. 889-2941.

Though you may not know it, you probably see an image of one of Nashville's most famous citizens dozens of times every week. Who is this person whose face pops up so frequently? Andrew Jackson, the face on the $20 bill, and the man who built the Hermitage, a stately southern plantation home. Jackson moved to Tennessee in 1788 and became a prosecuting attorney. He served as the state's first congressman and later as a senator and judge. However, it was during the War of 1812 that he gained his greatest public acclaim as the general who led American troops in the Battle of New Orleans. His role in that battle helped Jackson win the presidency in 1828 and again in 1832.

Though the Hermitage now displays a classic Greek Revival facade, this is its third incarnation. Originally built in the Federal style in 1821, it was expanded and remodeled in 1831, and acquired its current appearance in 1836. Tours through the mansion and grounds are to the accompaniment of recordings that describe each room and

FROMMER'S FAVORITE NASHVILLE EXPERIENCES

A Day at Opryland   There's no doubt about it—a day spent at Opryland is a day well spent. Fun rides, lots of good music—there's something about big theme parks that brings out the kid in all of us. You don't even mind standing in all those lines.

An Evening at the Bluebird Café   With its excellent acoustics and two shows a night, the Bluebird is Nashville's most famous venue for country song writers. Only the best make it here, and many of the people who play the Bluebird wind up getting "discovered."

Cruising on the Cumberland   Cruising the Cumberland River on a paddlewheeler gives you a totally different perspective on Nashville. Add to the experience some good food and lively entertainment such as you get on the *General Jackson* showboat, and you have the makings of a very memorable excursion.

Attending the "Grand Ole Opry"   This live radio broadcast is an American institution that's as entertaining today as it was when it first went on the air almost 70 years ago. Luckily the current Grand Ole Opry House is quite a bit more comfortable than the old Ryman Auditorium where the "Opry" used to be held.

An Afternoon at the Country Music Hall of Fame and Museum   Lots of interesting displays chronicling the history of country music make this one of the most fascinating museums in Nashville. Even if you never thought you were a fan of country music, you may learn differently here.

section of the grounds. In addition to the main house, you'll also visit the kitchen, smokehouse, garden, Jackson's tomb, an original log cabin, the spring house, and nearby the Old Hermitage Church and Tulip Grove mansion.

Admission: $7 adults, $6.50 senior citizens, $3.50 children 6–18, free for children under 6.

Open: Daily 9am–5pm.

CHEEKWOOD, TENNESSEE BOTANICAL GARDENS & MUSEUM OF ART, 1200 Forrest Park Dr. Tel. 356-8000.

Once a private estate, Cheekwood today has much to offer both art lovers and garden enthusiasts. The museum and gardens are situated in a 55-acre park that's divided into several formal gardens and naturally landscaped areas. The museum itself is housed in the original Cheek family mansion, which was built in the Georgian style with many architectural details brought over from Europe. Among the mansion's most outstanding features is a lapis lazuli fireplace mantel. Within the building are collections of 19th- and 20th-century American art, Worcester porcelains, antique silver serving pieces, Oriental snuff bottles, and much period furniture.

The grounds are designed for strolling and there are numerous different gardens including a Japanese garden, a herb garden, a perennial garden, a dogwood garden, a magnolia garden, an iris garden, a peony garden, a rose garden, an azalea garden, and greenhouses full of orchids. You'll also find a gift shop and restaurant here on the grounds.

Admission: $5 adults, $4 senior citizens, $2 students.

Open: Mon–Sat 9am–5pm, Sun 1–5pm. **Closed:** New Year's Day, Thanksgiving, Christmas Eve, Christmas Day, New Year's Eve.

THE TENNESSEE STATE MUSEUM, Fifth Ave. between Union and Deaderick Sts. Tel. 741-2692.

To gain an understanding of Tennessee history, stop by this modern museum in the basement of the Tennessee Performing Arts Center. The museum houses a large display of Indian artifacts from the Mississipian period. The first whites to visit this region were long hunters (named for their long hunting trips west of the Appalachian Mountains) who arrived in the 18th century. The most famous long hunter was Daniel Boone, and you'll see a pocket knife that once belonged to him on display here. Other interesting artifacts on display include a knife and rifle that once belonged to Davy Crockett. Other displays focus on Presidents Andrew Jackson and James K. Polk, as well as Sam Houston, another Tennessean who went on to fame elsewhere.

There are numerous full-scale replicas of old buildings and period rooms such as a log cabin, a water-driven mill, a woodworking shop, an 18th-century print shop, and an 1855 parlor. The lower level of the museum is devoted mostly to the Civil War and Reconstruction.

One block west on Union Street, you'll find the museum's Military Branch, which houses displays on Tennessee's military activity from the Spanish-American War through World War II.

Admission: Free.

Open: Mon–Sat 10am–5pm, Sun 1–5pm.

CUMBERLAND SCIENCE MUSEUM, 800 Ridley Blvd. Tel. 862-5160.

It's hard to say which exhibit kids like the most at the Cumberland Science Museum, there are just so many fun interactive displays from which to choose in this modern, hands-on museum. Though the museum is primarily meant to be a fun way to introduce children to science, it can also be a lot of fun for adults. Kids of all ages can learn about technology, the environment, physics, and health as they roam the museum pushing buttons and turning knobs. The youngest kids will enjoy the Curiosity Corner, which is designed for children 10 and under. On weekends there are almost always special shows and demonstrations, and throughout the year the museum schedules special exhibits. In the Sudekum Planetarium, there are regular shows that take you exploring through the universe.

Admission: Museum, $6 adults, $4.50 senior citizens and children 3–12, free for children under age 3; planetarium $3; museum and planetarium, $7 adults, $5.50 senior citizens and children 3–12.

Open: June–Aug, Mon–Sat 9:30am–5pm, Sun 12:30–5:30pm; Sept–May, Tues–Sat 9:30am–5pm, Sun 12:30–5:30pm.

THE PARTHENON, Centennial Park, West End Ave. Tel. 862-8431.

Centennial Park, as its name implies, was built for the Tennessee Centennial Exposition of 1897, and this full-size replica of the Parthenon in Athens, was the exposition's centerpiece. However, the original structure was only meant to be temporary, and by 1921 the building, which had become a Nashville landmark, was in an advanced state of decay. In that year, the city undertook a reconstruction of their Parthenon and by 1931 a new, permanent building stood in Centennial Park. The building now duplicates the floor plan of the original Parthenon in Greece, and houses a 42-foot-tall statue of Athena Parthenos, the goddess of wisdom, prudent warfare, and the arts. This is the largest piece of indoor sculpture in the country. In addition to this impressive statue, there are original plaster castings of the famous Elgin marbles—bas-reliefs that once decorated the pediment of the Parthenon. Down in the basement galleries of the Parthenon, you'll find an excellent collection of 19th- and 20th-century American art. The Parthenon's two pair of bronze doors, which weigh in at 7.5 tons per door, are considered the largest matching bronze doors in the world.

Admission: $2.50 adults, $1.25 senior citizens and children.
Open: Tues–Sat 9am–4:30pm (extended hours in summer).

2. MORE ATTRACTIONS

ARCHITECTURAL HIGHLIGHTS

OPRYLAND HOTEL CONSERVATORY AND CASCADES, in the Opryland Hotel, 2800 Opryland Dr. Tel. 889-1000.

With more than 1,800 rooms, this place is big, but what makes it worth a visit are the two massive atriums that form the hotel's two main courtyards. Each of these atriums is covered with more than two acres of glass to form vast greenhouses full of tropical plants. There are rushing streams, roaring waterfalls, bridges, pathways, ponds, and fountains. There are also plenty of places to stop for a drink or a meal. In the evenings a harpist plays in the Cascades Atrium, and there is also a light show on this atrium's fountain.

Admission: Free.
Open: Daily 24 hours.

TENNESSEE STATE CAPITOL, Charlotte Ave. between Sixth and Seventh Aves. Tel. 741-2692.

The Tennessee State Capitol, which was completed in 1859, is a classically proportioned Greek Revival building and sits on a hill on the north side of downtown Nashville. The Capitol is built of local Tennessee limestone and marble that was quarried and cut by slaves and convict laborers. President and Mrs. James K. Polk are both buried on the capitol's east lawn. Several of the rooms within the building have been furnished in the style of the 19th century. There are also several ceiling frescoes and many ornate details. You can pick up a guide to the Capitol at the Tennessee State Museum.

Admission: Free.
Open: Daily 9am–4pm.

CAR COLLECTIONS

CAR COLLECTOR'S HALL OF FAME, 1534 Demonbreun St. Tel. 255-6804.

Though this antique and classic car museum advertises itself as having the cars of the country-music stars, it also has quite a few other beautiful old vehicles. Included here are a 1962 Lincoln Continental used by John F. Kennedy, a Cadillac Eldorado that belonged to Elvis, Webb Pierce's silver-dollar 1962 Bonneville, a 1982 Buick Riviera specially built for Tammy Wynette, and an MG-TD that belonged to Louise Mandrell. There are a total of about 45 cars on display at any given time.

Admission: $4.95 adults, $3.25 children, free for children under 6.
Open: June–Aug, daily 8am–9pm; Sept–May, daily 9am–5pm.

MUSIC VALLEY CAR MUSEUM, 2611 McGavock Pike. Tel. 885-7400.

Located across the road from the Opryland Hotel, this car museum contains dozens of antique cars, hot rods, and many cars that were once owned by famous country stars. You can see a Cadillac that belonged to Dolly Parton and yet another car that once belonged to Elvis (this one a limousine).

Admission: $3.50 adults, $3 senior citizens, $1.50 children 6–12, free for children under 6.
Open: Memorial Day–Labor Day, daily 8am–9pm; Labor Day–Memorial Day, daily 9am–5pm.

HISTORIC BUILDINGS & MONUMENTS

BELMONT MANSION, 1900 Belmont Blvd. Tel. 269-9537.

This pink-and-white Italianate villa was built in the 1850s by Adelicia Acklen, who was at the time one of the wealthiest women in the country. She had made her fortune smuggling cotton through the Union army blockade during the Civil War. The Belmont Mansion was originally built as a summer home, and yet no expense was spared in its construction. On your tour of the mansion, you'll see 15 rooms filled with period antiques, artwork, and marble statues. The grand salon is the most elegant and elaborate room ever built in an antebellum home. In the gardens surrounding the home, you'll find the largest collection of 19th-century garden ornaments in the United States.

Admission: $4 adults, $1 children 6–12, free for children under 6.

Open: June–Aug, Mon–Sat 10am–4pm, Sun 2–5pm; Sept–May, Tues–Sat 10am–4pm.

FORT NASHBORO, 170 First Ave. N. No phone.

Though it's much smaller than the original, this reconstruction of Nashville's first settlement includes several buildings that authentically reproduce what life in this frontier outpost would have been like in the late 18th century. The current fort consists of a log palisade inside of which are several log cabins, each of which is decorated with a few pieces that reflect activities pursued by early Tennessee settlers. The fort is located on the edge of Waterfront Park.

Admission: Free.

Open: Daily 9am–5pm.

HISTORIC TRAVELERS REST, 636 Farrell Pkwy. Tel. 832-2962.

Built in 1799, Traveler's Rest, as its name implies, once offered gracious Southern hospitality to travelers passing through a land that had only recently been settled. Among the period furnishings in this restored Federal-style farmhouse you'll see the largest public collection of pre-1840 Tennessee-made furniture. Travelers Rest was built by Judge John Overton, who, along with Andrew Jackson and another local man, founded the city of Memphis. Overton also served as Andrew Jackson's campaign manager when Jackson ran for president.

Admission: $5 adults, $2 children 6–16.

Open: June–Aug, Mon–Sat 10am–5pm, Sun 1–5pm; Sept–May, Mon–Sat 9am–4pm, Sun 1–4pm. **Directions:** Take I-65 south from downtown, get off at the Harding Place exit, and follow the signs.

HISTORIC MANSKERS STATION FRONTIER LIFE CENTER, Moss-Wright Park, Caldwell Rd. Tel. 859-FORT.

Tennessee's earliest non-Indian history comes to life here in a reconstruction of a fort built in 1779 by Kasper Mansker and settlers whom he had led to this spot. Today the fort is peopled by costumed interpreters who demonstrate the skills and activities of those 18th-century settlers. Cooking fires send smoke curling from the chimneys of log cabins while weavers spin wool into yarn and woodworkers build rough-hewn furniture. In March, May, July, September, October, November, and December there are living-history camps held on weekends. During these camps, costumed camp participants live in the style of the pioneers for a few days. In

IMPRESSIONS

Tennessee summer days were not made for work; in fact, many a resident had doubted that they were made at all, but that they sprang to life from the cauldrons of hell.
—CARL ROWAN, *SOUTH OF FREEDOM*, 1952

---

addition to the fort, Historic Manskers Station also includes the Bowen-Campbell House. Built between 1785 and 1787, this is the oldest brick house in middle Tennessee and is furnished with 18th-century antiques.

Admission: $3 adults, $2 students.

Open: Mar–Dec, Tues–Sat 9am–4:45pm. **Closed:** Jan–Feb.

MUSEUMS & GALLERIES

MUSEUM OF BEVERAGE CONTAINERS AND ADVERTISING, 1055 Ridgecrest Dr. Tel. 859-5236.

A beer can and soda can collection gone mad, this museum contains more than 30,000 beverage containers, making it the world's largest such collection. There are also plenty of beer and soda advertisements.

Admission: $2 adults, free for children under 13.

Open: Mon–Sat 9am–5pm, Sun 1–5pm. **Directions:** Take I-65 north to Exit 98, turn right, and proceed 1.3 miles to the museum.

MUSEUM OF TOBACCO ART AND INDUSTRY, 800 Harrison St. Tel. 271-2349.

In this small museum operated by the United States Tobacco Manufacturing Company you'll find an amazing array of antique pipes (including peace pipes), snuff bottles, tobacco jars, old tobacco advertisements, tobacco tins, and cigar-store Indians. This museum is located just north of the Tennessee State Capitol off Eighth Avenue North.

Admission: Free.

Open: Mon–Sat 9am–4pm.

VAN VECHTEN GALLERY, Fisk University, 1000 17th Ave. N. Tel. 329-8543.

This small art museum at the corner of Jackson Street and D. B. Todd Boulevard on the Fisk University campus houses part of famous photographer Alfred Steiglitz's art collection. The collection was donated by the photographer's widow, Georgia O'Keeffe, and contains not only photos by Steiglitz and paintings by O'Keeffe, but pieces by Picasso, Cézanne, Toulouse-Lautrec, Renoir, and Diego Rivera as well. Though the collection is small, it's well worth a visit.

Admission: By donation.

Open: Tues–Fri 10am–5pm, Sat–Sun 1–5pm.

NEIGHBORHOODS

THE DISTRICT, Broadway, Second Avenue, and Printer's Alley.

The District is Nashville's restored downtown section and is divided into three areas. Along Broadway between the Cumberland River and Fifth Avenue you'll find several of country music's most important sites, including the Ryman Auditorium (home of the "Grand Ole Opry" for many years), Tootsie's Orchid Lounge (where "Opry" performers often dropped by for a drink), Gruhn guitars, the Ernest Tubb Record Store, and the Merchants restaurant. Second Avenue was traditionally the warehouse district, serving riverboats on the Cumberland River. Today this street, between Broadway and Union Street, is lined with antiques stores, gift-shop arcades, restaurants, and at least five places where you can hear live music.

MUSIC ROW, along 16th and 17th Aves. between Demonbreun St. and Grand Ave.

This is the very heart of the country-music recording industry and is home to dozens of recording studios and record-company offices. This is also where you'll find the Country Music Hall of Fame and Museum, the Country Music Wax Museum, and several country-music gift shops and small private museums. The neighborhood is a combination of old restored homes and modern buildings that hint at the vast amounts of money generated by the country-music industry. This is one of the best areas in town for spotting country-music stars. Keep your eyes peeled.

PARKS, GARDENS & ZOOS

GRASSMERE WILDLIFE PARK, 3777 Nolensville Rd. Tel. 833-0632.

This modern wildlife park just south of downtown Nashville houses only animals that are indigenous to Tennessee. In the naturalistic habitats, you'll see river otters, bison, elk, black bear, gray wolves, bald eagles, and cougars, as well as other smaller animals. In the park's aviary, you can walk among many of the state's songbirds, and at the Cumberland River exhibit, you'll see the fish, reptiles, and amphibians.

Admission: $5 adults, $3 senior citizens and children 3–12, free for children under 3.

Open: Memorial Day–Labor Day, daily 10am–6pm (last admission at 5pm); Labor Day–Memorial Day, daily 10am–5pm (last admission at 4pm). The park stays open for one hour after the last admission.

NASHVILLE ZOO, 1710 Ridge Road Circle, Joelton. Tel. 370-3333.

Located on 150 acres of rolling hills near Nashville, this zoo has more than 800 residents representing 150 animal species. The naturalistic settings are home to a surprisingly wide variety of animals from around the world. You'll see snow leopards, giraffes, tree frogs, llamas, lemurs, white tigers, and many other animals.

Admission: $5.50 adults, $3.50 senior citizens and children 3–12, free for children under 3.

Open: May–Memorial Day, daily 9am–5pm; Memorial Day–Labor Day, daily 9am–6pm; Labor Day–Apr, daily 10am–5pm.

Directions: Take I-24 about 15 miles northwest of downtown Nashville to Exit 31.

3. COOL FOR KIDS

Nashville is full of things for kids to see and do, and many of these are attractions already listed above under "The Top Attractions" and "More Attractions." Below I have mentioned again several attractions with special appeal for kids:

Opryland USA   This theme park on the outskirts of the city is an absolute "must" for children.

Cumberland Science Museum   Kids can push buttons, turn knobs, and hardly even notice that they're learning about science while they have a blast.

The Tennessee State Museum   Old Indian arrowheads, Davy Crockett's rifle, and Daniel Boone's pocket knife may still get kids oohing and ahhing.

Nashville Zoo   Lions and tigers and bears, oh my!

Grassmere Wildlife Park   Don't let the kids miss the antics of the river otters.

NASHVILLE TOY MUSEUM, 2613 McGavock Pike. Tel. 883-8870.

Railroad buffs, toy train enthusiasts, and children of all ages will enjoy this huge collection of antique toys. The emphasis is on toy trains, and there's a large model train layout that can keep kids and adults fascinated for hours. Among the several large collections in the museum, there are shelves full of old toy trains, antique model cars, miniature boats and ships, dolls, and teddy bears.

Admission: $3.50 adults, $1.50 children.

Open: Memorial Day–Labor Day, daily 9am–9pm; Labor Day–Memorial Day, daily 9am–5pm.

WAVE COUNTRY, Two Rivers Pkwy. Tel. 885-1092.

This water park is located just off Briley Parkway about a mile from Opryland USA and is a summertime "must" for kids of all ages. There's a huge wave pool and a whole bunch of water slides.

Admission: $5 adults, $4 children 5–12, free for children under 5; half price for everyone after 4pm.

Open: Memorial Day–Labor Day, daily 10am–8pm.

GRAND OLD GOLF, 2444 Music Valley Dr. Tel. 871-4701.

With three miniature-golf courses, bumper boats, and a video arcade, this place is sure to be a hit with your kids. It's located not far from Opryland USA, so when you can't afford another day in the big theme park, bring the little ones here.

Admission: $5 adults, $4 senior citizens, $2.50 children under 9.
Open: Mon–Thurs 10am–10pm, Fri–Sat 10am–midnight, Sun noon–10pm.

---

4. SPECIAL-INTEREST SIGHTSEEING

FOR THE COUNTRY-MUSIC FAN

THE OLD "GRAND OLE OPRY"

RYMAN AUDITORIUM AND MUSEUM, 116 Fifth Ave. N. Tel. 254-1445.

Known as the "Mother Church of Country Music," the Ryman Auditorium is the single most historic site in the world of country music. It was here that the "Grand Ole Opry" was held between 1943 and 1974. Originally built in 1892 as the Union Gospel Tabernacle by riverboat captain Tom Ryman, this building served as an evangelical hall for many years. However, by the early 1900s, the building's name had been changed to honor its builder and a stage had been added. That stage, over the years, saw the likes of Sarah Bernhardt, Enrico Caruso, Katherine Hepburn, Will Rogers, and Elvis Presley. However, it was not until 1943 that the "Grand Ole Opry" began broadcasting from the Ryman Auditorium. In 1974 the "Grand Ole Opry" moved to a new theater at Opryland USA, and the Ryman, which had been listed on the National Register of Historic Places since 1971, became a shrine to the "Grand Ole Opry" and country music. Visitors can sit in the old wooden church pews that were used for decades, have a look in the old dressing rooms, and take the stage themselves.

As this book goes to press, the Ryman Auditorium is closed for renovations with plans to reopen in the summer of 1994. As part of the renovation, the old theater is being prepared to once again become a theater offering live-music performances. Before visiting, be sure to find out if the auditorium has reopened.

Admission: $2.50 adults, $1 children 12 and under.
Open: Daily 8:30am–4:30pm.

MUSEUMS & GIFT SHOPS

BARBARA MANDRELL COUNTRY, 1510 Division St. Tel. 242-7800.

Fans of Barbara Mandrell can learn all about her life and career across the street from the Country Music Hall of Fame. In addition to loads of personal items (guitars, clothes, photos), there's a reproduction of Barbara's bedroom and a video tour of her log home. Other videos chronicle Barbara's life and career. The huge gift and Christmas shop here is considered one of the best in Nashville for country-music fans. Visitors can even make a recording in a studio on the premises.

Admission: $6.50 adults, $2.25 children 6–12, free for children under 6.

Open: Daily 9am–5pm.

GEORGE JONES GIFT SHOP, Demonbreun St. Tel. 255-9119.

Though this is primarily a country-music gift shop, you'll also find a small collection of George Jones memorabilia, including gold records, old photos, and clothing and jewelry once worn by George Jones.

Admission: Free.

Open: May 15–Oct, daily 8am–10pm; Nov–May 14, daily 8am–6pm.

HANK WILLIAMS, JR., MUSEUM AND GIFT SHOP, 1524 Demonbreun St. Tel. 242-8313.

Despite the "Jr." in the name, this museum and gift shop are dedicated to both Hanks, father and son. You'll see old Cadillacs that belonged to both of these stars, stage outfits, guitars, old photos, and many other pieces of memorabilia pertaining to these two giants of country music.

Admission: $4 adults and senior citizens, free for children under 17.

Open: Mar–Sept, daily 8am–10pm; Oct–Feb, daily 8am–5pm.

HOUSE OF CASH, 700 Johnny Cash Pkwy., Hendersonville. Tel. 824-5110.

If the special Johnny Cash room in the Country Music Hall of Fame and Museum didn't give you enough of the man in black's past, head out to Hendersonville, northeast of downtown Nashville (take I-65 to the Saundersville Road exit). In addition to learning more about Johnny Cash, his wife, June Carter, and the famous Carter family, you'll get to see a motorcycle that belonged to Buddy Holly, Buffalo Bill's Winchester rifle, Al Capone's chair, John Wayne's six-shooter, and many other interesting items.

Admission: $6 adults, $1 children 6–12.

Open: Mon–Sat 9am–4:30pm.

JIM REEVES MUSEUM, 1023 Joyce Lane. Tel. 226-2065 or 226-2062.

Jim Reeves' smooth voice and mellow music have done much to spread the popularity of country music around the world. Here, in a 1794 plantation home you can see a very thorough display chronicling this star's career. Included in the exhibits are a 1960 Cadillac El Dorado that Reeves once drove, guitars and musical instruments used by Reeves and his band, and some rare film footage of Reeves in performance. You'll find the museum at the corner of Gallatin Road and Briley Parkway.

Admission: $4 adults, $3.50 senior citizens, $2 children 6–12, free for children under 6.

Open: Daily 9am–5pm.

KITTY WELLS/JOHNNY WRIGHT FAMILY COUNTRY

JUNCTION, 240 Old Hickory Blvd., Madison. Tel. 865-9118.

This little place is first and foremost a gift shop, but if you're a fan of these two country music old-timers, be sure to drop by. Exhibits include a replica of Kitty's kitchen, model train layouts, a 1957 Cadillac used in the film *Coal Miner's Daughter,* and plenty of old photos and awards. You'll find this gift shop and museum in nearby Madison.

Admission: Free.

Open: Mon–Fri 9am–5pm, Sat 9am–4pm. **Directions:** Take I-65 north to Exit 92 (Old Hickory Boulevard).

TWITTY CITY, 1 Music Village Blvd., Hendersonville. Tel. 822-6650.

Though Conway Twitty died in 1993, his home and 10 acres of manicured grounds are still a major Nashville attraction. Actually, Twitty City is more of a theme park than a home. On the guided tours here, you'll visit Conway's Showcase, a computerized display that traces the star's long music career, and then have a look inside Twitty's mansion.

Admission: $8 adults, $4.50 children 6–12, free for children under 6.

Open: Daily 9am–5pm. **Directions:** Head north on I-65, take Exit 95, and follow the signs.

WILLIE NELSON AND FRIENDS SHOWCASE MUSEUM, 2613A McGavock Pike. Tel. 885-1515.

This museum is filled with displays on Willie Nelson and many other country-music stars as well. You'll see Nelson's guitars, his gold and platinum records, and many of his personal items, such as his pool table. Other stars featured in exhibits here include Elvis Presley, Roy Orbison, Patsy Cline, Audie Murphy, Web Pierce, and Mel Tillis. The museum is inside the Music Valley Gift Emporium, which is Nashville's largest gift shop, and is located across the road from the Opryland Hotel.

Admission: $3.50 adults, $2.50 senior citizens, $1.50 children 7–12, free for children under 7.

Open: Memorial Day–Labor Day, daily 8am–10pm; Labor Day–Memorial Day, daily 9am–5pm (closing hours sometimes vary).

LIVE TELEVISION BROADCASTS

THE NASHVILLE NETWORK, 2806 Opryland Dr. Tel. 883-7000.

This cable-television network, which has its studios near Opryland USA, is a country-music-oriented network that's broadcast into 57 million homes. Each week numerous live and recorded shows are taped here, and it's possible to join the audience at one of these programs. The most popular is "Nashville Now," a performance-and-interview program that's broadcast live each night. For reservations to be part of the "Nashville Now" audience, phone 889-6611.

Admission: $5.

Open: Daily.

WAX MUSEUMS

COUNTRY MUSIC WAX MUSEUM AND MALL, 118 16th Ave. Tel. 256-2490.

So you spent all day on Music Row and didn't see even one of your favorite country-music stars. Don't despair—just stop by this wax museum at the top of Music Square and see the next best thing. There are more than 60 wax figures of famous country stars, and they're all dressed in outfits once owned by the stars themselves.

Admission: $4 adults, $1.75 children.

Open: June–Aug, daily 9am–8pm; Sept–May, daily 9am–5pm (closing time sometimes varies).

MUSIC VALLEY WAX MUSEUM OF THE STARS, 2515 McGavock Pike. Tel. 883-3612.

While you're out in the Opryland USA area, you can check out Nashville's other country-music wax museum, which features wax figures of more than 50 famous stars. Out in front of the museum, more than 200 stars have left their footprints, handprints, and signatures in concrete.

Admission: $3.50 adults, $3 senior citizens, $1.50 children 6–12, free for children under 6.

Open: Memorial Day–Labor Day, daily 8am–10pm; Labor Day–Memorial Day, daily 9am–6pm (closing time sometimes varies).

5. ORGANIZED TOURS

CITY TOURS

Country & Western/Gray Line Tours, 2416 Music Valley Dr. (tel. 883-5555, or toll free 800/251-1864), a Gray Line affiliate offers a dozen or more different tours ranging in length from four hours to a full day. On the "Discover Nashville" tour, you'll ride past the homes of such country stars as Tammy Wynette, Ronnie Milsap, Hank Williams, Eddy Arnold, Porter Wagoner, and Minnie Pearl. You'll also see many historic and country-music-related Nashville sights. There's a strictly historical tour, sunset tours, and combinations. Tour prices range from $16 to $60 for adults and $8 to $40 for children.

Grand Ole Opry Sightseeing Tours, 2810 Opryland Dr. (tel. 889-9490), is the official tour company of Opryland USA, though their tours take in more than just Opryland. Several of the tours offered by this company include drives past homes of country-music stars. The "Country Legends" tour includes a visit backstage at the "Grand Ole Opry" or the set of "Nashville Now." Tours cost $16, free for children under 7.

Johnny Walker Tours, 97 Wallace Rd. (tel. 834-8585), splits its tours past stars' homes into two three-hour tours. One tour goes past homes (and former homes) of Johnny Cash, Conway Twitty, Roy Orbison, Col. Tom Parker, and the Osborne Brothers, with a stop in Music Valley and the Opryland complex. The other main tour goes past such homes as those of Dolly Parton, George Jones, Tammy Wynette, Brenda Lee, Roseanne Cash, and Webb Pierce, and includes a visit to Music Row. Tour charges are $17 to $25 for adults, $8.50 to $12.50 for children 4 to 11, and free for children under 4.

RIVERBOAT TOURS

Operated by Opryland USA, the ✪ *General Jackson* **SHOW-BOAT,** 2812 Opryland Dr. (tel. 889-6611), is the biggest and most elegant of Nashville's paddleboats, and is also the biggest showboat in the world. The *General Jackson* is 300 feet long, has four decks, and harkens back to the days when riverboats were the most sophisticated way to travel. Cruises include plenty of entertainment, including country music and comedy routines on daytime cruises and a Broadway-style musical revue during the evening dinner cruises. Other evening cruises include a Dixieland band and live rock and country dance bands. The *General Jackson* departs from the dock at Opryland USA. A two-hour day or night cruise costs $14.95; three-hour dinner cruises are $36.95 for adults and $28.95 for children 4 to 11.

The paddlewheelers of the **Belle Carol Riverboat Co.,** 106 First Ave. S. (tel. 244-3430, or toll free 800/342-2355), are not nearly as glamorous as the *General Jackson,* but they'll still give you a glimpse of what it was like to travel by riverboat. These small sternwheelers depart from Riverfront Park in downtown Nashville and the Music Valley Dock near Opryland. There are sightseeing cruises and dinner cruises. A late-night party cruise offered on Friday and Saturday nights between May and October offers two hours of dancing to live Top-40 music. Reservations are required for dinner and brunch cruises. The daily sightseeing cruise costs $10.95 for adults and $8.20 for children under 12; the Sunday brunch cruise goes for $17.95 for adults and $13.15 for children under 12; the prime rib dinner cruise is $32.95 for adults and $21.85 for children under 12; and the party cruise costs $10.95 per person.

A HISTORY TOUR

Between May 15 and October 15, you can get an earful of Nashville history on the walking tour offered by **Historic Nashville,** 172 Second Ave. N., Suite 112 (tel. 244-7835). The tours are a fairly easy walk through the historic downtown area known as the District. The tour costs $5 for adults and $3 for senior citizens and students.

WALKING TOUR — DOWNTOWN NASHVILLE

Start: Riverfront Park at the intersection of Broadway and First Avenue. (There's an inexpensive public parking lot here that's one of the cheapest and most convenient places to park in downtown Nashville.)
Finish: Printer's Alley.

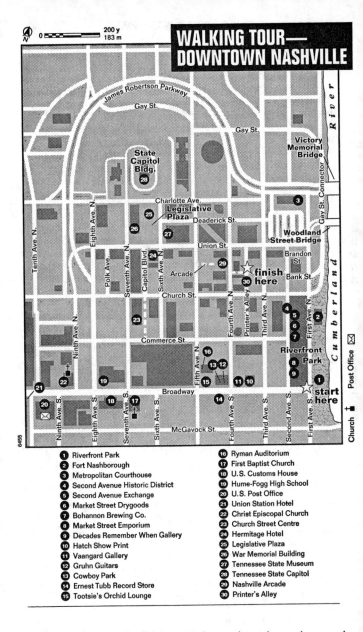

WALKING TOUR—
DOWNTOWN NASHVILLE

0 — 200 y
0 — 183 m

1 Riverfront Park
2 Fort Nashborough
3 Metropolitan Courthouse
4 Second Avenue Historic District
5 Second Avenue Exchange
6 Market Street Drygoods
7 Bohannon Brewing Co.
8 Market Street Emporium
9 Decades Remember When Gallery
10 Hatch Show Print
11 Vaangard Gallery
12 Gruhn Guitars
13 Cowboy Park
14 Ernest Tubb Record Store
15 Tootsie's Orchid Lounge
16 Ryman Auditorium
17 First Baptist Church
18 U.S. Customs House
19 Hume-Fogg High School
20 U.S. Post Office
21 Union Station Hotel
22 Christ Episcopal Church
23 Church Street Centre
24 Hermitage Hotel
25 Legislative Plaza
26 War Memorial Building
27 Tennessee State Museum
28 Tennessee State Capitol
29 Nashville Arcade
30 Printer's Alley

Time: Anywhere from three to eight hours, depending on how much time you spend in the museum, shopping, or dining.

Best Times: Tuesday through Friday, when both the Tennessee State Museum and the Tennessee State Capitol are open to the public.

Worst Times: Sunday, Monday, and holidays, when a number of places are closed.

Though Nashville is a city of the New South and sprawls in all directions with suburbs full of office parks and shopping malls, it still has a downtown where you can do a bit of exploring on foot. The downtown area includes the historic area known as the District, which is comprised of three distinct areas. Within these three areas of downtown are many turn-of-the-century commercial buildings that have been preserved and now house restaurants, clubs, and interesting shops. Because Nashville is the state capital, the downtown also has many impressive government office buildings.

Start your tour at the intersection of Broadway and First Avenue at:

1. **Riverfront Park,** which is on the banks of the Cumberland River. The park was built as part of Nashville's bicentennial celebration, and is where the Nashville Trolleys start their circuits around downtown and out to Music Row. If you should grow tired of walking at any time during your walk, just look for a trolley stop and ride the trolley back to the park.

   Walk north along the river to:

2. **Fort Nashboro.** This is a reconstruction of the 1780 fort that served as the first white settlement in this area.

   Continue up First Avenue to Union Street and turn left. Across the street is the:

3. **Metropolitan Courthouse,** which also houses the Nashville City Hall. Built in 1937, the imposing building incorporates many classic Greek architectural details. Of particular interest are the bronze doors, the etched-glass panels above the doors, and the lobby murals. At the information booth in the lobby, you can pick up a brochure detailing the building's many design elements.

   If you now head back down Second Avenue, you'll find yourself in the:

4. **Second Avenue Historic District.** Between Union Avenue and Broadway are numerous Victorian commercial buildings, most of which have now been restored. Much of the architectural detail is near the tops of the buildings, so keep your eyes up.

REFUELING STOP Second Avenue has several excellent restaurants where you can stop for lunch or a drink. **The Old Spaghetti Factory,** 160 Second Ave. N., is a cavernous place filled with Victorian antiques. There's even a trolley car parked in the middle of the main dining room. A couple of doors down is **Mère Bulles,** at 152 Second Ave. N., an outpost of urban chic where you can taste New Southern cuisine.

There are several interesting antiques and crafts stores along Second Avenue. Next door to The Old Spaghetti Factory you'll find the:

5. **Second Avenue Exchange,** a warehouse full of antiques and collectibles.

   A few doors down from Mère Bulles is:

6. **Market Street Drygoods.** In this old dry-goods store, you'll

find more than 40 vendors selling Tennessee crafts, handmade jewelry, and antiques.

Two doors farther down, you come to the:

7. **Bohannon Brewing Co.,** Nashville's first microbrewery. You can tour the brewery and taste samples of their beer and ale.

Farther down the street, watch for the:

8. **Market Street Emporium,** a collection of specialty shops that also includes an artist's studio and the Windows on the Cumberland restaurant. Next door is:

9. **Decades, Remember When Gallery,** a shop selling collectibles and antiques with a focus on the 1950s and old advertising signs.

At the corner of Second Avenue and Broadway, turn right. Between Third and Fourth Avenues, watch for:

10. **Hatch Show Print.** This is the oldest poster shop in the United States and still prints its posters on an old-fashioned letterpress printer. The most popular posters are those advertising the "Grand Ole Opry."

At the corner of Broadway and Fourth Avenue is the:

11. **Vaangard Gallery,** an art gallery specializing in works by local artists.

Cross Fourth Avenue and you'll come to:

12. **Gruhn Guitars.** This is the most famous guitar shop in Nashville and specializes in used and vintage guitars. Next door is:

13. **Cowboy Park.** The cowboy sculptures in this rather informal park were created by artist Olin Calk and are made of recycled garbage.

REFUELING STOP If you didn't stop for lunch on Second Avenue, now would be a good time. Directly across the street is **The Merchants** restaurant, at 401 Broadway, a favorite Nashville power-lunch spot. The atmosphere is sophisticated and the food is New American cuisine.

If you stay on this side of the street, you'll pass the:

14. **Ernest Tubb Record Store.** This store was once the home of the "Midnight Jamboree," a country-music radio show that took place after the "Grand Ole Opry" was over on Saturday nights.

Back on the opposite side of Broadway is:

15. **Tootsie's Orchid Lounge,** one of the most famous bars in Nashville. "Grand Ole Opry" musicians used to duck into Tootsie's before, during, and after the show at the Ryman. There's live country music all day long at Tootsie's.

From Tootsie's, turn right on Fifth Avenue and in a few steps you'll come to the front door of the:

16. **Ryman Auditorium,** where the "Grand Ole Opry" was held from the 1943 to 1974. This building was originally built as a tabernacle to host evangelical revival meetings, but because of its good acoustics and large seating capacity it became a popular setting for theater and music performances.

After leaving the Ryman Auditorium, walk back down to the corner of Broadway and Fifth Avenue, cross Broadway, and turn to your right. At the corner of Seventh Avenue, you'll find the:

17. **First Baptist Church,** a modern building that incorporates a Victorian Gothic church tower built between 1884 and 1886. The church's congregation wanted a new church, but didn't want to give up the beautiful old tower. This is the compromise that was reached.

Across Seventh Avenue is the:

18. **U.S. Customs House,** which is now leased as private office space. This Victorian Gothic building was built in 1877 and displays fine stonework and friezes. The imposing structure, with its soaring tower and arched windows, could be in any European city.

Directly across the street is the:

19. **Hume-Fogg High School,** which was built between 1912 and 1916. The building incorporates elements of English Tudor and Gothic design.

Two blocks farther up Broadway you'll see a decidedly different style of architecture. The:

20. **U.S. Post Office** building was designed with elements of both neoclassical and art deco architectural styling. This building's beauty lies in its detail work rather than in its overall design. Be sure to step inside the lobby and observe some of the interior details.

The post office shares a parking lot with the:

21. **Union Station hotel.** This Victorian Romanesque Revival building was built in 1900 as Nashville's main passenger railroad station, but in 1986 was renovated and reopened as a luxury hotel. The exterior stone walls incorporate many fine carvings, and the lobby is the most elegant historic space in Nashville.

Head back the way you came and cross over to the opposite side of Broadway at Ninth Avenue. Here you'll find:

22. **Christ Episcopal Church,** which was built between 1887 and 1892. The building is in the Victorian Gothic style and is complete with gargoyles. This church also has Tiffany stained-glass windows.

Continue back down Broadway and at Seventh Avenue, head north to Commerce Street and take a right. If you turn into the lobby of the Nashville Stouffer Hotel and go up to the mezzanine, you'll find a glass-enclosed walkway leading to:

23. **Church Street Centre.** This modern indoor shopping mall is one of the recent commercial developments calculated to attract people back into downtown Nashville.

From Church Street Centre's front door, head north up Capitol Boulevard. At the corner of Union Street is the:

24. **Hermitage Hotel.** This is Nashville's last grand old hotel, and though the guest rooms are far from luxurious, the lobby exudes beaux arts extravagance, with a stained-glass skylight and marble columns and floor.

Across Union Street from the Hermitage Hotel is the:

25. **Legislative Plaza,** a large public plaza that's a popular lunch spot for downtown officeworkers. Fronting onto this plaza is the:

26. **War Memorial Building,** which was built in 1925 to honor soldiers who died in World War I. The centerpiece of this neoclassical building is an atrium holding a large statue titled *Victory.* This building also houses the Tennessee State Museum Military Branch.

   On the opposite side of the plaza is the:

27. **Tennessee State Museum,** which is in the basement of the same building that houses the Tennessee Performing Arts Center. This museum contains an extensive and well-displayed collection of artifacts pertaining to Tennessee history.

   Returning to the Legislative Plaza and continuing to the north across Charlotte Street will bring you to the:

28. **Tennessee State Capitol.** This Greek Revival building was built between 1845 and 1859. Be sure to take a look inside where you will find many beautiful architectural details and artworks.

   If you walk back across the Legislative Plaza and take a left on Union Street and then a right on Fifth Avenue (cross to the far side of the street), you'll come to the west entrance of the:

29. **Nashville Arcade.** This covered shopping arcade was built in 1903 and is modeled after an arcade in Italy. There are only a few such arcades left in the United States, and unfortunately, no one has yet breathed new life into this one.

   Walk through the arcade and continue across Fourth Avenue. The alley in front of you leads to:

30. **Printer's Alley,** which for more than a century has been a center for evening entertainment. Today things are much tamer than they once were, but you can still find several nightclubs featuring jazz and country music.

6. SPORTS & RECREATION

SPECTATOR SPORTS

AUTO RACING   Stock cars race weekly at the **Nashville Motor Raceway,** on the Tennessee State Fairgrounds. The race season runs from April through November, and races are held on Saturday nights. For more information, phone 726-1818.

   The **Music City Raceway,** 3302 Ivy Point Rd. in Goodletsville, is the place to catch National Hot Rod Association (NHRA) drag-racing action. The dragstrip has races on Friday and Saturday between March and October. Admission is $7 for adults; children enter free.

BASEBALL   The **Nashville Sounds** are a farm team of the Chicago White Sox and play at Greer Stadium, 534 Chestnut St., off Eighth Avenue South. Admission ranges from $3 general to $7 for reserved box seats. For schedule and ticket information, phone 242-4371.

GOLF TOURNAMENTS   The **Sara Lee Classic LPGA Golf Tournament** is held each year in early May and features 144 of the world's top woman golfers. The tournament is held at the Hermitage Golf Course on Old Hickory Boulevard. Admission is free on Monday and Tuesday, goes up to $5 Wednesday through Friday, and is $10 on Saturday and Sunday. For more information, phone 847-5017.

HOCKEY   The **Nashville Knights** (tel. 255-PUCK) is a minor-league farm team of the NHL and plays at the Nashville Municipal Auditorium, 417 Fourth Ave. N. Tickets are $6.50 for general admission and $8.50 for reserved seats.

HORSE SHOWS   Horse shows are important events in the Nashville area's calendar of special events. The biggest and most important horse show of the year is the **Annual Tennessee Walking Horse National Celebration.** This show takes place 40 miles southeast of Nashville in the town of Shelbyville and is held each year in late August and early September. For information on dates, schedules, and ticketing, contact the Celebration, P.O. Box 1010, Shelbyville, TN 37160 (tel. 615/684-5915).

The city's other big horse event is the annual running of the **Iroquois Steeplechase** in early May. This amateur steeplechase is held in Percy Warner Park in the Belle Meade area and is a benefit for the Vanderbilt Children's Hospital. For more information, contact Friends of Children's Hospital, 2424 Garland Ave., Nashville, TN 37212 (tel. 615/322-7450).

RECREATION

GOLF   Nashville has seven municipal golf courses and several more private courses that are open to the public. These include **Forrest Crossing,** 750 Riverview Dr. (tel. 794-9400); **Harpeth Hills,** 2424 Old Hickory Blvd. (tel. 373-8202); the **Hermitage Golf Course,** 3939 Old Hickory Blvd., (tel. 847-4001); **McCabe Golf Park,** 46th Avenue North at Murphy Road (tel. 297-9138); **Nashboro Village,** 2250 Murfreesboro Rd. (tel. 367-2311); the **Percy Warner Golf Course,** Percy Warner Park, Forrest Park Drive off Belle Meade Boulevard in Belle Meade (tel. 356-2767); **Rhodes Golf Center,** 2400 MetroCenter Blvd. (tel. 242-2336); the **Riverview Golf Course,** South 17th and Sevier Streets (tel. 226-9331); the **Shelby Golf Course,** South 20th and Fatherland Streets, which is close to downtown (tel. 862-8474); and the **Two Rivers Golf Course,** Two Rivers Parkway and McGavock Pike, (tel. 889-2675).

HORSEBACK RIDING   If you want to go for a ride through the Tennessee hills, there are a couple of nearby places where you can rent a horse. The **Ramblin Breeze Ranch,** 400 Knight Rd., Whites Creek (tel. 876-1029), is just seven miles north of downtown Nashville and rents horses for $10 an hour. **Ju-Ro Stables,** 7149 Cairo Bend, Lebanon (tel. 449-6621), is located about 25 miles east of Nashville and charges the same rate.

SWIMMING   Though most of the hotels and motels listed in this book have pools, if you'd rather go jump in a lake, head for **J. Percy Priest Lake.** You'll find this large man-made lake just east of downtown Nashville at Exit 219 off I-40. Stop by the information center to get a map showing the designated swimming areas (there are three).

TENNIS   Nashville has dozens of municipal tennis courts all over the city. You can find out the location of the nearest public courts by picking up a map at any public library or by contacting the **Metropolitan Board of Parks and Recreation** (tel. 862-8400) Monday through Friday between 8am and 4:30pm. For indoor courts there's the **Thomas F. Frist Centennial Sportsplex Tennis Center,** 25th Avenue North at Brandau Avenue (tel. 862-8480).

CHAPTER 7

NASHVILLE SHOPPING

1. THE SHOPPING
   SCENE
2. SHOPPING A TO Z

With its many country-music stars and fans, Nashville has become a great shopping city. Whether you're looking for handmade stage outfits costing thousands of dollars or a good deal on a pair of shoes at a factory-outlet store, you'll find plenty of shopping opportunities in Nashville.

1. THE SHOPPING SCENE

As in most cities of the South, the shopping scene in Nashville is spread out over the width and breadth of the city. Most of the city's best shopping is to be found in the many large new shopping malls scattered around the newer suburbs. However, there are also many interesting and exclusive shops in the West End area. In downtown Nashville, you'll find gift and souvenir shops, antiques stores, and music instrument and record stores that cater to country musicians and fans. Second Avenue North, in the historic downtown area known as the District, is a great place to browse for antiques and collectibles.

Country-music fans will find plenty of opportunities to shop for western wear. There are dozens of shops specialising in the *de rigueur* attire of country music. You probably can't find a better selection of cowboy boots anywhere outside Arizona, and if your tastes run to sequined denim shirts or skirts, you'll find plenty to choose from.

2. SHOPPING A TO Z

ANTIQUES

DECADES, REMEMBER WHEN GALLERY, 110 Second Ave. N. Tel. 254-4887.

 Collectibles from the 1950s are the specialty of this Second Avenue store, but they also have lots of advertising signs dating back much earlier. With a warehouse worth of space, the store can sell such large pieces as old store ice chests advertising various soft drinks.

DOWNTOWN ANTIQUE MALL, 612 Eighth Ave. S. Tel. 256-6616.

Among the many stalls in this historic warehouse building you'll find lots of Civil War memorabilia. There are also plenty of other antiques as well.

MADE IN FRANCE, 3001 West End Ave. Tel. 329-9300.

Though not everything here is antique, you will find quite a few European antiques. The store is an interior-design shop specializing in traditional and contemporary European accent pieces such as handmade throw pillows, old birdcages, and many other small and large decorative items.

ART

IMAGINE GALLERY, 2308 West End Ave. Tel. 320-5670.

Located across from Vanderbilt University, this gallery specializes in limited-edition artwork by John Lennon, Jerry Garcia, Miles Davis, and Rolling Stones guitarist Ronnie Wood. In addition to prints, they also have T-shirts, Jerry Garcia ties, and collectible posters.

LOCAL COLOR GALLERY, 1912 Broadway. Tel. 321-3141.

This gallery specializes in works by local and Tennessee artists. Watercolors and other paintings comprise the largest portion of the works on sale here, but you'll also find ceramics and sculptures.

WOODCUTS, 1613 Jefferson St. Tel. 321-5357.

If you're interested in artworks by African-American artists, this is the place to visit in Nashville. Prints, posters, note cards, and greeting cards comprise the majority of the offerings here, though they also do framing. The shop is adjacent to Fisk University.

BOOKS

DAVIS-KIDD BOOKSELLERS, 4007 Hillsboro Rd. Tel. 385-2645.

For the best and biggest selection of books in Nashville, head south of downtown to the Green Hills area where you'll find this big bookstore. The store has regular book signings and there's a good café on the second floor.

ELDER'S BOOK STORE, 2115 Elliston Place. Tel. 327-1867.

This dusty old shop looks as if some of the antiquarian books on sale were first stocked when they were new. Every square inch of shelf space is jammed full of books and there are stacks of more books seemingly everywhere you turn. This place is a book collector's dream come true.

CRAFTS

AMERICAN ARTISAN, 4231 Harding Rd. Tel. 298-4691.

Stocking only the finest of contemporary American handcrafts from around the country, American Artisan is Nashville's best place to shop for original fine crafts. There are intricate baskets, elaborate ceramic pieces, colorful kaleidoscopes, one-of-a-kind jewelry, and beautiful wood furniture. All exhibit the artist's eye for creativity.

TENNESSEE MEMORIES, 2182 Bandywood Dr. Tel. 298-3253.

Located in the Fashion Square shopping plaza next to the Mall at Green Hills, this small store is filled with crafts from around the state. You'll find everything from birdhouses with license plates for roofs to pottery, from walking sticks to rocking chairs.

DEPARTMENT STORES

CASTNER KNOTT, 618 Church St. Tel. 256-6411.

This is one of Nashville's two upscale department stores and is well known for its personable employees and wide selection of fine lines. Other stores can be found at the Cool Springs Galleria mall, 1790 Galleria Blvd. (tel. 771-2100); Bellevue Center mall, 7616 U.S. 70S (tel. 646-5500); Donelson Plaza, 2731 Lebanon Rd. (tel. 883-8551); the Mall at Green Hills, 2133 Hillsboro Rd. (tel. 383-3300); Harding Mall, 4070 Nolensville Rd. (tel. 832-6890); Hickory Hollow Mall, 917 Bell Rd. (tel. 731-8500); and Rivergate Mall, 1000 Two Mile Pkwy., Goodlettsville (tel. 859-5251).

DILLARD'S, in the Bellevue Center mall, 7624 U.S. 70S. Tel. 662-1515.

With stores throughout the South, Dillard's is recognized as one of the nation's leading upscale department stores. They carry many leading brands and have stores at several malls around Nashville. Other locations include the Mall at Green Hills, 3855 Green Hills Village Dr. (tel. 297-0971); Hickory Hollow Mall, 5248 Hickory Hollow Pkwy. (tel. 731-6600); Rivergate Mall, Two Mile Parkway, Goodlettsville (tel. 859-2811); and Cool Springs Galleria mall, 1796 Galleria Blvd. (tel. 771-7101).

DISCOUNT SHOPPING

GENESCO PARK, 1415 Murfreesboro Rd. Tel. 367-7000.

Located across the road from the airport, this outlet shopping mall offers lots of good shopping for discounted clothes, shoes, and household goods.

OUTLETS LTD. MALL, River Rock Blvd. Tel. 895-4966.

Located about 30 minutes south of Nashville near the city of Murfreesboro, this outlet shopping mall still draws a lot of Nashville shoppers. You'll find several shoe stores, and men's and women's fashion stores. To reach the mall, take I-24 south and get off at Exit 78.

FASHIONS

DANGEROUS THREADS, 105 Second Ave. N. Tel. 256-1033.

As the name implies, these are not your ordinary clothes. Primarily a shop for rock musicians, Dangerous Threads deals mostly in black clothes, with the assorted studs or rhinestones here and there. If you're young and want some cutting-edge, dangerous threads, check it out. A second store is located at 2201 Elliston Place (tel. 320-5890).

WESTERN WEAR

LORETTA LYNN'S WESTERN STORE, 16th Ave. and Demonbreun St. Tel. 256-2814.

If you're looking for plain old, ordinary working-folks western wear, this is the place. Prices are pretty good and so is the selection. There's another Loretta Lynn store at 435 Donelson Pike (tel. 889-5582), near the airport.

MANUEL EXCLUSIVE CLOTHIER, 1922 Broadway. Tel. 321-5444.

This is where the stars get their style. If you're a fan of country music, you've already seen plenty of Manuel's work, though you probably didn't know it at the time. Unless you're an established performer, you probably won't be able to afford anything here, but it's still great fun to have a look at the spendy duds Manuel creates. Everything is impeccably tailored, with the one-of-a-kind pieces often covered with rhinestones.

NOUVEAU WEST, 2817 West End Ave. Tel. 329-1317.

Located in the Park Place Shopping Center, this store sells men's and women's high fashions with a southwestern flare. Hand-tooled leather and beaded fringe are specialties here, and you'll find a wide selection of boots, belts, vests, pants, shirts, blouses, and jackets. This is where to find Ammons custom boots, which are some of the finest available.

RIFLEFIRE!!, 1801 21st Ave. S. Tel. 297-6241.

Though not quite as pricey as Manuel, Riflefire!! is another favorite of country-music stars. The fashions here are tastefully flashy and many have a distinct southwestern flavor. Cottons and suedes in rich colors, ultra-fancy cowboy boots, and painted silk shirts are just some of the specialty items you can find here. There's also plenty of jewelry, including lots of bolo ties, to go with your new Riflefire!! clothes.

SHOES & BOOTS

BOOT COUNTRY, 2412 Music Valley Dr. Tel. 883-2661.

Cowboy boots, more cowboys boots, and still more cowboy boots. That's what you'll find at this boot store. Whether you want a basic pair of work boots or some fancy python-skin show boots, you'll find them here. Boot Country has several other locations around the city: 1183 Gallatin Rd. (tel. 824-5176), two miles north of Rivergate Mall; 5252 Hickory Hollow Pkwy. (tel. 731-7722), in the Hickory Hollow Mall; 798 Old Hickory Blvd. (tel. 377-1326), in Brentwood; and 99 White Bridge Rd. (tel. 356-4707).

BOOT FACTORY, 1415 Murfreesboro Rd. Tel. 367-7660.

If the price of boots in the boot stores has your jaw draggin' the floor, head on over to this boot-factory outlet in the Genesco Park outlet mall. The prices are significantly lower. In addition to a wide selection of slightly imperfect boots, factory overruns, and discontinued boots, there's a full line of western wear.

WOMEN'S

CHICO'S, 4009 Hillsboro Rd. Tel. 292-0902.

This store's fashionable casual clothing, much of it with an ethnic flavor, appeals to younger women and the young at heart. Most of the fashions here are from natural fibers and everything is cut to be comfortable and easy-going.

COCO, 4239 Harding Rd. Tel. 292-0362.

This ladies' boutique sells designer sportswear, dresses, and accessories, and features such lines as Ellen Tracy and Emmanuel. Both the fashions and the clientele tend to be rather upscale.

SCARLET BEGONIA, 2805 West End Ave. Tel. 329-1272.

Ethnic fashions, jewelry, and fine crafts from around the world prove that there is life beyond country Nashville. The emphasis here is on South American clothing and the quality is much higher than you'll find in the average import store.

MEN'S

EVERETT HOLZAPFEL, 4514 Harding Rd. Tel. 383-0365.

If you suddenly realize that you forgot your Brooks Brothers suit and are planning to attend the symphony while in Nashville, all is not lost. Head out to the Belle Meade Plaza shopping center where you'll find this exclusive men's clothing store.

R. JOSEPH MENSWEAR, 2010 Glen Echo Rd. Tel. 298-2100.

At the Glendale in Green Hills shopping plaza you'll find more European and classic American styles for men. The collection of ties here is one of the best in the city.

CHILDREN'S

CHOCOLATE SOUP, 3900 Hillsboro Rd. Tel. 297-1713.

Kids love the name and parents love the clothes. Colorful play clothes, mostly in cotton, are the specialty here. There's also a good selection of toys, stuffed animals, and the like.

HELEN'S CHILDREN'S SHOP, 4102 Hillsboro Rd. Tel. 292-3576.

White christening outfits and classic ball gowns for little girls are the stock in trade at this shop selling Southern gentility for children.

GIFTS/SOUVENIRS

Nashville abounds in souvenir shops purveying every manner of country-themed souvenirs. The greatest concentration of these shops is in the Music Row area, and many of them specialize in particular country-music performers. Many of the gift shops also have backroom museums where you can see personal belongings or memorabilia of a particular star. These museums are often just an excuse to get you into the big souvenir shop out front, but if you're a fan, you'll enjoy touring the exhibits and maybe picking up a souvenir. See "Special-Interest Sightseeing" in Chapter 6, "What to See and Do in Nashville," for further information.

ALABAMA BAND GIFTS & SOUVENIRS, 118 16th Ave. S. Tel. 256-1373.

The band Alabama may no longer be the major act they once were, but you can still catch them on videos played at this gift shop dedicated to souvenirs emblazoned with the Alabama name. You'll find the shop upstairs in the Country Music Wax Museum mall building.

CONWAY TWITTY'S COUNTRY STORE & RECORD SHOP, 1530 Demonbreun St. Tel. 256-8299.

Though Conway died in 1993, his store lives on and still has a great selection of Twitty recordings as well as a large selection of other country music.

GEORGE STRAIT'S TEXAS CONNECTION, 118 16th Ave. S. Tel. 256-2490.

This shop is located in the Country Music Wax Museum building and deals almost exclusively in George Strait souvenirs.

RANDY TRAVIS GIFT SHOP, 1514 Demonbreun St. Tel. 255-1434.

Housed in one of the last old homes along this section of Demonbreun Street, this shop is full of Randy Travis souvenirs and country crafts. There's also a room full of Travis memorabilia, including the converted bread truck Travis used when he first started touring.

JEWELRY

FACTORY JEWELERS, 4805 Old Hickory Blvd. Tel. 391-0920, or toll free 800/248-3064.

Though the name may not inspire great confidence, this is the largest jewelry store in Tennessee. In addition to the immense selection of gold, diamond, gemstone, and pearl jewelry at wholesale prices, the store also houses the Gem and Mineral Museum of Tennessee. You'll find the store not far from the Hermitage on the east side of town.

LINDSEY JEWELERS, 4009 Hillsboro Rd. Tel. 383-6363.
Located in the same shopping plaza that houses Davis-Kidd Booksellers, this jewelry store caters to a much more sophisticated clientele than the above-mentioned store.

MALLS/SHOPPING CENTERS

BELLEVUE CENTER, 7620 U.S. 70S. Tel. 646-8690.
Though this isn't the largest shopping mall in Nashville, for several years it has been considered the best place to shop in Nashville. Department stores include Dillard's and Castner Knott, the city's two most upscale department stores. There are also more than 115 specialty shops. Among the mall's stores are quite a few that are found nowhere else in Nashville. These include Abercrombie & Fitch, Banana Republic, and Godiva Chocolatier.

CHURCH STREET CENTRE, Seventh Ave. and Church St. Tel. 254-4260.
Right in the heart of downtown Nashville, adjacent to the Stouffer Hotel and the Nashville Convention Center, you'll find a modern shopping mall with three floors of specialty shops and a food court. If you're visiting in town and show your hotel room key at the customer-service desk, you can get a booklet with $200 worth of coupons.

COOL SPRINGS GALLERIA, 1800 Galleria Blvd. Tel. 771-2128.
South of Nashville off I-65 is one of the city's newest shopping malls. Here you'll find three major department stores and more than 100 specialty stores. This mall is a 10- or 15-minute drive from downtown Nashville.

HICKORY HOLLOW MALL, 5252 Hickory Hollow Pkwy., Antioch. Tel. 731-4500.
More than 180 specialty shops, a 15-restaurant food court, and four major department stores make this the largest shopping mall in the Nashville area. You'll find the mall south of downtown at Exit 60 off I-24 east.

THE MALL AT GREEN HILLS, Hillsboro Rd. and Abbott Martin Rd. Tel. 298-5478.
Closer to downtown than the Bellevue Center mall, the Mall at Green Hills is almost equally exclusive and is one of Nashville's busiest malls. Among the mall's exclusive shops are Brooks Brothers, Laura Ashley, Lillie Ruben, and the Nature Company. Surrounding the mall are several more small shopping plazas full of interesting shops.

RIVERGATE MALL, 1000 Two Mile Pkwy. Tel. 859-3456.
If you're looking for shopping in northern Nashville, head up I-65N to Exit 95 or 96. The Rivergate Mall includes four department stores and more than 160 boutiques, specialty shops, and restaurants.

MARKETS

NASHVILLE FARMER'S MARKET, 618 Jackson St. Tel. 862-6765.
Just north of the Tennessee State Capitol building in downtown you'll find Nashville's sprawling Farmer's Market. Trucks loaded with fresh produce roll in early every morning and set up their displays, and even if you're not in the market for a case of okra, you'll find that the atmosphere here is colorful. The market opens at 5am and stays open until 9pm daily. On the weekends there's also a flea market here.

NASHVILLE FAIRGROUNDS FLEA MARKET, Tennessee State Fairgrounds, Fourth Ave. Tel. 383-7636.
This huge flea market is held the fourth weekend of every month (except September and December) and attracts more than 1,500 vendors selling everything from cheap jeans to handmade crafts to antiques and collectibles. You'll find the fairgrounds just a few minutes south of downtown.

MUSIC RECORDINGS

THE GREAT ESCAPE, 1925 Broadway. Tel. 327-0646.
This old store adjacent to the Vanderbilt campus caters to the record and comic-book needs of college students and other collectors and bargain-seekers. The used-records section has a distinct country slant, but you can also find other types of music as well. This is a big place and the selection is great. There's another Great Escape at 111 N. Gallatin Rd. (tel. 865-8052), near Opryland.

ERNEST TUBB RECORD SHOPS, 417 Broadway. Tel. 255-7503.
Whether you're looking for a reissue of an early Johnny Cash album or the latest from Garth Brooks, you'll find it at Ernest Tubb. These shops sell exclusively country-music recordings on CD, cassette, and record. You'll find other Ernest Tubb stores at 2414 Music Valley Dr. (tel. 889-2474), and at 1516 Demonbreun St. (tel. 244-2845).

MUSICAL INSTRUMENTS

S. FRIEDMAN LOAN OFFICE, 420 Broadway. Tel. 256-0909.
This lower Broadway pawnshop has been in business since 1897 and is the best place in the city to look for classic used guitars and other music equipment. You might even be able to pick up a guitar that once belonged to a star.

GRUHN GUITARS, INC., 400 Broadway. Tel. 256-2033.

This is Nashville's biggest guitar dealer and stocks classic used and collectible guitars as well as reissues of musicians' favorite instruments. If you're serious about your sound, this is the place to shop. Where else can you find a 1953 Les Paul ($5,350) or a 1938 Martin D-28 ($25,000)?

NASHVILLE NIGHTS

In Nashville, live music is ubiquitous. Not only are there dozens of clubs featuring live country music, as you'd expect, but there is also a very lively rock-music scene. There are also several jazz, blues, and folk clubs, nightclubs featuring dinner shows, songwriters' showcases, and family theaters featuring country music and comedy. And, of course, there's the "Grand Ole Opry," country music's radio grandpa.

There is also music in some unexpected places. You can catch a show before you even make it out of the Nashville International Airport where there are regularly scheduled performances by country bands. If you hop the right trolley (they operate around downtown and from downtown to Music Row), you can catch some live country music while you cross town. Street corners, parking lots, closed-off streets, bars, hotel lounges—there's no telling where you might run into some great live music. The city is overflowing with talented musicians and they play where they can, much to the benefit of visitors to Nashville.

If I've given you the impression that Nashville is a city of live *popular* music only, let me point out that Nashville also has a symphony orchestra, opera company, ballet company, the state's largest professional theater company, and several smaller community theaters.

The **Nashville Scene** is the city's arts-and-entertainment weekly. It comes out on Thursday and is available at restaurants, clubs, convenience stores, and other locations. Just keep your eyes peeled. Every week on Friday, *The Tennessean,* Nashville's morning daily, publishes **"Weekend,"** a guide to the weekend's entertainment scene. The **Music City USA Entertainment Guide** is a weekly calendar of events that's aimed primarily at tourists and can be found at the Nashville Tourist Information Center, hotels, and some shops around downtown Nashville.

If you're here for country music, Music Valley is where you'll want to be. This area on the east side of Nashville is where you'll find Opryland USA (a musical theme park), the Grand Ole Opry House, the Roy Acuff Theater, the Jim Ed Brown Family Theater, the Nashville Palace, and the Ernest Tubb Record Store Midnight Jamboree.

However, it's the downtown area known as the District and the warehouse district a few blocks south that are the heart of the Nashville entertainment scene. Here you'll find the Tennessee Performing Arts Center and the greatest concentration of clubs. Within the District, the most famous entertainment street is Printer's Alley, which has been known as an entertainment center since shortly after the Civil War. Nightclubs in the alley between Church and Union Streets have hosted performances by such celebrities as Chet Atkins and Willie Nelson. Today Printer's Alley has several nightclubs featuring a variety of musical styles.

Tickets to major concerts and sporting events can be purchased through **Ticketmaster** (tel. 737-4849, or toll free 800/333-4849 outside Nashville). Ticketmaster has desks in the following locations: all Castner Knott department stores, Turtle's Records stores, Tower Video, the Tennessee Performing Arts Center box office, and Vanderbilt University's Sarratt Center. Though you can use a credit card when making telephone purchases, most desks accept cash only. A service charge is added to all ticket sales.

1. THE PERFORMING ARTS

THE MAJOR PERFORMING ARTS COMPANIES

OPERA & CLASSICAL MUSIC

NASHVILLE OPERA, Tennessee Performing Arts Center, 505 Deaderick St. Tel. 292-5710.
Though this small regional opera company currently does only two shows each season, it does a very respectable job. Some operas are performed in the original language and some are performed in English. Recent seasons have included *Tosca* and *Madama Butterfly*.
Admission: Tickets, $10–$37.50.

NASHVILLE SYMPHONY ORCHESTRA, Tennessee Performing Arts Center, 505 Deaderick St. Tel. 329-3033.
Though this orchestra has gone through financial difficulties in recent years, it has managed to hang on and is still providing Nashville with the city's most rewarding orchestral performances. Each season sees a mix of contemporary American orchestral music, classical pieces, and a pops series. There's also a children's series each year.
Admission: Tickets, $7–$50.

DANCE COMPANIES

NASHVILLE BALLET, Tennessee Performing Arts Center, 505 Deaderick St. Tel. 244-7233 for information.
With musical accompaniment by the Nashville Symphony Orchestra, this ballet company stages energetic and imaginative presentations of classical and contemporary works. The 1993–94 season

---

THE MAJOR CONCERT & PERFORMANCE HALLS

Chevrolet/GEO Celebrity Theater, in Opryland, 2802 Opryland Dr. (tel. 889-6611).

Grand Ole Opry House, 2804 Opryland Dr. (tel. 889-3060).

Nashville Municipal Auditorium, 417 Fourth Ave. N. (tel. 862-6390).

Starwood Amphitheater, 3839 Murfreesboro Pike (tel. 641-5800).

Tennessee Performing Arts Center (TPAC), 505 Deaderick St. (tel. 741-7975).

---

included performances of *Giselle* and *The Nutcracker,* plus two productions that each included four shorter pieces.
   Admission: Tickets, $10–$23.

THEATER COMPANIES

ACTORS' PLAYHOUSE OF NASHVILLE, 2318 West End Ave. Tel. 327-0049.

This tiny 68-seat theater located above Papa John's Pizza offers some of Nashville's more thought-provoking performances. The theater was renovated in 1993 and is now looking better than ever. A recent schedule included Samuel Becket's *Waiting for Godot* and David Mamet's *Oleanna,* as well as *Cyrano de Bergerac* and *Vincent.* There are also regular late-night performances.
   Admission: Tickets, $4–$10.

AVANT GARAGE COMEDY REPERTORY THEATRE, Church Street Center Mall, Seventh Ave. and Church St. Tel. 256-3560.

The name says it all, doesn't it? No morbid dramas here, just outrageous comedy in an avant-garde vein. Leave the Neil Simon to TPAC—this stuff is out there.
   Admission: Tickets, $12 adults, $8 students, $6 children under 7.

CIRCLE PLAYERS, Tennessee Performing Arts Center, 505 Deaderick St. Tel. 383-7469.

With more than 45 years of performances behind it already, Circle Players is Nashville's top community theater company and does six productions per season. The 1993–94 season included such standards as *Sweet Charity* and *Noises Off,* but also the gospel-music show *Black Nativity* and *The Piano Lesson,* a Pulitzer Prize-winning drama.
   Admission: Tickets, $10.

TENNESSEE REPERTORY THEATER, Tennessee Performing Arts Center, 505 Deaderick St. Tel. 244-4878.

This is Tennessee's largest professional theater company and stages five crowd-pleasing productions each season. The season runs from September through May and includes dramas, musicals, and comedies. A mix of old favorites and newer works makes for a varied program.
Admission: Tickets, $12–$26.

PERFORMING ARTS SERIES

FRIENDS OF MUSIC, Tennessee Performing Arts Center, 505 Deaderick St. Tel. 254-0469.

This series brings a diverse array of music to Nashville each year. The season, which runs from October to March, usually includes four productions. The 1993–94 season included the Mozart Orchestra of Hamburg, the Paragon Ragtime Orchestra, a Slavic music-and-dance ensemble, and a performance of *A Midsummer Night's Dream* by the London Ballet Theatre.
Admission: Tickets, $16–$25.

GREAT PERFORMANCES AT VANDERBILT, Vanderbilt University, Langford Auditorium, 21st Ave. S. Tel. 322-2471.

Each year Vanderbilt University schedules more than a dozen internationally acclaimed performing-arts companies from around the world. The emphasis is on chamber music and modern dance, but touring theater productions and classical ballet companies are also scheduled. Performances are held at Langford Auditorium, which is behind the Vanderbilt Hospital. The 1993–94 season included shows by the Lar Lubovitch Dance Company, Martha Graham Dance Company, the Vivaldi Orchestra of Moscow, and Cloris Leachman performing *Grandma Moses: An America Primitive.*
Admission: Tickets, $12–$18.

TPAC BROADWAY SERIES, Tennessee Performing Arts Center, 505 Deaderick St. Tel. 741-7975.

The best of Broadway, past and present, takes the stage at the Tennessee Performing Arts Center. During a season that runs from November through July there are six scheduled productions. The 1993–94 season included both *Les Misérables* and *Phantom of the Opera.*
Admission: Tickets, $21–$42.

MAJOR CONCERT HALLS & ALL-PURPOSE AUDITORIUMS

NASHVILLE MUNICIPAL AUDITORIUM, 417 Fourth Ave. N. Tel. 862-6390.

Though the acoustics are some of the worst in the city, this big hall gets a lot of business, especially from rock concerts. This is also the home of the Nashville Knights hockey team.
Admission: Tickets, $7–$25.

STARWOOD AMPHITHEATRE, 3839 Murfreesboro Pike. Tel. 641-5800.

✪ In the summer, this is *the* place in Nashville for concerts by big-name performers. Pop, country, jazz, rock, ethnic, and classical music all benefit from being performed under the stars. There is reserved seating as well as space on grassy slopes where you can spread out a blanket and have a picnic.

Admission: Tickets, $15–$30.

TENNESSEE PERFORMING ARTS CENTER (TPAC), 505 Deaderick St. Tel. 741-7975.

✪ This state-of-the-art performance center includes three theaters—the Andrew Johnson, the Andrew Jackson, and the James K. Polk. Together these three spaces are able to accommodate large and small productions. Performance companies that appear here include the Nashville Ballet, Nashville Symphony, Nashville Opera, Tennessee Repertory Theatre, Circle Players, and Friends of Music. The TPAC, as it's known by locals, is located almost directly across the street from the Tennessee State Capitol in downtown Nashville. The box office is open Monday through Friday from 10am to 5pm and on Saturday from noon to 4pm, and a half hour prior to shows.

Admission: Ticket prices vary with the series (see the listings above).

THEATERS & FAMILY ENTERTAINMENT

CHEVROLET/GEO CELEBRITY THEATER AT OPRYLAND, 2802 Opryland Dr. Tel. 889-6611.

This theater is inside the Opryland USA theme park and to attend most concerts you'll have to first pay admission to the park. However, there are occasionally concerts that do not require park admission. Country music is the specialty of this theater and there are concerts almost every night from April through October. The 1993 schedule included performances by such stars as Tammy Wynette, Tanya Tucker, Emmylou Harris, Crystal Gayle, Sammy Kershaw, Eddie Rabbitt, and Ricky Skaggs. Shows are at 5 and 7:30pm.

Admission: Tickets, $5.50 with paid park admission, $12 without paid park admission.

GENERAL JACKSON SHOWBOAT, 2802 Opryland Dr. Tel. 889-6611.

✪ If you'd like to combine some evening entertainment with a cruise on the Cumberland River, the *General Jackson* is the boat not to miss. This reproduction paddlewheeler is huge and brings back the glory days of river travel. The dinner-cruise show is a Broadway-style musical revue, while the "Southern Nights" cruise includes dancing under the stars to live country and Top-40 music. During the day, there are also cruises that include live country music and comedy shows.

Admission: Tickets, $36.95 for the dinner cruise, $14.95 for the "Southern Nights" cruise.

GRAND OLE OPRY HOUSE, 2804 Opryland Dr. Tel. 889-3060.

★ The "Grand Ole Opry" is the country's longest continuously running radio show and airs every weekend from this theater at the Opryland USA theme park. Over the years the "Grand Ole Opry" has had several homes, and though the Ryman Auditorium in downtown Nashville is the Opry's most famous venue, this theater is more modern and comfortable. The "Grand Ole Opry" show is a mix of country music and humor that has proved its popularity for nearly 70 years. Over the decades, the "Opry" has featured nearly all the greats of country music, and in fact many of them got their start on the Opry's stage. There's no telling who you might see at any given performances of the "Grand Ole Opry," but the show's membership roster includes Bill Monroe, Travis Tritt, Garth Brooks, Lorrie Morgan, Porter Wagoner, Ricky Skaggs, and many others. Nearly all "Grand Ole Opry" performances sell out, and though it's often possible to get last-minute tickets, you should try to order tickets as far in advance as possible.

Shows are given as follows: in April, on Friday at 7:30pm, on Saturday at 6:30 and 9:30pm, and a Sunday matinee at 3pm; in May, September, and October, on Friday and Saturday at 6:30 and 9:30pm, and a Sunday matinee at 3pm; June to August, matinees on Tuesday and Thursday at 3pm, on Friday and Saturday at 6:30 and 9:30pm, and a Sunday matinee at 3pm; and November to March, on Friday at 7:30pm and on Saturday at 6:30 and 9:30pm.

Admission: Tickets, $11–$15.

JIM ED BROWN FAMILY THEATER, 2620 Music Valley Dr. Tel. 885-5701.

Country music and comedy are a combination patented by the "Grand Ole Opry" and adhered to by this theater, which is named for a former Opry regular. Shows are held Tuesday through Sunday from 7 to 10pm.

Admission: $10 adults, $5 children.

MUSIC VILLAGE USA, 44 Music Village Blvd., Hendersonville. Tel. 822-0600.

This theater across the street from Twitty City in Hendersonville is home to the LeGarde Twins, who give several performances daily of their blend of country, gospel, bluegrass, and comedy. Matinees last 30 minutes while evening performances are 90 minutes. Shows are Monday through Saturday at 11am, 3:30pm, and 7pm (evening show by reservation only).

Admission: $5.

DINNER THEATER

CHAFFIN'S BARN DINNER THEATRE, 8204 Tenn. 100. Tel. 646-9977.

This big old Dutch colonial barn is a bit of a drive out of the city, but that never stops Nashvillians, who enjoy the chance to spend an evening enjoying theater in the country. The theater offers 10 different shows a year, each of which plays for about a month. The dinner is an all-you-can-eat country buffet and plays are generally classic musicals and contemporary comedies. Dinner-performances are Tuesday through Sunday, and reservations are required.

To reach Chaffin's Barn, either head out West End Avenue and keep driving, or take I-40 west to Exit 199 (Old Hickory Boulevard) and head south to Old Harding Road.

Admission: Tickets, Dinner and show, $28–$30 adults, $15 children under 13; show only, $20.

TELEVISION SHOWS

THE NASHVILLE NETWORK, 2806 Opryland Dr. Tel. 883-7000.

This cable-television network is dedicated to country music and reaches more than 57 million homes. The network's most popular show is "Nashville Now," a live 90-minute program that includes performances of country music and interviews with country stars. Reservations are necessary to attend a broadcast of "Nashville Now"; call 889-6611. Other shows with live audiences that you can join include "Crook and Chase," "The Statler Brothers' Show," and "American Music Shop."

Admission: Tickets, $5 for "Nashville Now," free for other shows.

2. THE CLUB & MUSIC SCENE

FOR MUSIC

COUNTRY

BLUEBIRD CAFE, 4104 Hillsboro Rd. Tel. 383-1461.

Over the past few years, this little club has developed a national reputation for showcasing up-and-coming country songwriters. Surprisingly, you'll find the Bluebird not in the District or on Music Row but in a suburban shopping plaza across the road from the Mall at Green Hills. There are usually two shows a night. At 7pm they have music in the round, during which four singer-songwriters play some of their latest works. After 9pm there's a cover charge and more established acts take the stage. This is *the* place in Nashville to catch the music of people you'll be hearing from in coming years.

Admission: $5–$6.

ERNEST TUBB RECORD SHOP MIDNIGHT JAMBOREE, 2414 Music Valley Dr. Tel. 889-2474.

The Ernest Tubb Record Shop on Broadway was for many years the site of a late-night radio show that featured performances by musicians who had just finished playing across the street at the "Grand Ole Opry" (Ryman Auditorium). When the "Opry" moved out to Opryland on Music Valley Drive, the midnight jamboree moved too. Now you can catch the show, which features "Opry" acts

and country-music newcomers, at this newer Ernest Tubb store. Arrive by 11:30pm on Saturday night if you want to get a seat.
Admission: Free.

NASHVILLE PALACE, 2400 Music Valley Dr. Tel. 885-1540.

If you're in town to do the country thang and you just spent the day at Opryland, caught the "Grand Ole Opry," and are wondering what to do next, this is it! The Nashville Palace is open nightly with live country-and-western music, a dance floor, and a full restaurant. This is where Randy Travis got his start.
Admission: $5.

TOOTSIE'S ORCHID LOUNGE, 422 Broadway. Tel. 726-3739.

This country bar has certainly seen better days, but it has been a Nashville tradition since the days when the "Grand Ole Opry" was still performing in the Ryman Auditorium just around the corner. In those days "Opry" stars used to duck into Tootsie's for a drink. Today you can see signed photos of the many stars who have downed a drink or two at Tootsie's. There's free live country music here almost any time of day or night.
Admission: Free.

SONGWRITERS' VENUES

The most famous of Nashville's songwriter's clubs is the Bluebird Café, listed above. In addition, many hotels have songwriter's nights in their lounges. Be sure to check at your hotel. The following are some of the places around Nashville that showcase songwriters one or more nights a week.

BELL COVE CLUB, 151 Sunset Dr., Hendersonville. Tel. 822-7074.

Located out in Hendersonville, this club has songwriters' show-cases on Thursday and Sunday nights. Tuesday is cowboy/cowgirl poetry night. An added bonus here is the view across Old Hickory Lake, especially at sunset.
Admission: Free–$7.

DOUGLAS CORNER, 2106A Eighth Ave. S. Tel. 298-1688.

This is one of the top venues for songwriters trying to get a break in Nashville, and it occasionally has shows by those who are established as well. The club is located a few minutes south of downtown.
Admission: $2–$10.

JACK'S GUITAR BAR, 2185 Nolensville Rd. Tel. 726-3855.

This country-music bar has a songwriters' night on Tuesday and an afternoon showcase on Sunday. Wednesday, Friday, and Saturday nights there's also live music.

Admission: Free Tues, Thurs, and Sun; $2 Wed and Fri–Sat.

SILVER DOLLAR SALOON, 100 Second Ave. N. Tel. 256-9962.

Located in the heart of the District, the Silver Dollar features a small listening room hosting established and up-and-coming songwriters. Despite the name, kids are welcome here. There's also a blues jam on Friday and Saturday nights.

Admission: Free.

FOLK & BLUEGRASS

BLUE SKY COURT, 412 Fourth Ave. S. Tel. 256-4562.

The '60s meet the '90s at the Blue Sky Court. During the day, folks hang out over espresso catching up on their Sartre or playing board games. But at night, live entertainment takes the stage. There's acoustic folk music most nights, with a couple of comedy nights thrown in each week for good measure.

Admission: $3.

MULLIGAN'S PUB, 117 Second Ave. N. Tel. 242-8010.

This is Nashville's only true Irish pub and features live acoustic folk music on the weekends. The pub atmosphere may seem a bit out of place in Nashville, but then you'll find country-music pubs in Dublin. There's good Irish food and cold pints.

Admission: Free.

STATION INN, 402 12th Ave. S. Tel. 255-3307.

If your country-music tastes run to bluegrass straight from the hills, try this club down in the warehouse district south of Broadway in downtown. The big stone building is pretty nondescript, but keep looking and you'll find it.

Admission: Free Sun–Thurs, $5 Fri–Sat.

ROCK

ACE OF CLUBS, 114 Second Ave. S. Tel. 254-ACES.

If you love to dance, deal yourself an Ace of Clubs. It's big, it's loud, and there's always a full house. Other nights of the week there's live rock with local performers and lesser-known national acts such as NRBQ and Maria McKee. Best of all, you don't have to be feeling flush to enjoy an evening here. Admission charges are surprisingly low. You'll find the Ace of Clubs in the District. Year after year, Nashvillians name the Ace of Clubs the city's best place to dance.

Admission: $2–$12.

12TH & PORTER, 114 12th Ave. N. Tel. 254-7236.

Located just off Broadway behind the offices of *The Tennessean*, Nashville's daily newspaper, 12th & Porter is impossible to miss. It's that turquoise-and-black building with the retro look. This place has a hip, urban feel and books alternative rock bands. The clientele here is primarily gay.

Admission: $5–$10.

328 PERFORMANCE HALL, 328 Fourth Ave. S. Tel. 259-3288.

Housed in an old warehouse a few blocks south of Broadway, the 328 Performance Hall is one of Nashville's most popular spots for live rock. It's a great space and manages to book acts such as Los Lobos, as well as the best of the regional rock scene.
Admission: $6–$12.

JAZZ & BLUES

THE MERCHANTS, 401 Broadway. Tel. 254-1892.

The Merchants is best known around Nashville as *the* downtown power-lunch spot, but it's also the best place in town to hear live jazz. The atmosphere is a mix of Southern elegance and contemporary Mediterranean sophistication. There's live music on Wednesday and Thursday from 6:30 to 10:30pm, on Friday from 7:30 to 11pm, and on Saturday from 8:30pm to 12:30am.
Admission: Free.

MERE BULLES, 152 Second Ave. N. Tel. 256-1946.

Under the same management as the Merchants, Mère Bulles also features the best in live jazz amid a contemporary urban atmosphere. Don't confuse this with Club Mère Bulles, which is the rock club in the basement of this restaurant. There's live jazz Thursday through Sunday nights, with piano music for the dinner hours.
Admission: Free.

3RD & LINDSLEY BAR & GRILL, 818 Third Ave. S. Tel. 259-9891.

Eight blocks south of Broadway, in a new office complex surrounded by old warehouses, you'll find Nashville's premier blues club. The atmosphere may lack the sleaze and smoke that you'd expect of a real blues club, but the music is true to the blues.
Admission: Free Sun–Thurs, $4–$6 Fri–Sat.

NIGHTCLUBS/CABARETS

BOOTS RANDOLPH'S, 209 Printer's Alley. Tel. 256-5500.

Printer's Alley is the heart of downtown Nashville's entertainment district, and Boots Randolph's place is the most popular nightclub in the alley. Randolph, best known for his album *Yakkety Sax,* plays regularly at 9pm. You can come early and have dinner here, or just attend the show.
Admission: $9.

THE CAPTAIN'S TABLE, 313½ Church St. Tel. 251-9535.

The Captain's Table has been in business since 1968 and offers three dinner shows nightly plus a late-night show. The house band plays the latest country hits, as well as old favorites. Over the years, the stage at the Captain's Table has hosted such well-known performers as Brenda Lee, Hank Williams, and Willie Nelson. Out front is a sign that lists all the many celebrities who have performed or eaten here.

Admission: $5 entertainment charge, plus dinners in the $12–$18 range.

COMEDY CLUBS

ZANIES COMEDY SHOWCASE, 2025 Eighth Ave. S. Tel. 269-0221.

This is Nashville's only exclusively comedy club and has shows on Friday and Saturday nights at 8:30 and 10:30pm, and on Sunday at 8:30pm only.

Admission: $6–$8.25.

DANCE CLUBS/DISCOS

COUNTRY

RODEOS DANCE CLUB, 1031 Murfreesboro Pike. Tel. 399-2666.

The DJs at Rodeos play the hottest new country tunes while all the urban cowkids kick up their heals on the biggest dance floor in town. You'll find this place not far from Wrangler's.

Admission: $3 Thurs–Sat after 8pm.

SOUTHFORK SALOON, 2265 Murfreesboro Pike. Tel. 361-9777.

Here's another club claiming to have the biggest dance floor in Nashville, and it's also located on Murfreesboro Pike. If you haven't tried country dancing yet, you can take free lessons here Sunday through Thursday from 7 to 9pm.

Admission: Free Sun–Thurs, $3 Fri–Sat.

WRANGLER'S, 1204 Murfreesboro Pike. Tel. 361-4440.

This is the most popular country dance club in Nashville and has been around for more than a decade. If you've never tried two-steppin', you can get free dance lessons several nights a week and then join the action on the gigantic dance floor. Murfreesboro Pike is an extension of Lafayette Street, which begins at Eighth Avenue just south of Broadway.

Admission: Free Sun–Wed, $2 Thurs–Sat.

ROCK

CLUB MERE BULLES, 150 First Ave. N. Tel. 256-CLUB.

The name means "Mother Bubbles," and a bubbly atmosphere definitely prevails at this cavernous club. Located in the District, Club Mère Bulles is downstairs from the restaurant of the same name.

Crowds are a lively mix of locals and tourists and the music is primarily Top 40, with a mix of recorded and live music.

Admission: $3 Tues–Wed and Sun, $5 Thurs–Sat. Free admission with dinner at either Mère Bulles or the Merchants.

GAY CLUBS

THE CHUTE, 2535 Franklin Rd. Tel. 297-4571.

It may have taken k.d. lang to let Nashville know that gays like, and make, country music too, but at the Chute, everybody already knew it well. This is where to head when you want to do a bit of western dancing to the latest country hits. They even give dance lessons.

Admission: $3 Fri–Sun.

CONNEXTION, Fifth Ave. S. and Demonbreun St. Tel. 742-1166.

This club has brought a touch of New York sophistication to the Nashville club scene. Located in a big old warehouse of a building just south of Broadway, Connextion attracts primarily a well-dressed, well-paid crowd. There are late-night shows on the weekends, and the club's restaurant is open until after midnight.

Admission: $3 Wed–Thurs and Sun, $5 Fri–Sat.

3. THE BAR SCENE

The Nashville bar scene is for the most part synonymous with the Nashville restaurant scene. Because an establishment has to serve food in order to serve liquor, if you want a cocktail, step into almost any moderately priced or expensive restaurant. The first thing you're likely to see is a bar.

RESTAURANT BARS

FAISON'S, 2000 Belcourt Ave. Tel. 298-2112.

On a summer evening, there's no better place for a cold drink than Faison's patio bar. It's shaded by a big old tree, and a few feet away there's a fountain bubbling away—quintessential plantation atmospherics. Was that Tennessee Williams I just saw?

JAMAICA, 1901 Broadway. Tel. 321-5191.

With its tropical decor and huge saltwater aquariums, this is one of the most colorful bars in Nashville. It attracts students from Vanderbilt University as well as music-industry types from Music Row.

JIMMY KELLY'S, 217 Louise Ave. Tel. 329-4349.

The bar isn't very large, but you can feel as though you're part of a

Nashville tradition when you have a drink here. The place is always lively, and the clientele tends to be older and well-to-do.

THE OLD SPAGHETTI FACTORY, 160 Second Ave. N. Tel. 254-9010.

⭐ Sure it's touristy, but if you think Victoriana is the height of romance, you won't want to miss out on bringing a date here. It's hard to believe that this elegant room was once a warehouse.

SUNSET GRILL, 2000A Belcourt Ave. Tel. 386-3663.

If you're lucky this place may still be the trendiest bar in town when you make the Nashville scene. Great drinks, lively atmosphere, and lots of beautiful people.

PIANO BARS

106 CLUB, 106 Harding Place. Tel. 356-1300.

⭐ I can think of no more romantic place to start or end a night on the town in Nashville than in the lounge of this Belle Meade restaurant. Subtle lighting, original paintings on the wall, quiet conversations, and superb jazz played on the baby grand. The music starts at 7:30pm and goes on until midnight.

WILD BOAR, 2014 Broadway. Tel. 329-1313.

The Wild Boar is Nashville's most expensive and exclusive restaurant, but it also has a great piano bar where you *won't* have to spend $80 to enjoy the atmosphere. It's always a good idea to dress as if you were coming to dinner here.

SPORTS BARS

BOX SEAT, 2221 Bandywood Dr. Tel. 383-8018.

Located next to the Mall at Green Hills, the Box Seat is a favorite of local college athletes and is a great place to catch a Vanderbilt football game on the tube.

SPORTSMAN'S GRILL, 5405 Harding Rd. Tel. 356-6206.

With a bit more style than your average sports bar, the Sportsman's Grill comes closer to a "Cheers" sort of atmosphere. There's lots of dark wood and brass, and the beers and burgers keep the crowds content. A second Sportsman's is located at 1601 21st Ave. (tel. 320-1633).

GAY & LESBIAN BARS

Two popular gay men's clubs—Connextion and 12th & Porter—are mentioned above in "The Club and Music Scene."

CHEZ COLETTE, 300 Hermitage Ave. Tel. 256-9134.

Lesbians looking for a place to have a drink and meet like-minded Nashvillians should head south a few blocks from Broadway to the city's most popular women's bar. Hermitage Avenue is an extension of First Avenue South. Straight women are also welcome here.

RALPH'S RUTLEDGE HILL TAVERN, 515 Second Ave. S. Tel. 256-9682.

This friendly lesbian tavern is in the heart of Nashville's main nightclub district and is only a short distance from Chez Colette. Once again, straight women are also welcome.

4. MORE ENTERTAINMENT

The best theater in town is the **Fountain Square 14,** 2298 MetroCenter Blvd. (tel. 254-3144), a few miles north of downtown. For foreign and art films, give a call to Vanderbilt University's **Sarratt Cinema** (tel. 322-2425).

CHAPTER 9

EASY EXCURSIONS FROM NASHVILLE

1. FRANKLIN & SCENIC U.S. 31

2. DISTILLERIES, WALKING HORSES & A CIVIL WAR BATTLEFIELD

3. LORETTA LYNN'S RANCH

After you've had your fill of Nashville's country-music scene, it may be time for a change of scenery and a taste of the real country. Head in any direction from Nashville and you hit the Tennessee hills. These are the hills that are famous for their walking horses and sour-mash whiskey. They also hold some historic old towns and Civil War battlefields that are well worth visiting.

---

1. FRANKLIN & SCENIC U.S. 31

South of Nashville, U.S. 31 leads through the rolling Tennessee hills to the historic towns of Franklin and Columbia. This was the heart of the middle Tennessee plantation country and there are still many antebellum mansions along this route. If you contact the **Williamson County Tourism Office,** City Hall (P.O. Box 156), Franklin, TN 37065-0156 (tel. 615/794-1225), before heading out this way, they'll send you a guide to U.S. 31 and its many mansions. However, none of these historic homes is open to the public and you may want to take U.S. 31 anyway and read later about the homes you saw along the way. You'll pass by more than a dozen old plantation homes before you get to Franklin.

The start of the scenic section of U.S. 31 is in Brentwood at Exit 74 off I-65. Alternatively, you can take I-65 straight to Franklin (Exit 65) and then take U.S. 31 back north to Nashville.

WHAT TO SEE & DO

FRANKLIN

Once in Franklin, which is 20 miles south of downtown Nashville, stop in at the tiny **Heritage Foundation Visitor Information Center,** on East Main Street (tel. 790-0378), open Monday through Friday from 9am to 5pm. Here, in a former doctor's office that was built in 1839, you can pick up the guide to antebellum mansions along U.S. 31. You can also pick up a self-guided walking-tour map of the town. Franklin's entire 15-block downtown and quite a few other buildings around town have been listed on the National Register of Historic Places.

Franklin is best known in Tennessee as the site of the bloody Battle of Franklin during the Civil War. During this battle, which took place on November 30, 1864, more than 6,000 Confederate and 2,000 Union soldiers were killed. Today Franklin calls itself both the prettiest historic town in the South and the new antiques capital of Tennessee. Both of these statements come pretty close to the mark. Nearly the entire town, both commercial buildings around the central square and residential buildings in surrounding blocks, has been restored, giving the town a charming 19th-century air. The best thing to do in Franklin is just stroll around admiring the restored buildings and browse through the many antiques stores and malls. Many of the town's antiques malls are located not in the historic downtown, but in the several new shopping plazas at the I-65 interchange. You can pick up a map of local antiques stores at the tourist information center.

CARNTON PLANTATION, 1345 Carnton Lane. Tel. 794-0903.

Built in 1826 by Randal McGavock, a former mayor of Nashville, Carnton Plantation is a beautiful neoclassical antebellum mansion. During the Battle of Franklin, one of the bloodiest battles of the Civil War, this plantation home served as a Confederate hospital. When the fighting was over on November 30, 1864, thousands of soldiers lay dead or dying. Two years later the McGavock family donated two acres of land to be used as a cemetery for Confederate soldiers who had died during the Battle of Franklin. There are more than 1,500 graves in the McGavock Confederate Cemetery, which makes this the largest private Confederate cemetery in the country.

The stately old home, with its seven square columns and porches that stretch the length of both floors in the front of the house is in the slow process of being restored and houses many original pieces of furniture and other antiques.

Admission: $3 adults, $2.50 senior citizens, $1.50 children 3–12.

Open: Apr–Oct, Mon–Sat 9am–5pm, Sun 1–5pm; Nov–Mar, Mon–Sat 9am–4pm, Sun 1–4pm.

CARTER HOUSE, 1140 Columbia Ave. Tel. 791-1861.

The Carter House was built in 1830, only four years after Carnton Plantation was constructed, and during the Battle of Franklin it served as the Union army command post. All the while the Carter family hid in the cellar of the house. In addition to getting a tour of the restored home, you can spend some time in the museum, which contains many Civil War artifacts. A video presentation about the battle that took place here in Franklin will provide you with a perspective for touring around the town.

Admission: $4 adults, $1.50 children.

Open: Apr–Oct, Mon–Fri 9am–5pm, Sun 1–5pm; Nov–Mar, Mon–Fri 9am–4pm, Sun 1–4pm.

COLUMBIA

Continuing south from Franklin on U.S. 31 will bring you to the town of Columbia in about 26 miles. Along the way, you'll see a dozen or so historic antebellum homes and in Columbia itself, there are more old homes and three districts listed on the National Register of Historic Places. However, the most important building in Columbia is the James K. Polk home.

From Columbia, you can head back north on U.S. 31, take U.S. 412/Tenn. 99 east to I-65, or head west on Tenn. 50 to the Natchez Trace Parkway. This latter road is a scenic highway administered by the National Park Service. If you still have time enough, you may want to continue south for a while on the Natchez Trace Parkway before turning around and heading back to Nashville.

JAMES K. POLK HOUSE, 301 W. Seventh St., Columbia. Tel. 388-2354.

This modest home was where James K. Polk, the 11th president of the United States, grew up and where he was living when he began his legal and political career. Though Polk may not be as familiar a name as those of some other early presidents, Polk did achieve two very important goals while in office. He negotiated the purchase of California and settled the long-standing dispute between the United States and England over where to draw the border of the Oregon Territory. The house is filled with antiques that belonged both to Polk's parents when they lived here and to Polk and his family during their time in the White House. In a separate building, there is an exhibit of political and Mexican War memorabilia.

Admission: $2.50 adults, $2 senior citizens, $1 students.

Open: Apr–Oct, Mon–Sat 9am–5pm, Sun 1–5pm; Nov–Mar, Mon–Sat 9am–4pm, Sun 1–5pm.

WHERE TO DINE

CHOICES & BENNETT'S CORNER, 108 Fourth Ave. S. Tel. 791-0001.

Cuisine: AMERICAN/INTERNATIONAL. **Reservations:** Accepted only for parties of five or more.

$ Prices: All dishes $5–$7.50. AE, CB, DC, DISC, MC, V.

Open: Lunch Mon–Sat 11am–2pm; dinner Mon–Thurs 5:30–9pm, Fri–Sat 5:30–10pm.

This big restaurant is my favorite Franklin lunch spot. Its a sprawling place with several dining rooms, all of which are decorated just the way you would expect them to be in a town full of antique malls and craft shops. There are antique farm implements hanging on the walls, and lots of dried flower arrangements. You can get good southern pork barbecue but for the most part, the menu features such contemporary dishes as Cajun salad, grilled chicken in a pesto Alfredo sauce, and vegetarian burritos. Up on the second floor you'll find the lounge known as Bennett's Corner. Here you can get a cocktail and listen to live music on weekend evenings. As part of the decor here on the second floor, there is a re-creation of an old interurban trolley. Within the same building and directly opposite the restaurant's hostess station is the Merridee's Breadbasket bakery and restaurant, where you can get great pastries, breads, soups, and sandwiches.

2. DISTILLERIES, WALKING HORSES & A CIVIL WAR BATTLEFIELD

Though Tennessee was the last state to secede from the Union, the Civil War came early to the state, and three years of being on the front lines left the state with a legacy written in blood. More Civil War battles were fought in Tennessee than in any other state except Virginia, and the bloodiest of these was the Battle of Stones River, which took place 30 miles south of Nashville near the city of Murfreesboro. Today this battle is commemorated at the **Stones River National Battlefield.**

In the two decades that followed the war Tennessee quickly recovered and developed two of the state's most famous commodities—Tennessee sippin' whiskey and Tennessee walking horses. Another 45 miles or so south of Murfreesboro, you can learn about both of these time-honored Tennessee traditions.

For those of you who are not connoisseuers of **sour-mash whiskeys,** Tennessee whiskey is *not* bourbon. This latter whiskey, which is named for Bourbon County, Kentucky, where it was first distilled, is made much the same way but is not charcoal-mellowed the way fine Tennessee sour-mash whiskey is. The famous **Tennessee walkers** are horses that are trained to walk with a distinctive high-stepping gait. Tennessee walkers make excellent show horses and can be seen going through their paces at various annual shows in the Nashville area.

Start this driving tour by heading south from Nashville on I-24.

WHAT TO SEE & DO

STONES RIVER NATIONAL BATTLEFIELD, U.S. 41/70S. Tel. 893-9501.

On New Year's Eve 1862, what would become the bloodiest Civil War battle west of the Appalachian Mountains began just north of Murfreesboro along the Stones River. Though by the end of the first day of fighting the Confederates thought they were assured a victory, Union reinforcements turned the tide against the rebels. By January 3, the Confederates were in retreat and 23,000 soldiers lay dead or dying on the battlefield. Today 351 acres of the battlefield are preserved. The site includes a national cemetery and the Hazen Brigade Monument, which was erected in 1863 and is the oldest Civil War memorial in the United States. In the visitor center, you'll find a museum full of artifacts and details of the battle.
Admission: Free.
Open: Daily 8am–5pm.

GEORGE DICKEL DISTILLERY, Cascade Rd., Tullahoma. Tel. 857-9313.

To reach this distillery, take Exit 105 off I-24 and follow the signs for about 10 miles. The George Dickel Distillery has seen its share of ups and downs over the years. Though George Dickel was ready to set up his still in 1860, the Civil War interrupted his plans, and he didn't get around to distilling his first bottle of whiskey until the 1870s. When Prohibition rolled around, he got shut down, and because Prohibition stayed in effect until 1958 in this neck of the woods, it was a long time before the George Dickel Distillery began fermenting sour mash again. You can tour the distillery and learn about its history, see how the whiskey is made, and then stop in at Miss Annie's General Store to shop for souvenirs, gifts, and antiques. However, don't bother looking for the bottles of George Dickel's finest—you can't buy it here. Though the distillery is perfectly legal, Coffee County is a "dry" county, which means that you can't buy alcoholic beverages anywhere in the county. It's probably all for the better this way since you've still got a bit of driving to do.

Admission: Free.
Open: Mon–Fri 9am–3pm.

JACK DANIEL'S DISTILLERY, Tenn. 55, Lynchburg. Tel. 759-4221.

To reach this most famous of American distilleries, take Tenn. 55 southwest for 10 miles to the town of Lynchburg. Old Jack Daniel (or Mr. Jack, as he was known hereabouts) didn't waste any time setting up his whiskey distillery after the Civil War came to an end. Founded in 1866, this is the oldest registered distillery in the United States and is on the National Register of Historic Places. This is still an active distillery and you can tour the facility and see how Jack Daniel's whiskey is made and learn how it gets such a distinctive flavor. There are two secrets to the manufacture of Mr. Jack's famous sour-mash whiskey. The first of these is the water that comes gushing—pure, cold, and iron free—from Cave Spring. The other is the sugar maple that's used to make the charcoal. In fact it is this charcoal, through which the whiskey slowly drips, that gives Jack Daniel's its renowned smoothness.

After touring the distillery, you can glance in at the office used by Mr. Jack and see the safe that did him in. Old Mr. Jack kicked that safe one day in a fit of anger and wound up getting gangrene for his troubles. We can only hope that regular doses of Tennessee sippin' whiskey helped ease the pain of his last days. You, however, will taste nary a dram of Mr. Jack's water of life. Moore County, like Coffee County, is dry. Oh, the injustice of it all!

Admission: Free.
Open: Daily 8am–4pm.

TENNESSEE WALKING HORSE MUSEUM, Calhoun and Evans Sts., Shelbyville. Tel. 684-5915.

From Lynchburg, head 3 miles northeast on Tenn. 55 and then turn north onto Tenn. 82 for 13 miles. The Tennessee walking horse, named for its unusual walking gait, is considered the world's premier breed of show horse, and it is here in the rolling hills of middle Tennessee that most of these horses are bred. Through the use of interactive videos, hands-on exhibits, and other displays, this museum presents the history of the Tennessee walking horse. Though the exhibits here will appeal primarily to horse enthusiasts, there is also much for the casual visitor to learn and enjoy. The annual Tennessee Walking Horse National Celebration, held each August here in Shelbyville, is one of middle Tennessee's most important annual events.

Admission: $3 adults, $2 senior citizens and children 7–12, free for children under 7.

Open: Mon–Sat 9am–5pm.

WHERE TO DINE

MISS MARY BOBO'S BOARDING HOUSE, Main St., Lynchburg. Tel. 759-7394.
Cuisine: SOUTHERN. **Reservations:** Required, well in advance.
$ Prices: All dishes $5–$10. No credit cards.
Open: Lunch seatings Mon–Fri at 1pm, Sat at 11am and 1pm.
This restaurant, housed in an antebellum-style mansion built slightly postbellum in 1866, opened for business in 1908. You'll feel as if you should be wearing a hoop skirt or top when you see the grand, white mansion, with its columns, long front porch, and balcony over the front door, but casual, contemporary clothes are just fine. Be prepared for filling portions of good, southern home-cooking, and remember, lunch here is actually midday dinner. Miss Mary's is very popular, and you generally need to book a weekday lunch two to three weeks in advance; for a Saturday lunch, you'll need to make reservations two to three *months* in advance.

3. LORETTA LYNN'S RANCH

Loretta Lynn is one of country music's biggest stars and even before being immortalized in the highly acclaimed movie *Coal Miner's Daughter* she was familiar to a generation of country-music fans. Today Loretta lives on a 3,500-acre ranch about 65 miles southwest of Nashville and a few miles off I-40. The huge Loretta Lynn's Ranch, Hurricane Mills, TN 37078 (tel. 296-7700), includes the entire village of Hurricane Mills, where you can visit Loretta's Gift Shop & Museum. The museum is in the old grist mill and includes lots of memorabilia from Loretta's long career. Between April and October there are daily tours through Loretta and her husband Mooney's 100-year-old plantation home. To see how far the famous singer came in her life, you can visit a reconstruction of Loretta's Butcher Holler home where she lived as a coal miner's daughter. Several times each summer Loretta gives concerts here at the ranch. If you're a fan, you may want to schedule your visit to coincide with one of these concerts. Call ahead to find out when concerts are scheduled this year. Tickets to tour Loretta's home and museum cost $10.50 (children 6 and under are free).

The ranch is a popular summer vacation spot and includes rental cabins and an RV park, snack bars, and several craft and gift stores. Ranch activities include canoeing, hiking, fishing, swimming (in a pool), hayrides, miniature golf, volleyball, horseshoes, and softball. In addition to the concerts Loretta gives each summer, there are daily live country-music performances, Saturday horse shows, and Saturday-night dances. The Loretta Lynn Restaurant, which serves buffet and à la carte southern meals, is just off I-40 at Exit 143.

INTRODUCING MEMPHIS

Memphis is a city overlooked by America. Nashville stole the Tennessee limelight with its country music. New Orleans, with its Mardi Gras, Cajun food, steamy jazz, and French Quarter, has forged a romantic aura that draws people from around the country. But ask the average American what makes Memphis special and they *might* be able to tell you that this is where Elvis Presley's Graceland is located. What they're less likely to know is that Memphis is the birthplace of the blues, rock 'n' roll, and soul music.

This is the city where W. C. Handy put down on paper the first written blues music, the city where Elvis Presley walked into Sun Studio and asked if he could make a record as a gift for his mother, the city where Otis Redding and others sang what was in their hearts and crafted the sound of soul music at Stax/Volt Records.

Memphis today is a pilgrimage site for both fans of rock 'n' roll and fans of the blues. This is not just because Elvis's famous Graceland is here or because W. C. Handy spent time playing on Beale Street. Much more than that draws these music pilgrims. It was here in Memphis that Elvis, Carl Perkins, and Jerry Lee Lewis all got their starts singing a new sound called rockabilly, a sound that would later become known as rock 'n' roll. Years earlier, beginning just after the turn of the century, W. C. Handy—and later, B. B. King, Muddy Waters, Ma Rainey, and others—merged the gospel singing and cotton-field work songs of the Mississippi Delta into a music called the blues.

Walking down Beale Street today, or sitting in the Sun Studio Café, you're almost as likely to hear French and German as English. British, Irish, and Scottish accents are all common in a city known throughout Europe, and the United States, as the birthplace of much of American music.

---

1. GEOGRAPHY, HISTORY & CULTURE

GEOGRAPHY

Located at the far-western end of Tennessee, Memphis sits on a bluff overlooking the Mississippi River. Directly across the river is Arkan-

WHAT'S SPECIAL ABOUT MEMPHIS

Activities
- [ ] Paddlewheeler cruises on the Mississippi.
- [ ] Memphis Ducks land and water tours of Memphis in army-surplus amphibious vehicles.

After Dark
- [ ] Beale Street, the most important street in the history of blues music and home to nearly a dozen nightclubs.
- [ ] Overton Square, Memphis's midtown entertainment district, with several nightclubs and restaurants.
- [ ] The Orpheum Theatre, a restored vaudeville theater that now serves as the city's main performing arts center.

Buildings
- [ ] Graceland, Elvis Presley's famous mansion.
- [ ] The Pyramid, Memphis's new stainless-steel arena built to resemble an Egyptian pyramid.

For the Kids
- [ ] Libertyland, a patriotic theme park in midtown Memphis.
- [ ] The Children's Museum of Memphis, with many interactive displays.

Literary Shrines
- [ ] In nearby Henning, the boyhood home of Alex Haley, who won a Pulitzer Prize for his novel *Roots*.

Museums
- [ ] The National Civil Rights Museum, housed in the Lorraine Motel, site of the assassination of Dr. Martin Luther King, Jr.

- [ ] The Mississippi River Museum, a fascinating history museum that focuses on life on the Mississippi.
- [ ] Dixon Gallery and Gardens, with an excellent collection of impressionist and post-impressionist paintings.

Music History
- [ ] The home of W. C. Handy, the first person to write down and publish a blues song.
- [ ] Sun Studio, where Elvis Presley, Jerry Lee Lewis, Carl Perkins, Roy Orbison, and Johnny Cash first recorded and originated rock 'n' roll music.

Natural Attractions
- [ ] Old Man River—the Mississippi—which makes its muddy way past Memphis.

Offbeat Oddities
- [ ] The Peabody Ducks, which spend their day in a marble fountain in the lobby of the Peabody Hotel, marching in at 11am and out at 5pm.
- [ ] The statue of Elvis on Beale Street, which is covered with graffiti dedicated to the "king."

Shopping
- [ ] A. Schwab Dry Good Store, an old-fashioned store that has been in business since 1876.

sas, and only a few miles to the south is Mississippi. The area, which was long known as the "fourth Chickasaw bluff," was chosen as a strategic site by French, Spanish, and finally American explorers and soldiers. The most important reason for choosing this site for the city was that the top of the bluff was above the high-water mark of the Mississippi, and thus was safe from floods.

With the Mississippi Delta region beginning just south of Memphis, the city has played an important role as the main shipping port for cotton grown in the delta. During the heyday of river transportation in the 19th century, Memphis became an important Mississippi River port, which it remains today. This role as river port has given the city a link and kinship with other river cities to the north.

Thus, with its importance to the cotton trade of the Deep South and its river connections to the Mississippi port cities of the Midwest, Memphis has developed some of the characteristics of both regions. Memphis today is not entirely of the South and not entirely of the Midwest. It is a city in-between.

DATELINE

- **1541** Hernando De Soto views the Mississippi River from the fourth Chickasaw bluff, site of today's Memphis.
- **1682** La Salle claims the Mississippi Valley for France.
- **1739** The French governor of Louisiana orders a fort built on the fourth Chickasaw bluff.
- **1795** Manuel Gayoso, in order to expand Spanish lands in North America, erects Fort San Fernando on the Mississippi River.
- **1797** Americans build Fort Adams on the ruins of Fort San Fernando and the Spanish flee to the far side of the river.
- **1818** The Chickasaw Nation cedes western Tennessee to the United States.
  (continues)

HISTORY

FROM INDIAN DAYS TO THE 20TH CENTURY Habitation of the bluffs of the Mississippi dates back nearly 15,000 years, but it was between A.D. 900 and 1600, during the Mississippian period, that these native peoples of the region reached a cultural zenith. During this 700-year period, people congregated in large, permanent villages. Sun worship, a distinctive style of artistic expression, and mound building were the main characteristics of this culture. The mounds, which are today the most readily evident reminders of this native heritage, were built as foundations for temples and can still be seen in places such as the Chucalissa Museum. However, by the time the first Europeans arrived in the area, the mound-builders had disappeared and had been replaced by the Chickasaw Indians.

The fourth Chickasaw bluff is a 100-foot-tall cliff overlooking the Mississippi River. As early as 1541 Spanish explorer Hernando De Soto stood atop this bluff and looked down on the mighty Mississippi River. More than 100 years later, in 1682, French explorer Sieur de La Salle claimed the entire Mississippi River valley for his country. However, it would be more than 50 years before the French built a permanent outpost in this region.

In 1739 the French built Fort Assumption on the fourth Chickasaw bluff. From this spot they hoped to control the Chickasaw tribes, who had befriended the English. By the end of the 18th century the Louisiana territory had passed into the hands of the Spanish, who erected Fort San Fernando on the bluff over the Mississippi. Within two years, the Spanish had decamped to the far side of the river and the U.S. flag flew above Fort Adams, which had been built on the ruins of Fort San Fernando.

A treaty negotiated with the Chickasaw Nation in 1818 ceded all of western Tennessee to the United States. Within the year, Memphis was founded as a speculative land investment by John Overton, Gen. James Winchester, and Andrew Jackson (who would later serve as president of the United States). The town was named for the capital of ancient Egypt, a reference to the Mississippi being the American Nile. However, it would take the better part of the century before the city began to live up to its grand name.

The town of Memphis was officially incorporated in 1826, and for the next two decades grew slowly. In 1845, the establishment of a naval yard in Memphis gave the town a new importance. Twelve years later the Memphis and Charleston Railroad linked Memphis to Charleston, South Carolina, on the Atlantic coast. Thus the town became a shipping and trading center.

In the years prior to the outbreak of the Civil War, the people of Memphis were very much in favor of secession, but it was only a few short months after the outbreak of the war that Memphis fell to Union troups. Both the Union and the Confederacy had seen the importance of Memphis as a supply base, and yet the Confederates had been unable to defend their city when, on June 6, 1862, steel-nosed ram boats easily overcame the Confederate fleet guarding Memphis. The city quickly became a major smuggling center as merchants sold to both the North and the South.

However, within two years of the war's end, tragedy struck Memphis. Cholera and yellow fever epidemics swept through the city killing hundreds of residents. This was only the first, and the mildest, of such epidemics to plague Memphis over the next

DATELINE

- **1819** The town of Memphis founded.
- **1826** Memphis incorporated.
- **1840s** Cheap land makes for boom times in Memphis.
- **1857** The Memphis and Charleston Railroad completed, linking the Atlantic and the Mississippi.
- **1862** Memphis falls to Union troops but becomes an important smuggling center.
- **1870s** Several yellow fever epidemics leave the city almost abandoned.
- **1879** Memphis's charter revoked and the city is bankrupt.
- **1880s** Memphis rebounds.
- **1890s** Memphis becomes the largest hardwood market in the world, attracting African Americans seeking to share in the city's boom times.
- **1892** The first bridge across the Mississippi south of St. Louis opens in Memphis.
- **1893** Memphis regains its city charter.
- **1909** W. C. Handy, a Beale Street bandleader, becomes the father of the blues when he writes the first blues song for mayoral

(continues)

DATELINE

candidate E. H. "Boss" Crump.

• **1916** The nation's first self-service grocery store opens in Memphis.

• **1940** B. B. King plays for the first time on Beale Street, at an amateur music contest.

• **1952** Jackie Brenston's "Rocket 88," regarded by many as the first rock 'n' roll recording, released by Memphis's Sun Studio.

• **1954** Elvis Presley records his first hit record at Sun Studio.

• **1960** Stax Records, a leader in the soul-music industry of the 1960s, founded.

• **1968** Dr. Martin Luther King, Jr., assassinated at the Lorraine Motel.

• **1977** Elvis Presley dies at Graceland, his home on the south side of Memphis.

• **1991** The National Civil Rights Museum opens in the former Lorraine Motel.

• **1992** Memphis elects its first African-American mayor.

11 years. In 1872 and 1878, yellow fever epidemics killed thousands of people and caused nearly half the city's population to flee. In the wake of these devastating outbreaks of the mosquito-borne disease, the city was left bankrupt and nearly abandoned.

However, some people remained in Memphis and had faith that the city would one day regain its former importance. One of those who had faith in the city was Robert Church, a former slave, who bought real estate from people who were fleeing the yellow fever plague. He later became the South's first African-American millionaire. In 1899, on a piece of land near the corner of Beale and Fourth streets, Church established a park and auditorium where African Americans could gather in public.

In the years following the Civil War, freed slaves from around the South flocked to Memphis in search of jobs. Other African-American professionals, educated in the North, also came to Memphis to establish new businesses. The center for this growing community was Beale Street. With all manner of businesses, from lawyers' and doctors' offices to bars and houses of prostitution, Beale Street was a lively community. The music that played in the juke joints and honky tonks began to take on a new sound that derived from the spirituals, field calls, and work songs of the Mississippi Delta cotton fields. By the first decade of the 20th century, this music had acquired a name— the blues.

THE MUSIC OF MEMPHIS Though the blues developed from work songs and spirituals, their roots went back much farther, to traditional musical styles of Africa. These musical traditions, brought to America by slaves, had gone through an interpretation and translation out in the cotton fields and in the Christian churches that became one of the few places that African Americans could gather. By the 1890s, freed slaves had brought their music of hard work and hard times into the nightclubs of Memphis.

It was here, on Beale Street, that African-American musicians began to put together the various aspects of the traditional musical styles of the Mississippi Delta. In 1909, one of these musicians, a young bandleader named

William Christopher Handy, was commissioned to write a campaign song for E. H. "Boss" Crump, who was running for mayor of Memphis. Crump won the election, and "Boss Crumps Blues" became a local hit. W. C. Handy later published his tune under the title "Memphis Blues." With the publication of this song, Handy started a musical revolution. The blues, which developed about the same time that jazz was first being played down in New Orleans, became one of the first truly American musical styles and later gave rise to both rock 'n' roll and soul music.

Beale Street became a center for musicians, who flocked to the area to learn the blues and showcase their own musical styles. Over the next four decades, Beale Street produced many of the country's most famous blues musicians. Among these was a young man named Riley King, who won praise during an amateur music contest. In the 1940s King became known as the Beale Street "Blues Boy," the initials of which he incorporated into his stage name when he began calling himself B. B. King. Today, B. B. King's Blues Club is Beale Street's most popular nightclub. Several times a year, King does shows at the club, and the rest of the year blues bands keep up the Beale Street tradition. Other musicians to develop their style and their first followings on Beale Street include Furry Lewis, Muddy Waters, Albert King, Bobby "Blue" Bland, Alberta Hunter, and Memphis Minnie McCoy.

By the time B. B. King got his start on Beale Street, the area was beginning to lose its importance. The Depression shut down a lot of businesses on the street, and many never reopened. By the 1960s there was talk of bulldozing the entire area to make way for an urban-renewal project. However, in the 1970s an interest in restoring old Beale Street developed. Beginning in 1980, Memphis and business investors began renovating the old buildings between Second and Fourth Streets. New clubs and restaurants opened and Beale Street once again became Memphis's main entertainment district. Today it's not just the blues, but rock, reggae, country, jazz, gospel, and folk that get played in Beale Street clubs.

Since the earliest days of Beale Street's musical popularity, there had been whites who visited the street's primarily African-American clubs. However, it wasn't until the late 1940s and early 1950s that a few adventurous white musicians began incorporating into their own music the earthy sounds and lyrics they heard on Beale Street. One of these musicians was a young man named Elvis Aaron Presley.

Elvis Presley was a delivery-truck driver in 1954 when he walked into Memphis's Sun Studio, to record a song as a birthday present for his mother. Studio owner Sam Phillips had been recording such Beale Street blues legends as B. B. King, Howlin' Wolf, Muddy Waters, and Little Milton, but his market had been limited to the African-American population. He was searching for a way to take the blues to a mainstream (that is, white) audience, and a new sound was what he needed. That new sound soon showed up at his door. Phillips produced what many music scholars regard as the first rock 'n' roll record when, in 1952, he recorded Jackie Brenston's "Rocket 88." Two years later Elvis Presley showed up at Sun Studio, and when Phillips heard his music, the studio owner knew that he had found what he was looking for. Within a few months of Elvis's visit to Sun

Studio, three other musicians—Carl Perkins, Jerry Lee Lewis, and Johnny Cash—showed up independently of one another. Each brought his own interpretations of the cross-over sound between African-American blues and country (or hillbilly) music. The sounds these four musicians crafted soon became known as rockabilly music, the foundations of rock 'n' roll. Roy Orbison would also get his start here at Sun Studio.

With his growing success, Elvis, who was from Tupelo, Mississippi, decided to stay in Memphis. In the late 1950s he purchased a traditional plantation-style home on the southern outskirts of the city. The house had been named Graceland by its previous owner and Elvis kept the name. Since Elvis's death in 1977, Graceland has become a pilgrimage site for the king's fans.

RECENT TIMES   The music that expressed itself as the blues was the expression of more than a century of struggle and suffering by African Americans. By the middle of the 20th century, that long suffering had been given another voice—the civil rights movement. One by one, school segregation and other discriminatory laws and practices of the South were challenged. Equal treatment and equal rights with whites was the goal of the civil rights movement, and the movement's greatest champion and spokesman was Dr. Martin Luther King, Jr., whose assassination in Memphis threw the city into the national limelight in April 1968.

In the early months of 1968, the sanitation workers of Memphis, most of whom were African Americans, went out on strike. In early April, Dr. King came to Memphis to lead a march by the striking workers. Dr. King stayed at the Lorraine Motel, just south of downtown. On April 4, the day the march was to be held, Dr. King stepped out onto the balcony of the motel and was gunned down by an assassin's bullet. Dr. King's murder did not, as perhaps had been hoped, end the civil rights movement. The Lorraine Motel is now the National Civil Rights Museum. The museum preserves the room where Dr. King was staying the day he was assassinated and also includes many evocative exhibits on the history of the civil rights movement.

By the time of Dr. King's murder, downtown Memphis was a classic example of urban decay. The city's population had moved to the suburbs in the post–World War II years and the inner city had quickly become an area of abandoned buildings and empty storefronts. However, beginning in the 1970s, a growing desire to restore life to downtown Memphis saw renovation projects undertaken. By the 1980s the renewal process was well under way. Beale Street was restored and became an entertainment district. The most visible example of downtown's regrowth is the 32-story stainless-steel Pyramid, a multipurpose arena on the north edge of downtown. Connecting the Pyramid and Beale Street is a new old-fashioned trolley that runs down Main Street.

Despite these investments, the redevelopment of downtown Memphis is still proceeding very slowly. The downtown mall along the route of the trolley tracks lacks the sort of upscale shops that can lure people away from suburban shopping malls. Downtown Memphis at this time has only a tenuous grasp on new life, but there's hope for the future.

The suburbs are still where the city's wealthier residents make their homes, have their businesses, and do their shopping. Consequently, Memphis is a sprawling city with a population of nearly a million people in the metropolitan area. The section of the city known as East Memphis is today the business and shopping heart of the city. High-rises sprout from suburban neighborhoods, in effect creating a new Memphis away from the river. This new Memphis is making its fortunes not on cotton, but on a diversified manufacturing and shipping economy that promises to keep the city healthy and growing into the 21st century.

ART, ARCHITECTURE & CULTURAL LIFE

For nearly 100 years, Memphians have taken pride in their music. The blues and rock 'n' roll are the sounds that have defined Memphis music and made it a city known to music lovers all over the world (see above for a brief history of Memphis's musical styles and performers).

Memphis has not done as well as many other cities in preserving its architectural heritage. The downtown has only a few blocks of historic districts that have retained the architecture of the late 19th century. These historic districts include the Pinch district north of downtown, Cotton Row, and Beale Street—all areas that have been, or are in the process of being, renovated. Several unrestored buildings exhibit beautiful and unusual tilework on their facades. So keep your eyes peeled for hidden architectural treasures when walking around downtown.

To the east of downtown the Victorian Village historic district features several ornate, brick Victorian homes. Heading farther east, in the area around Overton Park, are streets lined with beautiful old mansions in a wide variety of architectural styles.

The city's single most architecturally distinctive structure is the Pyramid, the 32-story stainless-steel arena that rises at the north end of downtown. Built to resemble an Egyptian pyramid, this coliseum opened in 1991, and though it quite frequently fades into the hazy gray skies over Memphis, on a clear day the Pyramid shimmers in the sun with a blue sky making it stand out all the more.

Memphis, as was mentioned above, is a city between two regions, with ties to both the South and to the Midwest. Ever since the end of the Civil War, the city has been attracting African Americans from throughout the South. This has made the city one of those with the

IMPRESSIONS

I'd rather be here than any place I know.
—W. C. Handy, referring to Beale Street

highest percentages of African-American residents. This very concentration of people provided fertile ground for the musical experimentation and expression that gave the world the blues.

For the most part, Memphis today has the feel of a city of the New South. Bolstered by the migration of northern companies to the Sunbelt, Memphis has attracted a variety of new industries that are turning the city from one of regional importance into one of national importance. However, the city has not lost its southern charm, nor has it strayed far from its cotton roots. A gracious southern style still pervades life in Memphis.

2. FAMOUS MEMPHIANS

Kathy Bates (b. 1948) A Memphis native who won an Academy Award for best actress for her role in the film *Misery*, which was based on a Stephen King novel. Bates also appeared in the popular film *Fried Green Tomatoes*.

W. C. Handy (1873–1958) This Beale Street bandleader was the first person to write down and publish the blues music that originated in the Mississippi Delta, and so he is considered the father of the blues. His most famous tunes include the "Memphis Blues" and the "St. Louis Blues."

B. B. King (b. 1925) Blues music pioneer King developed his first following on Beale Street after winning an amateur music contest. His initials stand for Beale Street "Blues Boy." He is best known for his rendition of the song "Lucille."

Tim McCarver (b. 1941) Born in Memphis, McCarver played baseball for the St. Louis Cardinals and the Boston Red Sox before going on to become a popular sportscaster and sports writer.

Elvis Presley (1935–77) Born poor in Tupelo, Mississippi, Elvis Presley went on to become arguably the most famous rock 'n' roller in history. He got his start, and helped originate rock 'n' roll music, at the tiny Sun Studio in Memphis. Graceland, his former home, is one of the most popular attractions in Memphis.

IMPRESSIONS

Energetic, clean, and preoccupied with its almost incredible industrial expansion, Memphis seems—despite its Beale Street, its heavy Negro population, its Cotton Carnival, and a commanding position as the Deep South's cotton-trade center—more like a bustling midwestern city than the mecca of Mississippi planters.
—HODDING CARTER, 1947

Cybill Shepherd (b. 1950) This multitalented performer has been a stage, film, and television actress. Shepherd was born in Memphis and still lives there today. Her most famous roles have been in *The Last Picture Show* and on the TV series "Moonlighting."

Danny Thomas (1914–91) Beloved TV and film personality, Thomas founded the St. Jude Children's Research Hospital in Memphis.

3. FOOD & DRINK

Memphis calls itself the **pork barbecue** capital of the world. This is quite a claim in a region that just about lives on pork barbecue. For those of you who are not from the South, let me give you a short barbecue primer. Southern pork barbecue is, for the most part, just exactly what its name says it is—pork that has been barbecued over a wood fire. There are several variations on barbecue, and most barbecue places offer the full gamut. My personal favorite is pulled shoulder, which is a barbecued shoulder of pork from which meat is pulled by hand after it's cooked. What you end up with on your plate is a pile of shredded pork to which you can add your favorite hot sauces. Barbecued ribs are a particular Memphis specialty and these come either dry-cooked or wet-cooked. If you order your ribs dry-cooked, it's up to you to apply the sauce, but if you order it wet-cooked, the ribs will have been cooked in a sauce. Barbecue is traditionally served with a side of cole slaw and perhaps some baked beans or potato salad.

The city's other traditional fare is good **old-fashioned American food**—here, as in Nashville, known as "meat and three," a term that refers to the three side vegetables that you get with whatever type of meat you happen to order. This is very simple food, and even in the most famous "meat-and-three" restaurants, your vegetables are likely to come out of a can. Perhaps because of the southern affinity for traditions, Memphians both young and old flock to "meat-and-three" restaurants for meals just like mom used to fix.

While "meat-and-three" places fill the budget-dining niche in Memphis, up at the other end of the scale you'll find restaurants serving New American or New Southern cuisine. This is the South's nod of the head to the pioneering culinary work done in California. Regional ingredients get new treatments that have their roots in the Mediterranean, the Southwest, and even Asia. Once again, pork shows up on a lot of menus, though prepared with quite a bit more attention than your basic barbecue. Last, you'll also find quite a bit of **Cajun food** here in Memphis, which isn't surprising when you look at a map and see how close New Orleans is.

The most important thing to remember about drinking in Memphis is that, because of state laws, you'll only find cocktail bars in restaurants and hotels. If you happen to be a fan of brew pubs, you'll find a couple in the metropolitan area.

4. RECOMMENDED BOOKS, FILMS & RECORDINGS

BOOKS

GENERAL For information on books that include some of the history of Memphis see "Recommended Books, Films, and Recordings" in Chapter 2. If you're interested in the civil rights movement and the life and death of Dr. Martin Luther King, Jr., you may want to read *At the River I Stand: Memphis, the 1968 Strike and Dr. Martin Luther King, Jr.* (Carlson Publishing, 1989), by Joan Turner Beifuss. This is a rather weighty work.

FICTION John Grisham's novels *The Firm* (Doubleday, 1991) and *The Client* (Doubleday, 1993) provide a sense of the city and at the same time provide suspenseful entertainment. Both books are set amid the Memphis legal world.

MUSIC A lot has been written about the blues over the years, and consequently a lot has been written about Memphis and the nearby Mississippi Delta. *Rythm Oil, A Journey Through the Music of the American South* (Vintage, 1993), by Stanley Booth, is a collection of articles that have appeared in other publications. Over the years, Booth has traveled the world in pursuit of stories on the blues and interviews with famous blues musicians. *The Land Where the Blues Began* (Pantheon Books, 1993), by Alan Lomax, is a thick but very readable account of the Mississippi Delta's blues music. The book includes plenty of interviews and song lyrics. Beale Street is where the blues finally became a force in the world of American music, and in *Beale Black & Blue* (Louisiana State University Press, 1981) Margaret McKee and Fred Chisenhall tell the history of Beale Street and the people who made it famous.

One of those Beale Street figures was B. B. King, the reigning king of the blues. Charles Sawyer's *The Arrival of B. B. King* (Da Capo Press, 1980), though a bit dated, tells the story of the Beale Street "Blues Boy." *Woman with a Guitar: Memphis Minnie's Blues* (Da Capo Press, 1992), by Paul and Beth Garon, is a biography of another of Beale Street's early blues singers.

In the early 1950s, Sun Studio in Memphis recorded some of the world's first rock 'n' roll music. Among the artists to record here were Jerry Lee Lewis, Roy Orbison, Carl Perkins, and Elvis Presley. *Great Balls of Fire* (Mandarin Paperbacks, 1989), by Myra Lewis with Murray Silver, is a biography of Jerry Lee Lewis, the rocker whose career died when he married his 13-year-old cousin. *Dark Star: The Roy Orbison Story* (Carol Publishing Group, 1990), by Ellis Amburn, is a biography of the enigmatic Orbison. The book is drawn from interviews with Orbison's friends and family and includes a lot on the early days at Sun Studio.

Elvis There has probably been more written about Elvis Presley (and I don't just mean in the tabloids) than about any other rock star in history. To start out, you might look for *Elvis, The King Lives* (Gallery Books, 1990), a large-format picture book with text by John Alvarez Taylor. For a good, basic biography, read Jerry Hopkins's two books *Elvis: A Biography* (Warner Books, 1971) and *Elvis: The Final Years* (Playboy Books, 1981). For those who are curious what it was like to be Mrs. Elvis, there's the *New York Times* bestseller *Elvis and Me* (Berkley Books, 1986), by Priscilla Presley. Much controversy surrounded the death of Elvis and his adoring fans were loath to learn that "the king" was a drug addict. In *The Death of Elvis: What Really Happened* (Delacorte Press, 1991), authors Charles C. Thompson II and James P. Cole dig deep into the cause of Elvis's death and the subsequent cover-up. However, it was *Elvis: What Happened?* (World News Corporation, 1977), by Red West, Sonny West, and Dave Hebler as told to Steve Dunleavy, which was published shortly before Elvis's death, that caused such a stir. The book is a sleazy exposé of Elvis's drug and sex habits.

FILMS

Though it did not have nearly the complexity of John Grisham's novel, the movie version of *The Firm* (1993), starring Tom Cruise, was a suspense-filled film and a big summer hit. On the heels of this film's success, shooting began on Grisham's more recent novel *The Client,* due out during this book's lifetime. And Jim Jarmusch's wry *Mystery Train* prominently features the mythic, if seamy, underbelly of Memphis.

RECORDINGS

Having given rise to the blues, rock 'n' roll, and soul music, Memphis is arguably the most important city in the United States when it comes to American music history. It was W. C. Handy who got the whole American music scene rolling when he wrote down the first published blues tune, "Memphis Blues," back in 1909. Over the years Handy's tunes were recorded by many artists. At a good record store you might be able to find some collections of old W. C. Handy tunes. Other Memphis blues artists to look for are "Ma" Rainey, Memphis Minnie McCoy, Furry Lewis, Albert King, Bobby "Blue" Bland, and Alberta Hunter.

By the late 1940s and early 1950s the Memphis music scene was hot again. Sun Studio, not far from Beale Street, was where blues musicians B. B. King, Muddy Waters, Howlin' Wolf, and Little Milton all got their start. However, it was not these African-American artists who would bring Sun Studio and Memphis its greatest claim to fame, but a handful of white singers who took the blues and merged them with the country-music sound. What came out of this merger was a sound called rockabilly. The names of the Sun Studio rockabilly artists have become familiar to people all over the world—Carl Perkins, Jerry Lee Lewis, Roy Orbison, Johnny Cash, and, most famous of all, Elvis Presley. The sound these musicians independently created was the foundation for rock 'n' roll, though it's another Sun Studio recording artist who is credited with releasing the first rock 'n' roll tune. His name was Jackie Brenston, and his 1952 record was titled "Rocket 88." Many Sun Studio tunes are available on reissues, and over the years these first rock 'n' roll songs have been recorded by dozens of musicians.

In the early 1960s Memphis once again entered the popular music limelight when Stax/Volt Records gave the country its first soul music. Otis Redding, Isaac Hayes, Booker T and the MGs, Johnny Taylor, William Bell, and Karla Thomas were among the musicians who got their start at this Memphis recording studio.

CHAPTER 11

PLANNING A TRIP TO MEMPHIS

Whether you're visiting Memphis as part of a trip to Nashville or heading specifically to this sprawling city on the Mississippi, you're likely to have some questions before you arrive. This chapter will help you to answer such important questions as "What will it cost?" and "How do I get there?".

1. INFORMATION & COSTS

SOURCES OF INFORMATION

The **Visitor's Information Center,** at 340 Beale St., Memphis, TN 38103 (tel. 901/543-5333), is open Monday through Friday from 9am to 5pm, on Saturday from 9am to 6pm, and on Sunday from noon to 5pm; in the summer months, the center is open until 6pm every day. You can drop in to get free brochures on attractions and lodgings or to speak to someone at the staffed counter.

At the airport, there are information boards with telephone numbers for contacting hotels and getting other helpful telephone numbers.

For information on other parts of Tennessee, contact the **Tennessee Department of Tourism Development,** P.O. Box 23170, Nashville, TN 37202-3170 (tel. 615/741-2158).

For information about travel insurance, packing for your trip, and tips for travelers with special interests or needs, see Chapter 2, "Planning a Trip to Nashville."

COSTS

What will a vacation in Memphis cost? Of course it all depends on how much you want to spend and how comfortable you want to be. If your standards are high and you like to stay in the best hotels and eat at gourmet restaurants, you may find yourself spending upward of $130 per person per day (maybe $70 per person on a room and $60 for three meals). However, if you have less money to spend, you can get a motel out in East Memphis for around $40 a night double, and eat well for $25 or less per day for a total outlay of around $45 per person per day. Of course, you can also spend anything in between these two extremes.

When it comes time to pay your bills, you'll find that a credit or charge card is most convenient, although traveler's checks are accepted at hotels, motels, restaurants, and most stores. If you plan to rent a car, know that you'll need a credit or charge card at almost every rental agency for the deposit.

WHAT THINGS COST IN MEMPHIS	U.S. $
Taxi from the airport to the city center	16.00
Taxi from the airport to Poplar Street (East Memphis)	14.25
Bus ride between any two downtown points	1.15
Local telephone call	.25
Double room at the Peabody (deluxe)	140.00
Double room at the Holiday Inn–Overton Square (moderate)	75.00
Double room at the La Quinta Inn (budget)	47.00
Lunch for one at Aubergine (moderate)	16.00
Lunch for one at Buntyn Restaurant (budget)	8.00
Dinner for one, without wine, at Raji (deluxe)	40.00
Dinner for one, without wine, at Automatic Slim's Tonga Club (moderate)	21.00
Dinner for one, without wine, at Salsa Cocina Mexicana (budget)	14.00
Bottle of beer	2.50
Coca-Cola	1.00
Cup of coffee or iced tea	.95
Roll of ASA 100 Kodacolor film, 36 exposures	4.90
Movie ticket	6.00
Theater ticket to the Orpheum Theatre	20.00–43.00

2. WHEN TO GO — CLIMATE & EVENTS

CLIMATE

Summer is the peak tourist season in Memphis, but this doesn't coincide with the city's best weather. During July, August, and often September, temperatures can be up around 100° F, with high humidity. Memphians say that May and October are the most pleasant months of the year. During spring and fall days are often warm and nights cool, though the weather can be changeable—so bring a variety of clothes. Heavy rains, which blow up suddenly from the gulf, can hit any time of year. Winters generally aren't very cold, but expect freezing temperatures so bring a coat.

Memphis's Average Monthly Temperatures and Rainfall

	Jan	Feb	Mar	Apr	May	June	July	Aug	Sept	Oct	Nov	Dec
Temp. (°F)	40	44	52	63	71	79	82	81	74	63	51	43
Temp. (°C)	4	7	11	17	22	26	28	27	23	17	11	6
Days of Rain	10	10	11	10	9	9	9	8	7	6	9	10

MEMPHIS CALENDAR OF EVENTS

JANUARY

☐ **Elvis Presley's Birthday Tribute,** Graceland. International gathering of Presley fans to celebrate the birthday of "The King." Call 332-3322. Around January 8.
☐ **Martin Luther King, Jr.'s Birthday,** citywide. Events to memorialize Dr. King take place on the nationally observed holiday. Call 521-9699. Around January 18th.

FEBRUARY

☐ **Kroger St. Jude International Tennis Championship,** Racquet Club of Memphis. World-class players compete in this famous tour event. Call 765-4400. Early February.

APRIL

☐ **Africa in April Cultural Awareness Festival,** downtown. A five-day-long festival centering around African music, dance, theater, exhibits, arts, and crafts. Call 785-2542. Mid-April.

MAY

✪ *Memphis in May International Festival   A month-long celebration of a different country each year with musical, cultural, and artistic festivities; business, sports, and educational programs; and food unique to the country. More than a million people come to almost 100 sanctioned events scheduled throughout the city. The most important happenings are the Memphis in May Beale Street Music Festival, the International Festival Tattoo, the World Championship Barbecue Cooking Contest, and the Sunset Symphony. The Ivory Coast will be honored in 1994 and Thailand in 1995.*

   ***Where:** Citywide. **When:** Month of May. **How:** Call Memphis in May (tel. 525-4611).*

☐ **Blues Memphis Week.** A week-long blues festival including the International Blues Summit, and ending with the Blues Music awards and post-show jam. For more information call the Blues Foundation at 527-BLUE. Early May.

☐ **Cotton Maker's Jubilee,** downtown. The largest African-American parade in the country and a midway are parts of this tribute to King Cotton. Call 774-1118. Early May.

☐ **Spring Memphis Music Festival,** Beale Street. Festival celebrating a wide range of contemporary Memphis music and musicians. Call 526-0110. Mid-May.

JUNE

☐ **Carnival Memphis,** citywide. Almost half a million people join in the family activities of exhibits, music, crafts, and events. Call 278-0243. Early June.

☐ **Germantown Charity Horse Show,** Germantown Horse Show Arena. Four-day competition for prizes. Call 754-7443. Second week in June.

☐ **Native American Holidays,** Halle Stadium on Mt. Moriah Road. Native Americans from Canada and the U.S. meet to participate in the Native American Inter-Tribal Association Plains-style dance competition. Third week in June.

JULY

☐ **WMC Star Spangled Celebration,** downtown and Mud Island. Fourth of July entertainment and fireworks. July 4.

☐ **Memphis Music and Heritage Festival,** Mud Island. A three-day celebration of the diversity of the South, sponsored by the Center for Southern Folklore. Call 525-3655. Second weekend in July.

☐ **Federal Express St. Jude Golf Classic,** Tournament Player's Club at Southwind. A PGA tour event which benefits St. Jude's Children's Hospital. End of July.

AUGUST

☐ **Elvis Week,** citywide. Festival commemorating the influences of Elvis. Call 332-3322. Second week in August.

☐ **Memphis Blues Festival,** Tom Lee Park. Musicians celebrate the blues. Call 526-9300. Mid-August.

SEPTEMBER

☐ **National Labor Day Weekend Blues Bash,** Beale Street. Winners of the National Amateur Blues Talent Contests perform. Call 527-BLUE. Labor Day weekend.

☐ **Mid-South Fair,** Mid-South Fairgrounds. Ten days of fun-filled rides, food, games, shows, a midway, and rodeo. Call 274-8800. Last week of September.

OCTOBER

☐ **Pink Palace Crafts Fair,** Audubon Park. Artists and performers in one of the largest craft fairs in Tennessee. Call 320-6320 or 320-6365. Early October.

☐ **Memphis Arts in the Park Festival,** Overton Park. Visual arts competition open to all artists. Call 761-1278. Mid-October.

NOVEMBER

☐ **Mid-South Arts and Crafts Show,** Memphis Cook Convention Center. Artists and craftspeople from over 20 states sell their handiwork. Third week in November.

DECEMBER

☐ **Merry Christmas Memphis Parade,** downtown. Christmas parade with floats and bands. Call 526-6840. Early December.

☐ **St. Jude Liberty Bowl Football Classic,** Liberty Bowl Memorial Stadium. Intercollegiate game that's nationally televised. Call 767-7700. Late December.

☐ **Bury Your Blues Blowout on Beale New Year's Eve Celebration,** Beale Street. New Year's Eve celebration both inside the clubs and outside on Beale Street. Call 526-0110. December 31.

3. GETTING THERE

BY PLANE

THE AIRPORT The **Memphis International Airport,** just off I-240 (tel. 901/922-8000), is located 11 miles south of downtown Memphis and 9 miles west of East Memphis.

THE MAJOR AIRLINES Memphis is served by the following airlines: American Airlines (tel. toll free 800/433-7300), Delta (tel. 901/762-4141, or toll free 800/221-1212), Northwest (tel. toll free 800/225-2525), TWA (tel. toll free 800/221-2000), United Airlines (tel. toll free 800/241-6522), and USAir (tel. toll free 800/428-4322).

REGULAR AIRFARES At the time of this writing, round-trip 14-day advance-purchase fares from New York to Memphis were about $347. Full coach fares were running about $820 and first-class fares were about $1,028. Round-trip 14-day advance-purchase fares from Los Angeles to Memphis were about $493. Full coach fares were about $1,176 and first-class fares about $1,806. For information on "bucket shops" and other options for bargain airfares, see Chapter 2, "Planning a Trip to Nashville."

BY TRAIN

Memphis is served by **Amtrak** (tel. toll free 800/872-7245) with a route that goes from New York through Chicago to Memphis. The *City of New Orleans* connects Memphis with Chicago. The round-trip fare between Chicago and Memphis is about $102. The Amtrak station in Memphis is located at 545 S. Main St. (tel. 521-1061).

BY BUS

Greyhound Lines (tel. toll free 800/231-2222) offers service to Memphis from around the country, and, in fact, Memphis is where Greyhound got started. The fare between Chicago and Memphis is $72 one-way and $129 round-trip. In Memphis, the Greyhound bus station is at 203 Union Ave. (tel. 523-2440).

BY CAR

Memphis is a crossroads of the South and is within an eight-hour drive of many major southern cities. **I-57** comes into Memphis from Chicago and the north. **I-55** leaves Memphis from the south, and goes nearly all the way to New Orleans. **I-40,** which runs across the entire country from east to west, connects Memphis to Nashville.

Here are some driving distances from selected cities (in miles): Atlanta, 414; Chicago, 534; Dallas, 466; Kansas City, 459; Nashville, 206; and New Orleans, 393.

PACKAGE TOURS

Tour companies that offer tours with stops in Memphis include **Globus** and **Cosmos Tourama.** Ask a local travel agent for information about these tours.

The **Delta Queen Steamboat Company,** 30 Robin St. Wharf, New Orleans, LA 70130-1890 (tel. 504/586-0631), offers paddlewheel steamboat tours that stop in Memphis.

Tours that focus on Memphis are offered by **Domenico Tours,** 751 Broadway, Bayonne, NJ 07002 (tel. toll free 800/554-8687); **Our Town Tours,** P.O. Box 148287, Nashville, TN 37214 (tel. 615/889-0525, or toll free 800/624-5170); and **Maupintour,** which works only with travel agents.

CHAPTER 12

GETTING TO KNOW MEMPHIS

- **1. ORIENTATION**
- **• NEIGHBORHOODS IN BRIEF**
- **2. GETTING AROUND**
- **• FAST FACTS: MEMPHIS**
- **3. NETWORKS & RESOURCES**

Once you hit town, you may be surprised and baffled by Memphis. This city is spread out, so getting around can be confusing and frustrating at first. Read this chapter, and your first hours in town should be less confusing. You'll also find in this chapter a lot of useful information that will help you throughout your stay.

1. ORIENTATION

ARRIVING

BY PLANE The **Memphis International Airport** (tel. 901/ 922-8000) is located approximately 11 miles south of downtown Memphis off I-240. From the airport to East Memphis, it's about 9 miles. The route into either downtown or East Memphis is on I-240 all the way. Generally, allow about 20 minutes for the trip between the airport and downtown, and 15 minutes between the airport and East Memphis—more during rush hour. For information on airlines serving Memphis, see "Getting There," in Chapter 11.

Getting into Town **Airport Express** (tel. 901/922-8238) operates a shuttle service between the Memphis International Airport and many area hotels. The ticket counter is located in Terminal B. They operate from about 7am to about 11pm seven days a week. Rates are $8 one-way and $15 round-trip. When you want to return to the airport, contact the front desk of your hotel for schedule information.

The Memphis Area Transit Authority (MATA) (tel. 274-MATA) operates **buses** between the airport and downtown Memphis. The buses run Monday through Saturday and the fare is $1.20. From the lower level at the airport, take no. 32A, the East Parkway bus (which operates about every 15 to 60 minutes Monday through Friday, depending on the time of day, and much less often on Saturday) to Airways and Winchester Roads. Transfer to no. 20, the Bellevue/ Winchester bus, which will take you to Front and Jefferson Streets downtown. This bus operates Monday through Friday about every 30 or 60 minutes, depending on the time of day; Saturday service is less frequent. If you want to take the bus, the best bet is to call MATA or ask a bus driver for the latest schedule information.

A **taxi** from the airport to downtown Memphis will cost about

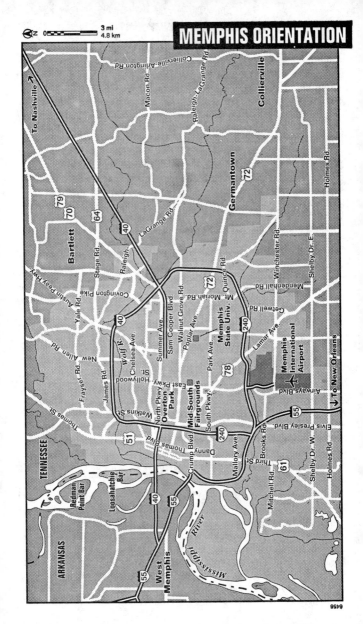

$16; to East Memphis it will cost about $14. There are usually plenty of taxis around, but if you can't find one, call Checker/Yellow Cab (tel. 577-7777) or City Wide Cab Company (tel. 324-4202). The flag-drop rate is $2.35; after that, it's $1.10 per mile. Each additional passenger is 25¢ extra.

BY TRAIN If you arrive in Memphis on an Amtrak train, you'll find yourself at the **Amtrak Station** at 545 S. Main St. (tel. 901/521-1061), near Calhoun Street. For information, call Amtrak (tel. toll free 800/872-7245).

BY BUS The **Greyhound Lines bus station** (tel. 901/523-2440) is at 203 Union Ave., within two blocks of the Peabody Hotel. For schedules and information, call Greyhound's main information line (tel. toll free 800/231-2222).

BY CAR The main routes into Memphis include **I-40,** which connects Memphis with Nashville and Raleigh to the east and Little Rock and Oklahoma City to the west. **I-55** passes through the southwestern corner of the city and connects Memphis to New Orleans in the south and to St. Louis and Chicago to the north.

If you're coming in from the east and trying to get to downtown Memphis, I-40 is slightly faster than I-240. From I-40, take Danny Thomas Boulevard, or take I-40 to I-240 and get off at Union Avenue. If you're heading to East Memphis, take I-240. Poplar Avenue is the main East Memphis exit.

TOURIST INFORMATION

At the airport, there are information boards with telephone numbers for contacting hotels and getting other helpful telephone numbers.

The **Visitor's Information Center,** at 340 Beale St., Memphis, TN 38103 (tel. 901/543-5333), is open Monday through Friday from 9am to 5pm, on Saturday from 9am to 6pm, and on Sunday from noon to 5pm. In the summer months the center is open until 6pm every day. You can drop in to get free brochures on attractions and accommodations or to speak to someone at the staffed counter.

CITY LAYOUT

Memphis was built on the east bank of the Mississippi River and is just above the Mississippi state line, consequently growth has had to be primarily to the east and, to a lesser extent, to the north. The inexorable sprawl of the suburbs has pushed the limits of the metropolitan area far to the east, and today the area known as East Memphis is the city's business and cultural center. Despite the fact that the city has a fairly small and compact downtown area, the sprawl of recent years has made getting around difficult for both residents and visitors. Traffic congestion on main east-west avenues is

---

IMPRESSIONS

If I could only find a white man who had the Negro sound and the Negro feel, I could make a million dollars.
—SAM PHILLIPS, OWNER OF SUN STUDIO, SHORTLY BEFORE ELVIS APPEARED AT THE STUDIO IN THE EARLY 1950S

bad throughout the day, so you're usually better off taking the Interstate around the outskirts of the city if you're trying to cross town.

In general, the city is laid out on a grid with a north-south axis. However, there are many exceptions, including downtown, which was laid out with streets parallel to the river and avenues running perpendicular to the river. Throughout the city you'll find that, in general, avenues run east-west and streets run north-south.

MAIN ARTERIES & STREETS Memphis is circled by **I-40,** which loops around the north side of the city, and **I-240,** which loops around the south side. **Poplar Avenue** and **Sam Cooper Boulevard/North Parkway** are the city's main east-west arteries, with Poplar having more businesses and more traffic. Sam Cooper Boulevard is also an alternative route into downtown if you don't want to take the Interstate. **Union Avenue** is the dividing line between the north and south sides of the city. Other important **east-west roads** include Central Avenue, Summer Avenue, and Park Avenue. Major **north-south arteries** include (from downtown heading eastward) Third Street/U.S. 61, I-240, Elvis Presley Boulevard/U.S. 51, Airways Boulevard/East Parkway, and Mendenhall Road. Other important roads include Summer Avenue, and Lamar Avenue.

Out **in East Memphis,** the main east-west arteries are Poplar Avenue and Winchester Road. The main north-south arteries are Perkins Road/Perkins Road Extended, Mendenhall Road, Hickory Hill Road, and Germantown Road.

FINDING AN ADDRESS "Good luck" is all I can say about finding an address in Memphis. Your best bet will always be to call someone first and ask for directions or the name of the nearest main cross street. Though the address numbering system increases the farther you get from downtown, it does not increase by a specific amount for each block. However, there are some general guidelines to get you in the general vicinity of where you're going. If an address is in the hundreds or lower, you should be downtown. If the address is an avenue or other east-west road in the 2000 to 4000 range, you'll likely find it in midtown; if the number is in the 5000 to 7000 range, you should be out in East Memphis. If the address is on a street, it will likely have a north or south prefix included. Union Avenue is the dividing line between north and south.

STREET MAPS The streets of Memphis can seem a bit baffling at times, so you'll definitely need to get a good map. You can get one from the **Visitor's Information Center,** at 340 Beale St., Memphis, TN 38103 (tel. 901/543-5333). If you arrive at the airport and rent a car, the rental company should be able to give you a basic map that will at least get you to your hotel or to the information center.

If you happen to be a member of **AAA,** you can get free maps of Memphis and the rest of Tennessee either from your local AAA office or from the Memphis office at 5683 S. Rex Rd. (tel. 901/761-5371); it's open Monday through Friday from 8:30am to 5:30pm. One other option is to stop in at a gas station, where there are usually a variety of maps available.

NEIGHBORHOODS IN BRIEF

More important than neighborhoods in Memphis are the city's general divisions. These major divisions are how the city defines itself.

Downtown   This, the oldest part of the city, is built on the bank of the Mississippi River and is today striving for a rebirth through a long and protracted labor. Though historic Beale Street, the city's main entertainment district, and a couple of excellent museums are located downtown, this is not a vibrant area. There are few good restaurants and even fewer good hotels.

Midtown   This is primarily a residential area, though it's also known for its numerous hospitals. The Overton Square area is Midtown's most active district and is the site of several good restaurants, nightclubs, and antiques stores. Midtown is also where you will find Overton Park, the Memphis Zoo and Aquarium, the Memphis Brooks Museum of Art, and many of the city's other main attractions. There are many large, stately homes on parklike blocks surrounding Overton Park.

East Memphis   Heading still farther east from downtown brings you to East Memphis, which lies roughly on either side of I-240 on the east side of the city. This is the city's most affluent and most newly developed region. It's characterized by wide avenues, numerous shopping malls and shopping centers (seemingly at every major intersection), new office complexes, and a few high-rise hotels and office buildings.

2. GETTING AROUND

BY PUBLIC TRANSPORTATION

BY BUS   The **Memphis Area Transit Authority (MATA)** (tel. 274-MATA) operates city-wide bus service. Bus stops are indicated by blue-and-white signs. For schedule information, ask a bus driver or call the MATA number above. The standard **fare** is $1.10 and exact change is required. Transfers cost 10¢, and there's a 50¢ discount for handicapped persons and senior citizens with ID cards. (To qualify for the discounted fare, however, you need to obtain a MATA ID card by bringing two forms of identification to the MATA Customer Service Center at 61 S. Main St. in the Mid-America Mall, open Monday through Friday from 8am to 5pm.

Discount Passes   In the past, during the summer MATA has offered a special tourist pass with unlimited rides. Call them at 722-7100 to see if the pass is available during your visit.

BY STREETCAR   The **Main Street Trolley** operates renovated 1920s trolley cars that run along a north-south route down the Main Street Mall from the Pyramid to the National Civil Rights Museum. It's a unique way to get around the downtown area. The fare is 50¢ each way, with a lunch hour special rate of 25¢ between 11am and

1:30pm. An all-day pass is $2; exact change is required and passengers may board at any of the 20 stations along Main Street. Trolleys are wheelchair-accessible.

BY TAXI

For quick cab service, call **Checker/Yellow Cab** (tel. 577-7777) or **City Wide Cab Company** (tel. 324-4202), or have your hotel or motel call one for you. The flag-drop rate is $2.35; after that it's $1.10 per mile. Each additional passenger is 25¢.

BY CAR

Memphis is a big sprawling city and the best—and worst—way to get around is by car. A car is nearly a necessity for traveling between downtown and East Memphis, yet traffic congestion can make this trip take far longer than you'd expect (45 minutes isn't unusual). East-west avenues and any road in East Memphis at rush hour are the most congested. Parking downtown is not usually a problem, but stay alert for tow-away zones and watch the time on your meter. Out in East Memphis, there is usually no parking problem.

CAR RENTALS　For the very best deal on a rental car, make your reservation at least one week in advance. It also pays to shop around and call the same companies a few times over the course of a couple of weeks. If you decide on the spur of the moment that you want to rent a car, check to see whether there are any weekend or special rates available. If you're a member of a frequent-flyer program, be sure to mention it: You might get mileage credit for renting a car. Currently, daily rates for a subcompact are around $35 and weekly rates are around $135.

All the major auto-rental companies and several independent companies have offices in Memphis. Some are located near the airport only, and some have offices both near the airport and in other areas of Memphis. Be sure to leave yourself plenty of time for returning your car when you head to the airport to catch your return flight. None of the companies has an office in the airport itself, so you'll have to take a shuttle van from the car drop-off point to the airport terminal.

Major car-rental companies in Memphis include: **Alamo Rent-A-Car** (tel. toll free 800/327-9633), near the airport at 2600 Rental Rd. (tel. 901/346-9777); **Budget Rent-A-Car** (tel. toll free 800/527-0700), near the airport at 2650 Rental Rd. (tel. 901/767-1000) and at 5133 Poplar Ave. (tel. 901/685-8888); **Dollar Rent-A-Car** (tel. toll free 800/800-4000), near the airport at 2031 E. Brooks Rd. (tel. 901/396-2495); **Enterprise Rent-A-Car** (tel. toll free 800/325-8007), near the airport at 2041 E. Brooks Rd. (tel. 901/345-8588) and 1969 Covington Pike (tel. 901/385-8588); **Hertz** (tel. toll free 800/654-1831), near the airport at 2560 Rental Rd. (tel. 901/345-5680); **Payless Rent-A-Car** (tel. toll free 800/PAYLESS), near the airport at 3420 Airways Blvd. (tel. 901/345-2440); and **Thrifly Car Rental** (tel. toll free 800/367-2277), near the airport at 2780 Airways Blvd. (tel. 901/345-0170).

PARKING The best place to park in downtown is on the cobblestones between Front Street and the Mississippi River (located between Union and Poplar Avenues). This is a free public parking lot right on the river. There is free on-street parking near Beale Street, while parking lots behind the Beale Street clubs are sometimes free and sometimes cost $3. Metered parking on downtown streets is fairly easy to find, but be sure to check the time limit on the meter. Also be sure to check whether or not you can park in a parking space during rush hour. Downtown parking is also available in municipal and private lots and parking garages.

DRIVING RULES A right turn at a red light is permitted after coming to a full stop, unless posted otherwise, but drivers must first yield to vehicles that have a green light or pedestrians in the walkway. Children under 4 years of age must be in a child's car seat or other approved child restraint when in the car.

Tennessee has a very strict DUI (Driving Under the Influence of alcohol) law, and recently passed a law which states that a person driving under the influence with a child under 12 years of age may be charged with a felony.

ON FOOT

Downtown Memphis is walkable. The rest of the city is not.

FAST FACTS **MEMPHIS**

Airport The Memphis International Airport (tel. 901/922-8000) serves the Memphis area; see "Orientation," earlier in this chapter.

American Express There is no American Express office in Memphis, but their representative is American and International Travel Services, with five local offices. Two of those offices are at 8 S. Third St. (tel. 525-0151) and 540 S. Mendenhall Rd. (tel. 628-1595), both open Monday through Friday from 8:30am to 5pm. There is a national number for American Express (tel. toll free 800/528-4800).

Area Code The telephone area code in Memphis is 901.

Babysitters Contact Annie's Nannies (tel. 755-1457 or 365-3655).

Business Hours **Banks** are generally open Monday through Friday from 8:30am to 5pm, with later hours on Friday. Office hours in Memphis are usually Monday through Friday from 8:30am to 5pm. In general, **stores** located in downtown Memphis are open Monday through Saturday from 10am to 5:30pm. Shops in suburban Memphis malls are generally open Monday through Saturday from 10am to 9pm and on Sunday from 1 to 5 or 6pm. **Bars** are allowed to stay open until 3am, but may close between 1 and 3am.

Car Rentals See "Getting Around," earlier in this chapter.

Climate See "When to Go," in Chapter 11.

Currency See "Preparing for your Trip," in the Appendix.

Currency Exchange   See "Preparing for Your Trip," in the Appendix.

Dentist   If you need a dentist while you're in Memphis, contact Dental Referral Service, Inc. (tel. 523-0526)

Doctor   If you should find yourself in need of a doctor, call the referral service at Baptist Memorial Hospital (tel. 362-8677).

Documents Required   See "Preparing for Your Trip," in the Appendix.

Driving Rules   See "By Car" in "Getting Around," earlier in this chapter.

Drugstores   There are about 30 Walgreen's Pharmacies in the Memphis area (tel. toll free 800/925-4733 for the Walgreen's nearest you). They're usually open Monday through Saturday from 8am to 10pm and on Sunday from 9am to 7pm.

Embassies/Consulates   See "Fast Facts: For the Foreign Traveler," in the Appendix.

Emergencies   For police, fire, or medical emergencies, phone 911.

Eyeglasses   If you have problems with your glasses while in Memphis, contact Memphis Optical, with several locations. The most convenient may be at 4697 Poplar Ave. (tel. 683-8226) and 5393 Elvis Presley Blvd. (tel. 398-9209). They also have a contact lens hotline (tel. 767-0440).

Hairdressers/Barbers   Gould's Styling Salons offer hairstyling for men and women, and have more than 10 locations around Memphis. Three convenient locations are the Park Place Salon, 1229 Park Place Center in the Park Place Mall (tel. 767-3888); the Oak Court Mall at Goldsmith's (tel. 766-2313); and the Hickory Ridge Mall (tel. 795-5591).

Holidays   See "Fast Facts: For the Foreign Traveler," in the Appendix.

Hospitals   The Baptist Memorial Hospital Medical Center is at 899 Madison Ave. (tel. 227-2727), and also has another location in East Memphis at 6019 Walnut Grove Rd. (tel. 766-5000). Saint Francis Hospital is at 5959 Park Ave. (tel. 765-1000).

Hotlines   The "Give Me Memphis" hotline (tel. 901/681-1111; Touch-Tone phone required) offers information on current music, entertainment, arts, sports, and other topics 24 hours a day. The Crisis Intervention number is 274-7477, and the Rape Crisis Center is 528-2161.

Information   See "Orientation," earlier in this chapter.

Laundry/Dry Cleaning   For self-service or drop-off service, Do-Duds Coin Laundries, at 1625 Madison Ave. (tel. 725-7552), is open from 7am to 10pm daily. Other locations are at 4541 Summer Ave. (tel. 683-5211) and 3004 Overton Crossing St. (tel. 358-6424). For dry-cleaning needs call on the Dryve Cleaners, a drive-in cleaner open Monday through Friday from 7am to 7pm and on Saturday from 8am to 5pm, with several locations in East Memphis. One is at 3361 Poplar Ave. (tel. 324-4466) and another is at 5180 Poplar Ave. (tel. 683-6816).

Libraries   The main branch of the Memphis/Shelby County Public Library, at 1850 Peabody Ave. (tel. 725-8800), is open Monday through Thursday from 9am to 9pm, on Friday and Saturday from

9am to 6pm, and on Sunday from 1 to 5pm. There are 21 other branches throughout Memphis.

Liquor Laws   The legal drinking age in Tennessee is 21. Bars are allowed to stay open until 3am every day. Beer can be purchased at a drug, grocery, or package store, but wine and liquor are sold through package stores only.

Lost Property   If you left something at the airport, call the airport police (tel. 922-8298). If you left something on a MATA bus, call 528-2870.

Luggage Storage/Lockers   There is a luggage storage facility at the Greyhound bus station at 203 Union Ave. (tel. 523-2440). Lockers cost $1 for 24 hours.

Mail   For general information about the post office, see "Post Office," below. If you need to receive mail while in Memphis, your best bet is to have it sent to the hotel where you'll be staying. Otherwise, try contacting the local American Express representative (see above), which will hold mail for American Express clients to pick up.

Maps   Maps of Memphis are available at the Visitor's Information Center at 340 Beale St.

Money   See "Preparing for Your Trip," in the Appendix.

Newspapers/Magazines   *The Commercial Appeal* is Memphis's daily and Sunday newspaper. The arts and entertainment weekly is *The Memphis Flyer,* and the monthly city magazine is *Memphis Magazine.*

Photographic Needs   For film processing and photo supplies, visit Wolf Camera and Video at the Oak Court Mall, 4465 Poplar Ave. This is a large photographic dealer and has many locations in the Memphis area.

Police   For police emergencies, phone 911.

Post Office   The main post office is at 555 S. Third St. (tel. 521-2186 or 521-2187). There's a branch in East Memphis at 5821 Park Ave. in the White Station area (tel. 683-8257). Both locations are open Monday through Friday from 8:30am to 5:30pm and on Saturday from 10am to noon. For other branches, check the blue pages in the Memphis phone book.

Radio   Memphis has more than 30 AM and FM radio stations. Some specialize in a particular style of music, including country, gospel, rhythm and blues, and jazz. WEVL at 89.9 FM plays diversified music such as alternative rock, rockabilly, and blues. National Public Radio (NPR) news and talk radio can be heard on 88.9 FM, and NPR classical programming can be heard at 91.1 FM.

Religious Services   For an extensive listing of churches, look under "Churches" in the Memphis yellow pages; they're arranged by locality. Alternatively, you can ask at your hotel for locations and hours of services.

Restrooms   There are restrooms available to the public at hotels, restaurants, and shopping malls.

Safety   Memphis is a large urban city, and all the normal precautions that apply in other cities hold true here. Take extra precaution with your wallet or purse when you're in a crush of people—pickpockets take advantage of crowds. At night, whenever possible, try to park your car in a garage, not on the street. When walking around town at night, stick to the busier streets. Outside of the Beale Street area and the area around the Peabody Hotel, downtown Memphis can be quite deserted at night.

Shoe Repairs   Master Shoe Rebuilders, 72 Union Ave. (tel. 527-0764), is located downtown next to the Peabody Hotel. In East Memphis, try Goldsmith's Department Store, in the Oak Court Mall at Poplar Avenue and Perkins Road (tel. 766-2312).

Taxes   The state sales tax is 8.25%. An additional room tax of 5% on top of the state sales tax brings the total hotel-room tax to a whopping 13.25%.

Taxis   See "Getting Around," earlier in this chapter.

Television   The six local television channels are 3 (CBS), 5 (NBC), 10 (PBS), 13 (ABC), 24 (Fox), and 30 (Independent), as well as Memphis Cablevision.

Time   Tennessee is in the central time zone—central standard time (CST) or central daylight time, depending on the time of year, making it two hours ahead of the West Coast and one hour behind the East Coast.

Tipping   In restaurants, 15% to 20% is the rule if service has been good. Taxi drivers expect about 10%. Airport porters and bellhops should be tipped about $1 per bag, and $1 per night is appropriate for chamber staff.

Transit Information   Call 274-MATA for the MATA bus system route and schedule information.

Weather   For information about the weather, phone the National Weather Service (tel. 756-4141).

3. NETWORKS & RESOURCES

FOR STUDENTS   If you don't already have one, get an official student ID from your school. Such an ID will entitle you to discounts at museums, theaters, and attractions around town.

There are about a dozen major colleges and universities in the Memphis area. The most prominent are **Rhodes College,** 2000 North Parkway (tel. 274-1800), which has a Gothic-style campus located opposite Overton Park; and **Memphis State University,** on Central Avenue (tel. 678-2000), located on a large campus in midtown Memphis.

FOR GAY MEN & LESBIANS   The *Triangle Journal News* (tel. 454-1411) is a monthly newspaper for gay men and lesbians, available at Davis-Kidd Booksellers and public libraries, among other places.

Meristem Bookstore, 930 S. Cooper St. (tel. 276-0282), carries lesbian and gay books and periodicals and is a resource center for the gay community.

The **Memphis Gay & Lesbian Community Center,** 1486 Madison Ave. (tel. 728-GAYS), is staffed by volunteers between 7:30 and 11pm nightly. Call them for descriptions of programs and activities.

FOR WOMEN The **Meristem Bookstore,** 930 S. Cooper St. (tel. 276-0282), is a feminist bookstore and information center for women.

The local **Rape Hotline** is 528-2161.

MEMPHIS ACCOMMODATIONS

Like many other southern cities, Memphis has yet to experience a large-scale move back into its downtown. Consequently, despite continued attempts at urban renewal, downtown Memphis, with the exception of Beale Street, is not a very lively—or attractive—part of the city.

There are only a few downtown hotels, and although a couple of these, including the elegant Peabody Hotel, are among the best in the city, most are far below the standards (and rates) of downtown hotels in other cities. Most of the city's better hotels, whether expensive or not, are to be found in East Memphis, which is more than 20 miles by Interstate from downtown Memphis. Luckily, East Memphis also happens to be where you'll find most of the city's better restaurants. If you're in town on business or with your family, you may prefer to get a room in East Memphis. However, if you're here to sample the Beale Street nightlife, then definitely consider staying downtown. The midtown area is another option, and is convenient to Beale Street, many midtown museums, and the East Memphis restaurants. Fans of Elvis, on the other hand, may want to stay in the Graceland area.

If you're looking to save money on your room, you may want to contact the **Memphis Hotel & Motel Reservation Service** (tel. toll free 800/206-5829), which is operated by Elvis Presley Enterprises (the same folks who run Graceland). This reservations service offers discounts at more than 40 Memphis hotels and motels. There's no charge for this service, and often they can find you a room when everyplace seems to be full. If you're making a last-minute booking, they'll always save you money.

If you show up in town without a room reservation, you may want to make the **Visitor's Information Center** on Beale Street your first stop. At this office, you can pick up coupons that will give you discounts at area hotels. They also have a room-reservation phone line here.

Virtually all hotels now offer no-smoking and handicapped-accessible rooms. Many larger hotels are also adding special rooms for hearing-impaired travelers and occasionally special rooms for women business travelers. When making a reservation, be sure to request the type of room you need.

If you'll be traveling with children, always check into policies on children staying for free. Some hotels let children under 12 stay free, while others set the cutoff age at 18. Still others charge you for the kids, but let them eat for free in the hotel's restaurant.

Almost all hotels offer special corporate and government rates.

However, in this chapter I have listed only the official published rates. You may be able to get the corporate rates simply by asking; it's always worth a try. Most of the more expensive hotels have lower weekend rates, while inexpensive hotels tend to raise their rates slightly on the weekend.

If you get quoted a price that seems exorbitantly high, you might have accidentally stumbled upon a special holiday or event rate. Such rates are usually in effect for major coliseum events and college football games. If this is the case, try scheduling your visit for a different date if possible. Barring this possibility, try calling around to hotels farther out of town, where rates aren't as likely to be affected by special events. In fact, at any time, the farther you get from major business districts the less you're likely to spend on a room. If you don't mind driving for 20 or 30 minutes, you can almost halve the amount you'll need to spend on a room. For more tips on finding the right place to stay at the right price, see the "Frommer's Smart Traveler: Hotels" feature in Chapter 4.

For the purposes of this book, I have placed hotels in the following **rate categories:** "Very Expensive," $125 and up for a double room; "Expensive," $90 to $125; "Moderate," $60 to $90; and "Inexpensive," less than $60. Please keep in mind, however, that the rates listed below do not include taxes, which in Memphis add up to a whopping 13.25% (8.25% sales tax and 5% room tax). In some cases, a hotel would actually be in the next higher rate category when taxes are figured in, and in such cases, I have listed these hotels in the higher category.

1. DOWNTOWN

VERY EXPENSIVE

THE PEABODY MEMPHIS, 149 Union Ave., Memphis, TN 38103. Tel. 901/529-4000, or toll free 800/PEABODY. 438 rms, 16 suites. A/C TV TEL

$ Rates: $115–$185 single; $140–$210 double; from $380 suite. Special packages available. AE, CB, DC, DISC, ER, MC, V. **Parking:** $5 per day.

For more than 120 years, the Peabody has been one of the finest hotels in the South, and today it's still the most luxurious hotel in Memphis. The stately lobby, though seemingly always bustling, is the picture of classic elegance. Marble columns, gilded mezzanine railings, hand-carved and burnished woodwork, and ornate gilded plasterwork on the ceiling give the lobby the air of a palace. However, the lobby's most prominent feature is its Romanesque fountain, which was carved from a single block of travertine marble. It's in this fountain that the famous Peabody ducks while away each day. The Peabody ducks are one of Memphis's biggest attractions and daily attract hundreds of people to the hotel (see Chapter 15 for details).

The elegance continues in the guest rooms, where in the deluxe rooms you'll find classic French styling, maple-burl armoires, and king-size beds. The bathrooms are beautifully designed with marble floors, a circular counter around the sink, and a nice assortment of deluxe toiletries. Up on the 12th floor you'll find the club level, which offers a few more amenities.

Dining/Entertainment: With four restaurants, the Peabody provides plenty of dining options. Chez Philippe, serving classic French cuisine amid palatial surroundings, has long been the best restaurant in Memphis (see Chapter 14 for details). Though Dux is not as sophisticated as Chez Philippe, it's still quite elegant and offers more excellent meals with an emphasis on Cajun food and mesquite broiling (see Chapter 14 for details). Mallards Bar is styled after a traditional oyster bar and serves quite a bit of shellfish, as well as sandwiches and pasta dishes, throughout the day. In the evenings, this is the hotel's main lounge and features live music, including a bit of jazz and blues. Cafe Expresso is a New York–style deli and Viennese pastry shop that evokes the cafés of Europe with its colorful tile floors and café tables. Up on the roof is a patio area known as the Skyway. During the summer months, this rooftop garden café is the site of Sunset Serenades, which feature live blues, jazz, rock, pop, and R&B music. Cover charge for these shows is $4 to $6, and a buffet meal is available. The Skyway is also the site of the hotel's Sunday brunch, which costs $16.95 for adults and $12.95 for children. Brunch is held from 10:30am to 3pm.

Services: Concierge, 24-hour room service, massage, valet/laundry service, shoeshine stand.

Facilities: Down in the basement is a complete athletic facility with a very elegant pool flanked by Roman columns. Other facilities include a steam room, sauna, and exercise room. Also in the hotel you'll find several shops and a beauty salon.

EXPENSIVE

HOLIDAY INN CROWNE PLAZA, 250 N. Main St., Memphis, TN 38103. Tel. 901/527-7300, or toll free 800/ HOLIDAY. Fax 901/526-1561. 403 rms, 10 suites. A/C TV TEL
$ Rates: $107 single or double; $250–$400 suite. AE, CB, DC, DISC, JCB, MC, V. **Parking:** Free.

Located at the north end of downtown, at the end of the Main Street trolley line, the 18-floor Holiday Inn Crowne Plaza is primarily a convention hotel. The grand lobby is built on a scale that reflects the size of the adjacent Cook Convention Center. Soaring ceilings, travertine marble floors, Oriental-motif carpets, and numerous seating areas provide plenty of spaces for private conversations.

My favorite rooms here are the corner rooms, which have angled walls that give the rooms a bit more character. However, the standard king rooms are also good bets. Both these types of rooms have sofas and plenty of room to move around. The top two floors are the hotel's concierge levels and offer such amenities as complimentary breakfast and afternoon hors d'oeuvres and cocktails, hairdryers and mini-refrigerators, and complimentary magazines and morning papers.

Dining/Entertainment: The Bistro, serving American and international fare, is the hotel's main restaurant. Located to one side

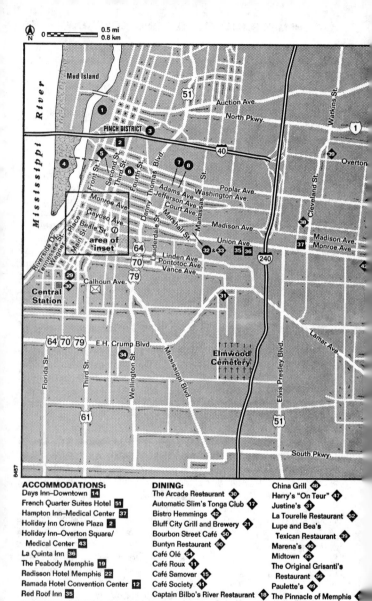

of the lobby, it's a casual sort of place. Breakfasts and coffee are served in the small Coffee Café. There's a small bar set up beside a fountain in one corner of the lobby, and also a larger, livelier lobby lounge. In yet another area of the lobby, up a few steps and overlooking a small garden, you'll find a piano bar where a limited menu is served.

Services: Room service, concierge, complimentary downtown shuttle, valet/laundry service.

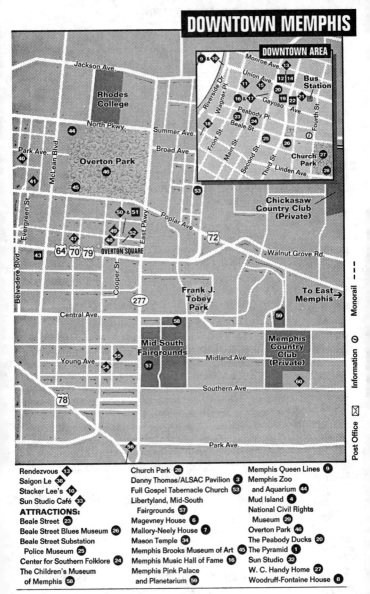

DOWNTOWN MEMPHIS

DOWNTOWN AREA

Rendezvous **13**	Church Park **28**
Saigon Le **38**	Danny Thomas/ALSAC Pavilion **3**
Stacker Lee's **10**	Full Gospel Tabernacle Church **53**
Sun Studio Café **33**	Libertyland, Mid-South
ATTRACTIONS:	Fairgrounds **57**
Beale Street **23**	Magevney House **6**
Beale Street Blues Museum **26**	Mallory-Neely House **7**
Beale Street Substation	Mason Temple **34**
Police Museum **25**	Memphis Brooks Museum of Art **45**
Center for Southern Folklore **24**	Memphis Music Hall of Fame **16**
The Children's Museum	Memphis Pink Palace
of Memphis **58**	and Planetarium **59**

Memphis Queen Lines **9**
Memphis Zoo
and Aquarium **44**
Mud Island **4**
National Civil Rights
Museum **29**
Overton Park **46**
The Peabody Ducks **20**
The Pyramid **1**
Sun Studio **32**
W. C. Handy Home **27**
Woodruff-Fontaine House **8**

Facilities: Large indoor pool (housed in a sunny glass-walled room that also includes an exercise area, hot tub, and sauna), gift shop, flower shop.

RADISSON HOTEL MEMPHIS, 185 Union Ave., Memphis, TN 38103. Tel. 901/528-1800, or toll free 800/333-3333. Fax 901/526-3226. 245 rms, 6 suites. A/C TV TEL

$ Rates: $95 single; $105 double; $135–$220 suite. AE, CB, DC, DISC, MC, V. **Parking:** $4 per day.

Located across the street from the Peabody, the Radisson is also housed in a restored building. In this case, the restoration included a modernization of the lobby's appearance, and today a seven-story atrium is filled with modern furnishings, a fountain, and live trees. However, the focal point of the lobby is the facade of a historic building that once stood on this site. The brick facade serves as a frame for the lounge.

Regular rooms are large and have modern furnishings and standard size bathrooms. However, if you're willing to spend a bit more money, you can opt for one of the spacious corner rooms. These rooms have three walls of windows, marble-topped coffee tables, and big bathrooms with two sinks. The king resort rooms are also good choices if you like space and convenience.

Dining/Entertainment: The Veranda Restaurant, with its white chairs and yellow walls, is a bright and cheerful place with a summery, garden feel. The menu features many southern favorites. In the gift shop you'll find an old-fashioned ice-cream parlor. Behind the historic building facade in the lobby is the Lobby Bar, a quiet place for a drink at the end of the day.

Services: Room service, complimentary airport shuttle.

Facilities: Outdoor pool, hot tub, sauna, small exercise room, gift shop.

MODERATE

RAMADA HOTEL CONVENTION CENTER, 160 Union Ave., Memphis, TN 38103. Tel. 901/525-5491, or toll free 800/2-RAMADA. Fax 901/525-5491, ext. 2322. 186 rms, 5 suites. A/C TV TEL
$ Rates: $58–$90 single; $68–$120 double; $135–$200 suite. AE, CB, DC, DISC, MC, V. **Parking:** Free.

This downtown Ramada, across the street from the Peabody, could definitely do with a renovation, but if you can overlook the soiled carpets in the halls, you'll find that the rooms are generally acceptable. The guest rooms, though not large, do have big windows and feature a bit of Asian styling in their decor.

Dining/Entertainment: Seasons on Broadway restaurant serves southern favorites such as catfish and fried chicken.

Services: Room service.

Facilities: Swimming pool.

INEXPENSIVE

BEST WESTERN RIVERBLUFF INN, 340 W. Illinois Ave., Memphis, TN 38106. Tel. 901/948-9005, or toll free 800/354-2604 or 800/528-1234. Fax 901/946-5716. 99 rms. A/C TV TEL
$ Rates: $42–$62 single or double. AE, CB, DC, DISC, MC, V. **Parking:** Free.

Though it's a short drive from the heart of downtown Memphis, this Best Western is the best choice in budget accommodations downtown. Located on a grassy bluff overlooking the Mississippi River, the older motel is adjacent to both a park with an old Indian mound and the National Ornamental Metal Museum. Guest rooms are large, have walls of windows, and were all recently redecorated. A rooftop restaurant offers views of the river to accompany inexpensive southern fare, and there's an outdoor pool as well. You'll find the motel adjacent to the Memphis-Arkansas Bridge at Exit 12-C off I-55.

DAYS INN–DOWNTOWN, 164 Union Ave., Memphis, TN 38103. Tel. 901/527-4100, or toll free 800/325-2525. Fax 901/527-6091. 106 rms. A/C TV TEL
$ Rates: $40–$45 single; $45–$65 double. AE, CB, DC, DISC, MC, V. **Parking:** $2.50 per day.

Located across the street from the Peabody Hotel, the Days Inn is downtown's most convenient budget lodging. The big, open lobby is absolutely empty, except for a little fountain over in one corner, but there's a restaurant off to the side. Guest rooms are a bit small and windows are small, so there isn't much sunlight, but if you plan to spend most of your time away from the room, you shouldn't notice these shortcomings. The proximity to Beale Street is the main appeal of this hotel, and guests tend to be young and accustomed to roughing it.

2. MIDTOWN

EXPENSIVE

FRENCH QUARTER SUITES HOTEL, 2144 Madison Ave., Memphis, TN 38104. Tel. 901/728-4000, or toll free 800/843-0353. Fax 901/278-1262. 105 suites. A/C TV TEL
$ Rates (including buffet breakfast): $95–$130 suite for one or two people. AE, CB, DC, DISC, MC, V. **Parking:** Free.

Located right in Overton Square, one of Memphis's entertainment districts, the French Quarter Suites Hotel draws on New Orleans for its architectural theme. The exterior of the building displays a characteristically French styling, while inside, a central atrium is surrounded by ornate wrought-iron railings in the style of the Big Easy's famous entertainment district.

All the rooms are furnished in a style befitting French New Orleans. There are half-canopied king-size beds in some rooms, and all the rooms have high ceilings and overhead fans. Double whirlpool tubs make the hotel popular with honeymooners. Many rooms have French doors opening onto private balconies.

Dining/Entertainment: The atrium lobby, with its gazebo bar, doubles as the hotel's lounge and features live jazz or Top-40 music Wednesday through Saturday night. Tucked in behind the gazebo is the Bourbon St. Café, open for three meals a day, including Sunday brunch, and serving a mixture of French and Cajun cuisines.

Services: Room service, valet/laundry service, complimentary newspaper, in-room coffee, and evening social hour.

Facilities: Outdoor pool, exercise room.

MODERATE

HOLIDAY INN–OVERTON SQUARE/MEDICAL CENTER, 1837 Union Ave., Memphis, TN 38104. Tel. 901/278-4100, or toll free 800/HOLIDAY. Fax 901/272-3810. 174 rms. A/C TV TEL

$ Rates: $65–$82 single; $75–$92 double. AE, CB, DC, DISC, MC, V. **Parking:** Free.

Though not as new or as well maintained as the East Memphis Holiday Inns, this midtown lodging is a good moderately priced choice if you're here on vacation and want to be close to both museums and nightclubs. You'll find the hotel at the corner of Union Avenue and McLean Boulevard. Guest rooms are pretty standard, with darker tones and older furnishings. Try to get a room on an upper floor so you can enjoy the views of the city at night.

Dining/Entertainment: The hotel plays up Memphis's rock 'n' roll history with lots of Elvis memorabilia in its Bluff City Diner and Bar, which is done in a combination of art deco and '50s-diner styling. The menu is suitably traditional with moderate prices.

Services: Room service, valet/laundry service, airport shuttle.
Facilities: Outdoor pool, exercise room.

INEXPENSIVE

HAMPTON INN–MEDICAL CENTER, 1180 Union Ave., Memphis, TN 38104. Tel. 901/276-1175, or toll free 800/HAMPTON. Fax 901/276-4261. 126 rms. A/C TV TEL

$ Rates (including continental breakfast): $43–$52 single; $49–$58 double. AE, CB, DC, DISC, MC, V. **Parking:** Free.

This Hampton Inn, right in the heart of the Memphis Medical Center area, is one of the most reliable choices you'll find this close to downtown and Beale Street. Though the guest rooms aren't too large, they are clean and comfortable. There's also a small outdoor pool.

LA QUINTA INN, 42 S. Camilla St., Memphis, TN 38104-3102. Tel. 901/526-1050, or toll free 800/531-5900. Fax 901/525-3219. 130 rms, 2 suites. A/C TV TEL

$ Rates (including continental breakfast): $43–$46 single; $47–$52 double; $62–$65 suite. AE, CB, DC, DISC, MC, V. **Parking:** Free.

S Southwestern styling may seem out of place in Memphis, but this La Quinta Inn is still a very comfortable lodging choice. The rooms are fairly large, and in the king rooms you'll get plenty of space, a recliner, and two phones. In the summer months you can relax in the outdoor pool. You'll find the motel just west of I-240 between Union and Madison Avenues.

RED ROOF INN–MEDICAL CENTER, 210 S. Pauline St., Memphis, TN 38104. Tel. 901/528-0650, or toll free 800/THE-ROOF. Fax 901/528-0659. 120 rms.

$ Rates: $32–$41 single; $38–$46 double. AE, CB, DC, DISC, MC, V. **Parking:** Free.

Red Roof Inns are very basic, no-frills motels. The three-floor motel has no elevator, so if you have trouble climbing stairs, be sure to request a ground-floor room. If you don't need a swimming pool, this motel will save you $10 or so over nearby motels that do have pools.

3. EAST MEMPHIS

VERY EXPENSIVE

ADAM'S MARK HOTEL, 939 Ridge Lake Blvd., Memphis, TN 38120. Tel. 901/684-6664, or toll free 800/444-ADAM. Fax 901/762-7411. 379 rms, 13 suites. A/C TV TEL

$ Rates: $125–$145 single; $135–$155 double; $195–$445 suite. Weekend and special packages available. AE, CB, DC, DISC, MC, V. **Parking:** Free.

The Adam's Mark Hotel, the most dramatic hotel in Memphis, is located just north of Poplar Avenue on the west side of I-240 (turn left at the bottom of the hill and go under the bridge). With its column of glass rising straight out of a semicircular pond, the Adam's Mark is impossible to miss. With the largest ballroom of any East Memphis hotel, the Adam's Mark is popular for conferences and conventions, but it's also a pleasant place to stay if you're here on vacation.

Because this building is circular, most of the guest rooms are wedge-shaped, which makes them attractively different from most hotel rooms. Imitation rosewood-and-ebony armoires and desks, combined with rattan chairs give the guest rooms a hint of Asian styling. Travertine floors and telephones in the bathrooms and a separate dressing room are features likely to be appreciated by both business travelers and vacationing families. The club-level rooms include continental breakfast, evening hors d'oeuvres, and access to a special lounge.

Dining/Entertainment: Down one level below the lobby (right at pond level) is the entertaining Bravo! Ristorante, which features Italian meals and singing waiters and waitresses who perform both opera and Broadway show tunes. Just off the main lobby is the large Satchmo's Lounge, which is marked by a bronze statue of old Satchmo (Louis Armstrong) himself. There is live jazz music here Tuesday through Saturday night. Also just off the lobby is a smaller sports bar.

Services: Room service, valet/laundry service, secretarial service, complimentary airport shuttle, express and video check-out.

Facilities: Outdoor pool, exercise room, gift shop.

EXPENSIVE

EAST MEMPHIS HILTON, 5069 Sanderlin Ave., Memphis, TN 38117. Tel. 901/767-6666, or toll free 800/HILTONS. Fax 901/767-6666, ext 167. 265 rms, 7 suites. A/C TV TEL

$ Rates: $89 single; $99 double; $109–$230 suite. Weekend specials available. AE, CB, DC, DISC, MC, V. **Parking:** Free.

Located 1½ miles west of I-240 just off Poplar Avenue at Mendenhall Road, the East Memphis Hilton is near several shopping malls and some very good restaurants.

Most rooms here are designed with the business traveler in mind and have two phones, radio/television speakers in the bathrooms, and large desks. Other features include small refrigerators and large windows. With their angled walls, the king rooms have the most distinctive styling and will appeal to anyone who's tired of identical hotel rooms.

Dining/Entertainment: With its brass rails and potted plants, the Sanderlin St. Café and Lounge is a combination of a fern bar and a country club restaurant. The atmosphere is, however, strictly casual, and the menu features moderately priced American fare.

Services: Room service, valet/laundry service.

Facilities: The indoor/outdoor pool is partially enclosed in a bright sun room filled with tropical plants. You'll also find a hot tub and tiny exercise room with only two machines.

EMBASSY SUITES, 1022 S. Shady Grove Rd., Memphis, TN 38120. Tel. 901/684-1777, or toll free 800/EMBASSY. Fax 901/685-8185. 220 suites. A/C TV TEL

$ Rates (including full breakfast): $99–$139 suite for one or two people. AE, CB, DC, DISC, MC, V. **Parking:** Free.

The lobby of this modern atrium hotel looks more like a botanical conservatory than a hotel lobby. There are tropical plants all around and a meandering stream, complete with waterfall, little beach, and giant goldfish. Not to be upstaged by the Peabody, this Embassy Suites even has a couple of resident ducks floating on the lobby stream.

All the guest rooms here are spacious two-room suites that have kitchenettes, dining tables, two televisions, two phones, and sofa beds.

Dining/Entertainment: Note that the rates here include a complete, cooked-to-order breakfast in the atrium dining area. In the evening there's a complimentary two-hour manager's reception featuring free drinks. There is also a moderately priced Italian restaurant serving lunch and dinner.

Services: Room service, valet/laundry service, airport transportation.

Facilities: Indoor pool, hot tub, sauna, exercise room with a good assortment of machines, gift shop.

HOLIDAY INN MEMPHIS EAST, 5795 Poplar Ave., Memphis, TN 38119. Tel. 901/682-7881, or toll free 800/833-4463. Fax 901/682-7881. 244 rms, 4 suites. A/C TV TEL

$ Rates: $67–$98 single or double; $240–$340 suite. AE, CB, DC, ER, JCB, DISC, MC, V. **Parking:** Free.

Located right at the interchange of I-240 and Poplar Avenue, the Holiday Inn Memphis East is convenient both to east-side businesses and to the Interstate when you're ready to head downtown. The lobby here is small and informal, but there is an attractive corner

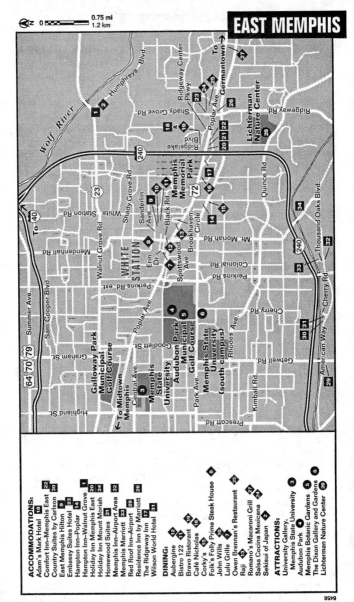

0.75 mi
1.2 km

ACCOMMODATIONS:
Adam's Mark Hotel 18
Comfort Inn-Memphis East 22
Country Suites by Carlson 30
East Memphis Hilton 9
Embassy Suites Hotel 23
Hampton Inn-Poplar 1
Hampton Inn-Walnut Grove 20
Holiday Inn Memphis East 34
Holiday Inn Mount Moriah 32
Homewood Suites 33
Memphis Inn-Airport Area 33
Memphis Marriott 29
Red Roof Inn-Airport 26
The Ridgeway Inn 17
Wilson World Hotel 31

DINING:
Aubergine 12
Bistro 122 19
Bravo Ristorante 9
Café Nicholas 15
Corky's 13
Folk's Folly Prime Steak House 9
John Wills 10
Lulu Grille 16
Owen Brennan's Restaurant 28
Raji 27
Romano's Macaroni Grill 24
Salsa Cocina Mexicana 2
Sekisui of Japan 11

ATTRACTIONS:
University Gallery,
 Memphis State University 3
Audubon Park 4
Memphis Botanic Gardens 5
The Dixon Gallery and Gardens 6
Lichterman Nature Center 26

6458

that's enclosed by a greenhouse wall overlooking a glass-block fountain.

When I last visited this hotel, it was undergoing a complete renovation of its guest rooms. When you check in, you should find attractively furnished modern rooms with new carpets and paint. There are special rooms for women business travelers, and in all the rooms you'll find coffee makers and clock radios.

Dining/Entertainment: In the Monterey Grill there are daily lunch specials as well as a Sunday champagne brunch and a Saturday-evening southern buffet dinner. Zeiggy's Lounge features weekday happy hour specials, DJ dance music on Friday and Saturday, and live happy hour jazz on Sunday.

Services: Room service, valet/laundry service, complimentary airport shuttle.

Facilities: The indoor pool here is the largest and most attractive in this neighborhood, though the adjacent outdoor sun deck is extremely noisy. You also have access to a hot tub, sauna, exercise room, and gift shop.

HOMEWOOD SUITES, 5811 Poplar Ave., Memphis, TN 38119. Tel. 901/763-0500, or toll free 800/CALL-HOME. Fax 901/763-0132. 145 suites. A/C TV TEL

$ Rates (including continental breakfast): $89–$149 suite for one or two people weekdays, $69–$130 weekends. AE, CB, DC, DISC, MC, V. **Parking:** Free.

Located at the interchange of Poplar Avenue and I-240, the Homewood Suites offers some of the most attractive and spacious accommodations in Memphis. The suites, which are arranged around an attractively landscaped central courtyard with a swimming pool and basketball court, resemble an apartment complex rather than a hotel. The beautiful and comfortable lobby has the feel of a mountain lodge and features pine furnishings, lots of natural wood trim, and attractive decorations and artwork.

Early American styling, with pine furnishings, set the tone in the suites. A comfortable living room features a wood-burning fireplace, while in the bedroom you'll find a contemporary wrought-iron bed and overhead fan. There are two televisions (and a VCR) in every suite, as well as full kitchens and big bathrooms with plenty of counter space.

Dining/Entertainment: Though there's no restaurant on the premises, you can pick up microwaveable meals in the hotel's convenience shop.

Services: Complimentary airport and local shopping shuttle, morning newspaper, and evening social hour; voice mail system, valet/laundry service.

Facilities: Outdoor pool, hot tub, basketball court, exercise room, convenience store, executive center.

RESIDENCE INN BY MARRIOTT, 6141 Poplar Pike, Memphis, TN 38119. Tel. 901/685-9595, or toll free 800/331-3131. 105 suites. A/C TV TEL

$ Rates (including continental breakfast): $84–$104 suite for one or two people. AE, CB, DC, DISC, MC, V. **Parking:** Free.

Though it's not as attractively designed as the nearby Homewood Suites, the Residence Inn offers many of the same conveniences and amenities.

Some suites have rooms that open onto the lobby, while others have tiny triangular balconies and windows to the outside. You can choose a studio or two-bedroom/two-bath suite. Whichever size suite you choose, you'll have plenty of space, including a full kitchen and perhaps a fireplace. The two-bedroom suites have loft sleeping areas.

Dining/Entertainment: There are no restaurants on the premises, but within 100 yards there are three excellent restaurants.

Services: Room service, passes to a local health club, complimentary newspaper and evening hospitality hour, grocery-shopping service.

Facilities: Outdoor pool, sports court, hot tub.

THE RIDGEWAY INN, 5679 Poplar Ave., Memphis, TN 38119. Tel. 901/766-4000, or toll free 800/822-3360. Fax 901/763-1857. 155 rms, 3 suites. A/C TV TEL

$ Rates: $119 single or double; $125–$175 suite. Weekend rates available. AE, CB, DC, DISC, ER, MC, V. **Parking:** Free.

You'll find the Ridgeway Inn just west of I-240 at the Poplar Avenue exit. Operated by the same company that runs the Peabody, this hotel offers comparable accommodations in a modern East Memphis hotel. With its European styling, the small lobby sets a classically sophisticated tone for this popular hostelry, which is a favorite of business travelers.

Guest rooms are comfortable and designed for the business traveler. In the king rooms you'll find a desk for working and a couch for relaxing. Furnishings are primarily reproductions of Early American pieces. Concierge-level rooms include a TV and hairdryer in the bathroom, continental breakfast, afternoon hors d'oeuvres, and evening turn-down service.

Dining/Entertainment: Terra-cotta floor tiles and gray-and-white checkerboard chairs and banquettes give Café Expresso a traditional Italian café look. However, the menu features deli sandwiches, continental dishes, and a wide selection of pastries. The adjacent Lobby Bar has a country-club feel that's more in keeping with the classic decor of the rest of the hotel.

Services: Room service, valet/laundry service.

Facilities: The outdoor pool here is, unfortunately, right beside busy Poplar Avenue and is usually too noisy to be at all relaxing. There's also an exercise room.

MODERATE

COMFORT INN–MEMPHIS EAST, 5877 Poplar Ave., Memphis, TN 38119. Tel. 901/767-6300, or toll free 800/221-2222. Fax 901/767-0098. 126 rms. A/C TV TEL

$ Rates (including continental breakfast): $49–$59 single; $54–$64 double. AE, CB, DC, DISC, ER, JCB, MC, V. **Parking:** Free.

Located right at the interchange of I-240 and Poplar Avenue, the Comfort Inn is an economical choice in this upscale East Memphis district. Guest rooms are fairly large and feature modern oak furniture and big windows.

Dining/Entertainment: George & David's is a casual and moderately priced restaurant serving American and southern dishes.

Facilities: Outdoor pool, small exercise room.

HAMPTON INN–POPLAR, 5320 Poplar Ave., Memphis, TN 38117. Tel. 901/683-8500, or toll free 800/HAMPTON. Fax 901/763-4970. 126 rms. A/C TV TEL

$ Rates (including continental breakfast): $54–$59 single; $64–$69 double. AE, CB, DC, DISC, MC, V. **Parking:** Free.

Located about a mile west of I-240 on Poplar Avenue, this Hampton Inn offers the sort of dependable accommodations that have made Hampton Inns so popular. The king deluxe rooms, which come with king-size beds, easy chairs, and a desk, are the best choice for business travelers, while the king study rooms, with a sofa bed, make a good choice for leisure travelers and families.

Facilities: The outdoor pool is surrounded by attractively landscaped gardens and is set back a bit from the street so it isn't too noisy.

HAMPTON INN–WALNUT GROVE, 33 Humphreys Center Dr., Memphis, TN 38120. Tel. 901/747-3700, or toll free 800/HAMPTON. Fax 901/747-3800. 120 rms. A/C TV TEL
$ Rates: $49–$59 single; $57–$67 double. AE, CB, DC, DISC, MC, V. **Parking:** Free.

Almost identical in design and level of comfort to the Hampton Inn on Poplar Avenue, this lodging is more convenient to I-240 and many newer East Memphis businesses. One of the city's best Japanese restaurants is in a shopping center adjacent to this hotel.

Facilities: Outdoor pool.

HOLIDAY INN–MOUNT MORIAH, 2490 Mt. Moriah Rd., Memphis, TN 38115. Tel. 901/362-8010, or toll free 800/HOLIDAY. Fax 901/368-0452. 198 rms. A/C TV TEL
$ Rates: $54–$79 single or double. AE, CB, DC, DISC, MC, V. **Parking:** Free.

Formerly a Ramada Inn, this East Memphis hotel is near one of the city's booming business and entertainment districts. There are several shopping malls, nightclubs, excellent restaurants, and movie theaters nearby. The guest rooms are slightly larger than average and are very clean and new. There are large TVs in all the rooms, as well as clock radios.

Dining/Entertainment: Rio Loco, as you might guess, serves Mexican food and the adjacent lounge has a small dance floor.

Services: Room service, complimentary airport shuttle.

Facilities: Outdoor pool; plans are under way for adding an exercise room.

INEXPENSIVE

LA QUINTA INN, 6068 Macon Cove Rd., Memphis, TN 38134. Tel. 901/382-2323, or toll free 800/531-5900. Fax 901/385-1941. 130 rms. A/C TV TEL
$ Rates (including continental breakfast): $47–$54 single; $53–$60 double. AE, CB, DC, DISC, MC, V. **Parking:** Free.

With their southwestern styling, La Quinta Inns look pleasantly out of place wherever they're found. This particular inn is east of Memphis at Exit 12 off I-40. This exit is a sort of budget hotel smörgåsbord, with more than half a dozen modern chains from which to choose. Though the guest rooms are fairly standard and lack the southwestern decor of the rest of the motel, they're quite comfortable. There's an outdoor pool.

MEMPHIS INN, 6050 Macon Cove Rd., Memphis, TN 38138. Tel. 901/373-9898. 105 rms. A/C TV TEL
$ **Rates:** $28–$32 single; $34–$38 double. AE, CB, DC, DISC, MC, V. **Parking:** Free.

S Though this motel is older than others at I-40's Exit 12, it does have a distinctive medieval styling (fake half-timbering and stone walls) that makes it an interesting choice. Some rooms have kitchenettes. Its other distinction is that it's the cheapest motel around that has a swimming pool. There's another Memphis Inn over near the airport.

RED ROOF INN, 6055 Shelby Oaks Dr., Memphis, TN 38134. Tel. 901/388-6111, or toll free 800/THE-ROOF. Fax 901/388-6157. 109 rms. A/C TV TEL
$ **Rates:** $31–$42 single; $37–$49 double. AE, CB, DC, DISC, MC, V. **Parking:** Free.
"No frills" means low rates at Red Roof Inns, and that's just what you'll get at this motel, which is just north of I-40 at Exit 12. Bathrooms are small here, but the rooms have desks, small tables, and plenty of counter space.

SUPER 8 MOTEL, 6015 Macon Cove Rd., Memphis, TN 38134. Tel. 901/373-4888, or toll free 800/800-8000. Fax 901/373-4888, ext. 305. 70 rms. A/C TV TEL
$ **Rates:** $36–$40 single; $43–$52 double. AE, CB, DC, DISC, MC, V. **Parking:** Free.
Super 8 motels are some of the most reliable budget motels in the country and this newer motel off I-40 at Exit 12 is no exception. Rooms are comfortable and have as much space as you're likely to need, but there are no frills.

4. THE AIRPORT & GRACELAND AREAS

VERY EXPENSIVE

MEMPHIS MARRIOTT, 2625 Thousand Oaks Blvd., Memphis, TN 38118. Tel. 901/362-6200, or toll free 800/627-3587. Fax 901/360-8836. 320 rms, 4 suites. A/C TV TEL
$ **Rates:** $129–$131 single; $146–$152 double; $165–$275 suite. Weekend specials available. AE, CB, DC, DISC, MC, V. **Parking:** Free.
Located just off I-240 about midway between the airport and the Poplar Avenue exit for East Memphis, this Marriott is just down the street from the Mall of Memphis, the largest shopping mall in the city. The large lobby, with its travertine and red marble floor, overlooks a courtyard garden.

Though most of the rooms are a bit smaller than you would hope, the king rooms are well laid out and have large work desks with phones, plus a second phone by the bed. Comfortable chairs and sofas mean that you won't spend your leisure time sitting on the bed.

Try for a higher floor to get a good view of the surrounding countryside. Special touches include four pillows on the beds and evening chocolates.

Dining/Entertainment: In the back of the lobby there's an elegant piano bar. The dark-wood bar and wall of wine to one side lend this lounge a classic air. Stacy's Grille, which is to one side of the lobby lounge, features a gardenlike decor with trellises and lots of potted plants. The menu focuses on southern favorites and some New American dishes. For evening entertainment there's Coco Locos, a tropical-theme dance lounge.

Services: Room service, complimentary airport shuttle, valet/laundry service.

Facilities: Indoor and outdoor pools, hot tub, sauna, exercise room.

EXPENSIVE

SHERATON INN MEMPHIS AIRPORT, 2411 Winchester Rd., Memphis, TN 38116. Tel. 901/332-2370, or toll free 800/365-2370. Fax 901/398-4085. 211 rms. A/C TV TEL

$ Rates: $72 single; $82 double; $59 single or double on weekends. AE, CB, DC, DISC, ER, MC, V. **Parking:** Free.

If you're in town on a quick business meeting or plan to arrive late at night, this Sheraton on the grounds of the airport is a good choice. All the rooms are well soundproofed so you don't have to worry about losing sleep because of the noise of jets. The rooms themselves are not very memorable, but many are set up for business travelers with a desk and comfortable chair.

Dining/Entertainment: Sports fans will be right at home in Parachutes, the hotel's small sports bar. In Delphine's a casually formal atmosphere prevails. Steaks and traditional American fare are the focus of the menu.

Services: Room service, valet/laundry service, complimentary airport shuttle.

Facilities: The outdoor pool is set in a pleasant (though sometimes noisy) sunken garden area between two wings of the hotel.

 FROMMER'S COOL FOR KIDS: HOTELS

Embassy Suites (see p. 172) The indoor pool and gardenlike atrium lobby provide a place for the kids to play even on rainy or cold days, and the two-room suites give parents a private room of their own.

Wilson World Hotel (see p. 180) The pool in the middle of the lobby is a hit with kids, as is the games room—no problem keeping the little ones entertained.

Two tennis courts and an exercise room make this one of the most resortlike hotels in town.

MODERATE

COUNTRY SUITES BY CARLSON, 4300 American Way, Memphis, TN 38118. Tel. 901/366-9333, or toll free 800/456-4000. Fax 901/366-7835. 120 suites. A/C TV TEL

$ Rates (including continental breakfast): $59–$79 suite for one or two people. AE, CB, DC, DISC, MC, V. **Parking:** Free.

A cheery, tiled lobby greets you as you step through the entrance of this all-suites hotel near the airport. Studios and one- and two-bedroom suites are available, and all have kitchens with microwave ovens and coffee makers. If you opt for a one-bedroom suite, you'll get a large kitchen, as well as a separate bedroom.

Dining/Entertainment: The complimentary breakfast is served in a bright sun room overlooking the pool area. Every Wednesday evening there's a cookout in the courtyard, but otherwise there's no restaurant on the premises.

Services: Complimentary evening social hour, fax and copy service, shopping service.

Facilities: A square pool, children's pool, and hot tub fill the hotel's courtyard and look particularly inviting at night. There's also a coin laundry.

MEMPHIS AIRPORT HOTEL & EXECUTIVE CONFERENCE CENTER, 2240 Democrat Rd., Memphis, TN 38132. Tel. 901/332-1130. Fax 901/398-5206. 380 rms, 8 suites. A/C TV TEL

$ Rates: $69 single; $74 double; $169–$275 suite. AE, CB, DC, DISC, MC, V. **Parking:** Free.

Step through the doors of this large hotel only minutes from the airport and you enter a vast, cavernous, and dimly lit lobby. With its glowing stained-glass gazebo, turned wooden railings, tiered fountains, and hardwood floors, it's the most unusual lobby in Memphis. The rooms themselves are rather spartan and dark, but are otherwise quite acceptable and have bright-red bathroom counters and two sinks. I prefer the king rooms, which have sofa beds and a bit more space to move around in.

Dining/Entertainment: Adding to the old Beale Street feel of the lobby is a big wooden bar and a couple of pool tables. Down by the pool is a restaurant serving moderately priced meals.

Services: Room service, complimentary airport shuttle.

Facilities: At the far end of the lobby, and down one level, is an indoor pool that features a four-story wall of stone that trickles water. A small bridge crosses the pool. An outdoor pool provides a sunnier place to swim in the summer months. Near the reception desk is a small room with a few video games. Other facilities include a tennis court and saunas.

RAMADA INN–SOUTHWEST AIRPORT, 1471 E. Brooks Rd., Memphis, TN 38116. Tel. 901/332-3500, or toll free 800/2-RAMADA. Fax 901/346-0017. 250 rms. A/C TV TEL

$ Rates: $50 single; $60 double. AE, CB, DC, DISC, MC, V.
Parking: Free.

Located close to both the airport and Graceland, this is another good bet for Elvis fans on a pilgrimage. Rates are slightly lower than at the Holiday Inn right next door, and the atmosphere is a bit more upscale. The lobby is surprisingly elegant, with a crystal chandelier, some antique furnishings, music-theme wall murals, and arched windows. The guest rooms don't live up to the promise of the lobby, but they're still adequate. Ask for one on the courtyard side of the building.

Dining/Entertainment: Trumpets Restaurant continues the elegant decor of the lobby with more arched windows, brick walls, and lots of polished wood trim. On the weekends, there's live country music at Dad's Place lounge, which is a large place with brick walls and lots of wood and brass. The Oak Room is a much quieter lounge.

Services: Room service, courtesy airport shuttle.

Facilities: There's a large outdoor pool in an attractive garden setting.

WILSON WORLD HOTEL, 2715 Cherry Rd., Memphis, TN 38118. Tel. 901/366-0000, or toll free 800/872-8366. Fax 901/366-6361. 178 rms, 72 suites. A/C TV TEL

$ Rates: $50–$55 single; $55–$60 double; $60–$70 suite. AE, CB, DC, DISC, MC, V. **Parking:** Free.

Though the facade looks rather plain, you'll be surprised at the glitziness of the atrium lobby in this moderately priced hotel. Just inside the front door is a sunken lounge area with a white grand piano on a stage above the bar. Behind this is a swimming pool flanked by two hot tubs. All the guest rooms have wet bars and small refrigerators. The suites are only slightly larger than the standard rooms, so unless you really need two rooms, I'd stick with a less expensive room.

Dining/Entertainment: A large, informal restaurant features live piano music several evenings a week. The meals are simple and the prices moderate. A snack bar provides light meals and lunches. For drinks, there's the sunken lounge by the front door.

Services: Room service, airport shuttle, valet/laundry service.

Facilities: Indoor pool, two hot tubs, exercise room, games room, gift shop, barber, beauty salon.

INEXPENSIVE

DAYS INN AT GRACELAND, 3839 Elvis Presley Blvd., Memphis, TN 38116. Tel. 901/346-5500, or toll free 800/325-2525. 60 rms, 1 suite. A/C TV TEL

$ Rates (including continental breakfast): $45–$60 single; $50–$85 double; $100 suite. AE, CB, DC, DISC, MC, V. **Parking:** Free.

With Graceland right across the street, it's no surprise that Elvis is "the king" at this budget motel. Just watch for the Elvis mural on the side of the building and the neon guitar sign out front, and you'll have found this unusual Days Inn. In the lobby, and on the room TVs, are 'round-the-clock Elvis videos, and there are posters of old Elvis movies on the walls in the guest rooms. Best of all, there's a guitar-shaped outdoor swimming pool.

HAMPTON INN—AIRPORT, 2979 Millbranch Rd., Memphis, TN 38116. Tel. 901/396-2200, or toll free 800/HAMPTON. Fax 901/396-7034. 128 rms. A/C TV TEL

$ Rates (including continental breakfast): $47–$54 single; $53–$60 double. AE, CB, DC, DISC, MC, V. **Parking:** Free.

Hampton Inns have gained a very faithful following because of their reliability and "satisfaction guaranteed" policy. If you aren't satisfied with your stay at a Hampton Inn, you don't have to pay. Rooms here are standard-issue motel modern, but they're always clean. You can choose between a king room that's designed with the business traveler in mind, or a double-queen room that's a good choice for families. There's a swimming pool here and an airport shuttle as well.

MEMPHIS INN, 4879 American Way, Memphis, TN 38118. Tel. 901/794-8300. 108 rms. A/C TV TEL

$ Rates: $38–$39 single or double. AE, CB, DC, DISC, MC, V. **Parking:** Free.

Stone facades and half-timbered walls give this hotel a pseudo-medieval flavor that sets it apart from other budget motels. Furnishings in the rooms are a bit old, but if you're used to budget motels that aren't part of a chain, this place should be fine for you. A bonus is that despite the low room rates, this place does have an outdoor pool. There's another Memphis Inn at Exit 12 off I-40.

RED ROOF INN, 3875 American Way, Memphis, TN 38118. Tel. 901/363-2335, or toll free 800/THE-ROOF. Fax 901/363-2335, ext. 444. 110 rms. A/C TV TEL

$ Rates: $37–$44 single; $43–$50 double. AE, CB, DC, DISC, MC, V. **Parking:** Free.

This economy motel, part of a chain in the eastern and midwestern United States, is about as basic as they come. The rooms are simply furnished and access is along open hallways. There's no elevator in the three-floor motel, so ask for a ground-floor room if you don't want to climb the stairs. You won't find a pool or coffee and doughnuts here, but you won't be paying extra for them either.

WILSON WORLD HOTEL—GRACELAND, 3677 Elvis Presley Blvd., Memphis, TN 38116. Tel. 901/332-1000, or toll free 800/WILSONS. Fax 901/332-2107. 129 rms, 60 suites. A/C TV TEL

$ Rates: $37 single; $42 double; $47–$52 suite. AE, CB, DC, DISC, MC, V. **Parking:** Free.

If your visit to Memphis is a pilgrimage to Graceland, there should be no question as to where to stay. This hotel has a gate right into the Graceland parking lot, with Elvis's home itself right across Elvis Presley Boulevard. In the lobby you'll find a big portrait of "the king," and decor that would fit right in at Graceland. The rooms, which have small refrigerators and microwaves, seem to have seen a few too many Elvis fans, but are generally clean and comfortable. You'll find a tiny indoor pool and a hot tub behind the lobby. There's also free popcorn in the lobby.

CHAPTER 14

MEMPHIS DINING

1. DOWNTOWN
2. MIDTOWN
3. EAST MEMPHIS
• FROMMER'S COOL
   FOR KIDS:
   RESTAURANTS
4. SPECIALTY DINING

Perhaps it's the proximity to New Orleans and the Mississippi Delta that has helped the Memphis restaurant scene develop. In culinary terms the 400 miles to the Big Easy are a mere regional hop, skip, and jump. Consequently, Cajun and Créole food in Memphis restaurants is almost as good as it is down in Paul Prudhomme's hometown. What may come as a bit more of a surprise is that Memphis manages to support several excellent French restaurants. Once again, this may be due to New Orleans's French influences. However, what Memphis can claim as its very own is slow-smoked, pulled-shoulder pork barbecue (see "Food and Drink" in Chapter 10), to which you can add the spicy sauces of your choosing—chili vinegar, hot sauce, whatever. If this doesn't appeal to you, then maybe Memphis's famous ribs will. These are cooked much the same way as the pork shoulder and come dry or wet—that is, with the sauce added by you (dry) or cooked in the sauce (wet).

You'll also find traditional southern and New American restaurants. New Southern restaurants serve contemporary creations using traditional southern ingredients mixed with international influences.

See the "Frommer's Smart Traveler: Restaurants" feature in Chapter 5 for tips on making the most of your dining expenses during your visit down south.

For the following listings I considered a restaurant "Expensive" if a meal without wine or beer would average $25 or more. "Moderate" restaurants serve complete dinners in the $15 to $25 range, and "budget" listings are those where you can get a complete meal for less than $15.

1. DOWNTOWN

EXPENSIVE

CHEZ PHILIPPE, in the Peabody Memphis hotel, 149 Union Ave. Tel. 529-4188.
   Cuisine: CONTEMPORARY FRENCH. **Reservations:** Required.
$ **Prices:** Appetizers $7.50–$14.00; main courses $19.50–$25.00; menu dégustation $29.95 per person. AE, MC, V.
   Open: Dinner only, daily 6–10pm.

★ A table set with a colorful flower arrangement and food ingredients displayed in chafing dishes is the first thing you'll see as you step through the wrought-iron gates into this extremely elegant restaurant in the Peabody Hotel. Lacy New Orleans–style metalwork, wide marble columns, and sparkling chandeliers are a dramatic backdrop for red carpeting and green Louis XIV chairs. The dining rooms are on three separate levels, which further adds to the palatial atmosphere at Chez Philippe. A harpist plays soothing melodies as you peruse the menu and the waiters head off to the wine cellar in search of vintage wines.

The menu is every bit the equal of the surroundings and you'll find a mix of contemporary French and New Southern dishes being offered. To start out your meal, you might order an appetizer of eggplant cake with artichokes, tomatoes, and anchovy vinaigrette or, bowing to southern tastebuds, hushpuppies stuffed with shrimp. The appetizers all sound so delicious that it's difficult to get past them to the entree section, but try. Under the main courses you'll find such dishes as breaded lamb medallions with black olives, tomato sauce, and herb-pastry leaves and roasted Maine lobster with marinated catfish, chive, and rosemary sauce.

JUSTINE'S, 919 Coward Place. Tel. 527-3815.

Cuisine: FRENCH. **Reservations:** Recommended.
$ Prices: Appetizers $8–$16; main courses $9–$20. AE, CB, DC, DISC, MC, V.
Open: Dinner only, Tues–Sat 5:30–10pm.

Justine's is the epitome of Memphis tradition and has been at this spot since before the neighborhood went downhill. There's no sign out front (I guess you're expected to be a regular), though the valet parking attendant in the middle of a district of run-down buildings is a dead giveaway. The restaurant is housed in an 1830s mansion that looks much like a small French villa. Wrought-iron gates stand to one side of the entrance and ivy climbs the pink exterior walls. Inside are numerous dining rooms on both floors and antiques seemingly everywhere. Crystal chandeliers and original works of art complete the elegant decor.

You can start your meal with a traditional French appetizer such as escargots à la bourguignonne (snails in garlic butter) or vichyssoise soup. Continue with a main dish of truites à la Florentine (trout with spinach) or shrimp, crabmeat, and mushroom casserole and you'll have a classic of French gastronomy. If you make your request in advance, the chef will prepare a rack of lamb for two. Top your dinner off with some cerise jubilees (flamed cherries over vanilla ice cream) or gâteau Alaska flamed with brandy. Voilà! the perfect French dinner.

MODERATE

AUTOMATIC SLIM'S TONGA CLUB, 83 S. Second St. Tel. 525-7948.

Cuisine: SOUTHWESTERN. **Reservations:** Recommended.
$ Prices: Appetizers $2.75–$6.95; main courses $10.95–$18.95. AE, MC, V.

Open: Lunch Mon–Sat 11am–2:30pm; dinner Mon–Thurs 5–10pm, Fri–Sat 5–11pm.

A trip to Automatic Slim's is not just a meal, it's an experience. You might wonder about the name. Well, "Automatic Slim" is from an old blues song, and the Tonga Club was a local teen hangout popular in the early '60s. Artists from New York and Memphis created the Memphian decor (they're credited on the menu) including zebra-print upholstered banquettes, slag-glass wall sconces, and colorfully upholstered bar stools. On the bar are large glass jars in which peaches and mixed fruit are soaking—you can order your vodka drink with some of this fruit-soaked vodka.

Tumbleweeds perched over the door set the scene for some imaginative southwestern cooking that combines surprising ingredients to create fresh tastes. I can assure you that the food is as creative as the atmosphere. The coconut-mango shrimp with pico de gallo and mesquite-grilled cilantro-lime chicken salad were two recent starters that combined some marvelous flavors. For a hearty main dish, try the Caribbean voodoo stew with mussels, shrimp, whitefish, and crab legs served with rice. Freshly squeezed juices and a vegetarian selection are available, and at lunch ask about the purple-plate special.

CAPTAIN BILBO'S RIVER RESTAURANT, 263 Wagner Place. Tel. 526-1966.

Cuisine: SEAFOOD. **Reservations:** Accepted only for parties of eight or more.

$ Prices: Appetizers $2.50–$5.95; main courses $9.95–$22.95. AE, CB, DC, MC, V.

Open: Dinner only, Sun–Thurs 5–10:30pm, Fri–Sat 5–11pm. (Lounge, Sun–Thurs 4:30pm–1am, Fri–Sat 4:30pm–2am.)

I've always been a sucker for big, fun restaurants. Sure they're usually full of tourists and the food isn't always the best, but some experiences just shouldn't be missed. Captain Bilbo's is just such a place. This huge old warehouse overlooking the river has been turned into a reconstruction of an old river wharf. Everywhere you look there are fascinating things hanging from the walls and ceilings. There's also a large lounge that features live rock and country music, dancing, and an oyster bar.

Most of the dishes here are based on old southern recipes, such as oysters Bienville (broiled oysters topped with a butter sauce full of shrimp, mushrooms, and scallions), or red beans and rice with ham and smoked sausage. Fish offerings include jerk grilled catch of the day with pineapple salsa, or catfish Atchafalaya (catfish filets topped with a tangy cream sauce full of crayfish tails).

DUX, in the Peabody Memphis hotel, 149 Union Ave. Tel. 529-4199.

Cuisine: STEAKS/SEAFOOD. **Reservations:** Recommended.

$ Prices: Appetizers $4.95–$8.95; main courses $13.95–$24.95. AE, CB, DC, DISC, MC, V.

Open: Breakfast Mon–Fri 6:30–10:30am, Sat–Sun 6:30–11:30am; lunch Mon–Fri 11:30am–2:30pm, Sat–Sun noon–2:30pm; dinner Sun–Fri 5:30–11pm, Fri–Sat 5:30pm–midnight.

Orchids on the tables, red and black wicker furniture, and large urns give Dux an elegant Asian atmosphere, and pressed-tin ceilings and angled mirrors add more touches of class. Of course there are duck images everywhere, for this restaurant is in the Peabody Hotel. Glance around at the well-polished wine glasses and wine bottles and you might find it hard to resist sampling from the extensive wine list.

When you sit down, delicious foccacia bread arrives in a basket, and if you order an appetizer such as a lobster taco with homemade salsa, smoked chicken quesadillas, or gulf oysters, you'll be on the right track. Many of the steak and seafood dishes on the menu are grilled over wood. When I visited, there was swordfish steak marinated in olive oil and fresh herbs and New York strip steak with melted Maytag bleu cheese, both of which were grilled. Have some warm southern fruit cobbler or chocolate strawberry flan to top off your dining experience.

BUDGET

THE ARCADE RESTAURANT, 540 S. Main St. Tel. 526-5757.

Cuisine: AMERICAN. **Reservations:** Not accepted.

$ Prices: Breakfast $3–$4; lunch $3.50–$6. No credit cards.

Open: Breakfast/lunch daily 7am–3pm.

Established in 1919, the oldest café in Memphis stands as a reminder of the early part of the century when this was a busy neighborhood, bustling with people and commerce. Although this corner is not nearly as lively as it once was, the restaurant is always full of loyal Memphians who stop by for the home-style cooking.

BLUFF CITY GRILL AND BREWERY, 235 Union Ave. Tel. 526-BEER.

Cuisine: NEW AMERICAN. **Reservations:** Not accepted.

$ Prices: Appetizers $3.95–$5.95; main courses $9.95–$14.95. AE, DISC, MC, V.

Open: Daily 11am–1am.

This downtown brewery used to be the Trailways bus station, but has now been remodeled into a cavernous contemporary beer hall with soft artistic lighting, plain wooden booths, and a raised-seating island in the middle. There are usually five beers on tap at any given time. The burgers and sandwiches here are tasty and go well with a pint, as does a reinterpretation of a New Orleans classic, the muffaletta pizza, which is made with olive salad, pepperoni, salami, and mozzarella. A recent menu also included sautéed grouper cakes with white wine and Cajun tartar sauce and jambalaya with vegetables. For dessert, s'mores, those childhood campfire treats, were reincarnated as a torte.

CAFE ROUX, 94 S. Front St. Tel. 525-7689.

Cuisine: CREOLE/CAJUN. **Reservations:** Not accepted, but you can call ahead to get your name at the top of the waiting list.

$ Prices: Appetizers $3.50–$7.50; main courses $5.50–$13.50. AE, DC, DISC, MC, V.

Open: Mon–Thurs 11am–10:30pm; Fri–Sat 11am–11:30pm; brunch Sun 11am–3pm.

Casual and inexpensive, Café Roux serves up good Créole and Cajun food amid surroundings that conjure up visions of the French Quarter in New Orleans. There are wrought-iron railings and battered brick walls. Appetizers such as Cajun popcorn or a "broth" of alligator-tail chili will set you up for something equally fiery to follow. Platters of rich and spicy gumbo chicken filé or catfish Acadian in a creamy crayfish-and-shrimp sauce come with a marinated salad, black-eyed peas, Cajun fried rice, and yam patties. If you have such a mind, a slice of crunchy pecan pie contrasts sweetly with the hot flavors.

There's a second Café Roux at 7209 Winchester Rd. (tel. 755-7689).

CAFE SAMOVAR, 83 Union Ave. Tel. 529-9607.

Cuisine: RUSSIAN. **Reservations:** Not required.
$ Prices: Appetizers $1.95–$7.95; main courses $7.95–$14.95. CB, MC, V.
Open: Lunch Mon–Fri 11am–2pm; dinner Tues–Thurs 5–9pm, Fri–Sat 5–10pm.

Russian immigrants Gregory and Sylvia Sadetsky own and operate this downtown café, which is located on busy Union Avenue. The restaurant is decorated with samovars, a balalaika, Russian dolls, and wall murals with Russian folk themes, but it's the Russian gypsy dancing on the weekends that really puts you in the mood for the Sadetskys' cooking. Zakuski is the appetizer to order. It includes eggplant caviar, lobio, herring, chicken-liver pâté, beet pkali, and marinated mushrooms. If you aren't too hungry, stick with the simple chicken-liver pâté. Russian favorites like golubzi (cabbage leaves stuffed with sweet-and-sour ground beef), Belorussian blinis (crêpes filled with chicken and topped with mushroom sauce), and the well-known piroshky (a pastry filled with chicken and vegetables) are all hearty dishes that won't leave you hungry in an hour.

STACKER LEE'S, 65 Riverside Dr. Tel. 523-8968.

Cuisine: CREOLE/SEAFOOD. **Reservations:** Not required.
$ Prices: Appetizers $4.75–$12.95; main courses $9.75–$15.75. AE, DC, DISC, MC, V.
Open: Mon–Thurs 11am–1am, Fri–Sat 11am–3am, Sun noon–1am.

Stacker Lee was a wild riverboat captain celebrated in the famous blues tune "Stagolee," and now he has a restaurant named after him as well. Located at the cobblestones at the foot of Union Avenue, Stacker Lee's is housed in an old towboat floating on the muddy waters of the Mississippi River. The old boat smells of diesel fumes below deck, but that only makes Stacker Lee's seem all the more authentic. The upper decks overlook the water and have an excellent view of the river. This is a fine place to stop for a drink and some peel-and-eat shrimp or Cajun popcorn shrimp. For something more substantial, try something Créole and spicy such as seafood gumbo, jambalaya, or Créole-style spaghetti. Whatever you choose, you can't lose.

SUN STUDIO CAFE, 710 Union Ave. Tel. 521-9820.

Cuisine: DINER. **Reservations:** Not accepted.

$ Prices: Main courses $2.25–$5.95. AE, DISC, MC, V.
Open: Daily 8:30am–6pm.

Located next door to the famous Sun Studio where Elvis Presley made his first recording, this historic café has long been a place for recording engineers and musicians to grab a bite to eat during sessions. Back in the 1950s when it was known as Mrs. Taylor's, the diner was where Sam Phillips signed most of his contracts. Old photos and memorabilia of famous diner customers of the past cover the walls. Try the famous Dixie fried-banana pie with ice cream. You can still get a good '50s-style cheeseburger or milkshake—and who knows, you might bump into Bono or Johnny Cash. The jukebox here is reputed to be the best in Memphis.

2. MIDTOWN

EXPENSIVE

LA TOURELLE RESTAURANT, 2146 Monroe Ave. Tel. 726-5771.

Cuisine: FRENCH. **Reservations:** Required Fri–Sat.
$ Prices: Appetizers $5–$12.50; main courses $19–$26; tasting menu $42; bistro menu $27.50. MC, V.
Open: Dinner Sun–Thurs 6–10pm, Fri–Sat 6–11pm; brunch Sun 11:30am–2pm.

The exterior of this turn-of-the-century house in the Overton Square neighborhood belies the elegance of the interior. Quiet soothing colors, linen tablecloths, tapestry upholstered chairs, and a ceiling fan stirring lace curtains set the mood for good French cuisine.

Dinner might begin with a mesclun salad of fresh chicory, dandelion, arugula, chervil, and oak lettuce or red snapper with a marvelous sauce of leeks, coriander, and saffron. For main dishes, chef Erling Jensen prepares classic yet contemporary dishes such as crispy sweetbreads with langoustines in an avocado-basil sauce that displays a wonderful melding of flavors. The tasting menu is a good value that enables you to try six different courses, including sorbet and a cheese tray. Sunday brunch is elegant; the menu features soup and salad courses, and such dishes as crab cakes with smoked red bell pepper sauce.

MARENA'S, 1545 Overton Park. Tel. 278-9774.

Cuisine: INTERNATIONAL/MEDITERRANEAN. **Reservations:** Recommended.
$ Prices: Appetizers $9.50–$23; main courses $8.50–$15.50. AE, DISC, MC, V.
Open: Dinner only, Mon–Thurs 6–8:30pm, Fri–Sat 6–9:30pm.

From looking at the outside of Marena's (an urban-looking brick building), you'd never guess that the interior, with its rich colors, could possibly conjure up images of a Vermeer painting come to life. However, the deep-blue walls and ceiling stenciling on the sienna-colored paneling, and dark-green tables give the interior a genuine medieval feeling. Add to this setting a few luminous contemporary bowls and subtle, indirect lighting and you have a restaurant worthy of a film set. On top of this, there's even live classical guitar music most nights of the week.

The menu here changes monthly, and draws on influences from all over the world. This ever-changing focus makes Marena's a fresh dining experience each time you visit. When I was last at Marena's, the focus was on Mediterranean cuisines, including Spanish, Algerian, and Middle Eastern. It was difficult to choose between an array of Algerian and Spanish appetizers, but the onions stuffed with ground meat, rice, and spices made a hearty and flavorful start. Algerian salad with a North African dressing of olive oil, lemon juice, spices, and garlic was a piquant precursor to an Algerian soup made with fish, potato, tomato, spice, herbs, onions, garlic, and egg. There were also plenty of succulent dishes to choose from. Chicken was prepared with North African spices and fish with olive oil, lemon, garlic, and cilantro. However, what most appealed to me was the unpronounceable jaji mhishfyi, a chicken breast stuffed with almonds and pistachios and served with pepper sauce.

MODERATE

BISTRO HEMMINGS, 25 S. Belvedere Blvd. Tel. 276-7774.
　Cuisine: NEW AMERICAN. **Reservations:** Recommended.
$ **Prices:** Appetizers $6.50–$11.25; main courses $12.95–$16.95. AE, CB, DC, DISC, MC, V.
　Open: Lunch Mon–Fri 11:30am–2pm; dinner Mon–Thurs 5pm–midnight, Fri–Sat 5pm–1am; brunch Sun noon–3pm. (Bar, Mon–Thurs noon–midnight, Fri–Sat noon–1am.)

One of the city's finest restaurants, the Bistro Hemmings offers low-key elegance amid a traditional setting of dark tones and brass accents. There's also a comfortable walled patio for dining outside in good weather. Service is attentive and the menu creative, using imaginative combinations of regional ingredients. However, wine tastings are offered on Thursday nights.

A full bar tucked into the back is a pleasant place to enjoy a starter such as home-smoked salmon or corn-fried oysters with a red-pepper rémoulade sauce. A traditional grilled loin of pork with a surprising chili-voodoo sauce was more appealing to those who like spicy food. Other outstanding dishes included roast duck with rosemary-cranberry sauce and pecan chicken with orange-brandy sauce. If you're feeling really decadent and you have the room, a piece of Jack Daniel's chocolate pecan pie, or a smooth crème brûlée with raspberries is a fitting flourish to this melange of tastes.

CAFE SOCIETY, 212 N. Evergreen St. Tel. 722-2177.
　Cuisine: NEW AMERICAN. **Reservations:** Recommended.
$ **Prices:** Appetizers $2.95–$6.50; main courses $9.95–$18.95. AE, DC, MC, V.
　Open: Lunch Sun–Fri 11:30am–2pm; dinner Sun–Thurs 5–10pm, Fri–Sat 5–11pm; brunch Sun 11:30am–2pm.
Named after a Parisian café and sporting minimalist paintings,

dark-wood paneling, and dark ceilings, this bistro has a clean, almost stark look that's softly illuminated by the small lamps on each table. As in a Parisian café, you'll find convivial conversations at the bar and outdoor seating on the street where you can sit and people-watch, a popular pastime anywhere. Start out with something Parisian, such as a dish of mussels niçois, or artichoke hearts wrapped in bacon and topped with parmesan cheese, followed up with one of the specials such as New Mexican sirloin, topped with cantaloupe salsa, or a catfish filet with basil-lime butter.

MIDTOWN, 2146 Young Ave. Tel. 726-9614.

Cuisine: NEW AMERICAN. **Reservations:** Not required.

$ **Prices:** Appetizers $3.75–$6.25; main courses $6.95–$12.95. AE, DISC, MC.

Open: Daily 11am–3am; brunch Sat–Sun 11am–3pm.

The Cooper-Young intersection has recently become the hippest corner in Memphis, and this big restaurant is part of the reason why. The clientele tends to be young and artistic, which is reflected in the restaurant's contemporary decor and purple, pink, turquoise, and black color scheme. Changing exhibits of works by local artists provide the only distractions in this minimalist setting.

The bright flavors of Mediterranean cuisines are what keep diners coming back again and again. The appetizers list recently included a warm salad of roasted peppers, red onion, potato, and corn with provençal seasonings. A potato-and-spinach terrine, surrounded with arugula and fontina and dressed with a garlic vinaigrette was also quite tasty. Main dishes included catfish rolled in sesame seeds and sautéed in a ginger sauce and herb chicken with chardonnay sauce and fresh herbs. Rounding out the menu are several sandwiches and pastas. I'm a sucker for crème brûlée, and the Midtown's, made with Grand Marnier, is particularly good.

PAULETTE'S, 2110 Madison Ave. Tel. 726-5128.

Cuisine: FRENCH/HUNGARIAN. **Reservations:** Recommended.

$ **Prices:** Appetizers $2.50–$6.95; main courses $8.85–$18.95. AE, CB, DC, DISC, MC, V.

Open: Mon–Thurs 11am–10pm, Fri–Sat 11am–11:30pm, Sun 11am–10pm.

Overton Square is midtown's main entertainment area and Paulette's is the square's best restaurant. The decor is a cross between classic French country inn and baronial mansion. There are primitive antiques, a high stuccoed ceiling with exposed beams and skylights, cane-back chairs, copper pans hanging on walls, traditional European paintings, and hexagonal terra-cotta tiles. In the lounge, a pianist plays soothing jazz on Wednesday evenings and during Sunday brunch.

You can accompany your traditional Hungarian gulyas with uborka salata (cucumber salad in a sweet vinegar dressing), which is topped with sour cream. Though eastern European dishes are a specialty, hearty French fare rounds out the menu. The menu also usually includes a couple of excellent vegetarian dishes such as asparagus soufflé or broccoli fromage, which is baked in phyllo dough. Though the dessert list is quite extensive, you should be sure that someone at your table orders the Kahlúa-mocha pie, made with a pecan-coconut crust.

BUDGET

BUNTYN RESTAURANT, 3070 Southern Ave. Tel. 458-8776.

Cuisine: AMERICAN. **Reservations:** Not accepted.

$ Prices: Main courses $4.30–$6.50. No credit cards.

Open: Mon–Fri 11am–8:30pm.

Since the 1930s, Buntyn has had a loyal clientele of regulars from the surrounding neighborhood. However, these days you'll also see people from all over the city and all over the world crammed into the crowded restaurant. What everyone comes for is the good, old-fashioned home-cookin' just like ma used to make. Service is super-fast, and a basket of corn muffins and big homemade southern-style biscuits appear on your table as soon as you sit down. Lunches and dinners may be calf's liver smothered in onions, fried chicken, or homemade meatloaf. Portions are large and are served with your choice of two vegetables from a long list that includes fried okra, turnip greens, purple-hull peas, and lime-cream salad. A trip to Buntyn is truly an old-fashioned southern experience.

CAFE OLÉ, 959 S. Cooper St. Tel. 274-1504.

Cuisine: SOUTHWESTERN. **Reservations:** Not required.

$ Prices: Appetizers $1.95–$6.75; main courses $6.25–$12.95. AE, CB, DC, MC, V.

Open: Mon–Thurs 11am–10pm, Fri 11am–11pm, Sat 11:30am–11pm, Sun 11:30am–10pm.

Walls painted to mimic a crumbling effect, Mexican folk art, and leopard-print booths provide a casual setting for this neighborhood restaurant in the up-and-coming Cooper-Young area. A full bar in the back is usually crowded with neighbors toasting each other with cervezas. In this friendly environment carnivores and vegetarians can find something tempting on the menu without too much difficulty. Lunch specials are inexpensive and usually include a few rather uncommon dishes such as tamale pie and black-bean-and-spinach enchiladas with tomatillo sauce. Along with the usual Mexican standards—enchiladas and burritos—there are southwestern specialties such as cowboy steak, which is served with beer-battered onion rings and pico de gallo, and shrimp diablo (shrimp sautéed in chili butter and beer).

CHINA GRILL, 2089 Madison Ave. Tel. 725-9888.

Cuisine: CHINESE. **Reservations:** Recommended on weekends and for parties of four or more.

$ Prices: Appetizers $1–$4.50; main courses $4.50–$11. DISC, MC, V.

Open: Sun–Thurs 11:30am–10pm, Fri–Sat 11:30am–11pm.

A bright purple-and-turquoise exterior, exposed brick walls, and comfy booths contrast pleasantly with Chinese lamps, wood carvings, and an ornately carved bar. The contrast is a metaphor for the food served here. Traditional Chinese cooking meets New American to produce the likes of butterfly shrimp with lemon-dill sauce or tea-smoked duck and napa cabbage in a soy-and-honey dressing. One of the more popular vegetable dishes is string beans Szechuan style, and there's a good selection of other vegetable dishes as well. Kung pao dishes and General Tao's chicken are standard offerings. Specialties include sake-ginger fish, a melding of Japanese and Chinese ingredients, and crayfish with black-bean sauce, a tribute to a southern staple. Dim sum is served on Saturday, and a luncheon buffet special for $4.50 is served on weekdays.

HARRY'S "ON TEUR," 2015 Madison Ave. Tel. 725-6059.

Cuisine: CAJUN. **Reservations:** Recommended.
$ **Prices:** Appetizers $3.95–$4.95; main courses $5.95–$9.95. MC, V.
Open: Lunch Mon–Sat 11am–3pm; dinner Mon–Sat 5:30–10pm.

"On Teur" is kind of a play on the word *entrepreneur* and being "on tour." Harry's place is a funky little restaurant on a seedy block near Overton Square, but that's part of the magic about the place—the home-cooking is surprisingly good. Ordering is interesting because Harry has a way with words as well as with cooking—try a "samich" called the Big Easy. It's made with homemade New Orleans chaurice sausage, onions, and voodoo mustard on a hoagie roll. How about an amber Jack-n-Jill? It's made with pecan-smoked amberjack and is served with a sauce of white wine, apples, and thyme. The shrimp N'awlins is spicy and comes with a satisfying Cajun sauce. You can bring your own wine or liquor, but you can't buy it here.

LUPE AND BEA'S TEXICAN RESTAURANT, 394 N. Watkins St. Tel. 726-9877.

Cuisine: TEX-MEX/CUBAN. **Reservations:** Not accepted.
$ **Prices:** Appetizers $1.95–$5.95; main courses $4.95–$7.95. DISC, MC, V.
Open: Lunch Mon–Sat 11am–2pm; dinner Mon–Thurs 5–9pm, Fri–Sat 5–10pm.

This colorful little place stands out like a sore thumb, so you just can't miss it. There are strobe lights and neon announcing the restaurant's presence, and inside there's kitschy stuff everywhere. This has to be the friendliest Tex-Mex joint in town, and you'll leave full and feeling as if you just made new friends. Bea's Texican enchilada specials include a beef enchilada, and a cheese-and-onion enchilada, both of which are served with a side of guacamole and refried beans. The Lupe and Bea's special, tamales Texicanos, is two tamales with Texas chili and topped with Cheddar cheese. There are even some delicious Cuban dishes such as guiso de calamares con camaron (squid and shrimp) and Cuban lechon asado (grilled pork). You can bring your own wine.

SAIGON LE, 51 N. Cleveland St. Tel. 276-5326.

Cuisine: VIETNAMESE/CHINESE. **Reservations:** Not accepted.
$ **Prices:** Appetizers 85¢–$5; main courses $3.50–$13.95. AE, DISC, MC, V.

Open: Mon–Thurs 11am–10pm, Fri–Sat 11am–10:30pm, Sun 10am–5pm.

S This popular lunch spot is in an urban neighborhood close to the medical center district and is popular with hospital workers. Friendly service and generous portions of Chinese and Vietnamese dishes are the standards here. The kung pao beef is spicy, and the vegetable egg foo yung contains lots of vegetables. Even though the restaurant serves good Chinese food, it's becoming more popular for its Vietnamese food, which includes flavorful noodle, meat, fish, and vegetable dishes such as charcoal-broiled pork, eggrolls with vermicelli, and clear noodle soup with barbecued pork, shrimp, and crabmeat. At $2.85, the lunch special may be the best bargain in town.

3. EAST MEMPHIS

EXPENSIVE

FOLK'S FOLLY PRIME STEAK HOUSE, 551 S. Mendenhall Rd. Tel. 762-8200.
    Cuisine: STEAK/SEAFOOD. **Reservations:** Recommended.
$ **Prices:** Appetizers $2.75–$8; main courses $14.50–$35. AE, MC, V.
    Open: Dinner only, Mon–Fri 6–11pm, Sat 6pm–midnight, Sun 6–10pm.

You'll find Folk's Folly just off Poplar Avenue—it's the corner building with the royal-blue awning. Before you ever make it in the front door, you'll likely get a good idea of what this place is all about. Just off the parking lot is a tiny butcher shop that's part of the restaurant. In the meat cases inside, you'll see the sort of top-quality meats they serve here (the likes of which you'll never see at your

---

F FROMMER'S COOL FOR KIDS: RESTAURANTS

Captain Bilbo's River Restaurant *(see p. 184)* This cavernous renovated warehouse, with views of the Mississippi, is done up to look like an old cotton-shipping wharf. Kids will have a great time examining all the cool stuff.

Buntyn Restaurant *(see p. 190)* It's old and it's crowded and it's always lively. This Memphis "meat-and-three" restaurant will let your kids choose their poison (I mean vegetables). Meals are old-fashioned American favorites that kids love.

neighborhood Piggly-Wiggly). If you have access to a kitchen, you can buy steaks by the pound here and take it home to cook. However, I prefer to have the folks at Folk's do the cooking for me—they do a better job.

Steaks are the specialty of the house, and steaks are what they do best. However, you can start your meal with anything from blackened catfish to potato skins or even fried pickles. The prime cuts of beef are aged sirloins, filet mignons, and T-bones. Seafood offerings include Alaskan king crab legs and jumbo Maine lobsters.

RAJI, 712 W. Brookhaven Circle. Tel. 685-8723.
Cuisine: FRENCH/INDIAN. **Reservations:** Required.
$ Prices: Fixed-price dinner $25 for three courses, $40 for five courses. MC, V.
Open: Dinner only, Mon–Sat 6–11pm.

On a side street in a little house fronted by oak trees, chef Raji Jallepalli has for several years been serving up some of the most amazing combinations of continental and Indian cuisines. Tables set with white linen fill the elegant and simple dining room, which is a bit reminiscent of an old-fashioned suburban house. However, it's not the decor at Raji that brings people back again and again, but rather the often dramatically presented meals.

On my most recent visit to Raji, the evening's fixed-price dinner began with foie gras with fresh figs and Napoleon brandy. This was followed by blue-crab salad with fresh mint, cilantro, and essence of lime in sauvignon blanc. There was a choice of three main courses, which included sautéed scallops in a lentil crêpe with curried carrot-ginger sauce, pan-seared yellow-fin tuna with mirepoix of cucumber and tamarind vinaigrette, and sweetbreads braised in cashew-nut–curry-leaf emulsion with confit of ginger and serrano peppers. Just because there are only three choices doesn't mean that decision-making will be easy at Raji. Topping off this gustatory symphony was a simple raspberry tart, a fitting finale.

MODERATE

AUBERGINE, 5007 Black Rd. Tel. 767-7840.
Cuisine: CONTEMPORARY FRENCH. **Reservations:** Recommended.
$ Prices: Appetizers $3.50–$12; main courses $14–$20. AE, MC, V.
Open: Lunch Mon–Sat 11:30am–2:30pm; dinner Mon–Sat 6–9:30pm.

This intimate restaurant in a small building in the parking lot of a large older shopping plaza is run by the husband-and-wife team of Gene and Juliana Bjorklund. Gene studied in France and puts his own twists on French cuisine, preferring a smaller menu for the personal touch. The Bjorklunds call this the mom-and-pop establishment of the '90s because it exists through the efforts of their family, each of whom contributes different services to the running of the restaurant. Colorful faux-painted walls and beautifully spotlit artful flower arrangements create a comfortable and contemporary setting.

With a menu that contains unusual combinations of ingredients, Aubergine hopes to persuade traditionalist Memphians to try more adventurous dining. Begin your meal here with an appetizer of napoleon of foie gras and caramelized Granny Smith apples or perhaps oysters with watercress and seawater aspic. This is a good place to try both fish and wild game in season. Specialties such as roasted red snapper with tomato confit, garlic flakes, and pearl onion rings are currently among the more popular dishes. For dessert you might try something more traditional such as Memphis chocolate pyramid cake or something daring such as roasted bananas with orange juice and white-pepper ice cream.

BISTRO 122, 5101 Sanderlin Dr. Tel. 761-0663.

Cuisine: NEW AMERICAN. **Reservations:** Recommended.

$ Prices: Appetizers $5.25–$6; main courses $12.95–$19.50. AE, DC, MC, V.

Open: Lunch Mon–Fri 11am–2pm; dinner Mon–Sat 5–10pm.

What do this restaurant, located in the Sanderlin Shopping Center, and a Parisian bistro have in common? The answer is an unrushed and pleasant atmosphere, and a chance to linger over dessert and coffee or a good bottle of wine—and there are many to choose from.

You can start a meal with warm brie and turkey on a croissant or roast lamb with horseradish, or try one of the pastas. There are combinations such as angel-hair pasta with olives, capers, tomatoes, and fresh herbs—excellent when prefaced with an onion soup made "the old way." Braised lamb with garlic and rosemary might help you reminisce about the last time you were in Paris. Try the marquise au chocolat, a flourless chocolate cake, if you're a chocoholic.

CAFE NICHOLAS, 5469 Poplar Ave. Tel. 767-8704.

Cuisine: FRENCH/AMERICAN. **Reservations:** Recommended on weekends.

$ Prices: Appetizers $2.50–$8; main courses $11.50–$15. AE, DC, MC, V.

Open: Dinner only, Tues–Sat 5–10pm.

A green awning over the door gives the entryway a touch of class, an impression that's further enhanced by an interior of deep-green walls, lace curtains, and big gilt-framed pictures. The gentility of the South is apparent both here and in the cuisine, a combination of Louisiana cooking and country French fare. Traditional food, with a few nouveau ingredients to give it some style, in an elegant setting is what makes this place stand out.

Well-prepared Louisiana-style gulf shrimp with garlic-lemon butter and herbs, topped with a rémoulade sauce, is a good choice for an appetizer. Roast pork or strips of chicken breast are brightened by a fajita seasoning and are served over a dish of fettuccine. At the time of this writing, there were plans to begin serving lunch from 11am to 2pm.

JIM'S PLACE EAST, 5560 Shelby Oaks Dr. Tel. 388-7200.

Cuisine: SEAFOOD/STEAK. **Reservations:** Recommended.
$ **Prices:** Appetizers $6.75–$8.95; main courses $13.50–$20. AE, MC, V.
Open: Lunch Mon–Fri 11am–2pm; dinner Mon–Fri 5–9:30pm, Sat 5–10pm.

The first Jim's Place opened way back in the early 1900s and was located downtown. However, today's restaurant is located in an old mansion on several acres of parklike grounds. Old menus and photos greet you in the lobby whereupon the host may escort you through room after room of rarefied atmosphere and tables at which sit Memphis's social elite.

What has kept people faithful to Jim's Place these many years is quite simply the best southern cooking around as well as excellent Greek food. In the former category, you could have a plate of chicken croquettes that are more chicken than potato and accompany them with a heaping bowl of fresh turnip greens. In the latter category, there are specialties such as spanakopeta (phyllo dough filled with spinach), greek salad, moussaka, and souflima (rotisseried pork). This is also a good place to try such southern favorites as Maryland crab cakes, oysters fried Louisiana style in cornmeal, or catfish (broiled, grilled, or fried). A chocolate-mousse pie on a silver tray was irresistible.

LULU GRILLE, 565 Erin Dr., White Station Plaza. Tel. 763-3677.
Cuisine: INTERNATIONAL/MEDITERRANEAN. **Reservations:** Recommended.
$ **Prices:** Appetizers $4.50–$7.95; main courses $7.50–$19.50. AE, CB, DC, DISC, MC, V.
Open: Mon–Fri 11am–10pm, Fri–Sat 11am–11pm.

Set back in a corner of an older shopping center, the Lulu Grille has a country French look with copper pots hanging from the walls and lace café curtains on the big windows. There's a patio for nice weather, and the sculpted trees give it a very Parisian feel. A small bar serves as a hangout for restaurant regulars. The menu includes Mediterranean dishes and other light meals, as well as steaks and fish. However, Lulu's is best known for its outrageous desserts, such as big chocolate cakes, crème brûlée (you can get it to take out), and caramel-fudge brownies. To supplement your dessert, try an unusual bread appetizer that includes orange rye, rosemary, and walnut bread served with pickles, herbed goat cheese, olives, and artichokes. For a more substantial supplement, try the fat-free linguini in marinara. Lighter fare might also mean a simple olive-and-egg sandwich or a zucchini, squash, eggplant, and goat-cheese sandwich extravaganza.

THE ORIGINAL GRISANTI'S RESTAURANT, 1489 Airways Blvd. Tel. 458-2648.
Cuisine: ITALIAN. **Reservations:** Recommended for large parties.
$ **Prices:** Appetizers $4.95–$6.95; main courses $9.25–$23.95. AE, DC, DISC, MC, V.
Open: Lunch Mon–Fri 11am–2pm; dinner Mon–Thurs 5–10pm, Fri–Sat 5–11pm

★ Located on a busy parkway, this restaurant is unique in a couple of ways. First, this is a totally smoke-free restaurant, which in tobacco-growing Tennessee is tantamount to high treason. Second, the restaurant has the largest wine list in the city. Rare wines, including a 1791 bottle of red wine—the oldest red wine known—are perched in display cases over the booths. Diners are even invited to browse the wine cellar. Wines are the passion of owner "Big John" Grisanti, who once paid the highest price ever for a bottle of wine and then held a benefit tasting. This is Big John's family place and has been around since 1909. A gallery of family pictures are on display to prove it. Big John holds court here every night but Wednesday, when he and his wife go out to eat. He'll chat you up and make you feel like an old friend.

Those in-the-know come here for delicious traditional Italian dishes such as crispy and cheesy eggplant parmesan and pollo e carciofi. You'll also find such favorites as homemade ravioli and the elfo special—spaghetti with garlic, gulf shrimp, mushrooms, and parmesan cheese—as well as steaks and seafood.

OWEN BRENNAN'S RESTAURANT, in the Regalia Shopping Center, 6150 Poplar Ave. Tel. 761-0990.
    Cuisine: CAJUN/CREOLE. **Reservations:** Recommended Fri–Sat and for parties of more than four.
$ Prices: Appetizers $3.95–$5.95; main courses $9.95–$15.95. AE, DC, DISC, MC, V.
    Open: Sun–Thurs 11am–10pm, Fri–Sat 11am–11pm; brunch Sun 11am–3pm.

Decorated with the green, gold, and purple colors of Mardi Gras, this restaurant is large and so is its dark wooden bar. New Orleans–style grillwork contrasts with cream-colored walls and dark wood, all of which is presided over by a huge Mardi Gras jester and other Mardi Gras float decorations. The elegant regional atmosphere is just what producers of the film *The Firm* were looking for when they set a scene here. Chairs in the lounge area have bronze plaques on them to show where Gene Hackman and Tom Cruise sat during the filming.

The cuisine here is flamboyant Cajun and Créole, blazing like the colors of Mardi Gras. I can never get enough Cajun food when I'm in Memphis and like to order as much blackened fish or chicken as I can. Here they serve it with vegetables and "dirty" rice. Shrimp and crayfish étoufée is marvelously spicy and rich, and for those of you who enjoy salads, blackened fish and chicken can come on a crunchy bed of salad greens. "The Ultimate New Orleans Jazz brunch" is served here on Sunday from 11am to 3pm, with a live jazz band and champagne on the house at noon.

ROMANO'S MACARONI GRILL, 6705 Poplar Ave. Tel. 753-6588.
    Cuisine: ITALIAN. **Reservations:** Priority waiting list only.
$ Prices: Appetizers $3.95–$7.95; main courses $6.95–$15.95. AE, CB, DC, DISC, MC, V.
    Open: Lunch Mon–Fri 11am–2:30pm, Sat–Sun 11am–3:30pm; dinner Mon–Thurs 5–10pm, Fri 5–11pm, Sat 3:30–11pm, Sun 3:30–10pm.

Upon entering this restaurant at the Carrefour at Kirby Wood shopping plaza, the eye is immediately caught by a display of green, red, and white pasta draped over display cases of beautifully arranged ingredients—pastas, chunks of cheese, chops, vegetables. Archways and ceiling are artfully strung with lightbulbs and hundreds of bottles of wine are meticulously arranged on one wall, making it all look like a marketplace in Naples. Adding to the effect are propped-open window shutters that give the dining room a cool blue glow.

When you take a table, there's a gallon jug of wine on it for you to help yourself—just let the waiter know later how many glasses you've had. Dishes tend to have heartier ingredients in the winter and lighter ingredients in the summer. A large open kitchen supplies a good list of antipastos, including steamed mussels with saffron and fried mozzarella with marinara sauce. Pizzas here are baked in wood-burning ovens and pasta dishes are covered with ingredients such as shrimp, pine nuts, sun-dried tomatoes, asiago and feta cheeses, olives, and clam sauce.

SEKISUI OF JAPAN, in Humphrey's Center, 50 Humphreys Blvd., Suite 14. Tel. 747-0001.
   Cuisine: JAPANESE. **Reservations:** Recommended on weekends.
$ **Prices:** Appetizers $1.50–$13.95; main courses $8.50–$24.95. MC, V.
   Open: Lunch Mon–Fri 11:30am–2pm; dinner Sun–Thurs 5–9:30pm, Fri–Sat 5–10:30pm (bar open until midnight Fri–Sat).

This is yet another of Memphis's many excellent restaurants to be found in shopping plazas. Sekisui is noisy and active on the weekends, unlike some Japanese restaurants which seem to ooze an air of tranquility. You can even catch Japanese TV programs on the bar's TV; the evening we visited it was sumo wrestling night. There are "leg wells" under some tables so you can look as though you're sitting cross-legged on the floor even though you're not. Water dripping from fountains and a little brook running through the middle of the restaurant provide a relaxing traditional touch.

The sushi bar prepares platters of assorted sushi, from a small appetizer to a huge sushi boat that includes octopus, conch, snapper, and flying fish roe sushi. Tempura, teriyaki, kushiyaki, and yakizakana dinners come with rice, soup, and salad. For something different for dessert, try some tempura ice cream. Another smaller sushi bar and smaller, more intimate tatami rooms are in the back.

BUDGET

CORKY'S BAR-B-Q, 5259 Poplar Ave. Tel. 685-9744.
   Cuisine: BARBECUE. **Reservations:** Not accepted.
$ **Prices:** Main courses $6–$7. AE, CB, DC, DISC, MC, V.
   Open: Mon–Thurs 11am–9:30pm, Fri–Sat 11am–10:30pm, Sun 11:30am–9:30pm.

From the rock 'n' roll tunes piped about the premises (indoors and out) to the people inside having a good time, all here is jolly and noisy, with the extra bonus of aromatic barbecue perfuming the airways. Elbow your way past the crowds for some of that Memphis-style pulled pork shoulder, ribs, brisket, or chicken, all of which come cooked either wet or dry. There's always an argument as to which is the best barbecue restaurant in Memphis, and this one is always a strong contender. Photographs and letters from satisfied customers line the rough-paneled lobby, where you might have to wait for a table.

JOHN WILLS, 5101 Sanderlin Dr. Tel. 761-5101.
   Cuisine: BARBECUE. **Reservations:** Recommended in winter.
$ **Prices:** Appetizers $4.25–$7.95; main courses $7.50–$12.95. AE, MC, V.
   Open: Daily 11am–10pm.
The rich aroma of cooking barbecue greets you as you walk into this big delicatessen-style restaurant with black and white floor tiles. Located in the Sanderlin Center shopping plaza, John Wills offers its version of Memphis-style barbecue—crunchy brown on the outside and lean white in the middle. Barbecue plates feature pork ribs or shoulder, or beef ribs or brisket, and any of these come with all the fixin's. Barbecued shrimp, catfish, and chicken are also on the menu.

SALSA COCINA MEXICANA, in the Regalia Shopping Center, 6150 Poplar Ave. Tel. 683-6325.
   Cuisine: MEXICAN. **Reservations:** Accepted only for parties of six or more.
$ **Prices:** Appetizers $3.75–$5.95; main courses $5.75–$11.95. AE, DC, DISC, MC, V.
   Open: Mon–Sat 11am–10:30pm.
This Sonora-style Mexican restaurant serves creamy refried beans, a fabulous salsa piquante, and great margaritas, too. Service is attentive—they really care that you enjoy your meal. Discreet Mexican music plays in the background. High ceilings with textiles stretched below create an atmosphere of a contemporary pueblo, and even the neon beer signs are in Spanish. Quesa flameado—chorizo sausage covered with mushrooms and melted cheese, then flamed—is a special dish to try. When big platters of enchiladas, guacamole, salsa, beans, and rice show up at your table, you'll know that you've come to the right place.

4. SPECIALTY DINING

A LOCAL FAVORITE

RENDEZVOUS, 52 S. Second St. Tel. 523-2746.
   Cuisine: BARBECUE. **Reservations:** Not required.
$ **Prices:** Appetizers $3.95–$8; main courses $7.25–$9.95. AE, CB, DC, MC, V.
   Open: Tues–Thurs 4:30pm–midnight; Fri–Sat noon–midnight.
The entrance to this Memphis institution for the preservation of great barbecue is tucked away down General Washburn Alley, which is across from the Peabody Hotel. The Rendez-

vous has been in downtown Memphis since 1948, and has a well-deserved reputation for serving top-notch barbecue. You can see it being prepared in an old open kitchen as you walk in, but more important, your sense of smell will immediately perk up as the fragrance of hickory-smoked pork wafts past. You'll also be intrigued by all manner of strange objects displayed in this huge but cozy cellar. The museumlike atmosphere includes old bottles, tobacco boxes, beer steins, lanterns, farm equipment, musical instruments, murals, old photos, and even an arrowhead collection. Whether you like pork or beef barbecue, there will certainly be something on the menu to please you. There are even charcoal-broiled lamb riblets as an appetizer.

HOTEL DINING

BOURBON STREET CAFE, in the French Quarter Suites Hotel, 2144 Madison Ave. Tel. 728-4000.
   Cuisine: CAJUN. **Reservations:** Recommended.
$ **Prices:** Appetizers $1.95–$7.95; main courses $9.95–$16.95. AE, CB, DC, DISC, MC, V.
   Open: Breakfast Mon–Fri 6:30–10am, Sat 7–10am; lunch Mon–Sat 11am–2pm; dinner Sun–Thurs 5–10pm, Fri–Sat 5–11pm; brunch Sun 11:30am–3pm.

You'll find this surprisingly sophisticated little restaurant just off the French Quarter's high-ceilinged lobby, which, with its ornate wrought-iron railings, lives up to the New Orleans name. The restaurant, too, provides a pleasant taste of the Big Easy with its excellent Cajun dishes. You'll feel as though you should be paying far more than you will when you see the plush tapestry-cloth armchairs, large traditional paintings, and a glass case full of wines.

An extensive appetizer menu includes the likes of lobster bisque, Cajun popcorn crayfish, gumbo, and even a shrimp, crayfish, and sausage quiche. If none of these appeals to you, perhaps a Cajun chicken salad will. A good selection of pastas includes Cajun ravioli with crayfish, which I find nearly impossible to resist. All the steaks are good, but I like the Bourbon Street steak, which is made with a pepper, garlic, and brandy sauce. There's always a good selection of seafood dishes as well. A lunch buffet is served for $6.95.

BRAVO! RISTORANTE, in the Adam's Mark Hotel, 939 Ridge Lake Blvd. Tel. 684-6664.
   Cuisine: ITALIAN. **Reservations:** Recommended.
$ **Prices:** Appetizers $4.50–$6.50; main courses $10.50–$19.25; fixed-price meal $15.95. AE, CB, DC, DISC, MC, V.
   Open: Breakfast Mon–Sat 6:30–10am; lunch Mon–Sat 11:30am–6pm; dinner Sun–Thurs 6–10pm, Fri–Sat 6–11pm.

There may not be a more entertaining restaurant in Memphis. Bravo!, as its name suggests, offers up nightly encore performances by singing waiters and waitresses. The restaurant is located down on the ground level of the shimmering Adam's Mark Hotel, which is Memphis's glitziest hotel. Take a table amid huge faux-marble columns and you should have a view through a wall of glass to the pond and gardens just outside. All in all, Bravo! has the feeling of a Roman villa without being ostentatious.

Both the menu and the wine list are fairly long, so no matter what your tastes in Italian cooking, you should find something to satisfy you. I like to start out with the prosciutto and melon and follow this with a Caesar salad. For a main dish I usually opt for a pasta dish such as tagliatelle alla scaligera, which is made with prosciutto, peas, parmesan, and wild mushrooms. Those with a heartier appetite may enjoy the piccata of veal marsala that's made with parsley, lemon, and a marsala sauce. However, I have to say that the fixed-price dinner is the best deal on the menu.

DINING WITH A VIEW

THE PINNACLE OF MEMPHIS, 100 N. Main St. Tel. 523-2098.
   Cuisine: CONTINENTAL. **Reservations:** Recommended the day before.
$ **Prices:** Appetizers $2.50–$6.95; main courses $11.95–$17.95. DISC, MC, V.
   Open: Lunch Mon–Fri 11am–2pm; dinner Fri–Sat 5–9pm.
Way up on the 38th floor of a downtown skyscraper is this modest revolving restaurant where the views are by far the best in town. If you're trying to get your bearings, this is a great place to have lunch. The view will give you a feeling for the Memphis area. Spread out below is the big muddy Mississippi River spanned by several bridges and flanked by the shining Pyramid. The dining room takes about an hour to revolve, which gives you time to see the entire city and, if you're here for dinner, catch a good sunset and see the city lights come on. It's popular with the lunch crowd, and now open for dinner. The menu includes traditional dishes such as chicken Oscar and beef Wellington. Although the menu is rather basic, baked brie with honey and almonds and mushrooms stuffed with crabmeat are a couple of standout appetizers.

BREAKFAST/BRUNCH

If a restaurant serves Sunday brunch, I have noted it in the listings above, but a few deserve additional mention. **Owen Brennan's Restaurant,** 6150 Poplar Ave. (tel. 761-0990), serves a lavish buffet from 11am to 3pm. There's even a live jazz band providing entertainment. **La Tourelle Restaurant,** 2146 Monroe Ave. (tel. 726-5771), serving brunch from 11:30am to 2pm, and **Bistro Hemmings,** 25 S. Belvedere Blvd. (tel. 276-7774), serving from noon to 3pm, are both elegant settings for a gourmet brunch. More casual places include **Café Society,** 212 N. Evergreen St. (tel. 722-2177), with brunch from 11:30am to 2pm, and **Midtown,** 2146 Young Ave. (tel. 726-9614), which serves brunch on both Saturday and Sunday from 11am to 3pm.

LATE-NIGHT RESTAURANTS

If hunger strikes at a late hour, there are a number of places to head to in Memphis. Although none is open all night long, you can still get something a lot more exciting than a hamburger up until 3am at several places. See above for full details on the following restaurants: **Rendezvous,** 52 S. Second St. (tel. 523-2746); **Bluff City Grill and Brewery,** 235 Union Ave. (tel. 526-BEER); **Stacker Lee's,** 65 Riverside Dr. (tel. 523-8968); **Bistro Hemmings,** 25 S. Belvedere Blvd. (tel. 276-7774); and **Midtown,** 2146 Young Ave. (tel. 726-9614).

CHAPTER 15

WHAT TO SEE & DO IN MEMPHIS

Just as in Nashville, music is at the heart of Memphis, and many of the city's main attractions are related to Memphis's musical heritage. It was here on Beale Street that the blues first gained widespread recognition, and it was here at Sun Studio that rock 'n' roll was born. W. C. Handy, the father of the blues, lived here for many years, and Elvis Presley made his Memphis home—Graceland—a household word. You'll find the history of the Memphis sound on exhibit at several museums around the city, including a couple that are devoted exclusively to music. However, there's more to Memphis than music. The fine arts, Mississippi River life, the civil rights movement, and even Egyptian artifacts are all part of the museum offerings in Memphis. Also, every few years Memphis puts on an exclusive show of international importance. Called "Wonders: The Memphis International Cultural Series," these shows have in the past focused on Napoleon, Catherine the Great, the Ottoman Empire, and Rameses the Great. The Wonders series is held in the Memphis Cook Convention Center. When planning a trip to Memphis, always check with the tourist information office to find out if one of these exhibits will be going on during your visit. Advance reservations are always recommended for these shows.

SUGGESTED ITINERARIES

IF YOU HAVE ONE DAY   Elvis fans will want to spend most of the day at Graceland. Afterwards, you can visit Sun Studios, and then head over to Beale Street to see the Elvis statue and catch some live music. Blues and rock fans may want to follow the same itinerary but spend less time at Graceland and more on Beale Street and at the Memphis Music Hall of Fame. If you aren't a music fan, spend your day visiting Mud Island and the Mississippi River Museum. You could then go for a riverboat cruise or take a tour with the Delta Ducks. Later stroll down Beale Street, and then visit the National Civil Rights Museum. Either in the morning or in the afternoon, try to catch the march of the Peabody ducks.

IF YOU HAVE TWO DAYS If you did Graceland on your first day, visit Mud Island and the National Civil Rights Museum on day two. Otherwise, you might head out to midtown and visit the Memphis Brooks Museum of Art, the Dixon Gallery and Gardens, and Memphis Pink Palace museum.

IF YOU HAVE THREE DAYS On your third day, depending on your personal interests, you could visit the restored Magevney, Mallory-Neely, and Woodruff-Fontaine houses—three of Memphis's historic homes. You could also head south to the Chucalissa Museum to learn about the Native Americans who once lived in this area, and then visit the University Gallery to learn about ancient Egyptian culture.

1. THE TOP ATTRACTIONS

GRACELAND, 3675 Elvis Presley Blvd. Tel. 332-3322, or toll free 800/238-2000.

Even before Paul Simon made Graceland a household word for non-Elvis fans, this little southern mansion was the destination of thousands of lovestruck pilgrims searching for the ghost of Elvis. To paraphrase Simon, for reasons I couldn't explain, there was some part of me that wanted to see Graceland the first time I visited Memphis.

Purchased in the late 1950s for $100,000, Graceland today is far more than the former home of one of rock 'n' roll's greats, it is Memphis's biggest attraction and resembles a small theme park or shopping mall in scope and design. There are his two personal jets (the *Lisa Marie* and the *Hound Dog II*), the Elvis Presley Automobile Museum, the Sincerely Elvis collection of Elvis's personal belongings, the *Walk a Mile in My Shoes* video, and, of course, Graceland itself.

Visitors are fed through the complex by a staff of guides that spout memorized descriptions of each of the rooms that are open to the public (the second floor, site of Elvis's bedroom, is off-limits). After touring the house, you get to see Elvis's office, his racquetball building, a small exhibit of personal belongings, memorabilia, and awards, and finally, Elvis's grave. Then it's back across Elvis Presley Boulevard where you can watch a film about "the king" and visit the other Graceland attractions. True fans will want to do it all.

Admission: Graceland Mansion Tour, $8 adults, $7.20 senior citizens, $4.75 children 4–12; Elvis Presley Automobile Museum, $4.50 adults, $4.05 senior citizens, $2.75 children 4–12; Elvis's airplanes, $4.25 adults, $3.80 senior citizens, $2.75 children; Sincerely Elvis Museum, $2.75 adults, $2.50 senior citizens and children 4–12; the Platinum Tour (includes admittance to all Graceland attractions), $16 adults, $14.40 senior citizens, $11 children 4–12. Tour reservations are taken 24 hours in advance.

Open: Memorial Day–Labor Day, daily 7:30am–6pm; Labor

Day–Memorial Day, daily 8:30am–5pm (the mansion tour does not operate Tues Nov–Feb). **Closed:** New Year's, Thanksgiving, and Christmas Days. **Bus:** 13.

HISTORIC BEALE STREET, Front St. to Fourth St.

To fans of blues music, Beale Street is the most important street in America. It was here that the blues was born and here that the blues is still alive. Though the roots of the blues stretch back to the African musical heritage of slaves brought to the United States, it was here on Beale Street that African-American musician W. C. Handy was performing when he penned "The Memphis Blues," which is accepted as the first published blues song. At the time Handy was singing the blues, Beale Street was one of the most important streets in the South for African-Americans. After the Civil War, Memphis's Beale Street was one of the centers for African-Americans in the South. It was here that many of the most famous musicians in the blues world got their start—W. C. Handy, B. B. King, Furry Lewis, Rufus Thomas, Isaac Hayes, Alberta Hunter.

Today, though much of downtown Memphis has been abandoned to suburban sprawl, Beale Street continues to draw fans of blues and popular music in general. Nightclubs line the street between Front Street and Fourth Street. The Orpheum Theatre, once a vaudeville palace, is now the performance hall for Broadway road shows and the New Daisy Theatre features performances by up-and-coming bands and once-famous performers. Historic markers up and down the street relate the area's colorful past, and two bronze statues commemorate the city's two most important musicians—W. C. Handy and Elvis Presley. In addition to the many clubs featuring nightly live music, there are two museums (the Beale Street Blues Museum and the Center for Southern Folklore) and the museumlike A. Schwab Dry Goods store.

THE PEABODY DUCKS, in the Peabody Memphis hotel, 149 Union Ave. Tel. 529-4000.

It isn't often that one encounters live ducks in the lobby of a luxury hotel. However, in Memphis, ducks are *de rigueur* at the elegant Peabody Hotel. Each morning several ducks take the elevator down from their penthouse home, waddle down a red carpet, and hop into the hotel's travertine marble Romanesque fountain. And each evening they waddle back down the red carpet and take the elevator back up to the penthouse. During their entry and exit, the ducks waddle to the tune of the "King Cotton March," and attract large crowds of curious onlookers.

The Peabody ducks first took up residence in the lobby in the 1930s when the hotel's general manager, as a joke, put some of his live duck decoys in the hotel's fountain. The ducks were a hit, and since then have become a beloved fixture at the Peabody.

Admission: Free.

Open: The ducks march in at 11am and out at 5pm. **Bus:** All downtown buses.

NATIONAL CIVIL RIGHTS MUSEUM, 450 Mulberry St. Tel. 521-9699.

FROMMER'S FAVORITE MEMPHIS EXPERIENCES

A Cruise on the Mississippi Paddlewheelers are for many people the most immediately recognizable symbol of the Mississippi, and no visit to Memphis, or any other city on Ole Man River, is complete without a cruise on the Big Muddy.

A Night Out on Beale Street This is where the music called the blues took shape and gained its first national following. Today, as in the past, Beale Street is home to numerous nightclubs where music fans can hear everything from blues to zydeco.

Wandering Through the Mississippi River Museum This is the only museum in the country dedicated to life on the Mississippi River and features several life-size walk-through exhibits such as a paddlewheeler, a Civil War ironclad gunboat, and an old Beale Street honky tonk.

A Concert at the Mud Island Amphitheater Summer sunsets over the Mississippi are best appreciated when watching a famous performer give a concert at this amphitheater on Mud Island. Rock, pop, and country music are the mainstays here.

Lounging in the Lobby of the Peabody The Peabody Hotel is one of the most elegant hotels in the South, and anyone can indulge in that elegance for the price of a drink in the lobby bar. Of course, you'll also be sharing the lobby with the famous Peabody ducks.

Browsing Through the A. Schwab Dry Goods Store Even if you hate shopping, you may enjoy this store, which opened in 1876 and has changed little since then. Battered wooden floors and tables covered with an unimaginable array of stuff make this more of a museum than a store. However, everything is for sale, and you'll find some of the offerings absolutely fascinating.

Dr. Martin Luther King, Jr., had come to Memphis in early April of 1968 in support of the city's striking garbage collectors. He was staying at the Lorraine Motel as he always did when visiting Memphis. On April 4, he stepped out onto the balcony outside his room and was shot dead by James Earl Ray. The assassination of King struck a horrible blow to the American civil rights movement and incited riots in cities across the country. However, despite the murder of the movement's most important leader, African-Americans continued to struggle for the equal rights that were guaranteed to them under the U.S. Constitution.

IMPRESSIONS

For some reason I cannot explain, there's some part of me wants to see Graceland.
—PAUL SIMON, *GRACELAND*

Saved from demolition, the Lorraine Motel was completely remodeled and today serves as the nation's memorial to the civil rights movement. In evocative displays, the museum chronicles the struggle of African-Americans from the time of slavery to the present. Multimedia presentations and live-size, walk-through tableaux include historic exhibits: a Montgomery, Alabama, public bus such as the one on which Rosa Parks was riding when she refused to move to the back of the bus; a Greensboro, North Carolina, lunch counter; and the burned shell of a freedom ride Greyhound bus.

Admission: $5 adults, $4 senior citizens, $3 children 6–12, free for children under 6.

Open: Mon and Wed–Sat 10am–5pm, Sun 1–5pm (to 6pm Sun June–Aug). **Bus:** 11 or 19. **Trolley:** Main Street Trolley.

MUD ISLAND, Mud Island Rd. Tel. 576-7241.

If you have seen any pre-1900 photos of the Memphis waterfront, you may have noticed that something's missing from the photos—Mud Island. This island first appeared in 1900 and became permanent in 1913. In 1916 the island joined with the mainland just north of the mouth of the Wolf River, but a diversion canal was dug through the island to maintain a free channel in the Wolf River. Today this young island is home to a 52-acre park that includes several attractions. To learn all about the river, you can follow a five-block-long scale model of 900 miles of the Mississippi River. Called the **River Walk,** the model is complete with flowing water, street plans of cities and towns along the river, and informative panels that include information on the river and its history.

Eventually this model river flows past New Orleans, through the delta, and into the Gulf of Mexico, which happens to be a huge public swimming pool with an unobstructed view of the Memphis skyline.

After gaining an understanding of the scope and scale of the Mississippi River, visit the **Mississippi River Museum,** which is the most entertaining museum in Memphis. More than 10,000 years of river history are chronicled in several engrossing life-size reconstructions. The *Belle of the Bluffs* re-creates the front half of an 1870s steamboat: Cotton bales are stacked on the lower deck and water laps at the hull. An ironclad Union gunboat, under fire from a Confederate gun emplacement, is another of the museum's evocative displays. The music of the Mississippi is the focus of one of the museum's largest exhibits. Memphis blues, New Orleans jazz, early rock 'n' roll, and Elvis are all subjects of these displays.

World War II historians won't want to miss a visit to the **Memphis Belle,** one of the most famous B-17s that fought in World War II. After having a look at the famous plane, you can watch a documentary on the *Memphis Belle,* which was also the subject of a popular film a few years back. On the first Sunday of each month there are guided tours of the interior of the plane.

Evenings during the summer, the **Mud Island Amphitheater** hosts top-name performers.

Admission: Grounds and Mississippi River Museum, $6 adults, $4 senior citizens and children under 12; grounds only, $2 adults, $1 senior citizens and children under 12. Parking costs $3.

Open: Grounds, daily 10am–5pm (last admission at 3pm); museum, Tues–Sun 10am–5pm (last admission at 3:30pm); swimming pool/beach, late May to early Sept, Tues–Sun 11am–5pm. **Directions:** To reach Mud Island, you can drive by way of Auction Avenue just north of the Pyramid, or take the monorail from Front Street at Adams Avenue. The monorail operates daily during the spring and summer months and on weekends only in the autumn (also on the evening of Mud Island Amphitheater concerts in the autumn).

MEMPHIS BROOKS MUSEUM OF ART, Overton Park, 1934 Poplar Ave. Tel. 722-3500.

First opened in 1916 as the Brooks Memorial Art Gallery, this is the oldest art museum in Tennessee, and today contains one of the largest art collections of any museum in the Mid-South. With more than 7,000 pieces in the permanent collection, the Brooks frequently rotates works on display. The museum's emphasis is on European and American art of the 18th through the 20th century, with a very respectable collection of Italian Renaissance and baroque paintings and sculptures as well. Some of the museum's more important works include pieces by Auguste Rodin, Pierre Auguste Renoir, Thomas Hart Benton, and Frank Lloyd Wright. In addition, there are usually two or three special exhibits mounted at any given time.

Admission: Tues–Thurs and Sat–Sun, $4 adults, $2 students and senior citizens, free for children under 6; Fri, by donation (pay what you wish).

Open: Tues–Sat 10am–5pm, Sun 11:30am–5pm. **Bus:** 22L, 41, or 50.

DIXON GALLERY AND GARDENS, 4339 Park Ave. Tel. 761-5250.

The South's finest collection of French and American impressionist and post-impressionist artworks are the highlight of this exquisite little museum. The museum, art collection, and surrounding 17 acres of formal and informal gardens once belonged to Margaret and Hugo Dixon, who were avid art collectors. After the deaths of the Dixons, their estate opened to the public as an art museum in 1974 and became one of Memphis's most important museums. The permanent collection includes works by Henri Matisse, Pierre Auguste Renoir, Edgar Degas, Paul Gauguin, Mary Cassat, J. M. W. Turner, and John Constable. With strong local support, the museum frequently hosts temporary exhibits of international caliber. Twice a year the Memphis Symphony Orchestra performs outdoor concerts in Dixon's formal gardens.

You'll find the Dixon Gallery and Gardens across the street from the Memphis Botanic Garden.

Admission: $5 adults, $4 senior citizens, $3 students, $1 children under 12.

Open: Tues–Sat 10am–5pm, Sun 1–5pm. **Bus:** 52SF.

MEMPHIS PINK PALACE AND PLANETARIUM, 3050 Central Ave. Tel. 320-6320.

"The Pink Palace" was the name locals gave to the ostentatious pink-marble mansion built by grocery-store magnate Clarence Saunders shortly after World War I. It was Saunders who had revolutionized grocery shopping with the opening of the first Piggly Wiggly self-service market in 1916. Unfortunately Saunders went bankrupt before he ever finished his "Pink Palace," and the building was acquired by the city of Memphis for use as a museum of cultural and natural history. In 1977 the museum moved into an adjoining modern annex. Today the original marble mansion is not open to the public.

Among the exhibits here you can wander through a reproduction of the maze of aisles that constituted an original Piggly Wiggly. Other walk-through exhibits include a pre–Piggly Wiggly general store and an old-fashioned pharmacy with a soda fountain. Memphis is a major medical center and, not surprisingly, this museum has an extensive medical-history exhibit. On a lighter note, there's a hand-carved miniature circus that goes into animated action between 10:30 and 11am Monday through Saturday and from 2:30 to 3pm on Saturday and Sunday.

In the planetarium, there are frequently changing astronomy programs as well as rock 'n' roll laser shows (the annual August Elvis laser show is the most popular).

The museum was once again undergoing a major expansion when I last visited, and by the time you arrive, you may be able to take in a film in a new IMAX theater or join a class in the new learning center.

Admission: Museum, $4 adults, $3.50 senior citizens, $2.50 children 5–12, free for children under 5 and for everyone Thurs 5–8pm; planetarium, $3 adults, $2.50 senior citizens, $2 children 5–12 (children under 2 not admitted).

Open: Sept–May, Mon–Wed and Fri 9am–4pm, Thurs 9am–8pm, Sat 10am–5pm, Sun 1–5pm; June–Aug, Mon–Wed and Fri 10am–5pm, Thurs 10am–8pm, Sat 10am–5pm, Sun 1–5pm. **Bus:** 50C.

2. MORE ATTRACTIONS

ARCHITECTURAL HIGHLIGHTS

THE PYRAMID, 1 Auction Ave. Tel. 521-9675.

Memphis, named for the ancient capital of Egypt, has since its founding evoked its namesake in various buildings and public artworks. The city's most recent reflection of its adopted Egyptian character is the 32-story, stainless-steel Pyramid, Memphis's answer to the sports domes that have been built in so many cities across the country. With a base the size of six football fields and a height greater than that of the Astrodome or the Superdome, the Pyramid seats 22,500 people. Self-guided tours of the public areas and guided tours of the backstage areas are held throughout the year.

Admission: Walk-through, $2.50 adults, $1.50 senior citizens and children 4–11; guided tours, $3.75 adults, $2.75 senior citizens and children 4–11.

Open: Tours, Apr 17–Labor Day, Mon–Sat 10am–4pm, Sun noon–4pm. Labor Day–Nov 1, Sun–Thurs guided tours only, at noon, 1pm, and 2pm; Fri–Sat 10am–4pm. Nov 2–Apr 16, guided tours only, daily at noon, 1pm, and 2pm. **Bus:** 40 or 52. **Trolley:** Main Street Trolley.

HISTORIC BUILDINGS

MAGEVNEY HOUSE, 198 Adams Ave. Tel. 526-4464.

This diminutive wooden house not far from the skyscrapers of downtown Memphis is one of the oldest buildings in the city. It was here that the first Catholic mass in Memphis was held. Purchased by Irish immigrant Eugene Magevney in 1839, the house is today furnished as it might have been in the 1850s. Among the furniture on display in the house are several pieces that belonged to the Magevneys.

Admission: Free.

Open: Tues–Sat 10am–4pm; guided tours every 30 minutes (last tour at 3:30pm). **Bus:** 2.

MALLORY-NEELY HOUSE, 652 Adams Ave. Tel. 523-1484.

The centerpiece of the Victorian Village Historic District, the Mallory-Neely House is an imposing Italianate mansion built in 1855. Remodeled shortly before 1900, the three-story, 25-room home is an example of how wealthy Memphians lived in the latter half of the 19th century. Elaborate plasterwork moldings, ornate ceiling paintings, and a classically Victorian excess of decoration serve as a visually stunning backdrop for rooms full of original furnishings.

Admission: $4 adults, $3 senior citizens and students.

Open: Apr–Dec, Tues–Sat 10am–4pm, Sun 1–4pm; guided tours every 30 minutes (last tour at 3:30pm). **Closed:** Jan–Mar. **Bus:** 2.

WOODRUFF-FONTAINE HOUSE, Victorian Village, 680 Adams Ave. Tel. 526-1469.

Located adjacent to the Mallory-Neely House, the Woodruff-Fontaine House displays an equally elaborate Victorian aesthetic, in

IMPRESSIONS

The seven wonders of the world I have seen, and many are the places I have seen. Take my advice, folks, and see Beale Street first.
    —W. C. HANDY

this case influenced by French architectural styles. Built in 1870, the 16-room home has been fully restored and houses period furnishings. Mannequins throughout the house display the fashions of the late 19th century.

Admission: $5 adults, $4 senior citizens, $2 students.

Open: Mon–Sat 10am–4pm, Sun 1–4pm; guided tours every 30 minutes (last tour at 3:30pm). **Bus:** 2.

AN INDUSTRIAL TOUR

COORS BREWING COMPANY MEMPHIS BREWERY, 5151 E. Raines Rd. Tel. 368-BEER.

The Coors Brewery is open for tours throughout the year. The tours last about 40 minutes and conclude with a chance to sample some of the brewery's products. The tasting room, called the Coors Belle, is designed to resemble an old paddlewheel riverboat.

Admission: Free.

Open: Memorial Day–Labor Day, Mon–Sat 10am–4pm; Labor Day–Memorial Day, Mon–Sat noon–4pm. **Bus:** 10S.

MUSEUMS & GALLERIES

BEALE STREET SUBSTATION POLICE MUSEUM, 159 Beale St. Tel. 528-2370.

This might be the only 24-hour museum in the country—and is an active police station as well. The little museum is dedicated to crime and police activities in and around Memphis. There are old newspaper clippings tracing the assassination of Dr. Martin Luther King, the subsequent rioting, and the eventual arrest of James Earl Ray. Among the other displays are a collection of weapons (including homemade guns) used in local crimes, mug shots dating back to the early part of the century, and plenty of photos of Memphis's men and women in blue.

Admission: Free.

Open: Daily 24 hours. **Bus:** 2.

CENTER FOR SOUTHERN FOLKLORE, 152 Beale St. Tel. 525-3655.

This small and rather informal museum is dedicated to the preservation and presentation of southern culture. The emphasis is frequently on Memphis and the city's various musical traditions. When I last visited the exhibit was on rockabilly music in Memphis during the early 1950s. The center also offers tours of Beale Street and a short film about Beale Street musicians of the past.

Admission: $2 adults, $1 senior citizens and students; film screening $1 extra.

Open: Mon–Thurs 10am–8pm, Fri–Sat 10am–midnight. **Bus:** 2.

CHUCALISSA MUSEUM, 1987 Indian Village Dr. Tel. 785-3160.

Located south of Memphis off U.S. 61 and adjacent to the T. O.

Fuller State Park, the Chucalissa Museum is built on the site of a Mississippian Period (A.D. 900–1600) Native American village. Dioramas and displays of artifacts discovered in the area provide a cultural history of Mississippi River valley Native Americans. These people reached their highest level of cultural development during the Mississippian Period, when large villages were constructed on bluffs above the Mississippi. This culture was characterized by sun worship, mound building, and a distinctive artistic style that can be seen in many of the artifacts displayed here. The reconstructed village includes several family dwellings, a shaman's hut, and a chief's temple atop a mound in the center of the village compound. There is an annual Choctaw tribal festival held here at the museum.

Admission: $3 adults, $2 senior citizens and children 4–11, free for children under 4.

Open: Tues–Sat 9am–5pm, Sun 1–5pm.

DANNY THOMAS/ALSAC PAVILION, St. Jude Children's Research Hospital, 332 N. Lauderdale St. Tel. 522-0661.

The St. Jude Children's Research Hospital was founded by comic actor Danny Thomas to treat children with catastrophic illnesses, and over the years Thomas helped raise millions of dollars for the hospital. Thomas is buried in the pavilion, which now serves as both a tribute to Thomas's career and the hospital's history.

Admission: Free.

Open: Mon–Fri 10am–4pm, Sat–Sun 11am–4pm. **Bus:** 52.

NATIONAL ORNAMENTAL METAL MUSEUM, 374 W. California Ave. Tel. 774-6380.

Set on parklike grounds on a bluff overlooking the Mississippi, this small museum is dedicated to ornamental metalworking in all its forms. There are sculptures displayed around the museum's gardens, a working blacksmith shop, and examples of ornamental wrought-iron grillwork such as is seen on balconies in New Orleans. Sculptural metal pieces and jewelry are also prominently featured both in the museum's permanent collection and in temporary exhibits. Be sure to take a look at the ornate museum gates. They were created by 160 metalsmiths from 17 countries and feature a fascinating array of imaginative rosettes. Just across the street is a community park that includes an ancient Native American mound.

Admission: $2 adults, $1 senior citizens, students, and children 5–18, free for children under 5.

Open: Tues–Sat 10am–5pm, Sun noon–5pm. **Directions:** To reach the museum, take Crump Boulevard or I-55 toward the Memphis-Arkansas Bridge and get off at Exit 12-C (Delaware Street), which is the last exit in Tennessee; the museum is two blocks south.

UNIVERSITY GALLERY, Memphis State University, Central Ave. Tel. 678-2224.

Memphis takes its name from the ancient capital of Egypt, and here in the gallery of Memphis State University you can view artifacts from ancient Memphis. An outstanding little collection of Egyptian art and artifacts makes this one of the most interesting museums in Memphis. Among the items on display, there's even a loaf of bread dating from between 2134 and 1786 B.C. A hieroglyphic-covered sarcophagus contains the mummy of Iret-Iruw, who died around 2,200 years ago. Numerous works of art and funerary objects show the high level of skill achieved by ancient Egyptian artists. In addition to the Egyptian exhibit, there's a small collection of African masks and wood carvings.

Admission: Free.

Open: Tues–Fri 9am–5pm, Sat–Sun 1–5pm. **Bus:** 50C, 50S, or 61.

PARKS, GARDENS & THE ZOO

AUDUBON PARK, bounded by Park Ave., Perkins Rd., Southern Ave., and Goodlet St. Tel. 325-5759.
Slightly larger than Overton Park, (see below) Audubon Park contains the W. C. Paul Arboretum, the Memphis Botanic Garden, Theatre Memphis, and the Audubon Park Municipal Golf Course.

Bus: 42 or 52SF.

LICHTERMAN NATURE CENTER, 5992 Quince Rd. Tel. 767-7322.
This 65-acre nature preserve serves as both an environmental education center and a wildlife sanctuary. Within the preserve's hardwood forest can be found 350 species of plants, 200 species of birds, 45 species of reptiles and amphibians, and 35 species of small mammals. You can see some of these many plants and animals on the various trails that meander through forests and fields and past marshes, ponds, and a lake. The impressive log Interpretive Center was built in 1928 by wealthy Memphis resident Clarence Saunders, who opened the nation's first self-service grocery store. This is both a pleasant place for a quiet stroll and a great place to let kids learn about the environment.

Admission: $3 adults, $2 students and seniors, free for children under 3.

Open: Tues–Sat 9:30am–5pm, Sun 1–5pm. **Bus:** 52B.

MEMPHIS BOTANIC GARDEN, in Audubon Park, 750 Cherry Rd. Tel. 685-1566.
With 20 formal gardens covering 96 acres, this is quite a large botanic garden and requires a bit of time to visit properly. You'll find something in bloom at almost any time of year, and even in winter the Japanese garden offers a tranquil setting for a quiet stroll. In April and May the Ketchum Memorial Iris Garden, one of the largest in the country, is in bloom, and during May, June, and September the Municipal Rose Garden is alive with color. A special Sensory Garden is designed with the disabled in mind and has plantings that stimulate all five senses. Other gardens include azalea and dogwood gardens, a cactus and herb garden, an organic vegetable garden, a daylily garden, and a tropical conservatory.

Admission: $2 adults, $1.50 seniors, $1 children 6–17 and students, free for children under 6, free for everyone Tues 12:30am–closing.

Open: Nov–Feb, Mon–Sat 9am–4:30pm, Sun 11am–4:30pm; Mar–Oct, Mon–Sat 9am–6pm, Sun 11am–6pm. **Bus:** 42 or 52SF.

MEMPHIS ZOO AND AQUARIUM, in Overton Park, 2000 Galloway Ave. Tel. 726-4775.

Memphis's Egyptian heritage is once again called upon in the imposing and unusual entranceway to the Memphis Zoo. Built to resemble an ancient Egyptian temple, the zoo's entry is covered with traditional and contemporary hieroglyphics. Leading up to this grand entry is a wide pedestrian avenue flanked by statues of some of the animals that reside at the zoo. Once home to Volney, the famous MGM Studios lion that appeared at the beginning of thousands of motion pictures, the Memphis Zoo has recently remodeled its big-cat compound to provide a more naturalistic setting for its lions, snow leopards, and other big felines. The primate area is also in the process of being remodeled and should be completed by the time you visit; this area will include a monkey island in the center of a pond. In addition to the 2,800 animals in residence at the zoo, there is an area of children's carnival rides.

Admission: $5 adults, $3 seniors and children.

Open: Apr–Sept, daily 9am–5pm; Oct–Mar, daily 9am–4:30pm. **Bus:** 53S.

OVERTON PARK, bounded by Poplar Ave., East Parkway, North Parkway, and McLean Blvd. Tel. 325-5759.

This is one of Memphis's largest parks and includes not only the Memphis Zoo and Aquarium, but the Memphis Brooks Museum of Art, the Memphis College of Art, the Overton Park Municipal Golf Course, tennis courts, hiking and biking trails, and an open-air theater. The park's large, old shade trees make this a cool place to spend an afternoon in the summer, and the surrounding residential neighborhoods are some of the wealthiest in the city.

Bus: 22L, 41, or 50.

3. COOL FOR KIDS

Many of Memphis's main attractions will appeal to children as well as to adults, but there are also quite a few places that are specifically for kids. Among those attractions that kids find particularly interesting or entertaining are the following (for details, see "The Top Attractions" and "More Attractions," above):

Memphis Pink Palace and Planetarium A life-size mechanical triceratops, a real mastodon skeleton, and a miniature mechanical circus are most popular with the kids, but they can also learn about the stars at the planetarium.

Memphis Zoo Not only are there lots of animals, but there are carnival kiddie rides as well.

Lichterman Nature Center There's no better place in Memphis for kids to learn about the wonders of nature.

Chucalissa Museum A chance to walk through a real archeologist's trench and run around exploring a reconstructed Native American village will certainly thrill most children.

The Peabody Ducks The waddling little quackers get to

spend each day in the lobby of the posh Peabody Hotel, which is sure to have your kids pleading for a duck as a house pet.

Mud Island The swimming pool here, shaped like the Gulf of Mexico, is huge and is at the end of a massive scale model of the Mississippi River.

A CHILDREN'S MUSEUM

CHILDREN'S MUSEUM OF MEMPHIS, 2525 Central Ave. Tel. 458-2678.

Located adjacent to the Liberty Bowl Memorial Stadium, this children's museum is housed in a cavernous old building. Inside, kids can run wild as they learn how life in the adult world actually works. There's a real fire engine for them to climb on, a police motorcycle, and a car for them to drive. In the museum's kid-size city, your children can go shopping for groceries or stop by the bank to cash a check. Call to find out what special programs are being offered during your visit.

Admission: $5 adults, $4 children.

Open: Tues–Sat 9am–5pm, Sun noon–5pm. **Bus:** 2 or 50C.

AMUSEMENT PARKS & FAMILY FUN CENTERS

ADVENTURE RIVER, 6889 Whitten Bend Cove. Tel. 382-WAVE.

Summers can be hot and muggy in Memphis, and there's no better way to cool off with the kids than at Adventure River, a 25-acre aquatic park that includes a wave pool, speed water slides, winding tube-type water slides, and a lazy river down which you can float.

Admission: $13 plus tax.

Open: May, Sat 10am–8pm, Sun 10am–6pm; Memorial Day weekend–Labor Day weekend, daily 10am–8pm. **Closed:** Early Sept–Apr.

CELEBRATION STATION, 5970 Macon Cove Rd. Tel. 377-6700.

Located just off I-40 at Exit 12, this family fun center has more to offer than either of its competitors mentioned here. In addition to the miniature golf, go-karts, batting cages, and video games, there are kiddie rides, arcade games, bumper boats, and a pizza restaurant.

Admission: Play-all-day pass, $6 adults Mon–Thurs, $10 Fri–Sun; $5 children.

Open: Sun–Thurs 10am–10pm, Fri–Sat 10am–midnight. **Bus:** 53B.

LIBERTYLAND, Mid-South Fairgrounds, 940 Early Maxwell Blvd. Tel. 274-1776 or 274-8800.

Kids of all ages will enjoy the many rides at this amusement park in midtown Memphis. There's the Revolution roller coaster that does a 360° loop, a water slide, the giant Sea Dragon, and of course a Ferris wheel. There are also live song-and-dance performances at five different theaters. The smallest kids have their own special play areas at Tom Sawyer Island and the Kids' Korner. There's even a historic 1909 Grand Carousel.

Admission (including all shows, kids' rides, and some other rides): $7 per person $4 after 4pm, free for senior citizens and children under 4; $8 additional for thrill rides

Open: May–June 13 and Aug 28–Sept 6, Sat 10am–9pm, Sun noon–9pm; June 14–Aug 27, Wed–Fri and Sun noon–9pm, Sat 10am–9pm. The park is also open during the Mid-South Fair, late Sept to early Oct. **Closed:** Oct–Apr. **Bus:** 2, 50S.

PUTT-PUTT GOLF & GAMES, 5484 Summer Ave. Tel. 386-2992.

Located on the east side of town just off I-40, this miniature golf and games complex claims to be the largest of its kind in the world, and whether or not that claim is true, your kids will find plenty to do. There are 54 holes of miniature golf, a driving range, baseball batting cages, a go-kart track, swimming pool, video games room, and picnic tables.

Admission: All-day passport, $10 Mon–Fri, $12 Sat–Sun; other individual game or daily special rates are also available.

Open: Mon–Thurs 8am–11pm, Fri–Sat 8am–1am. **Bus:** 53.

4. SPECIAL-INTEREST SIGHTSEEING

FOR ROCK & BLUES LOVERS

If you're going to Memphis you're going to **Graceland,** but there are also several other museums and historic sites important in the history of rock and blues music. **Beale Street** is where the blues began and today, after a period of abandonment, this downtown street is once again a busy entertainment district. Today visitors can hear blues, rock, jazz, country, and even Irish music on Beale Street. To learn more about the various musical styles that originated along the Mississippi River, visit the **Mississippi River Museum** on Mud Island where there are several rooms full of exhibits on New Orleans jazz, Memphis blues, rockabilly, and Elvis. The **Center for Southern Folklore,** on Beale Street, sometimes has special exhibits pertaining to the Memphis music scene. All of these places were more fully described earlier in this chapter.

In addition to being the birthplace of the blues and city that launched Elvis and rock 'n' roll into the heart of the American identity, Memphis played an important role in **soul music** during the 1960s. It was here that Isaac Hayes and Booker T and the MG's recorded at Stax Studio. Other musicians who launched their careers from Memphis include Muddy Waters, Albert King, Al Green, Otis Redding, Sam and Dave, Sam the Sham and the Pharaohs, and the Box Tops.

Below are some other sites that music fans may want to visit while in Memphis:

BEALE STREET BLUES MUSEUM, 329 Beale St. Tel. 527-6008.

If your interest lies in the blues rather than early rock 'n' roll music, this is your museum. From the slavery days to the 1940s, the music of the American South is documented with an emphasis on the music that made Beale Street the most important street in the South. The museum is housed in the old Daisy Theater, which has an unusual bandshell entry that's still distinctive today. Exhibits include old photos and recordings, videos of famous performers, musical instruments, and displays on W. C. Handy, slavery, cotton, and riverboats.

Admission: $5 adults, $2 children under 13.
Open: Mon–Thurs 10am–6pm, Fri–Sat 10am–9pm, Sun noon–6pm. **Bus:** 2.

MEMPHIS MUSIC HALL OF FAME, 97 S. Second St. Tel. 525-4007.

Operated by the same people who run the Beale Street Blues Museum, this museum picks up where the other leaves off.

Among the displays here are numerous instruments used by some of the most famous Memphis musicians, with a focus on Elvis. However, all of Memphis's music from World War II to the present is chronicled. In the 1960s and early 1970s Memphis was one of the centers for soul-music recording, and you can learn more about the musicians who made Stax Studio every bit as important as Sun Studio. Videos provide rare glimpses of famous performers, and there are also plenty of recordings, posters, old photos, advertisements, and original recording equipment.

Admission: $5 adults, $2 children 7–13.
Open: Mon–Sat 10am–5pm, Sun noon–5pm. **Bus:** All downtown buses.

SUN STUDIO, 706 Union Ave. Tel. 521-0664.

If Elvis Aaron Presley hadn't come to Sun Studios in the early 1950s to record a song as a birthday present for his mother, musical history today might be very different. It was owner and recording engineer Sam Phillips who, in the early 1950s, first recorded such local artists as Elvis Presley, Jerry Lee Lewis, Roy Orbison, and Carl Perkins, who were creating a sound that would in a few years become known as rock 'n' roll. Over the years Phillips also helped start the recording careers of blues greats B. B. King and Howlin' Wolf, and country giant Johnny Cash. Sun Studio is still an active recording studio, and for $49.95 you can rent 30 minutes of studio time and cut your own tape. Next door is the Sun Studio Café, a 1950s-style diner that has long been a musicians' hangout.

Admission: $5 adults, $3.25 children 4–12, free for children under 4.
Open: Sept–May, daily 10:30am–5:30pm; June–Aug, daily 9:30am–6:30pm. **Bus:** 10, 13, 20, 34, 46, 56, 58, or 67.

W. C. HANDY HOME, Beale St. at Fourth St. Tel. 522-8300 or 527-2583.

Though Handy's small wood-frame home did not originally stand on Beale Street, it was moved here a few years ago as part of the plan

IMPRESSIONS

Beale Street is the life to me. We that play the blues, we're proud of it. It's somethin' religious.
—B. B. KING

---

to revive Beale Street. A visit to the Handy House will help you to learn more about Handy, his life, and his music.

Admission: $2.
Open: Mon–Sat 10am–6pm, Sun 1–5pm. **Bus:** 2.

AFRICAN-AMERICAN HERITAGE

One of the most significant, and saddest, events in African-American history took place in Memphis—the assassination of Dr. Martin Luther King, Jr. The Lorraine Motel, where King was staying when he was shot, is now the **National Civil Rights Museum.** Long before the civil rights movement brought King to Memphis, the city had become one of the most important cities in the South for African-Americans. After the Civil War and the abolition of slavery, Memphis became a magnet for African-Americans, who came here seeking economic opportunities, and **Beale Street** was where they headed to start their search. Beale Street's most famous citizen was W. C. Handy, the father of the blues, who first put down on paper the blues that had been born in the cotton fields of the Mississippi delta. W. C. Handy Park, with its statue of the famous blues musician, is about halfway down Beale Street, and Handy's small house is now on Beale Street also. In the **Beale Street Blues Museum** you can learn more about Handy and other famous African-American blues musicians who found a place for their music on Beale Street. Other museums with exhibits on African-American musicians in Memphis include the **Mississippi River Museum** and the **Memphis Music Hall of Fame.** Other famous African-American Memphians are the focus of an exhibit at the **Memphis Pink Palace Museum and Planetarium.** All these places are detailed earlier in this chapter.

Following are some other sites with significance in the African-American heritage of Memphis and the nation.

CHURCH PARK, Beale and Fourth Sts.

This park, which was also once the site of a large auditorium, was established by Robert R. Church, a former slave and Memphis businessman who became the city's first black millionaire. The park was a gathering place for African-Americans in the early 1900s when restrictive "Jim Crow" laws kept them out of other city parks.

Admission: Free.
Open: Daily dawn–dusk. **Bus:** 2.

FULL GOSPEL TABERNACLE CHURCH, 787 Hale Rd. Tel. 396-9192.

Gospel music was part of the inspiration for the blues that W. C. Handy wrote, and that music came from the churches of the African-American community. The tradition of rousing musical accompaniment in church continues at many of the city's churches, but none is more famous than this church, which is where one-time soul-music star Al Green is now a minister.

Open: Call for hours. **Bus:** 53B.

MASON TEMPLE, 930 Mason St. Tel. 578-3800.

This is the international headquarters of the Church of God in Christ and was where Dr. Martin Luther King, Jr., gave his "I've been to the mountaintop" speech shortly before his death.

Open: The church is open to the public, but call for hours. **Bus:** 13 or 17.

5. ORGANIZED TOURS

RIVER TOURS

Though the economic heart of Memphis has moved to the eastern suburbs, this is still a Mississippi River town and no visit to Memphis would be complete without spending a bit of time on Old Man River. The **Memphis Queen Line** (tel. 527-5694) operates five paddlewheelers, all of which leave from a dock by "the cobblestones" at the foot of Monroe Avenue, downtown. During the summer months there are 1½-hour sightseeing cruises, sunset dinner cruises, moonlight cruises, and moonlight party cruises. The dinner cruises include live Dixieland and big-band music.

The 1½-hour sightseeing cruise costs $8 for adults, $7.50 for senior citizens, $4.50 for children 4 to 11, and free for children under 4; the sunset dinner cruise costs $25 on weekdays, $28.50 on Friday and Saturday; and the moonlight cruise, $10 at the gate, $7.50 before 6pm.

CITY TOURS

If you decide to do an organized tour of Memphis, ✪ **Delta Duck Tours,** in the Radisson Hotel, 185 Union Ave. (tel. 527-6823 or 527-7320), is the company to use. Instead of piling into a stuffy van or bus, you'll ride around in a World War II surplus amphibious vehicle known as a Duck. These open-sided transports have colorful awnings and are equally at home on the water or on the street. The downtown tours take you past Memphis landmarks and then splash you into the river for a different perspective on the city. You just won't find a more enjoyable city tour. Tours cost $10.95 for adults, $9.95 for senior citizens, and $8.95 for children.

You'll find half a dozen or more horse-drawn carriages operated by **Carriage Tours of Memphis** (tel. 527-7542 or 525-1710) lined up in front of the Peabody Hotel most evenings. The carriages will hold at least four people and you can tour the downtown area, passing by Beale Street and Cotton Row. Tours cost $20 per half hour.

If you're just in town for a short time, or if you prefer to let someone else do the planning and navigating, **Stardust Tours/ Gray Line of Memphis,** 2050 Elvis Presley Blvd. (tel. 948-8687) will shuttle you around the city and make sure that you don't miss any important sights. There are half-day city tours as well as a tour that picks you up at your hotel and takes you to Graceland (though basically the tour company is only providing transportation to Graceland). A "Blues, Booze, & Barbeque Tour" spends four hours exploring Beale Street and includes a barbecue dinner, admission to two clubs, plus four drinks. Tours run $16 to $55 for adults, $8 to $31 for children 5 to 11.

Blues City Tours of Memphis, 164 Union Ave. (tel. 522-9229), offers tours similar to the Gray Line tours. There is a half-day city tour that takes you past all the city's most important attractions. There are also Graceland tours, shopping tours, two different Beale Street night-on-the-town tours, and a casino tour to Mississippi. The city tour costs $15 for adults and $9 for children; the Elvis Graceland Tour, $23 for adults and $18 for children; after-dark tours, $27 to $32 for adults and $27 for children; a shopping tour, $15 for adults and $9 for children; the casino tour, $20 per person.

WALKING TOUR — DOWNTOWN MEMPHIS

Start: The Peabody Hotel, on the corner of Union Avenue and Second Street.

Finish: The cobblestones on the bank of the Mississippi at the foot of Monroe Street.

Time: Approximately two hours, not including time spent at museums, shopping, meals, and other stops. It's best to plan on spending the whole day doing this walking tour.

Best Times: Spring and fall, when the weather isn't so muggy.

Worst Times: Tuesday, when the National Civil Rights Museum is closed.

Start your tour of Memphis's main historic districts at the posh:

1. **Peabody Hotel,** which is famous as the home of the Peabody Ducks, which spend their days contentedly floating on the water of a marble fountain in the hotel's lobby. The ducks make their grand, red-carpet entrance each morning at 11am and the crowds of onlookers begin assembling before 10:30.

REFUELING STOP By the time the crowds thin out and you've had a chance to ogle the Peabody's elegant lobby, you may already be thinking about lunch. Before starting your walking tour, you can fortify yourself at **Rendezvous,** 52 S. Second St., one of Memphis's favorite barbecue spots, or head over to **Café Roux,** 94 Front St., which specializes in Cajun and Créole cooking.

From the Peabody, walk one block west to Main Street, which is a pedestrian mall down which runs an old-fashioned trolley. Turn left, and in two blocks, you'll come to:

2. Beale Street, which is where W. C. Handy made the blues the first original American music when he wrote down on paper "The Memphis Blues." Today this street of restored buildings is Memphis's main evening entertainment district.

On the corner of Main and Beale, you can't miss the:

3. Orpheum Theatre. Originally built as a vaudeville theater in 1928, the Orpheum features a classic theater marquee and beautiful interior decor. Today it's Memphis's main performing arts center.

Across Main Street from the theater stands a:

4. statue of Elvis Presley. The nine-foot-tall statue is a must for Elvis fans. The statue is covered with "I love you Elvis" graffiti. The sound box of the guitar the statue is holding has also become a repository for notes to the ghost of Elvis.

Continuing east on Beale Street to the corner of Second Street will bring you to the:

5. Center for Southern Folklore, a small and rather informal museum primarily devoted to exhibits on the history of Memphis music.

Diagonally across this intersection is the first of Beale Street's many nightclubs:

6. B. B. King's Blues Club. Named for the Beale Street Blues Boy himself, this is the most popular club on the street, and though B. B. King only plays here a few times a year, there is still great live blues here almost every night.

Just a couple of doors down, you'll pass the:

7. Beale Street Substation Police Museum, a 24-hour museum inside an active police station. The museum has exhibits on famous Memphis crimes and old police and criminal paraphernalia.

A few steps farther down the street, you'll come to the:

8. A. Schwab Dry Goods Store. This store has been in business at this location since 1876, and once inside, you may think that nothing has changed since the day the store opened. You'll find an amazing array of the odd and the unusual.

At Beale and Third Streets, you can sit down for a while in the:

9. W. C. Handy Park, where there always seems to be some live music. This park is also the site of a statue of Handy.

Continuing down the block you come to the:

10. New Daisy Theatre, a popular venue for contemporary music, including rock, blues, and folk. The backdrop for the theater's stage is a mural depicting Beale Street in the old days.

Across the street in the old Daisy Theatre is the:

11. Beale Street Blues Museum, which focuses on music made between the Civil War and the 1940s. The main focus, of course, is the blues that originated in Memphis in the early part of this century.

Back across the street, and a few doors down from the New Daisy Theatre, you'll find the:

12. Memphis Visitor's Information Center. If you haven't already been by here, stop in with any questions you may have.

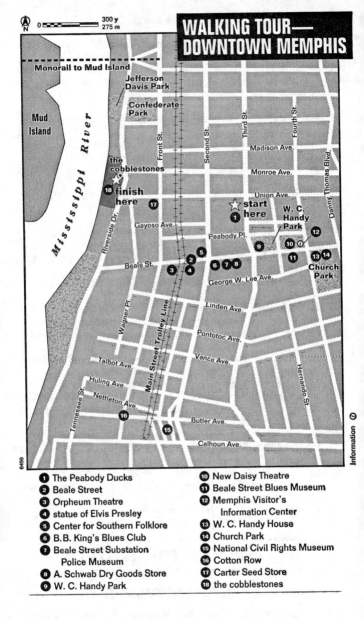

WALKING TOUR— DOWNTOWN MEMPHIS

Mud Island

Mississippi River

Monorail to Mud Island

Jefferson Davis Park

Confederate Park

Front St.

Second St.

Third St.

Fourth St.

Madison Ave.

Monroe Ave.

Danny Thomas Blvd.

Union Ave.

the cobblestones

18 finish here

17

⭐ start here

1

W. C. Handy Park

Gayoso Ave.

Peabody Pl.

9

10 **0**

12

Riverside Dr.

Beale St.

2 **5**

4

3

6 **7** **8**

11

13 **14**

Church Park

George W. Lee Ave.

Linden Ave.

Wagner Pl.

Main Street Trolley Line

Pontotoc Ave.

Vance Ave.

Hernando St.

Talbot Ave.

Huling Ave.

Tennessee St.

Nettleton Ave.

16

Butler Ave.

15

Calhoun Ave.

Information

6459

- **1** The Peabody Ducks
- **2** Beale Street
- **3** Orpheum Theatre
- **4** statue of Elvis Presley
- **5** Center for Southern Folklore
- **6** B.B. King's Blues Club
- **7** Beale Street Substation Police Museum
- **8** A. Schwab Dry Goods Store
- **9** W. C. Handy Park
- **10** New Daisy Theatre
- **11** Beale Street Blues Museum
- **12** Memphis Visitor's Information Center
- **13** W. C. Handy House
- **14** Church Park
- **15** National Civil Rights Museum
- **16** Cotton Row
- **17** Carter Seed Store
- **18** the cobblestones

Near the corner of Fourth Street is the restored:

13. W. C. Handy House. Though it wasn't always on this site, this house was where Handy lived when he was making a name for himself on Beale Street. Adjacent to this house is:

14. Church Park, which was given to the African-American citizens of Memphis in 1899 by Robert Church, a former slave who became the city's first African-American millionaire.

Now head back up Beale Street and take a left on Main. This is the street down which the trolley runs, so if you're feeling tired, you can hop on the trolley and take it south seven blocks to the end of the line. If you walk, turn left on Butler Street, and if you ride, walk east on Calhoun Street. In a very short block, you'll come to the:

15. **National Civil Rights Museum,** which is housed in the Lorraine Motel. It was here that Dr. Martin Luther King, Jr., was assassinated on April 4, 1968. The motel has been converted into a museum documenting the struggle for civil rights.

After visiting this museum, head west on Butler Street and turn right on Front Street. You will now be walking through:

16. **Cotton Row.** In the days before and after the Civil War, and continuing into the early part of this century, this area was the heart of the southern cotton industry. It was through the docks two blocks over that most of America's cotton was once shipped. This area of warehouses and old storefronts is now a designated historic district and many of the buildings have been renovated.

Just before you reach the corner of Front and Union Streets, watch for the:

17. **Carter Seed Store.** It's on the west side of the street and is sort of a small version of A. Schwab. The emphasis here is on agricultural supplies and seeds. The candy counter is straight out of the 19th century.

Take a left on Union Street and in two blocks you'll reach the banks of the Mississippi at an area known as:

18. **"the cobblestones."** This is a free public parking area and is where the Memphis Queen Lines paddlewheelers dock. The cobblestones were used as ballast by boats coming up the river to pick up cargoes of cotton.

REFUELING STOP Here at "the cobblestones," you'll find one of Memphis's only floating restaurants. **Stacker Lee's,** at 65 Riverside Dr., is popular not only as a restaurant but as an after-work bar. You can sit on the deck of this old towboat and watch the sun set over the Mississippi.

---

6. SPORTS & RECREATION

SPECTATOR SPORTS

AUTO RACING At the **Memphis International Motor-sports Park,** 5500 Taylor Forge Rd., Millington (tel. 358-7223), there is everything from drag racing to sprint-car racing to Atlantic Formula racing. The season runs from early spring to the autumn. Call for ticket and schedule information.

BASEBALL The **Memphis Chicks Baseball Club** is the farm team of the Kansas City Royals, and is the oldest pro team in the

Mid-South. The most famous former Chick is baseball and football star Bo Jackson. The Chicks play at Tim McCarver Stadium on the Mid-South Fairgrounds at the corner of East Parkway and Central Avenue. Call for ticket and schedule information (tel. 272-1687).

Nearby Millington is the site of **USA Baseball, AABC** (tel. 872-8326), the training facility for the U.S. Olympic baseball team.

BASKETBALL The **Memphis State University Tigers** regularly pack in crowds of 20,000 or more people when they play at the Pyramid. The Tigers often put up a good showing against nationally ranked NCAA teams, which makes for some exciting basketball. Call for ticket and schedule information (tel. 678-2337).

FOOTBALL The **Liberty Bowl Football Classic** is the biggest football event of the year in Memphis and pits two of the country's top college teams in a December post-season game. This game is held at the Liberty Bowl Memorial Stadium on the Mid-South Fairgrounds at the corner of East Parkway and Central Avenue. Call for more information (tel. 767-7700).

GOLF TOURNAMENTS The **Federal Express St. Jude Golf Classic,** a PGA charity tournament, is held each year in July at the **Tournament Players Club** at Southwind. Call for ticket and schedule information (tel. 388-5370).

GREYHOUND RACING Across the river in Arkansas, greyhounds race at the **Southland Greyhound Park,** 1550 N. Ingraham Blvd., West Memphis, Arkansas (tel. 501/735-3670, or toll free 800/467-6182). Matinees start at 1pm and evening races at 7:30pm. Admission ranges from $1 to $6 and parking is an additional 50¢ to $3. There's a shuttle that runs to the track from downtown Memphis hotels (check at your hotel for information).

HOCKEY The **Memphis Riverkings (CHL)** play at the Mid-South Coliseum between November and mid-March. Call for schedule and ticket information (tel. 278-9009). Tickets are available through Ticketmaster (tel. 274-7400).

HORSE SHOWS Horse shows are popular and the biggest of the year is the **Germantown Charity Horse Show** (tel. 754-7443), held each June at the Germantown Horse Show Arena, which is just off Poplar Pike at Melanie Smith Lane in Germantown. Other horse shows and rodeos are held throughout the year at **Shelby Farms Show Place Arena,** 105 Germantown Rd., Cordova (tel. 756-7433).

TENNIS TOURNAMENTS The **International Indoor Tennis Championships,** which are part of the Association of Tournament Players Tour, is held each year in February at the Racquet Club of Memphis. Call for ticket and schedule information (tel. 765-4400).

RECREATION

GOLF Memphis's public golf courses include the **Stoneridge Golf Course,** 3049 Davis Plantation Rd. (tel. 382-1886); the

Audubon Park Municipal Golf Course, 4160 Park Ave. (tel. 683-6941); the **Fox Meadows Park Municipal Golf Course,** 3064 Clark Rd. (tel. 362-0232); the **Galloway Park Municipal Golf Course,** 3815 Walnut Grove Rd. (tel. 685-7805); the **McKellar Park Municipal Golf Course,** 2440 Lake Dr. N. (tel. 346-0510); the **Pine Hill Park Municipal Golf Course,** 1005 Alice Ave. (tel. 775-9434); the **Davy Crockett Park Municipal Golf Course,** 4380 Range Line Rd. (tel. 358-3375); and the **T. O. Fuller State Park Golf Course,** 1500 Mitchell Rd. (tel. 543-7771).

HORSEBACK RIDING   Tennessee has long been known for its horses, and if you'd like to go for a ride on a Tennessee horse, head out to the east side of the city and **Shelby Farms Stables,** 7171 Mullins Station Rd. (tel. 382-4250), which is open daily from 8am to 7pm (from 7am in summer) and charges $7 an hour for rentals. Another option is to drive north to **Meeman-Shelby State Park,** off Tenn. 388 (tel. 876-5756), which is open daily from 8am to 7pm (8am to 4pm in winter) and charges $6 for an hour-long trail ride.

TENNIS   The **Memphis Parks Commission** (tel. 325-5755) operates dozens of public tennis courts all over the city. These public courts are open daily from 9am to 10pm. Some of the more convenient ones are Leftwich, 4145 Southern Ave. (tel. 685-7907); Ridgeway, 1645 Ridgeway Rd. (tel. 767-2889); and Riverside, 435 South Parkway (tel. 774-4340). Court fees for 1½ hours are $5 for singles and $9 for doubles. There are also public courts that are free, but operate on a first-come, first-served basis. These include Aububon, at Park Avenue and Goodlett Street; McKellar, at Airways Boulevard south of Wilson Road; and Southside, at 1736 Getwell Rd.

7. EASY EXCURSIONS

If you're in town for more than a few days, you may want to get out of the city and do a bit of exploring. Whether your interest is gambling or African-American history you'll find the following day trips worthwhile.

MISSISSIPPI CASINOS

Back in the heyday of paddlewheelers on the Mississippi, showboats and gamblers cruised the river, entertaining the masses and providing games of chance for those who felt lucky. In recent years, those days have returned to the Mississippi River as riverboats and floating casinos have opened in states bordering Tennessee. You still won't find any blackjack tables in God-fearing Tennessee, but you don't have to drive very far for a bit of Las Vegas–style action. In fact you don't have to drive at all, since **Casino Express buses** (tel. 901/324-9911) will pick you up at your Memphis hotel and take you straight to the new casinos across the state line in Tunica, Mississippi. Should you choose to drive, take either Tenn. 61 or I-55 south. If you take the Interstate, get off at the Senatobia exit and drive west on

Miss. 4. Once you reach Tunica, follow the signs to the Mhoon Landing, which is where the casinos are located. It's about 35 miles from Memphis to Tunica.

The tiny hamlet of **Tunica** sits in the flood plain of the Mississippi River surrounded by cotton fields, and there's nothing about this town that even remotely hints that it's an aspiring Las Vegas or Atlantic City. However, follow the signs out of town and within a few miles you'll top a levee and see before you all the glimmer and glitz of a miniature Las Vegas strip. What you'll also see is an armed guard at the front gate. This is gambling Mississippi style and lacks the casual, laid-back attitude of Las Vegas.

At the time I last visited Tunica, the **Splash Casino** (tel. toll free 800/949-DICE) was the only casino in operation. This sprawling place is partially built on a huge barge floating in the Mississippi River. Slot machines are the most popular game of chance here, but there are also plenty of blackjack tables, plus a handful of craps, poker, and roulette tables, as well as many other lesser-known games. The casino is open 24 hours a day and features live entertainment, a restaurant, and cocktails (as you'd expect).

Adjacent to the Splash Casino is the newer **Lady Luck Tunica Casino** (tel. 601/363-2250), which opened in late 1993. This place is much glitzier than Splash and has enough bright lights to compete with any Las Vegas casino. In fact this is the first real Las Vegas–style casino to open in Mississippi. The casino consists of two barges, one of which houses the gaming room, with its 650 slot machines and various other gambling tables. The other barge contains two restaurants.

Both casinos charge a whopping $10 admission, which is the biggest shock of gambling in Tunica. Before you reach the first slot machine, you're already in the hole.

ALEX HALEY'S HOME

Anyone who has read Alex Haley's book *Roots* (or was a fan of the TV miniseries) or who has an interest in African-American history will want to visit Haley's boyhood home. The **Alex Haley House & Museum** (tel. 738-2240) is located in the small town of Henning, which is about 45 miles north of downtown Memphis on U.S. 51.

Haley won a Pulitzer Prize for his book, which was a chronicle of Haley's search through his family's past. He was able to trace his roots back through the days of slavery to an ancestor back in Africa. In the process, he pieced together a story shared by many African-American families in the United States today.

The small house where Haley lived as a boy is now a museum containing memorabilia and old portraits of the Haley family. Nearby is the family burial site, where Haley and many of his ancestors, including Chicken George (the television series's most endearing character), are buried. The museum is open Tuesday through Saturday from 10am to 5pm and on Sunday from 1 to 5pm. Admission is $2.50 for adults and $1 for students.

MEMPHIS SHOPPING

Forget that quaint idea of strolling down the street window-shopping. This is the New South and that sort of thing just doesn't happen in Memphis. There are almost no downtown stores worth mentioning in this book (the downtown is still waiting to be gentrified), and out in the recently trendy neighborhoods in midtown Memphis you still find only a few stores worth visiting. For the most part, Memphis shopping means shopping malls, and most of the city's malls are out in East Memphis, a region of sprawling new, and mostly quite affluent, suburbs.

1. THE SHOPPING SCENE

As in Nashville and other cities of the New South, the shopping scene in Memphis is spread out. If you want to go shopping in this city, you'll need to arm yourself with a good map, get in the car, and start driving. The shopping malls and plazas (there are dozens) in East Memphis are where the majority of people head when they want to find quality merchandise. However, in recent years some interesting and trendy shops have been appearing in the midtown area, particularly around Overton Square and Cooper-Young area.

Hours   Shopping malls and department stores are generally open Monday through Saturday from 10am to 9pm and on Sunday from noon to 6pm.

2. SHOPPING A TO Z

ANTIQUES

Memphis's main antiques districts are at the intersection of Central Avenue and East Parkway, on Cooper Street between Overton Square and Young Street, and along Summer Avenue in East Memphis.

FLASHBACK, 2304 Central Ave. Tel. 272-2304.

With 1950s furniture becoming more collectible with each passing year, it should come as no surprise that Memphis, the birthplace of rock 'n' roll in the early 1950s, has a great vintage-furniture store. In addition to '50s furniture and clothing, this store sells stuff from the '20s, '30s, and '40s, including a large selection of European art deco furniture.

PINCH ANTIQUE MALL, 430 N. Front St. Tel. 525-0929.

Located in the Pinch Historic District adjacent to the Pyramid, this antique mall is the most convenient to downtown Memphis and is full of great stuff.

ROGERS MENZIES INTERIOR DESIGN, 766 S. White Station Rd. Tel. 761-3161.

The prices here reflect the clientele's means, and sumptuous antiques from Europe and Asia predominate. However, there are also throw pillows made from antique fabrics, French pâté urns, and other more affordable pieces.

ART

ALBERS FINE ART GALLERY, 1102 Brookfield Rd. Tel. 683-2256.

You won't find the works of any as-yet-undiscovered Memphis artists here, but you will find many established regional artists represented. The gallery is located down a side street off Poplar Avenue near the Ridgeway Hotel.

GALLERY THREE FIVE 0, 350 S. Main St. Tel. 526-6583.

This excellent little gallery is an African-American/multicultural gallery that displays art by local and regional artists, and sells African imports and arts from Kenya, Nigeria, and Ghana.

GESTINE'S, 156 Beale St. Tel. 526-3162.

This gallery features African-American art with a good cross-section of local, national, and international artists. Though there are prints, drawings, and photographs, the gallery is particularly strong on paintings. The gallery stays open until 10pm on Friday and Saturday.

KURTS BINGHAM GALLERY, 766 S. White Station Rd. Tel. 683-6200.

Located in a modern building with traditional French château styling, this gallery represents the finest regional and national artists, many of whom have works in museums around the country. You'll find this gallery just north of Poplar Avenue.

BOOKS

BOOKSTAR, 3412 Poplar Ave. Tel. 323-9332.

Housed in the converted Plaza Theatre, a big shopping-plaza movie theater, this is the city's biggest discount bookstore. All books are marked down 33%, including the latest *New York Times* hardcover and paperback bestsellers. Other Bookstar bookstores are located at Hickory Ridge Shopping Mall, 6279 Winchester Rd. (tel. 367-2829) and at Germantown Village Square, 7680 Poplar Ave. (tel. 757-7858).

BURKE'S BOOK STORE, 1719 Poplar Ave. Tel. 278-7484.

⭐ Located in a gentrifying neighborhood just west of Overton Park, Burke's specializes in used, old, and collectible books. However, they also have a good selection of new publications as well.

CRAFTS

AMERICAN CRAFTERS, Audubon Place, 4714 Spottswood Ave. Tel. 763-1638.

What antiques malls have done for antiques sales, American Crafters does for crafts. Various craftspeople lease spaces and sell their works throughout the year. This store is a good bet if you like traditional American crafts but you won't be in town during a craft show.

SOMETHING ELSE, INC., 381 N. Main St. Tel. 526-8873.

This is one of only a handful of downtown stores that you might want to seek out. Handcrafts and contemporary collectibles by regional artists are the specialty here and that includes jewelry, pottery, and hand-dyed silks, fused glass, photographs, and prints. They also have an espresso bar and serve pies and light meals. The store is right on the trolley line near the Pyramid.

DEPARTMENT STORES

DILLARD'S, in the Mall of Memphis, I-240 at Perkins Rd. Tel. 363-0063.

Dillard's is a Little Rock, Arkansas–based department store that has been expanding throughout the South. This is their biggest store in Tennessee and has a wide selection of moderately priced merchandise. Good prices and plenty of choices make this store a favorite of Memphis shoppers. You'll find other Dillard's department stores in the Raleigh Springs Mall (tel. 377-4020), the Oak Court Mall (tel. 685-0382), and the Hickory Ridge Mall (tel. 360-0077).

GOLDSMITH'S DEPARTMENT STORE, in the Oak Court Mall, 4545 Poplar Ave. Tel. 766-4199.

Goldsmith's department stores are the most upscale in Memphis. This particular location is probably the most convenient Goldsmith's for visitors to the city. Other stores can be found in the Hickory Ridge Mall, 6075 Winchester Rd. (tel. 369-1271); in the Raleigh Springs Mall, 3390 Austin Peay Hwy. (tel. 377-4473); and in the Southland Mall, 1300 E. Shelby Dr. (tel. 348-1271).

DISCOUNT SHOPPING

BELZ FACTORY OUTLET MALL, 3536 Canada Rd., Lakeland. Tel. 386-3180.

This direct factory-outlet mall has more than 50 stores. Savings at stores such as Bass, Gitano, Van Heusen, Corning, Revere, and Old Time Pottery range up to 75% off regular retail prices. You'll find the mall just off I-40 about 30 minutes from downtown Memphis.

WILLIAMS SONOMA CLEARANCE OUTLET, 4718 Spottswood Ave. Tel. 763-1500.

Williams Sonoma, one of the country's largest mail-order companies, has a big distribution center here in the Memphis area, and this store is where they sell their discontinued lines and overstocks. If you're lucky, you just might find something that you wanted but couldn't afford when you saw it in their catalog.

FASHIONS

BOSTON'S OF MEMPHIS, 6100 Primacy Parkway. Tel. 685-8595.

With two separate stores—one for men, one for women—side by side, Boston's of Memphis offers the well-to-do of Memphis a place to shop amid a clublike atmosphere—while you shop, you can sip a cup of coffee or a glass of wine. The men's shop carries primarily European designer lines. Along with Joan Franks, the women's shop is the most upscale women's fashion store in Memphis. Boston's is located south of Poplar Avenue and just off I-240.

PERCEPTIONS, 1525 Union Ave. Tel. 278-5935.

This midtown shop specializes in something for everyone. They carry men's and women's casual fashions that are both trendy and basic. There's also a good selection of jewelry and handbags.

SHOES & BOOTS

In addition to the following shoe and boot stores, you'll find an excellent selection of shoes at the **Dillard's** department store in the Mall of Memphis shopping mall.

DESIGNER SHOE WAREHOUSE, in Germantown Village Square, Germantown Pkwy. at Poplar Ave. Tel. 755-2204.

With savings of 20% to 50% off standard retail prices and an excellent selection of major-label shoes, it isn't surprising that this store closes two days each week (Tuesday and Wednesday) for restocking.

JOSEPH, 418 S. Grove Park Place. Tel. 767-1609.

You'll find the latest in fashionable women's shoes at this shop in the Laurelwood Collection shopping center.

THE SHOP FOR PAPPAGALLO, 4615 Poplar Ave. Tel. 761-4430.

If you're a fan of the Pappagallo line of shoes, you'll be in footwear heaven when you step through the doors of this Pappagallo store in the Laurelwood Collection shopping center at the corner of Poplar Avenue and Perkins Road. There's a second store at 2109 West St. in Germantown.

WOMEN'S

CACHE, in the Oak Court Mall, Poplar Ave. at Perkins Rd. Extended. Tel. 682-3935.

If you're in the market for eveningwear, this place, where they specialize in "that something special," is the shop to try for attractive glitzy and glamorous styles.

ELIZABETH EDWARDS, 6150 Poplar Ave. Tel. 761-1333.

Located in the upscale Regalia shopping center, this store carries a wide selection of daytime, cocktail, and evening dresses as well as casual sportswear by many well-known fashion designers.

GRAHAM & GUNN, in the Regalia shopping center, 6150 Poplar Ave. Tel. 684-1288.

This specialty shop caters to businesswomen, and carries its own private label as well as such lines as Albert Nipon. The emphasis here is on styles with flair that are also traditional and classic—the kind that you'll still want to pull out of your closet next year. You'll find silk blouses, skirts, blazers, and stylish suits, as well as some casual clothing.

JOAN FRANKS, 1072 W. Rex Rd. Tel. 685-9384.

⭐ Housed in a building constructed to resemble a miniature French château, Joan Franks is among the most exclusive women's fashion boutiques in Memphis. Only the finest lines are carried, and the simple designs are gorgeous and exquisitely made. Rich colors and lush fabrics, such as silks, velvets, and heavy rayons, predominate. There's an excellent assortment of extravagant jewelry for accessorizing your wardrobe. You'll find this shop off Poplar Avenue near the Ridgeway Hotel.

KITTIE KYLE KOLLECTION, 1511 Union Ave. Tel. 274-5223.

⭐ You'll find this great little shop in an older shopping center in the Medical Center neighborhood of midtown Memphis. The boutique represents small designers from around the country, with an emphasis on California styles. This is the place to find Joan Vass fashions in Memphis. There's also a wide selection of jewelry and accessories.

MIMI & ME, 434 S. Grove Park Rd. Tel. 761-7711.

The style of this shop is "California clean"—no frou-frou here. The beige and gold tones of the store's interior set off designs by Donna Karan, Emanuel, and Michael Kors. These are fashions for the working woman or those who can afford it. You'll find the store in the Laurelwood Center.

TIMNA, 5101 Sanderlin Centre. Tel. 683-9369.

Located in a shopping center adjacent to the East Memphis Hilton, Timna features hand-woven fashions and hand-painted silks by nationally acclaimed artists. A great selection of contemporary jewelry includes both fanciful pieces and more hard-edged "industrial" designs.

TRADER BOB'S, 1865 Madison Ave. Tel. 725-9236.

Young trendsetters will find the selection here to be among the best in Memphis—that is, if your tastes run to John Fluevog and Dr. Martens shoes, basic black (lace or leather), and other grunge fashions with femininity. These are basically the kind of clothes you need to be in your 20s to wear.

MEN'S

ALAN ABIS, in Chickasaw Oaks Plaza, 3086 Poplar Ave. Tel. 323-2255.

This indoor re-creation of an 18th-century village street is Memphis's most unusual shopping center, and is home to an excellent little men's boutique specializing in sophisticated European fashions for business and leisure.

OAK HALL, 555 Perkins Rd. Extended. Tel. 761-3580.

Conservative men's fashions, including such lines as Burberry's, Polo, Ralph Lauren, and Hermès, are the main focus at Oak Hall. However, there are also plenty of upscale casual fashions as well. Parking can be problem here.

CHILDREN'S

CHOCOLATE SOUP, 7730 U.S. 72E, Suite 6, Germantown Village Square, Germantown. Tel. 754-7157.

The clothes are colorful and mostly cotton, which should keep both parents and kids happy. There are also plenty of brightly colored toys and assorted things to keep kids entertained.

ONLY KIDS [OK], in the Regalia shopping center, 6150 Poplar Ave. Tel. 683-1234.

If you like to have the best for your children, this is the place to look. There's a wide selection of clothing and toys for infants to teenagers. Lines include Madame Alexander, Gund, Polo, Esprit de Corp, and Boston Traders.

GIFTS & SOUVENIRS

A. SCHWAB DRY GOODS STORE, 163 Beale St. Tel. 523-9782.

⭐ This store is as much a Memphis institution and attraction as it is a place to shop. With its battered wood floors and tables covered with everything from plumbing supplies to religious paraphernalia, A. Schwab is a step back in time to the days of general stores. The offerings here are fascinating, even if you aren't in the market for a pair of size 74 men's overalls. You can still check out the 44 kinds of suspenders, the wall of voodoo love potions and powders, and the kiosk full of Elvis souvenirs. What else will you find at Schwab's? The largest selection of hats in Memphis, bloomers, graniteware, reproductions of old advertising signs, crystal balls, millinery, gents' furnishings, hosiery, shoes, gloves, cloaks, and housewares—and that's just the start. Don't miss this place!

JEWELRY

MEDNIKOW, 474 Perkins Rd. Extended. Tel. 767-2100.

This is one of the largest and most highly respected jewelry stores in Memphis and offers exquisite diamond jewelry, Rolex watches, and other beautiful baubles.

WRIGHT JEWELERS, 3078 Poplar Ave. Tel. 454-1434.

You'll find this jewelry store in the Chickasaw Oaks Plaza

shopping mall. Both contemporary and antique jewelry is sold, and custom designs can be made.

MALLS/SHOPPING CENTERS

CHICKASAW OAKS PLAZA, 3092 Poplar Ave. Tel. 323-8777.

This indoor shopping center is built to resemble an 18th-century village street and houses 30 specialty shops, including gift shops, a small bookstore, and Alan Abis, a men's fashion store specializing in European styles.

HICKORY RIDGE MALL, Winchester Rd. at Hickory Hill Rd. Tel. 363-8471.

Located out in East Memphis, this large new mall includes three department stores (Dillard's, Goldsmith's, and Sears) and more than 120 specialty shops. To keep the kids entertained, there's a carousel.

LAURELWOOD COLLECTION SHOPPING CENTER, Poplar Ave. and Perkins Rd. Tel. 794-6022.

Tucked in behind an abandoned Sears store in an older shopping center, this newer shopping plaza houses several good clothing stores, Davis-Kidd Booksellers, and a candy store.

MALL OF MEMPHIS, I-240 at Perkins Rd. Tel. 362-9315.

This is Memphis's largest shopping mall and includes the largest Dillard's store in Tennessee, a J. C. Penney, and more than 150 specialty shops. There's also an ice skating rink, a multiscreen movie theater, and a sunny food court.

OAK COURT MALL, Poplar Ave. at Perkins Rd. Tel. 682-8928.

With both a Goldsmith's and a Dillard's and 80 specialty shops (including Godiva Chocolatier), this is the newest enclosed mall in Memphis. The mall surrounds a pretty little park full of animal sculptures, and the parking lot is full of big old shade trees. Together this attention to preserving a parklike setting makes this mall stand out from most malls.

PARK PLACE MALL, Park Ave. and Ridgeway Rd. Tel. 767-1200.

Located just east of I-240 at the Poplar Avenue exit, this mall and the adjacent shopping area is smaller than others around town, but benefits from several exclusive shops and some very good restaurants.

THE REGALIA, Poplar Ave. and Ridgeway Rd. Tel. 766-4217.

This small-but-elegant shopping center next door to the Embassy Suites Hotel and just off I-240 is home to several of the city's finest clothing stores and three great restaurants. The grand architecture of this shopping center is more reminiscent of a resort than of a shopping plaza.

SADDLE CREEK SHOPPING CENTER, Farmington Blvd. and Poplar Ave. Tel. 761-2571.

Located out in the heart of Germantown, Memphis's most affluent bedroom community, this shopping center is home to such familiar stores as Sharper Image, Banana Republic, Crabtree & Evelyn, Ann Taylor, GapKids, and Brentano's and similarly fashionable lesser-known stores.

MARKETS

MEMPHIS FLEA MARKET, Mid-South Coliseum, Mid-South Fairgrounds, East Parkway and Southern Avenue. Tel. 276-FLEA.

Held on the third weekend of every month, this huge flea market has been in business for more than 30 years. Vendors run the gamut from discount jeans and perfumes to antiques and other collectibles.

MUSICAL INSTRUMENTS

OLSWANGER MUSIC, 812 S. Highland Ave. Tel. 458-1557.

In business since 1946, Olswanger Music is where aspiring blues and rock musicians head when they need a new amp or the right guitar for that bluesy sound.

PYRAMID GUITARS, 1869 Madison Ave. Tel. 726-4633.

This is Memphis's oldest store specializing in vintage and used guitars. If you're looking for a classic so you can get that sound just right, this is the place. You'll find the store in midtown near Overton Square.

THE WAREHOUSE, 2766 Broad Ave. Tel. 323-8397.

This big warehouse full of new musical equipment is probably the best place in Memphis to shop for deals on musical instruments.

RECORD STORES

COLLECTORS MUSIC CORNER, 3521 Walker Ave. Tel. 454-9690.

If you're looking for a good selection of used albums, CDs, and cassettes, this is the place. Whatever your musical interest, you're likely to turn up something you've wanted for years.

EDDIE WORLD, 3072 Southern Ave. Tel. 458-5705.

Located right next door to the Buntyn Restaurant, Memphis's southern-cooking institution, Eddie World is a cluttered place filled with used jazz, blues, and rock CDs; vintage LPs, 45s, and even 78s; and 1950s furniture, local art, and other cool stuff.

MEMPHIS MUSIC, 149 Beale St. Tel. 526-5047.

This combination music and souvenir store specializes in the blues, with recordings by W. C. Handy, Leadbelly, Blind Lemon, and many of the other blues greats. There are also T-shirts with images of famous blues and jazz musicians printed on them.

RIVER RECORDS, 822 S. Highland. Tel. 324-1757.
This is the city's premier collector's record shop. They also sell baseball cards, comic books, CDs, and posters.

TOYS & KID STUFF

PINOCCHIOS, THE CHILDREN'S BOOK PLACE, 688 W. Brookhaven Circle. Tel. 767-6586.
This East Memphis store has the largest selection of children's books in the city. They also have some small toys and gifts for kids.

CHAPTER 17

MEMPHIS NIGHTS

1. THE PERFORMING ARTS

2. THE CLUB & MUSIC SCENE

3. THE BAR SCENE

4. MORE ENTERTAINMENT

For nearly 100 years Memphis has had one of the liveliest nightlifes in the South, and the heart and soul of that nightlife has always been Beale Street. Whether your interest is in the opera, ballet, or the blues, Broadway musicals, dinner theater, or rock, you'll find entertainment to your liking on Beale Street. You'll also find several theater companies performing in midtown near Overton Square, which is the city's other main entertainment district. In addition, there are live-music clubs all over the city.

To find out about what's happening in the entertainment scene while you're in town, pick up a copy of the **Memphis Flyer,** Memphis's arts and entertainment weekly, which comes out on Thursday. You'll find the *Memphis Flyer* in convenience, grocery, and music stores, some restaurants, and nightclubs. Alternatively, you can pick up the Friday edition of **The Commercial Appeal,** Memphis's morning daily newspaper. The "Playbook" section of the paper has very thorough event listings. If you're interest is strictly in music, look for **Shake Rattle & Roll,** a monthly guide to the Memphis music scene. You'll find this free magazine in nightclubs around town.

For tickets to sporting events and performances at the Pyramid, Mud Island Amphitheater, and the Mid-South Coliseum, you're best bet is to contact **Ticketmaster** (tel. 525-1515), which accepts credit- and charge-card payment for phone orders. Alternatively, you can stop by a Ticketmaster sales counter and pay cash for tickets. There are Ticketmaster counters at Piggly Wiggly grocery stores around Memphis, at Cat's CDs & Cassettes stores around the city, and at the Sound Warehouse, 4770 Poplar Ave.

1. THE PERFORMING ARTS

With Beale Street forming the heart of the city's nightclub scene, it seems appropriate that Memphis's main performance hall, the Orpheum Theatre, would be here also. A night out at the theater can also include a visit to a blues club after the show. During the summer, some of the best of Memphis's performing-arts events take place outside at the Mud Island Amphitheater and the Overton Park Shell.

THE MAJOR CONCERT & PERFORMANCE HALLS

Mid-South Coliseum, Mid-South Fairgrounds, East Parkway and Southern Avenue (tel. 274-3982).
Mud Island Amphitheater, Mud Island (tel. 576-7241).
Orpheum Theatre, 203 S. Main St. (tel. 525-3000).
Overton Park Shell, Overton Park, 1928 Poplar Ave. (tel. 274-6046).
The Pyramid, 1 Auction St. (tel. 521-9675).

MAJOR PERFORMING ARTS COMPANIES

OPERA & CLASSICAL MUSIC

MEMPHIS SYMPHONY ORCHESTRA, Vincent De Frank Music Hall, Memphis Cook Convention Center, Poplar Ave. and Main St. Tel. 324-3627.

Performing in the Cook Convention Center's recently renovated performance hall, the Memphis Symphony schedules a full season of classical, pops, and chamber-music concerts. Each year, the schedule also includes several performances by guest artists, often of international acclaim. In the past, Itzhak Perlman and Jean-Pierre Rampal have been among the guest performers.

Admission: Tickets, $12–$25.

OPERA MEMPHIS, Orpheum Theatre, 203 S. Main St. Tel. 678-2706.

For nearly 40 years this regional company has been staging the best of classical opera and Broadway musicals for appreciative Memphis audiences. In addition to staging four productions a year of such well-known operas as *The Magic Flute, Anna Bolena,* and *Don Carlo,* Opera Memphis also hosts concerts by such renowned artists as Leontyne Price and Joan Sutherland.

Admission: Tickets, $5–$41.

THEATER COMPANIES

CIRCUIT PLAYHOUSE, 1705 Poplar Ave. Tel. 726-5523.

The Circuit Playhouse in midtown is affiliated with the Playhouse on the Square and offers a very busy year-long season that includes 10 contemporary plays. Off-Broadway plays are the rule here, with the occasional première. Among the plays in the 1993–94 season were a world première, two children's plays based on the works of C. S. Lewis, and an exceptional mix of dramas, comedies, and a musical.

Admission: Tickets, $8–$10 adults, $7–$8 senior citizens, $6–$7 students.

GERMANTOWN COMMUNITY THEATRE, 3037 Forest Hill-Irene Rd. Tel. 754-2680.

One of the metropolitan area's best-loved theaters is this little community theater out in Germantown, which is one of Memphis's most affluent suburbs. Plays tend to be popular classics such as *The Taming of the Shrew* and *Cat on a Hot Tin Roof.* The annual *The Best Christmas Pageant Ever* is the theater's most popular performance of the year.

Admission: Tickets, $10–$14 adults, $8–$12 students Thurs and Sun.

MEMPHIS STATE UNIVERSITY THEATRE, 3745 Central Ave. Tel. 678-2565.

First-rate productions by students and faculty members have in the past been bolstered by performances by Memphis resident Cybill Shepherd. There are also regularly scheduled shows by visiting companies such as the San Francisco Mime Troupe. You'll find this theater in the Communications and Fine Arts Building at Memphis State University. The best place to park is in the big lot just across Central Avenue.

Admission: Tickets, $7–$10 general public, $5–$6.50 senior citizens and students.

PLAYHOUSE ON THE SQUARE, 51 S. Cooper St. Tel. 726-4656.

Located in the Overton Square entertainment district in midtown Memphis, the Playhouse on the Square is Memphis's only professional theater company. In this, their main theater, they stage such classics as *The Importance of Being Earnest, South Pacific,* and *Jesus Christ Superstar,* as well as more contemporary and daring dramas and comedies.

Admission: Tickets $12–$17 adults, $8–$13 senior citizens, $7–$9 students.

THEATRE MEMPHIS, 630 Perkins Rd. Tel. 682-8680.

With nearly 75 years of performances under its belt, this is one of the finest community theaters in the country. Over the years the theater, which is located on the edge of Audubon Park, has garnered numerous regional, national, and international awards for the excellence of its productions. There are two stages here—the 435-seat main theater and a 100-seat, black-box theater. The latter is where more daring productions are staged. In the Mainstage theater, expect the likes of *Phantom of the Opera* and *The Sound of Music,* while in the Little Theatre, more innovative productions are the rule.

Admission: Tickets, $10–$20 Mainstage, $8 Little Theatre.

DANCE COMPANIES

MEMPHIS CONCERT BALLET, Orpheum Theatre, 203 S. Main St. Tel. 763-0139.

This company has been providing Memphis with fine professional

ballet performances for nearly 20 years. The highlight of each season is the annual Christmas-season performance of *The Nutcracker*.
Admission: Tickets, $15–$30.

THEATERS, CONCERT HALLS & ALL-PURPOSE AUDITORIUMS

MUD ISLAND AMPHITHEATRE, Mud Island. Tel. 576-7241.

⭐ With the downtown Memphis skyline for a backdrop, the 5,000-seat Mud Island Amphitheatre is the city's main outdoor stage. The concert season runs from late spring to early autumn and includes many national acts with the emphasis on rock and country-music concerts. Though the monorail usually runs only during the summer months, outside of summer it operates on the evening of concerts in this amphitheater. Recent performers here have included Bob Dylan, Bonnie Raitt, Little Feat, and James Taylor.
Admission: Tickets, $10–$25.

ORPHEUM THEATRE, 203 S. Main Ave. Tel. 525-3000.

⭐ Built in 1928 as a vaudeville theater, the Orpheum was completely restored and renovated a few years back and now serves as Memphis's main performing-arts center. The ornate, gilded plasterwork on the walls and ceiling give the theater the elegance of a classic opera house and make this the most spectacular performance venue in the city. Should you have time or money for just one show while you're in town, try to make it anything here at the Orpheum. Touring Broadway musicals and performances by the Memphis Concert Ballet are among the theater's most popular shows.
Admission: Tickets, $20–$43.

OVERTON PARK SHELL, Overton Park, 1928 Poplar Ave. Tel. 274-6046.

Built by the Works Project Administration during the Great Depression, this classic bandshell is another popular site for outdoor summer concerts. This was where Elvis Presely made one of his first public appearances and where Janis Joplin made one of her last. Today the bandshell has been fully restored and each summer hosts a wide array of performances. You'll find the bandshell near the Memphis Brooks Museum of Art.
Admission: Tickets, Free–$7.

THE PYRAMID, 1 Auction St. Tel. 521-9675.

This 32-story stainless-steel pyramid is the third-largest pyramid in the world and is the most distinctive building in Memphis. As the city's main arena, it's where Memphis State University Tigers basketball games, rock concerts, and other large-scale performances are held. The Pyramid is at the north end of downtown near the banks of the Mississippi. Tours of the Pyramid are available (see Chapter 15, "What to See and Do in Memphis," for details).
Admission: Tickets, $8–$30.

2. THE CLUB & MUSIC SCENE

Beale Street is the center of Memphis's nightclub scene. This street where the blues gained widespread recognition is now the site of more than 10 nightclubs, plus a few other bars, restaurants, and theaters. The sidewalks and parks of Beale Street are also alive with music nearly every day of the week and almost any hour of the day or night.

COMEDY CLUBS

COMEDY ZONE, 2125 Madison Ave. Tel. 278-7861.
Located in the Overton Square entertainment district, this large club has a glitzy glass-block facade, an old-fashioned lobby bar, and a very plain performance hall. Comics from around the country perform throughout the week. There is also a resident improv company that performs on Wednesday and Sunday nights.
Admission: $8 Sun–Thurs, $10 Fri–Sat.

LAUGH FACTORY, 6063 Mt. Moriah Ext. Tel. 375-9000.
Located in a shopping center out in the suburbs of East Memphis, the Laugh Factory showcases local and national comedians. The walls are plastered with posters of old movie comedies and there's a bar in the front where you can hang out before or after laughing it up.
Admission: $6 plus two-drink minimum Sun–Thurs, $8 plus two-drink minimum Fri–Sat.

BLUES

B. B. KING'S BLUES CLUB, 143 Beale St. Tel. 527-5464 or 524-KING.
Yes, the "king of the blues" does play here occasionally, but not on a regular basis. However, any night of the week you can catch blazing blues played by one of the best house bands in town. Because of the name, this club frequently attracts famous musicians who have been known to get up and jam with whoever is on stage that night. Ruby Wilson and Little Jimmy King are two regulars here who are worth catching.
Admission: $3 Sun–Thurs, $5 Fri–Sat; up to $30 for special shows such as B. B. King performances.

BLUES CITY CAFE, 138-140 Beale St. Tel. 526-3637.
This club across the street from B. B. King's takes up two old storefronts, with live blues wailing in one room (called the Band Box) and a restaurant serving steaks in the other. Wednesday through Saturday nights, the Preston Shannon Band plays some of the best blues in town.
Admission: $2 Sun–Thurs, $3–$5 Fri–Sat.

KING'S PALACE CAFE, 162 Beale St. Tel. 521-1851.

Though this is primarily a restaurant serving good Cajun food, including a knock-out gumbo (it twice won the Memphis Gumbo Cookoff Championships), there's live jazz and blues nightly from 7pm to midnight.

Admission: Free.

RUM BOOGIE CAFE, 182 Beale St. Tel. 528-0150.

Dozens of autographed guitars, including ones signed by Carl Perkins, Stevie Ray Vaughan, Billie Gibbons of ZZ Top, Joe Walsh, George Thorogood, Albert Collins, and other rock and blues guitar wizards hang from the ceiling at the Rum Boogie. There's live music nightly, with the house band playing everything from blues to country Sunday through Thursday nights. On Friday and Saturday there are touring blues bands.

Admission: $2 Sun–Thurs, $5 Fri–Sat.

JAZZ

JOYCE COBB'S, 209 Beale St. Tel. 272-2910 or 525-0484.

Originally the Club Handy, where B. B. King got his start, Joyce Cobb's is now the best place on Beale Street to hear live jazz. Joyce Cobb herself performs Wednesday through Saturday nights. On Sunday afternoon from 3 to 6pm there's also live jazz, but later on Sunday evening, there are stand-up comics. On Monday night the Memphis Jazz Orchestra performs big-band music.

Admission: $5 in advance, $7 at the door.

ROCK, REGGAE & R&B

ALFRED'S, 197 Beale St. Tel. 525-3711.

This club on the corner of Third and Beale does a 1950s oldie review every Sunday night, while Wednesday through Saturday nights the house band plays more recent rock tunes.

Admission: $3–$6.

ANTENNA, 1588 Madison Ave. Tel. 276-4052.

This is one of Memphis's main alternative and heavy-metal rock clubs, so if you're looking for some hardcore grunge rock with lots of thrashing guitars, try this midtown club near Overton Square.

Admission: $3–$10.

NEW DAISY THEATER, 330 Beale St. Tel. 525-8979 or 525-8981.

With its stage-backdrop mural of P. Wee's Saloon and old Beale Street, the stage at the New Daisy has long been the place to see regional and national rock bands. The New Daisy also showcases musicians who have had past hits but who no longer draw big audiences (Janis Ian was playing when I was last in town).

Admission: $5–$22.50.

REGGAE CLUB INTERNATIONAL, 380 Beale St. Tel. 525-4528.

This huge club on the corner of Fourth Street is generally open only on Friday, Saturday, and Sunday nights with local and touring reggae bands performing.

Admission: $5–$10.

SIX-1-SIX, 616 Marshall St. Tel. 526-6552 or 526-1796.

Memphis's première rock club features local and national acts, with frequent shows by bands that include former members of famous bands. Recent acts to perform here have included Clarence Clemons (formerly with Bruce Springsteen's E Street Band) and Tumblin' Dice, which included among its members Mick Taylor (formerly of the Rolling Stones) and Ivan Neville.

Admission: $5–$15.

COUNTRY & FOLK

HERNANDO'S HIDEAWAY, 3210 Old Hernando Rd. Tel. 398-7496.

This old two-story brick building on the south side of the city near Graceland and the airport has for years been one of the city's old standbys for live country and rock music, which can be heard nightly.

Admission: Fri–Sat $3 men, $2 women; Sun–Thurs free.

JAVA CABANA, 2170 Young St. Tel. 272-7210.

Located just down from the corner of Cooper and Young Streets, this 1950s retro coffeehouse has live acoustic music on Tuesday, Wednesday, and Saturday night, and though you can't get alcohol here, you can get an espresso.

Admission: Free.

SILKY O'SULLIVAN'S, 183 Beale St. Tel. 522-9596.

Throughout the week there's a wide variety of music to be heard here at O'Sullivan's. There's a blues band on Monday night, and the rest of the week you might catch a bit of lighthearted piano music with a touch of humor to it. From spring through fall there's acoustic folk and rock out on the patio.

Admission: Free Sun–Thurs, $3 Fri–Sat.

DANCE CLUBS/DISCOS

ILLUSIONS, 3659 Mendenhall Rd., at Winchester Rd. Tel. 363-3646.

Located out in the suburbs of East Memphis, this big dance club has a different musical focus or theme each night. The crowd is mostly 20-something, and the music is modern dance tunes. On weekends there's a reduced admission for women, which promotes a singles-club atmosphere.

Admission: $3 Sun–Thurs ($1 with college ID), $1 Fri–Sat before 10pm, $3 for women and $5 for men after 10pm.

RED SQUARE, 1819 Madison Ave. Tel. 722-9003.

This club near Overton Square is Memphis's top alternative-music dance club. Just look for the big, red, square building on Madison

Avenue. Several nights a week there are beer busts that allow you to drink all the beer you want for a set admission of $5 or so.

Admission: $4 after 10pm for anyone 21 or older, $5 for anyone age 18–20.

3. THE BAR SCENE

BASIC BARS

AUTOMATIC SLIM'S TONGA CLUB, 83 S. Second St. Tel. 525-7948.

With the hippest decor in town, a great menu, and live music on the weekends, Automatic Slim's Tonga Club attracts the hip and upscale 30- and 40-something crowd.

THE BREWERY, at the Bluff City Grill & Brewery, 235 Union Ave. Tel. 526-BEER.

This is Memphis's only microbrewery and is housed in what was once the Trailways bus station. A cavernous hall serves as the brewery's restaurant, but in a side room is a long and winding bar where you can sample any or all of the five brews that are on tap at any given time.

KOKOMO BAY, 6532 Mt. Moriah Rd. Tel. 795-9882.

Located at the corner of Mt. Moriah and Hickory Hill Roads in East Memphis, Kokomo Bay is a tropical sort of place specializing in frozen drinks. There are 15 frozen-drink machines dispensing daiquiris of every color. The action here is usually later in the evening. On weekends there's live dance music.

LE CHARDONNAY, Cooper and Madison Sts. Tel. 725-1375.

Located directly behind T.G.I. Friday's in Overton Square, this is Memphis's original wine bar. The atmosphere is lively and the clientele tends to be casual young executive types.

THE PEABODY LOBBY BAR, in the Peabody Hotel, 149 Union Ave. Tel. 529-4000.

There's no more elegant place in Memphis for a drink, but be sure you drop in after the 5 o'clock crowds have departed after their attendance at the march of the Peabody ducks.

SLEEP OUT LOUIE'S, 88 Union Ave. Tel. 527-5337.

For the 30-something downtown office crowd, this is the place for an after-work drink and a few oysters on the half shell. The crowds fill the old-fashioned bar and spill out onto the patio. Be sure to check out the celebrity names on the many neckties hanging from the wall.

SPORTS BARS

THE SPORTS BAR & GRILL, 3569 S. Mendenhall Rd. Tel. 794-7626.

Though primarily a sports bar, with a couple of wide-screen televisions for catching the big games, this bar also has live music several nights a week, karaoke, and darts tournaments.

SPORTZ, 4760 Poplar Ave. Tel. 684-1145.

With 23 televisions, including two big-screens, a 40-foot-long bar, and some of the best burgers in town, this East Memphis sports bar is one of the most popular in the city.

GAY BARS

AMNESIA, 2866 Poplar Ave. Tel. 454-1366.

This is one of the newest gay bars in town, and is a contemporary, upscale sort of place.

J-WAG'S, 1268 Madison Ave. Tel. 725-1909.

This is Memphis's oldest gay bar and is open 24 hours a day. There are nightly drink specials and regular shows.

4. MORE ENTERTAINMENT

Most of Memphis's **movie theaters** are out in the suburban shopping centers of East Memphis. Among the more easily accessible of these are the **Winchester Court,** at Winchester Road and Kirby Parkway (tel. 681-2020); the **Ridgeway Four,** at Poplar Avenue and I-240 (tel. 681-2020); the **Highland Quartet,** at Poplar Avenue and Highland Avenue (tel. 681-2020); the **Mall of Memphis General Cinema,** at Perkins Road and American Way (tel. 794-2744); and the **Hickory Ridge Mall General Cinema,** at Hickory Hill Road and Winchester Road (tel. 794-0472).

FOR FOREIGN VISITORS

Country, blues, rock 'n' roll, soul—the music may be familiar, and, to a lesser extent, so too may be the cities of Nashville and Memphis. The myriad songs about Nashville make everyone an instant expert on Music City, and any fan of Elvis knows that Graceland is on Elvis Presley Boulevard. However, there is more to these two cities than what you've heard on the radio or seen in a music video or movie. As a foreign visitor, you may soon find that neither Nashville nor Memphis is quite like home. This chapter will help you to prepare for some of the uniquely American situations you are likely to encounter.

1. PREPARING FOR YOUR TRIP

INFORMATION

You can get tourist information on Nashville and the surrounding area by contacting the **Nashville Convention & Visitors Bureau,** 161 Fourth Ave. N., Nashville, TN 37219 (tel. 615/259-4700).

In Memphis, contact the **Memphis Visitor's Information Center,** at 340 Beale St., Memphis, TN 38103 (tel. 901/543-5333).

For information on other parts of Tennessee, contact the **Tennessee Department of Tourism Development,** P.O. Box 23170, Nashville, TN 37202-3170 (tel. 615/741-2158).

ENTRY REQUIREMENTS

DOCUMENTS Canadian nationals need only proof of Canadian residency to visit the United States. Citizens of Great Britain and Japan need only a current passport. Citizens of other countries, including Australia and New Zealand, usually need two documents: (1) a valid **passport** with an expiration date at least six months later than the scheduled end of their visit to the United States, and (2) a **tourist visa,** available at no charge from a U.S. embassy or consulate.

To get a tourist or business visa to enter the United States, contact the nearest American embassy or consulate in your country. If there is none, you'll have to apply in person in a country where there is a U.S. embassy or consulate. Present your passport, a passport-size photo of yourself, and a completed application, which is available through the embassy or consulate.

You may be asked to provide information about how you plan to finance your trip or show a letter of invitation from a friend with whom you plan to stay. Those applying for a business visa may be asked to show evidence that they will not receive a salary in the United States.

Be sure to check the length of stay on your visa; usually it's six months. If you want to stay longer, you may file for an extension with the Immigration and Naturalization Service once you're in the country. If permission to stay is granted, a new visa is not required unless you leave the United States and want to reenter.

The visitor arriving by air, no matter what the port of entry—San Francisco, Los Angeles, New York, Anchorage, Honolulu, or elsewhere—should cultivate patience and resignation before setting foot on U.S. soil. Getting through Immigration control may take as long as two hours on some days, especially summer weekends; and then it takes additional time to clear Customs. When planning connections between international and domestic flights, you should schedule at least two to three hours to allow for any delays.

In contrast, for the traveler arriving by car or by rail from Canada, the border-crossing formalities have been streamlined to the vanishing point. And for the traveler by air from Canada, you can sometimes go through Customs and Immigration at the point of departure, which is much quicker and less painful.

MEDICAL REQUIREMENTS   No inoculations are needed to enter the United States unless you're coming from, or have stopped over in, areas known to be suffering from epidemics, especially of cholera or yellow fever. Applicants for immigrant visas (and only they) must undergo a screening for AIDS and other medical conditions.

If you have a medical condition requiring treatment with prescription drugs, especially those containing narcotics, or injections with syringes, carry a valid signed prescription from your physician to allay any suspicions that you are smuggling drugs.

CUSTOMS REQUIREMENTS   Every adult visitor may bring in, free of duty: one liter of wine or hard liquor; 200 cigarettes or 50 cigars (but no cigars from Cuba) or two kilograms of smoking tobacco; and $100 worth of gifts. These exemptions are offered to travelers who spend at least 72 hours in the United States and who have not claimed these exemptions within the preceding six months. It is altogether forbidden to bring into the country foodstuffs (particularly cheese, fruit, cooked meats, and canned goods) and plants (vegetables, seeds, tropical plants, etc.). Foreign tourists may bring in or take out up to $10,000 in U.S. or foreign currency with no formalities; larger sums must be declared to Customs on entering or leaving.

INSURANCE

Unlike most other countries, the United States has no national health-care system yet, although plans for such a system have been a priority of the Clinton administration. Because the cost of medical care is extremely high, we strongly advise every traveler to secure health coverage before setting out. In addition, you may want to take out a travel policy that covers (for a relatively low premium) loss or theft of your baggage; trip-cancellation costs; guarantee of bail in case you are arrested; sickness or injury cost (medical, surgical, and hospital); and costs of accident, repatriation, or death. Such packages (for example, "Europe Assistance" in Europe) are sold by automobile clubs at attractive rates, as well as by insurance companies and travel agencies.

MONEY

CURRENCY & EXCHANGE The U.S. monetary system has a decimal base: one American **dollar ($1)** = 100 **cents** (100¢).

Dollar bills commonly come in $1 ("a buck"), $5, $10, $20, $50, and $100 denominations (the last two are not welcome when paying for small purchases and are not accepted in taxis). There are also $2 bills (seldom encountered).

There are six denominations of coins: 1¢ (one cent or "penny"), 5¢ (five cents or "nickel"), 10¢ (ten cents or "dime"), 25¢ (twenty-five cents or "quarter"), 50¢ (fifty cents or "half dollar"), and the rare (outside of Las Vegas, Nevada, and Atlantic City, New Jersey) $1 piece—both the older, larger silver dollars and the newer, small Susan B. Anthony coin.

For currency exchange in Nashville, go to the American Express Travel Service office at 4400 Harding Rd. (tel. 385-3535, or toll free 800/528-4800), open Monday through Friday from 9am to 5pm. The Third National Bank, 201 Fourth Ave. N. (tel. 748-4832), and the First American National Bank, First American Center, at Fourth Avenue and Union Street (tel. 748-2941), are both banks that exchange foreign currency.

To exchange money in Memphis, go to the National Bank of Commerce, 1 Commerce Sq. (tel. 523-3118), or Union Planters National Bank, 67 Madison Ave. (tel. 383-6733).

TRAVELER'S CHECKS Traveler's checks *in U.S. dollar denominations* are readily accepted at most hotels, motels, restaurants, and large stores. Traveler's checks in other than U.S. dollars will always have to be exchanged at a bank or currency-exchange office.

CREDIT & CHARGE CARDS The method of payment most widely used for paying hotel and restaurant bills and for making major purchases is the credit or charge card: The following are the major credit/charge cards listed in descending order of acceptance: VISA (BarclayCard in Britain), MasterCard (EuroCard in Europe, Access in Britain, Diamond in Japan), American Express, Discover, Diners Club, and Carte Blanche. You can save yourself trouble by using "plastic money," rather than cash or traveler's checks, in 95% of all hotels, motels, restaurants, and retail stores (except for those selling food or liquor). A credit or charge card can serve as a deposit for renting a car, as proof of identity (often carrying more weight than a passport), or as a "cash card," enabling you to draw money from banks that accept them. A few bed-and-breakfast inns levy a surcharge for the use of credit or charge cards.

The "foreign-exchange bureaus" so common in Europe are rare even at airports in the United States, and nonexistent outside major cities. Try to avoid having to change foreign money, or traveler's checks denominated other than in U.S. dollars; in fact, leave any currency other than U.S. dollars at home—it may prove more nuisance to you than it's worth.

SAFETY

GENERAL While tourist areas are generally safe, crime is on the increase everywhere, and U.S. urban areas tend to be less safe than those in Europe or Japan. Visitors should always stay alert. This is particularly true of large U.S. cities. It is wise to ask the city or area's tourist office if you are in doubt about which neighborhoods are safe. Avoid deserted areas, especially at night. Don't go into any city park at night unless there is an occasion that attracts crowds—for example, New York City's concerts in the parks. Generally speaking, you can feel safe in areas where there are many people, and many open establishments.

Avoid carrying valuables with you on the street, and don't display expensive cameras or electronic equipment. Hold on to your pocket-book, and place your billfold in an inside pocket. In restaurants, theaters, and other public places, keep your possessions in sight.

Remember also that hotels are open to the public, and in a large hotel, security may not be able to screen everyone entering. Always lock your room door; don't assume that once inside your hotel you are automatically safe and need no longer be aware of your surroundings.

DRIVING Safety while driving is particularly important. Question your rental agency about personal safety, or ask for a traveler safety tips brochure when you pick up your car. Obtain written directions, or a map with the route marked in red, from the agency showing how to get to your destination. And, if possible, arrive and depart during daylight hours.

Recently more and more crime has involved cars and drivers. If you drive off a highway into a doubtful neighborhood, leave the area as quickly as possible. If you have an accident, even on the highway, stay in your car with the doors locked until you assess the situation, or until the police arrive. If you are bumped from behind on the street or are involved in a minor accident with no injuries and the situation appears to be suspicious, motion to the other driver to follow you. *Never* get out of your car in such situations. You can also keep a pre-made sign in your car which reads: "PLEASE FOLLOW THIS VEHICLE TO REPORT THE ACCIDENT." Show the sign to the other driver and go directly to the nearest police precinct, well-lighted service station, or all-night store.

If you see someone on the road who indicates a need for help, do not stop. Take note of the location, drive on to a well-lighted area, and telephone the police by dialing 911.

Park in well-lighted, well-traveled areas if possible. Always keep your car doors locked, whether attended or unattended. Look around you before you get out of your car, and never leave any packages or valuables in sight. If someone attempts to rob you or steal your car, do not try to resist the thief/carjacker; report the incident to the Police Department immediately.

The Crime Prevention Division of the Police Department, City of New York, publishes a "Safety Tips for Visitors" brochure. It is translated into French, Spanish, Hebrew, German, Japanese, Dutch, Italian, Russian, Chinese, Portuguese and Swedish and contains general safety information. For a copy write to: Crime Prevention Division Office of D.C.C.A., 80-45 Winchester Blvd., Queens Village, NY 11427.

2. GETTING TO & AROUND THE U.S.

Travelers from overseas can take advantage of the APEX (Advance Purchase Excursion) fares offered by all the major U.S. and European carriers. Aside from these, attractive values are offered by Icelandair on flights from Luxembourg to New York and by Virgin Atlantic from London to New York/Newark.

Some large airlines (for example, TWA, American Airlines, Northwest, United, and Delta) offer travelers on their transatlantic and transpacific flights special discount tickets under the name **Visit USA,** allowing travel between any U.S. destinations at minimum rates. These tickets are not on sale in the United States, and must therefore be purchased before you leave your foreign point of departure. This system is the best, easiest, and fastest way of seeing the United States at low cost. You should obtain information well in advance from your travel agent or the office of the airline concerned, since the conditions attached to these discount tickets can be changed without advance notice.

For further information about travel to and around Nashville, Memphis, and Tennessee, see "Getting There" in Chapters 2 and 11 and "Getting Around" in Chapters 3 and 12.

 FOR THE FOREIGN TRAVELER

Accommodations It's always a good idea to make hotel reservations as soon as you know your trip dates. Reservations require a deposit of one night's payment. Hotels in both Nashville and Memphis tend to be particularly busy during the summer months and hotels book up in advance, especially on holiday weekends. If you don't have a reservation, it's best to look for a room in the midafternoon. If you wait until later in the evening, you run the risk that hotels will already be filled.

In the United States, major downtown hotels, which cater primarily to business travelers, commonly offer weekend discounts of as much as 50% to entice vacationers to fill up the empty hotel rooms. Note that rates in Nashville and Memphis tend to go up in the summer months when there's a greater demand. If you wish to save money and visit when the weather is not as hot and humid, you should consider visiting sometime other than summer. Spring and fall are when both cities are at their best, with the autumn months being slightly less rainy.

Auto Organizations   If you're planning to drive a car while in the United States and you're a member of an automobile organization in your home country, check before leaving to see if they have a reciprocal agreement with one of the large U.S. automobile associations such as the AAA. However, if you'll be driving only a rented car, the rental company should provide free breakdown service.

Business Hours   **Banks** are open Monday through Thursday from about 9am to 5pm, with later hours on Friday, and many banks are now open on Saturday also. There is also 24-hour access to banks through automatic teller machines. Most **offices** are open Monday through Friday from 8:30am to 5pm. Most **post offices** are open Monday through Friday from 8am to 5pm, and sometimes on Saturday mornings. In general, downtown **stores** open between 9 and 10am and close between 5 and 6pm, Monday through Saturday. Department stores and shopping malls are usually open from 10am to 9pm Monday through Saturday and from 1 to 6pm on Sunday. **Bars** are allowed to stay open until 3am, but may close after 1am.

Climate   See "When to Go," in Chapters 2 and 11.

Currency and Exchange   See "Money" in "Preparing for Your Trip," earlier in this chapter, for an explanation of U.S. currency and information on where you can exchange foreign currency.

Customs and Immigration   See "Entry Requirements" in "Preparing for Your Trip," earlier in this chapter.

Drinking Laws   The legal drinking age in Tennessee is 21. The penalties for driving under the influence of alcohol are severe.

Electricity   U.S. and Canadian wall outlets give electricity at 110–120 volts, 60 cycles, compared to 220–240 volts, 50 cycles, in most of Europe. Besides a 110-volt transformer, small appliances of non-American manufacture, such as hairdryers or shavers, will require a plug adapter with two flat, parallel pins.

Embassies and Consulates   All embassies are located in the national capital, Washington, D.C. Some consulates are located in major cities, and most nations have a mission to the United Nations in New York City. Listed here are the embassies and consulates of the major English-speaking countries—Australia, Canada, Ireland, New Zealand, and the United Kingdom. If you're from another country, you can get the telephone number of your embassy by calling "Information" in Washington, D.C. (tel. 202/555-1212).

The embassy of **Australia** is at 1601 Massachusetts Ave. NW, Washington, DC 20036 (tel. 202/797-3000), and there are Australian consulates in Chicago, Honolulu, Houston, Los Angeles, New York, and San Francisco.

The embassy of **Canada** is at 501 Pennsylvania Ave. NW, Washington, DC 20001 (tel. 202/682-1740), and there are Canadian consulates in Atlanta, Boston, Buffalo (N.Y.), Chicago, Cleveland, Dallas, Detroit, Los Angeles, Minneapolis, New York, San Francisco, and Seattle.

The embassy of the **Republic of Ireland** is at 2234 Massachusetts Ave. NW, Washington, DC 20008 (tel. 202/462-3939), and there are Irish consulates in Boston, Chicago, New York, and San Francisco.

The embassy of **New Zealand** is at 37 Observatory Circle NW, Washington, DC 20008 (tel. 202/328-4800), and there's a New Zealand consulate in Los Angeles.

The embassy of the **United Kingdom** is at 3100 Massachusetts Ave. NW, Washington, DC 20008 (tel. 202/462-1340), and there are British consulates in Atlanta, Chicago, Houston, Los Angeles, Miami, New Orleans, and New York.

Emergencies Call **911** to get the police, the fire department, or an ambulance. If you get into really desperate straits in Nashville, call Travelers' Aid of the Nashville Union Mission, 129 Seventh Ave. S. (tel. 780-9471), which is primarily a mission that helps destitute people. However, if you need help in making phone calls or getting home, they might be able to offer some assistance.

Gasoline (Petrol) In Tennessee, "self-service" gas stations are common and are less expensive than full-service stations.

Holidays On the following legal national holidays, banks, government offices, post offices, and many stores, restaurants, and museums are closed: January 1 (New Year's Day), third Monday in January (Martin Luther King Day), third Monday in February (President's Day, Washington's Birthday), Easter Sunday (variable; in March or April), last Monday in May (Memorial Day), July 4 (Independence Day), first Monday in September (Labor Day), second Monday in October (Columbus Day), November 11 (Veteran's Day/Armistice Day), last Thursday in November (Thanksgiving Day), and December 25 (Christmas Day).

The Tuesday following the first Monday in November is Election Day, and is a legal holiday in presidential-election years.

Information See "Preparing for Your Trip," earlier in this chapter.

Legal Aid The foreign tourist, unless positively identified as a member of the Mafia or of a drug ring, will probably never become involved with the American legal system. If you are pulled up for a minor infraction (for example, of the highway code, such as speeding), *never* attempt to pay the fine directly to the police officer; you may wind up arrested on the much more serious charge of attempted bribery. Pay fines by mail, or directly into the hands of the clerk of the court. If accused of a more serious offense, it's wise to say and do nothing before consulting a lawyer. Under U.S. law, an arrested person is allowed one telephone call to a party of his choice. Call your embassy or consulate.

Liquor Laws See "Drinking Laws," above.

Mail Mailboxes are blue with a red-and-white logo, and carry the inscription U.S. MAIL. The international airmail postage rates at the time of publication are 40¢ for a one-ounce letter and 30¢ for a postcard mailed to Canada. All other countries cost 50¢ (except Mexico, which is 35¢) for a half-ounce letter and 40¢ for a postcard.

Medical Emergencies   Dial 911 for an ambulance.

Post Office   In Nashville the downtown post office is at 901 Broadway (tel. 255-9447), with a branch office in the downtown arcade at 16 Arcade (tel. 255-3579). In Memphis the main post office is at 555 S. Third St. (tel. 521-2186 or 521-2187).

Radio and Television   Audiovisual media, with four coast-to-coast networks—ABC, CBS, NBC, and Fox—joined in recent years by the Public Broadcasting System (PBS) and a growing network of cable channels, play a major part in American life. In Nashville there are seven channels and in Memphis there are six. In addition there are the pay-TV channels showing recent movies or sports events. Both Nashville and Memphis have more than 30 local radio stations, each broadcasting a particular type of music—classical, country, jazz, Top-40, oldies—along with news broadcasts and frequent commercials.

Safety   Whenever you're traveling in an unfamiliar city or country, stay alert. Be aware of your immediate surroundings. Wear a moneybelt and don't flash expensive jewelry and cameras in public. This will minimize the possibility of your becoming a crime victim. Be alert even in heavily touristed areas and don't leave any valuables visible in your car. At night it's smart to stick to well-lit streets with late-night activity—ask at your hotel about the safety of the surrounding neighborhood. Nashville downtown areas tend to be deserted at night with the exception of lower Broadway, Second Avenue, and Printer's Alley. Downtown Memphis at night is fairly deserted except for the Beale Street area.

Taxes   In the United States there is no VAT (Value-Added Tax), or other indirect tax at a national level. Every state, and each city in it, is allowed to levy its own local tax on all purchases, including hotel and restaurant checks, airline tickets, etc. Tennessee's state sales tax is 8.25%, and this applies to goods and services (including all recreation, entertainment, and amusements, which usually include the tax in the price of a ticket). In Nashville, there is an additional room tax of 4%, which, with the sales tax, brings the total hotel-room tax to 12.25%; in Memphis the room tax is 5%, which brings the total hotel-room tax to a grand total of 13.25%.

Telephone, Telex, and Fax   Pay phones can be found on street corners, in bars, restaurants, hotels, public buildings, stores, service stations, etc. **Local calls** cost 25¢.

For **long-distance or international calls,** stock up on a supply of quarters; the pay phones will instruct you when, and in what quantity, you should put them into the slot. For direct overseas calls, first dial 011, followed by the country code (Australia, 61; Republic of Ireland, 353; New Zealand, 64; Great Britain, 44; and so on), and then by the city code (for example, 71 or 81 for London, 21 for Birmingham) and the number of the person you wish to call. For long-distance calls in Canada and the U.S., dial 1 followed by the area code and number you want.

Before calling from a hotel room, always ask the hotel phone operator if there are any telephone surcharges. These are best avoided by using a public phone, calling collect, or using a telephone charge card.

For **reverse-charge or collect calls,** and for **person-to-person calls,** dial 0 (zero, not the letter "O") followed by the area code and number you want; an operator will then come on the line and you should specify that you are calling collect, or person-to-person, or both. If your operator-assisted call is international, ask for the international operator.

For local **directory assistance (Information),** dial 555-1212; for long-distance information, dial 1, then the appropriate area code and 555-1212.

Like the telephone system, **telegraph and telex** services are provided by private corporations such as ITT, MCI, and above all, Western Union. You can bring your telegram in to the nearest Western Union office (there are hundreds across the country), or dictate it over the phone (a toll-free call, 800/325-6000). You can also telegraph money, or have it telegraphed to you very quickly over the Western Union system.

Almost all shops that make photocopies offer **fax** service as well.

Time   The United States is divided into six time zones. From east to west these are: eastern standard time (EST), central standard time (CST), mountain standard time (MST), Pacific standard time (PST), Alaska standard time (AST), and Hawaii standard time (HST). Always keep in mind the different time zones if you're traveling (or even telephoning) long distances in the United States. For example, noon in Nashville (CST) is 1pm in New York City (EST), 11am in Denver (MST), 10am in San Francisco (PST), 9am in Anchorage (AST), and 8am in Honolulu (HST). Daylight saving time is in effect from the first Sunday in April until the last Sunday in October, except in Arizona, Hawaii, part of Indiana, and Puerto Rico.

Tipping   In restaurants, if the service has been good, tip 15% to 20% of the bill. Taxi drivers expect about 10% of the fare. Airport porters and bellhops should be tipped about $1 per bag. For chamber service, $1 per night is an appropriate tip.

Toilets   Often euphemistically referred to as restrooms, public toilets can be found in bars, restaurants, hotel lobbies, museums, department stores, and service stations—and will probably be clean (although those at gas stations sometimes leave much to be desired). Note, however, that some restaurants and bars display a notice that "toilets are for the use of patrons only." You can ignore this sign, or better yet, avoid arguments by paying for a cup of coffee or soft drink, which will qualify you as a patron. The cleanliness of toilets at railroad stations and bus depots may be questionable; some public places are equipped with pay toilets which require you to insert one or two 10¢ coins (dimes) into a slot on the door before it will open.

White Pages and Yellow Pages   The local phone company provides two kinds of telephone directories. The general directory, called the White Pages, lists subscribers (business and personal residences) in alphabetical order. The inside front cover lists emergency numbers for police, fire, and ambulance, and other vital numbers (like the Coast Guard, poison control center, crime-victims hotline, etc.). The first few pages are devoted to community-service numbers, including a guide to long-distance and international calling, complete with country codes and area codes.

The second directory, the Yellow Pages, lists all local services, businesses, and industries by type, with an index at the back. The listings cover not only such obvious items as automobile-repair services by make of car and drugstores (pharmacies)—often by geographical location—but also restaurants by type of cuisine and location, bookstores by special subject, places of worship by religious denomination or location, and other information that the tourist might otherwise not readily find. The Yellow Pages also include city plans or detailed area maps, often showing postal Zip Codes and public transportation.

THE AMERICAN SYSTEM OF MEASUREMENTS

LENGTH

1 inch (in.)	=	2.54 cm				
1 foot (ft.)	=	12 in.	=	30.48cm	=	.305m
1 yard	=	3 ft.	=	.915m		
1 mile (mi.)	=	5,280 ft.	=	1.609km		

To convert miles to kilometers, multiply the number of miles by 1.61 (for example, 50 mi. × 1.61 = 80.5km). Note that this conversion can be used to convert speeds from miles per hour (m.p.h.) to kilometers per hour (km/h).

To convert kilometers to miles, multiply the number of kilometers by .62 (example, 25km × .62 = 15.5 mi.). Note that this same conversion can be used to convert speeds from kilometers per hour to miles per hour.

CAPACITY

1 fluid ounce (fl. oz.)	=	.03 liter		
1 pint	=	16 fl. oz.	=	.47 liter
1 quart	=	2 pints	=	.94 liter
1 gallon (gal.)	=	4 quarts	=	3.79 liter
	=	.83 Imperial gal.		

To convert U.S. gallons to liters, multiply the number of gallons by 3.79 (example, 12 gal. × 3.79 = 45.58 liters.)

To convert U.S. gallons to Imperial gallons, multiply the number of U.S. gallons by .83 (example, 12 U.S. gal. × .83 = 9.95 Imperial gal.).

To convert liters to U.S. gallons, multiply the number of liters by .26 (example, 50 liters × .26 = 13 U.S. gal.).

To convert Imperial gallons to U.S. gallons, multiply the number of Imperial gallons by 1.2 (example, 8 Imperial gal. × 1.2 = 9.6 U.S. gal.)

WEIGHT

1 ounce (oz.)		=	28.35 grams		
1 pound (lb.)	= 16 oz.	=	453.6 grams	=	.45 kilograms
1 ton	= 2,000 lb.	=	907 kilograms	=	.91 metric ton

To convert pounds to kilograms, multiply the number of pounds by .45 (example, 90 lb. × .45 = 40.5kg).

To convert kilograms to pounds, multiply the number of kilos by 2.2 (example, 75kg × 2.2 = 165 lb.).

AREA

1 acre	=	.41 hectare			
1 square mile (sq. mi.)	=	640 acres	=	2.59 hectares	= 2.6km

To convert acres to hectares, multiply the number of acres by .41 (example, 40 acres × .41 = 16.4ha).

To convert square miles to square kilometers, multiply the number of square miles by 2.6 (example, 80 sq. mi. × 2.6 = 208km).

To convert hectares to acres, multiply the number of hectares by 2.47 (example, 20ha × 2.47 = 49.4 acres).

To convert square kilometers to square miles, multiply the number of square kilometers by .39 (example, 150km × .39 = 58.5 sq. mi.).

TEMPERATURE

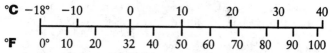

To convert degrees Fahrenheit to degrees Celsius, subtract 32 from °F, multiply by 5, then divide by 9 (example, 85°F − 32 × 5/9 = 29.4°C).

To convert degrees Celsius to degrees Fahrenheit, multiply °C by 9, divide by 5, and add 32 (example, 20°C × 9/5 + 32 = 68°F).

INDEX

ACCOMMODATIONS

NASHVILLE

MEMPHIS

RESTAURANTS
NASHVILLE

MEMPHIS

Please Send Me the Books Checked Below:

FROMMER'S COMPREHENSIVE GUIDES
(Guides listing facilities from budget to deluxe,
with emphasis on the medium-priced)

	Retail Price	Code		Retail Price	Code
☐ Acapulco/Ixtapa/Taxco 1993–94	$15.00	C120	☐ Morocco 1992–93	$18.00	C021
☐ Alaska 1994–95	$17.00	C131	☐ Nepal 1994–95	$18.00	C126
☐ Arizona 1993–94	$18.00	C101	☐ New England 1994 (Avail. 1/94)	$16.00	C137
☐ Australia 1992–93	$18.00	C002	☐ New Mexico 1993–94	$15.00	C117
☐ Austria 1993–94	$19.00	C119	☐ New York State 1994–95	$19.00	C133
☐ Bahamas 1994–95	$17.00	C121	☐ Northwest 1994–95 (Avail. 2/94)	$17.00	C140
☐ Belgium/Holland/Luxembourg 1993–94	$18.00	C106	☐ Portugal 1994–95 (Avail. 2/94)	$17.00	C141
☐ Bermuda 1994–95	$15.00	C122	☐ Puerto Rico 1993–94	$15.00	C103
☐ Brazil 1993–94	$20.00	C111	☐ Puerto Vallarta/Manzanillo/Guadalajara 1994–95 (Avail. 1/94)	$14.00	C028
☐ California 1994	$15.00	C134	☐ Scandinavia 1993–94	$19.00	C135
☐ Canada 1994–95 (Avail. 1/94)	$19.00	C145	☐ Scotland 1994–95 (Avail. 4/94)	$17.00	C146
☐ Caribbean 1994	$18.00	C123	☐ South Pacific 1994–95 (Avail. 1/94)	$20.00	C138
☐ Carolinas/Georgia 1994–95	$17.00	C128	☐ Spain 1993–94	$19.00	C115
☐ Colorado 1994–95 (Avail. 3/94)	$16.00	C143	☐ Switzerland/Liechtenstein 1994–95 (Avail. 1/94)	$19.00	C139
☐ Cruises 1993–94	$19.00	C107	☐ Thailand 1992–93	$20.00	C033
☐ Delaware/Maryland 1994–95 (Avail. 1/94)	$15.00	C136	☐ U.S.A. 1993–94	$19.00	C116
☐ England 1994	$18.00	C129	☐ Virgin Islands 1994–95	$13.00	C127
☐ Florida 1994	$18.00	C124	☐ Virginia 1994–95 (Avail. 2/94)	$14.00	C142
☐ France 1994–95	$20.00	C132	☐ Yucatán 1993–94	$18.00	C110
☐ Germany 1994	$19.00	C125			
☐ Italy 1994	$19.00	C130			
☐ Jamaica/Barbados 1993–94	$15.00	C105			
☐ Japan 1994–95 (Avail. 3/94)	$19.00	C144			

FROMMER'S $-A-DAY GUIDES
(Guides to low-cost tourist accommodations and facilities)

	Retail Price	Code		Retail Price	Code
☐ Australia on $45 1993–94	$18.00	D102	☐ Israel on $45 1993–94	$18.00	D101
☐ Costa Rica/Guatemala/Belize on $35 1993–94	$17.00	D108	☐ Mexico on $45 1994	$19.00	D116
☐ Eastern Europe on $30 1993–94	$18.00	D110	☐ New York on $70 1994–95	$16.00	D120
☐ England on $60 1994	$18.00	D112	☐ New Zealand on $45 1993–94	$18.00	D103
☐ Europe on $50 1994	$19.00	D115	☐ Scotland/Wales on $50 1992–93	$18.00	D019
☐ Greece on $45 1993–94	$19.00	D100	☐ South America on $40 1993–94	$19.00	D109
☐ Hawaii on $75 1994	$19.00	D113	☐ Turkey on $40 1992–93	$22.00	D023
☐ India on $40 1992–93	$20.00	D010	☐ Washington, D.C. on $40 1994–95 (Avail. 2/94)	$17.00	D119
☐ Ireland on $45 1994–95 (Avail. 1/94)	$17.00	D117			

FROMMER'S CITY $-A-DAY GUIDES
(Pocket-size guides to low-cost tourist accommodations and facilities)

	Retail Price	Code		Retail Price	Code
☐ Berlin on $40 1994–95	$12.00	D111	☐ Madrid on $50 1994–95 (Avail. 1/94)	$13.00	D118
☐ Copenhagen on $50 1992–93	$12.00	D003	☐ Paris on $50 1994–95	$12.00	D117
☐ London on $45 1994–95	$12.00	D114	☐ Stockholm on $50 1992–93	$13.00	D022

FROMMER'S WALKING TOURS
(With routes and detailed maps, these companion guides point out
the places and pleasures that make a city unique)

	Retail Price	Code		Retail Price	Code
☐ Berlin	$12.00	W100	☐ Paris	$12.00	W103
☐ London	$12.00	W101	☐ San Francisco	$12.00	W104
☐ New York	$12.00	W102	☐ Washington, D.C.	$12.00	W105

FROMMER'S TOURING GUIDES
(Color-illustrated guides that include walking tours, cultural and historic
sights, and practical information)

	Retail Price	Code		Retail Price	Code
☐ Amsterdam	$11.00	T001	☐ New York	$11.00	T008
☐ Barcelona	$14.00	T015	☐ Rome	$11.00	T010
☐ Brazil	$11.00	T003	☐ Scotland	$10.00	T011
☐ Florence	$ 9.00	T005	☐ Sicily	$15.00	T017
☐ Hong Kong/Singapore/			☐ Tokyo	$15.00	T016
Macau	$11.00	T006	☐ Turkey	$11.00	T013
☐ Kenya	$14.00	T018	☐ Venice	$ 9.00	T014
☐ London	$13.00	T007			

FROMMER'S FAMILY GUIDES

	Retail Price	Code		Retail Price	Code
☐ California with Kids	$18.00	F100	☐ San Francisco with Kids		
☐ Los Angeles with Kids			(Avail. 4/94)	$17.00	F104
(Avail. 4/94)	$17.00	F103	☐ Washington, D.C. with		
☐ New York City with Kids			Kids (Avail. 2/94)	$17.00	F102
(Avail. 2/94)	$18.00	F101			

FROMMER'S CITY GUIDES
(Pocket-size guides to sightseeing and tourist accommodations and
facilities in all price ranges)

	Retail Price	Code		Retail Price	Code
☐ Amsterdam 1993–94	$13.00	S110	☐ Montréal/Québec		
☐ Athens 1993–94	$13.00	S114	City 1993–94	$13.00	S125
☐ Atlanta 1993–94	$13.00	S112	☐ Nashville/Memphis		
☐ Atlantic City/Cape			1994–95 (Avail. 4/94)	$13.00	S141
May 1993–94	$13.00	S130	☐ New Orleans 1993–		
☐ Bangkok 1992–93	$13.00	S005	94	$13.00	S103
☐ Barcelona/Majorca/			☐ New York 1994 (Avail.		
Minorca/Ibiza 1993–			1/94)	$13.00	S138
94	$13.00	S115	☐ Orlando 1994	$13.00	S135
☐ Berlin 1993–94	$13.00	S116	☐ Paris 1993–94	$13.00	S109
☐ Boston 1993–94	$13.00	S117	☐ Philadelphia 1993–94	$13.00	S113
☐ Budapest 1994–95			☐ San Diego 1993–94	$13.00	S107
(Avail. 2/94)	$13.00	S139	☐ San Francisco 1994	$13.00	S133
☐ Chicago 1993–94	$13.00	S122	☐ Santa Fe/Taos/		
☐ Denver/Boulder/			Albuquerque 1993–94	$13.00	S108
Colorado Springs			☐ Seattle/Portland 1994–		
1993–94	$13.00	S131	95	$13.00	S137
☐ Dublin 1993–94	$13.00	S128	☐ St. Louis/Kansas		
☐ Hong Kong 1994–95			City 1993–94	$13.00	S127
(Avail. 4/94)	$13.00	S140	☐ Sydney 1993–94	$13.00	S129
☐ Honolulu/Oahu 1994	$13.00	S134	☐ Tampa/St.		
☐ Las Vegas 1993–94	$13.00	S121	Petersburg 1993–94	$13.00	S105
☐ London 1994	$13.00	S132	☐ Tokyo 1992–93	$13.00	S039
☐ Los Angeles 1993–94	$13.00	S123	☐ Toronto 1993–94	$13.00	S126
☐ Madrid/Costa del			☐ Vancouver/Victoria		
Sol 1993–94	$13.00	S124	1994–95 (Avail. 1/94)	$13.00	S142
☐ Miami 1993–94	$13.00	S118	☐ Washington,		
☐ Minneapolis/St.			D.C. 1994 (Avail.		
Paul 1993–94	$13.00	S119	1/94)	$13.00	S136

SPECIAL EDITIONS

	Retail Price	Code		Retail Price	Code
☐ Bed & Breakfast Southwest	$16.00	P100	☐ Caribbean Hideaways	$16.00	P103
☐ Bed & Breakfast Great American Cities (Avail. 1/94)	$16.00	P104	☐ National Park Guide 1994 (Avail. 3/94)	$16.00	P105
			☐ Where to Stay U.S.A.	$15.00	P102

Please note: if the availability of a book is several months away, we may have back issues of guides to that particular destination. Call customer service at (815) 734-1104.